Secret Societies

Secret Societies

edited by Norman MacKenzie

Crescent Books, Inc.

517 10508 X

Library of Congress Catalogue Card Number: 68-10787

This edition published by Crescent Books
a division of Crown Publishers, Inc.,
419 Park Avenue South, New York, N.Y. 10016

Printed in Yugoslavia by Mladinska Knjiga, Ljubljana

Uniform with this title

Astrology	Louis MacNeice
Gambling	Alan Wykes
The Supernatural	Douglas Hill and Pat Williams
Dreams and Dreaming	Norman MacKenzie
Medicine on Trial	Dannie Abse

Text Editor	Dorothy Kushler
Designers	Sheila Kasabova
	Valerie Leach
Assistant Designer	Jill Mackley
Research	Morwenna Arthy
	Desmond Green
	Ada Levenberg
	Jo Preston

Contents

Introduction

Secrecy plays an essential part in human life, as every child learns in growing up. There are always things other people conceal from us, just as there are always things we conceal from others. Without a degree of secrecy there would be no privacy, and without some semblance of privacy it would be impossible for human beings to live in society or to develop distinct personalities. The small child soon begins to feel that it lives in a world of its own, that its body, its actions, and its feelings are somehow different from those of its parents or its brothers and sisters, and that there are aspects of their lives that are mysterious and hidden. Secrecy, that is to say, is a condition of the individual's sense of identity.

This is a very important fact about human behavior. Secrecy is one of the means whereby we try to organize our personalities and to regulate our relationships with other human beings. If we grow up in a healthy and stable environment, we have a good chance of learning how to strike a balance between what we conceal and what we reveal, and how to be tolerant of the secrets of those around us. But many things can happen, especially in childhood, to upset that balance. We may, for instance, come to regard certain parts of our body as dirty or shameful. We may find that our parents have secrets we must not mention. Secrets may then assume an abnormal importance, as Sigmund Freud and other psychoanalysts have shown, because they are locked up in a private world of fantasy. One way of describing a neurotic individual is to say that his personality is distorted by such repressed secrets, of which he is no longer consciously aware, and which he is driven to act out in his daily life. Psychoanalysts believe that many neurotic symptoms can be traced back directly to the secret feelings and experiences of infancy, to discoveries that seemed threatening to the still weak and emerging identity of the child.

The psychology of secrecy is therefore vital to an understanding of human relationships, but our knowledge of it is still lamentably inadequate. We may suggest, for example, that a man who seems unduly given to conspiratorial behavior may well have had an upbringing that makes him put a premium on secrecy and feel that his personality will disintegrate without its protection. We may note that another individual seems less disposed to join secret organizations, but believes himself to be threatened by conspiracies. If people become obsessed with such ideas, and their case histories are revealed to psychiatrists, we may be able to see some of the intricate links between the way they have been brought up and the way they behave as adults. But in most cases, we can only observe what people actually do, and make the best guesses we can about why they do it.

This is true of all human behavior, but it applies with particular force to any activity that is secret. We can listen to a politician making a public speech, and we can learn a great deal about his motives simply by observing what he says and the way he says it. We cannot watch a Mau-Mau commander administering the oath of initiation to recruits, and before we can begin to understand the nature and meaning of his actions we have to go to a great deal of trouble merely to establish some basic facts about these activities. This difficulty is intensified when we are considering groups that have now disappeared, like the 12th-century Assassins or the Knights Templar. We have to discover facts that have deliberately been hidden, and to rely on fragments of knowledge that were revealed by accident or by disillusioned participants, misinformed observers, or malicious critics—with all the additional problems of inaccuracy that this involves. Yet, for all the difficulties, and perhaps because there are such difficulties to whet our interest, most of us find a curious fascination about secret societies. The very fact that they are secret endows them with a certain glamor; their deliberate dissimulation touches the springs of secrecy within each of us.

Let us consider Freemasonry. Anyone who lives in Britain or the United States is certain to have Freemasons among his acquaintances; there may be a Masonic temple in the center of town, or it may be known that a local Masonic lodge meets on given nights at a particular hotel. Nonmembers may attend dances or dinners organized by Masonic lodges, or hear of their charitable activities. Yet Masons learn to preserve the secrets of their "craft," and outsiders know little of Masonic beliefs and ritual. What attracts a man to join such a group? It is obviously not enough to dismiss such goings-on as a childish liking for dressing-up, as some people do, or solely as a means of holding together a clique of men who help each other out in business deals. Both these elements may be present in Freemasonry. But in themselves they do not explain why millions of men in Europe and in the United States join Masonic lodges and devote a good deal of time, energy, and money to Masonic activities. Groups of this kind are clearly meeting some deeply felt human need, and playing a role of some kind in the wider society that harbors them.

We may learn something about this role if we look at the part secret societies play in communities that are very different from our own. Secret societies are essential to the way of life of tribal groups in many parts of the world, because they are the means whereby boys are trained to become men, to acquire the values and learn the roles adult life demands. Such societies, as we shall see in the first chapter of this book, may be extremely complex, and may use all sorts of psychological pressure and physical penalties to preserve the secrecy of their rites. This collective discipline of secrecy may be as vital to tribal identity as personal secrecy and reticence is to the identity of the individual. Robert Lowie, the anthropologist, describes one such group in New Guinea:

"The Bukaua men mystify and terrorise the female population throughout a long boys' initiation festival, which includes circumcision. A demon, the women learn, craves their sons' flesh, but by bringing plenty of food they can appease the monster, who will regurgitate the youths he has swallowed. The hoax is bolstered up in various ways. According to the men's tale, the ogre bites or scratches the lads, which explains the marks from circumcision. Bull-roarers are whirled through the air, and the horrible sound produced thereby is supposed to be the demon's voice. The tyros themselves undergo a severe test. Their seniors lead them blindfolded, to their several months' retreat, where concealed guards frighten them with sounds and weapons. Just before the operation the men produce an awe-inspiring din by shouting, swinging bull-roarers, and rattling shells. When the novices finally discover the truth, they are forbidden—on pain of horrible punishments—to breathe a word to the uninitiated."

Many of the distinguishing marks of the secret society can be found in this brief passage—the initiation ritual, the ordeal, the oath, the myth or legend that supports the secrecy, and the segregation of the men from the women. Even such attenuated forms of secret society as the Oddfellows and the Elks retain these basic characteristics, and they will be found in most of the societies described in this book. But the nature of the secret itself, and the reasons for secrecy, will vary. They will obviously be different for a tribal group such as the Bukaua and for the small businessmen of a town in the American Middle West. They will be different again when we consider such political secret societies as that of the Carbonari, or the Irish Republican Brotherhood, which needed secrecy to ensure the physical safety of their members. They will be different again when we consider a Masonic lodge in London or New York.

Comparisons of this kind show us that there are many different kinds of secret organization. They also emphasize the fact that some human societies seem more prone than others to throw up such organizations. Though secret groups have existed throughout recorded history, in many parts of the world, they have flourished more vigorously at some times and places than at others. We are bound to ask why this should be so. It is tempting to say, for instance, that they are a very common phenomenon in tribal societies. So they are. But it is just as important to note that the secret society has played little part in the life of the Luo tribe in Kenya as it is to observe its importance among the Kikuyu. Secret societies have been powerful for centuries in China, and among Chinese communities settled overseas, but the Mongol people on China's northern frontier have apparently felt little need for organizations of this kind. This curiously uneven distribution of secret societies raises a number of interesting questions. We shall return to them later in this book, because they provide important clues to the conditions that foster conspiracies. But first we must define what we mean by a secret society.

Every organization has secrets of a kind. The hallmark of a secret society is that it places a premium upon secrecy and that its formal rituals are designed to seal that secrecy. In the case of such groups—for example, the Assassins, the Thugs, Mau Mau, or the Rosicrucians—we are dealing with a very special type of secrecy. We can say that without secrecy, the organization could not exist. It would either be destroyed by its enemies, or be unable to perform its allotted role, or simply fail to hold its members. The Mau Mau would illustrate the first category, the tribal societies of West Africa the second, and the Freemasons the third.

We may carry the point a little further. There are many different degrees of secrecy in the kind of associations people join, but among these associations we can distinguish four main types: the "open," the "limited," the "private," and the "secret." An open group is one to which anyone may belong; it has no secrets from its members or from outsiders. A limited group selects its members according to particular rules or objectives, but does not mind outsiders knowing its business. A private group is much more exclusive. Its membership is restricted, its affairs are not usually published, and some of its activities may be kept secret. A secret society, on the other hand, is organized around the principles of exclusiveness and secrecy. It places very strict limitations on recruitment and will often go to great lengths to screen its activities from the public gaze.

We must be wary of trying to force particular associations into these categories, for we know that there are many intermediate degrees of secrecy. But we can say a little more about each type. Open groups usually have a weak organization and ill-defined purposes. They may be a little more than assemblies of people who are temporarily thrown together—holidaymakers on a cruise, for instance—and who have no aims or activities that cannot become general knowledge. Limited groups are usually more stable; most voluntary organizations are of this type. People come together to raise money for charity, or to enjoy sport or some other recreation, or to meet the staff of the school their children attend. They have rules and officers and particular aims, and they usually publish summaries of their activities. But no great harm would come to the organization, or to its members, if all its affairs were made public.

With private associations, things are rather different. They may have good reasons for not encouraging publicity. For example, a business may want to protect its trade secrets from rivals; a political party may not want the press or its opponents to know all about its policies or its election plans; and a government always has a host of activities it wishes to keep to itself. Yet these are public organizations with private aspects. In other groups, such as an illegal political party operating underground, or a criminal society, secrecy is the condition of the group's existence, and is maintained as far as possible over the whole range of its activities.

It may be helpful to consider next the kinds of organization with which we will be dealing in this book—those whose whole outlook is colored by secrecy. There are the secret societies we find in tribal groups, such as the Poro in

West Africa. There are other ritualistic bands that have a predominantly religious character; the Thugs of India belong to this type. Military orders—which may have both political and religious motives—are represented by the Knights Templar. There are political conspiracies such as those of the revolutionary Carbonari of 19th-century Europe, the anarchists and Bolsheviks of Tzarist Russia, and the Fenians of Ireland. There are ritual brotherhoods and theosophical groups, such as the Freemasons and the Rosicrucians, and criminal bands—of which the Mafia is an outstanding example.

Even this short list is enough to make us realize how diverse are the aims of secret societies, and how many different conditions of men have found it necessary to belong to them. We might well ask, with the insights of modern psychology, whether some types of personality are attracted to secret organizations precisely because they are secret rather than because of their declared aims. There is no doubt that some kinds of personality are attracted to conspiratorial styles of life: there are many cases of people changing their affiliation from one secret organization to another whose structure is similar but whose purpose is antithetical. But we know so little about the members of secret organizations that are operating today, let alone those that are buried with the past, that we can only speculate about their motivations. For the most part, we have to confine ourselves to the external evidence—to look at what Sigmund Freud would have called the "manifest" rather than the "latent" characteristics of such groups.

When we do so, we can at least begin to find some useful ways of classifying what we know. We can start by observing that all secret organizations must have definite criteria by which they select some people for membership and exclude others. For instance, the majority of secret societies of which we know have been either exclusively or predominantly male. (Radical political conspiracies seem to be the main exception to this generalization.) They admit only men to membership, though they often allow women roles in a subordinate association. This is generally true of tribal secret societies, whose activities are closely linked with the rituals whereby boys graduate into manhood, and with the preservation of religious and political functions that are considered vital to the well-being of the tribe. In these circumstances, age also plays an important part. There are other exclusions such as racial limitations, which are quite common. The Ku Klux Klan, for example, denies membership to immigrants, Jews, Catholics, and Negroes. Thuggee was traditionally restricted to sons of Thugs, and the Mafia was confined to men of Sicilian birth.

We can also group secret societies by function, by examining their declared purposes, and what they actually do. Some of these functions have been mentioned already. They may be patriotic (as with the Loyal Order of Orange in Ulster), racialist (as with the Ku Klux Klan), political (as with the Carbonari, the Fenians, and the Bolsheviks), military (as with the Knights Templar and with such contemporary neo-military orders as the Knights of

Malta), or simply moralist (as with the modern Alcoholics Anonymous). Many secret societies, especially in the United States, are little more than benevolent or insurance societies, and their secret nature and ritual merely add glamor to these rather mundane activities. Others may be primarily concerned with a moral or spiritual discipline and their reticence may need to be explained in those terms. There are also bands of criminals who bind themselves more formally than the casual gang; traditions of bands of this kind, each with its own Robin Hood figure, are found not only in many European countries but also in China. There are also groups formed for professional or occupational reasons, like the stonemasons of the Middle Ages, or the early trade unions in Britain. (We must remember that the Tolpuddle Martyrs of Dorset were trade-union members convicted and deported in 1837 for administering illegal oaths of loyalty to recruits.) Finally, we should mention the many different secret societies in tribal communities, which seem to be a recognized and valuable component of the life of the whole tribe.

In the course of this book we shall be examining some of the different types of secret society, and we shall learn more about the conditions in which they have flourished, and the roles they have played. But it may be helpful at this stage to draw attention to some other characteristics that appear to be common to many of them, and that survive even in the secret groups we find in modern times. Almost all of them, for instance, are very hierarchical in structure, with an elaborate system of ranks and degrees through which the member progresses from novice to senior official. These ranks sometimes have high-sounding and even ridiculous names. Among the secret societies in contemporary America, for example, we find such officials as Chancellor Commander (the Knights of Pythias), Supreme Tall Cedar (Tall Cedars of Lebanon), Most Loyal Gander (Order of the Blue Goose), and Most Stalwart Sagamore (Stalwart Sagamores of the Iron Feather). Groups of this kind seem to deal in superlatives, and deliberately to build up archaic and elaborate nomenclatures. They give strange names to their regalia and their meeting places. The Fraternal Order of Eagles, as one might expect, meets in an Aerie, and the Tall Cedars of Lebanon in a Forest. The Negro society of the Grand Order of Galilian Fishermen meets in a Tabernacle, and the Patriotic and Protective Order of Stags in a Drove. It seems that once a group has separated itself from the wider community in which it flourishes it tries to differentiate itself even more by building up a self-contained and self-consistent environment of its own.

Another means of holding the group together is a specially created story of its origins. Sometimes these legends are traditional, and sometimes they are created to give a new society a claim to ancient lineage. It is hard to say how far the rank-and-file members take such myths seriously, and how far they are accepted as part of the collective fantasy that binds the solidarity of the group. One historian of Freemasonry, Albert G. Stevens, has described at least nine theories about its origin:

"Among the many theories as to the origin of modern Freemasonry the following have had many advocates: (1) that which carries it back through the mediaeval stone masons to the ancient Mysteries, or to King Solomon's Temple; (2) not satisfied with the foregoing, that which traces it to Noah, to Enoch and to Adam; (3) the theory that the cradle of Freemasonry is to be found in the Roman Colleges of Artificers of the earliest Christian era; (4) that it was brought into Europe by the returning Crusaders; (5) that it was an emanation from the Templars after the suppression of the order in 1312; (6) that it formed a virtual continuation of the Rosicrucians; (7) that it grew out of the secret society creations of the partisans of the Stuarts in their efforts to regain the throne of England; (8) that it was derived from the Essenes, and (9) from the Culdees."

Almost all these themes, we should note, are echoed in one part or another of the ritual or regalia of modern Freemasonry. We might even add a tenth theory, advanced by a student of Central American secret societies about fifty years ago, that Freemasonry owes its origin to the Mayas who, he claimed, transported their rites and ceremonies to the Nile and the Euphrates about 12,000 years ago, and founded the culture of the Middle East.

Freemasons are not the only group to lay claim to ancient origins. We shall see in a later chapter how the Rosicrucians, effectively founded in living memory by a Californian businessman, maintain that they are custodians of the lost secrets of mankind; and the Modern Woodmen of America, founded in 1883, have claimed that "the Woodsmen, in one form or another, existed centuries before the Golden Fleece or the Roman Eagle was dreamed of...."

Similar themes are sounded by the allegories and fables embodied in the rituals of many secret societies. Those that still flourish in Western Europe and the United States seem to draw upon sources that are largely biblical. The building of King Solomon's Temple plays a central part in Freemasonry; and the crucifixion of Christ, which was the theme of the third-degree Carbonari initiation ceremony, is reenacted by Masons who take the "Royal Arch" degree today. The parable of the Good Samaritan is found in a number of places, especially in the Independent Order of Odd Fellows; so is the story of David and Jonathan. The Maccabees related themselves to the Maccabean dynasty of the second and first centuries B.C., while the initiation drama of the Ancient Order of Foresters is based on the Robin Hood legend.

If we examine themes of this kind in detail, and consider the use that is made of them in the rituals of secret societies, we begin to see that they usually conform to certain broad patterns. A great deal of emphasis, for instance, is placed on the original initiation ceremony for the novice—as one would expect, since it is designed to draw a clear dividing line between the initiated and the uninitiated. In almost every case, the novice plays a similar dramatic role: he is treated as a stranger, a spy, a pilgrim, an alien, or some other outsider, who must submit to various tests. He is often made to take a symbolic journey, in the course of which he encounters threats and temptations. Those who know Mozart's opera *The Magic Flute* will be familiar with this dramatization of the ordeals of the prince Tamino, and his subjection to a discipline of silence.

Initiations often include a symbolic death and resurrection, and ceremonies of this kind seem to mark the full acceptance by the member of his new and changed status. He is, so to speak, a new man, with a new outlook, and a personality reshaped by the values of his new environment. Such an experience, which is by its nature incommunicable, may well be the most decisive feature of membership in any society. Indeed, when one strips the ritual and symbolism of secret societies to their core, it does seem as if they are ultimately aimed at securing some sort of conversion by an inner illumination. The transition to manhood in a tribal society is certainly something of this kind; so is admission to membership in a mystery cult, a religion, or a Masonic lodge. Even the initiation ceremonies of the Chinese criminal gangs in Hong Kong have the quality of a religious experience that translates the initiate out of his mundane world into a new kind of fellowship.

The great importance of this theme of rebirth is underlined by the frequency with which it appears in myths and religions in many parts of the world. The Swiss psychologist Carl Gustav Jung regarded this theme as an essential part of what he called the process of "individuation," the process whereby an individual grows up and takes on himself an adult role. But for Jung, this was something more than the secular process of finding a place in society. It was connected with man's need to find meaning in his life, and thereby come to terms with the mysteries of existence. This spiritual need, he suggested, often found expression in the feeling of being reborn.

We can discern something of this sort in all religions, and Jung spent much of his life tracing out the complex symbolic patterns through which it is expressed. The way altars are used; the employment of symbols such as the star, the cross, the circle, the eye, the lamb, the serpent, and the fish; the making of special costumes and paraphernalia; the reliance on chanting, prayer, processions, and silent meditation; all of these characteristics can be found in public organizations, as well as in private ones. The interesting question is why some men find the public ceremonies of their day unacceptable (though they may copy much of them in their private rituals) and feel they can find fulfilment only through membership in some exclusive group. Such a question cannot easily be answered, though it is vital to any consideration of the psychology of secrecy. Yet it may be useful to bear it in mind as we look at various types of secret society in this book. It is not possible to grasp the nature of membership in a secret society unless we appreciate that, essentially, it is a form of religious experience. Were this not the case, the elaborate and often fearful oaths with which secrecy is bound would be inexplicable. Many oaths of secrecy explicitly invoke death on the betrayer, and though this penalty has a purely symbolic value in many secret associations, it is significant that they retain this form of the oath, with its emotionally binding strength. The initiate will only subscribe to such oaths if he feels that they bind him by some deep and powerful sanction —that the integrity of his personality somehow depends on maintaining full and unquestioning membership of the group.

The rituals of many of the societies described in this book may seem anachronistic and bizarre; their beliefs may appear foolish, and their practices eccentric or even barbarous. But no one should underestimate the hold they have had on the minds of those who have felt the need to join them. When we look at a secret group under pressure, we see that its members may choose to die rather than to break the bonds that have united them.

1 Primitive secret societies

Anthropologists today are wary of the term *secret society*. They usually reserve the word *society* for the largest group of men and women they wish to deal with in tackling a particular problem of human relations. They may talk of "sub-societies" within this society, but they are more likely to use such words as "group," "association," "class," "clan," "lineage," and "family" to describe different agglomerations of people within their chosen society.

The word *secret* is more delicate. It bears, or is capable of bearing, a large number of meanings. To begin with, secrecy is certainly social, for a person cannot have a secret unless there is someone to keep it from. The excluded element, however, need not be very large. It can be limited to one person. No one person is wholly known to another, even when there is no specific secret involved. There is a halo of privacy surrounding each person beyond which it is "indiscreet" to go. This halo will be wider or more restricted according to the relationship involved, and it will also be of a different nature; man and wife have a different knowledge of each other than have man and mistress, or man and friend, colleague, inferior, and superior.

Any individual, then, is a "secret society" to himself. The nature of what he keeps secret will vary with societies and cultures. One's religious opinions or beliefs may be withheld from everyone except priest or confessor. One's bank manager may know more of one's economic affairs than does one's

The initiate's costume symbolizes his changed identity, and his independence of the ordinary world. This double mask, worn by Kwakiutl Indian initiates in a ritual dance, opens to show the carved face of a "spirit." The wearer manipulated the strings in order to demonstrate the supernatural powers he was supposed to have acquired.

wife. Even the most denuded of human societies has some concept of privacy. In the longhouse of the Bolivian Siriono, for instance, one can do anything as long as one faces the wall and the action is not "seen" by others. The German sociologist Georg Simmel has argued that in an advanced society, public affairs tend to become less and less secret, while private affairs tend to become more and more so. In simple societies, the situation is reversed. People live in such proximity that they are familiar with what we would call the "intimate" details of other people's private lives, while public affairs may have to be kept secret if they are to retain power and vitality. This may give us a clue to the nature of secret societies among advanced and simple folk respectively. In this discussion the relatively small size and lesser complexity of primitive societies is obviously going to count.

So far we have been talking of what is "naturally" secret either because it does not happen to have become known or because it forms part of an individual's "privacy." Let us now move closer to the secret proper and consider what is deliberately concealed.

People often keep things secret because the discovery of those things would endanger them physically or psychologically. For example, a group that is plotting against the wider society will be destroyed if its plot comes to light. There are secrets in the political and economic worlds: leaders may hide certain matters from the rest of the people as a whole. A finance minister cannot give away his budget before a set date. Specialists must have a kind of copyright of their crafts. Clearly, secrecy is often related to prestige.

In many primitive "secret societies," certain things are held to be secret when it is highly debatable that they can really remain so. When there is a secret organization that is joined by every man in a tribe at some time or another of his life, all the men will eventually be in the know. The men will often state that the secret must be kept from women and children, and talk of the penalty to be inflicted both on anyone who betrays it and on anyone who discovers it. But can one really believe that the women never know? What matters, then, is not so much the particular thing that is kept secret as the fact that some kind of secret is created, and that it pertains to the prestige and privileges of a sex or age group within the larger society. The secret here is a separating or distancing mechanism between a leading and a subordinate group in a situation where the total society is so small that nothing or very little could otherwise be distanced. Here we have an important point; very many of the primitive "secret societies" are based on age or sex distinctions.

In many human groupings there are some secret organizations of a religious nature. Here, we have a situation in which certain beliefs about the nature of the universe are kept not only from outsiders but also from other members of the society. Why should this be so? Clearly, priests and religious officials are powerful and prestigious, and secrecy adds to their prestige just as it adds to the prestige of politicians. One of the most dramatic elements in the ritual of many primitive "secret societies" is the ultimate disclosure to the initiates that the gods they have seen prancing about in the bush are their own teachers in disguise. By this time, however, the initiates have gone through a process of education that makes them understand the necessity of this, whereas, as children, they might merely have laughed and joked.

We are dealing here, then, not so much with power and prestige as with an educative process through which human beings gradually come to a knowledge of their society's beliefs and customs. We all recognize that there are matters we can appreciate only at a certain age, that certain aspects of experience must mature within us in order to make sense. If this is true of profane matters, it is very much more true of religious beliefs. Such Christian rites as baptism and confirmation are formal stages of the educative process; and such stages are usually much more formalized in primitive societies than they are among ourselves. Much of the work of the primitive "secret society" involves taking each generation through its religious paces in a series of ceremonies known as "rites of passage" in which the initiate is taken out of society for a while and then returned to it as a different person. This process often takes the form of a mimed death, followed by resurrection under a different name.

Initiation, however, is spiritual as well as material. The rite of passage is also the model for another process, admirably summarized in the New Testament statement: "Except a corn of wheat fall into the ground and die, it abideth alone: but if it die, it bringeth forth much fruit." It often seems as if a man has to deepen his experience by a great suffering, sometimes akin to death, and learn to give up much of what he clings to at any given moment, before he can obtain the release of enlightenment or the blessing of salvation. It also appears to anyone who has been through such an experience that the ultimate result is incommunicable. This suggests to us that a religious secret is often secret not because anything or anyone keeps it so, but because it cannot be known in any other way than by living through it. Franz Kafka summarized this when he wrote: "The true way goes over a rope which is not stretched at any great height but just above the ground. It seems more designed to make people stumble than to be walked upon." It cannot be mere chance that so many of the rituals of secret societies, both primitive and advanced, include tests of patience and fortitude, deliberately inflicted sufferings, disciplines of silence and heroism, followed by gradual revelation of mysteries concerned with the presence of dying in all living, which take away the sting of death and are followed by the candidate's return to the world as a resurrected being, an initiate. It often seems that a secret society undertakes the task of creating for the many such circumstances as may take a few fortunate men through to wisdom in a natural and unforced manner.

The secret has a disciplinary value, because it cannot be preserved without constant attention. Initiation teaches self-reliance in both physical and spiritual terms. It may have the function of cutting the bonds of reciprocity in

A 15th-century illustration to Dante's *Divine Comedy* depicts the poet and his guides passing through the fires of purgatory before they ascend the last stairway to Paradise. Initiation rituals often take the form of a symbolic pilgrimage; many include mimed ordeals by fire or by water, followed by the "rebirth" of the candidate as an initiate.

times of stress and peril, of maintaining the balance between closeness and distance that is necessary to all human beings. The initiate's "uniqueness" lies in this withdrawal from relationships with other people, which frees him from many of the constraints that bind the ordinary man in society. This may be why people who have reached the highest grades of any initiation often seem to assume privileges not enjoyed by ordinary members of the society and to act in a way that is virtually antisocial. The incest allowed only to sacred kings in ancient Egypt may have been a privilege of this nature.

A "secret society" is usually built, it does not grow. The building involved stresses the solidarity between members. It also has an aesthetic function in that creatively minded people will find an outlet in the elaboration of rituals and symbolic systems. Much of the art and poetry of a number of peoples is to be found within secret society ritual. The knowledge that is found in a secret society will be deeper, but not radically different from, the knowledge found in the tribe as a whole. Thus the division of knowledge may well be accepted, in traditional societies, as a legitimate aspect of the division of labor. In the fields of art and scholarship, a hierarchy of personal values can be opposed to one of mere expediency and a man may find compensation there for a lack of power in, say, the economic or political fields.

The nature of secret societies is easier to define in advanced societies than in primitive societies, where they seem to share so many of the educational, economic, political, ethical, and religious functions of society. Earlier anthropologists tended to invent *a priori* models of what a secret society should be, and to associate them with other social traits such as "totemism" or patriarchy; ultimately such schemes always fall under the weight of exceptions. We have very little reliable data on primitive "secret societies," because very few anthropologists have lent themselves to the only possible method of inquiry: being initiated into the society. Religion itself is an awkward subject, difficult to observe. It seems wiser now to say that secrecy may appear in any of a number of social situations for a number of different reasons rather than to try to force reality by attempting too closed a definition of the primitive secret society.

If we cannot clearly distinguish particular types, and the kind of society in which each type is likely to be found, we can take a number of examples set out on a scale. If we were to consider the whole society as a secret society at one end of the scale, and the individual as a secret society at the other, where would we find most examples? All men, or all women, or some men and some women? All aged, or all young, or some aged and some young? Can we really give an example of a whole society as a secret society? Some contemporary writers, like the French occultists Louis Pauwels and Jacques Bergier, have claimed that through science, mankind collectively can now achieve the equivalent of the philosopher's stone and the magus's powers. We may remember the Nazis' efforts to ascribe to whole peoples the character of a secret society, making them more prestigious in order to derive more power from destroying them, as in the case of the imagined Jewish conspiracy—the "Protocols of the Elders of Zion." One man as a secret society? Apart from the general examples we have given concerning the individual's privacy, and "discretion," there are particular officials in otherwise public religious bodies who are held to have some secret enabling them to serve as intercessors between a given divinity and the rest of society. Such are the officials looking after certain pre-Conquest divinities in confraternity chapels of the Highland Maya of Guatemala, chapels otherwise devoted to the entirely public cults of Catholic saints. As we have seen, in most primitive situations the secret society falls between these extremes and is reducible to sex or age categories.

In primitive societies we do not find many examples of secret societies designed to oppose or overthrow the existing regime. On the contrary, everything indicates that subgroups work toward the achievement of a healthy society, conjugating as many separate desires and actions as may be found in society at large. We must be satisfied with the paradox that certain groups are keeping things from nonmembers not only for their own good but also for the good of those nonmembers. This is a fundamental element in the constitution of all human groups; a rich life requires diversity, but at the same time, diversity cannot be allowed to run riot if the society as a whole is to endure.

The French sociologist Émile Durkheim studied the way in which different subgroups within a primitive society work toward the solution of this paradox by dividing up the world, and social functions, between the subgroups, and making each subgroup responsible to the whole society for that part of the total which it "owns." Among the Mende of Sierra Leone, for instance, the various secret societies are specialist institutions, looking after or "owning" various aspects of social life, and an individual pays them for helping him in some matter concerned with the aspect they own. In this case, the secret society—like any other subgroup—is obviously helping to shape the society as a whole. So, in the examples that follow, we shall find secret societies with general functions, such as education of the younger members of society as a whole, as well as specific functions, such as cŭring particular illnesses.

One of the primitive "secret societies" that has been most thoroughly investigated by anthropologists is the Poro, a generic term for an organization that exists among various tribal groups in Liberia, Sierra Leone, and Guinea. Rather than attempt to piece together, tribe by tribe, all the information we have, let us look briefly at those characteristics of the Poro that are common to all these tribes.

The Poro is both a tribal initiation through which adolescents are educated in the customs and beliefs of their tribe, and a secret society composed of men who have fuller knowledge of the mysteries involved and wield considerable power in their communities. Though interference by the colonial and Liberian governments has curtailed its power, the Poro still plays an important role

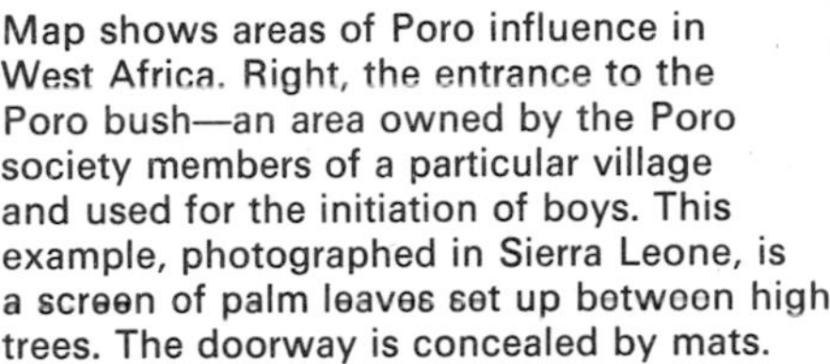
Map shows areas of Poro influence in West Africa. Right, the entrance to the Poro bush—an area owned by the Poro society members of a particular village and used for the initiation of boys. This example, photographed in Sierra Leone, is a screen of palm leaves set up between high trees. The doorway is concealed by mats.

in tribal life. It is certainly very old; some have suggested that the place-name *Purrus campus*, which appears on the medieval maps based on Ptolemy's, means "Poro bush." The first reliable references to the Poro occur in Hispanic and Portuguese sources of the 16th and 17th centuries.

The institution *Poro* is distinguished from a *poro*, which is its bush school. Such schools are set up at some distance from a village by the Poro elders when they decide that there are enough boys of the right age. In the old days a poro might last as long as three or four years; today, the period might be curtailed to a few weeks. A place was set apart in the bush with an entrance that screened proceedings from the view of women and uninitiated boys. Masked men were sent out to bring the boys in from the village. The death and resurrection theme, so typical of initiation, is well marked here: in some cases, a bladder full of chicken blood was tied to the boy's stomach, and members pretended to spear him as they tossed him over the screen into the poro enclosure. The learning the boys were to acquire was believed to emanate from ancestors, and they now "died" into the spirit world, supposedly being swallowed by a crocodile spirit. They ate white clay and smeared themselves with it, white being regarded as the color of spirits. A kind of bull-roarer, together with certain kinds of music held to represent the voices of spirits, provided the sound track for the benefit of the uninitiated. Most of the masked

Left, a Liberian *Gbetu*—an important spirit impersonator attached to Poro. Regarded as the representative of the Poro elders, he appears at all major ceremonials with two attendants (one holds a flag, the other a horn or musket and a speaker). Above, Mende girls who have been initiated into *Bundu*—a women's society that has links with Poro—display the scar marks made at their initiation. Right, at the close of a Poro initiation rite in Sierra Leone, officials of the society parade around the village with three new initiates. The initiates are covered with white clay and vines; each holds a cornstalk in his hand.

figures represented spirits. As in most initiations, the candidates soon learned that the masks were not in fact spirits, but men like themselves. This was confirmed at the end of the poro when boys saw a man dancing with a mask on his face but no costume to hide his body. The dance was carried out as carefully as ever, and at the end a sacrifice was made to the mask to indicate that it was the mask, not the wearer, that mattered.

Initiation is usually vouched for by some sort of physical sign. In the poro this consisted of circumcision and scarification, though circumcision alone was held to be sufficient in a few tribes. The scar marks made by priests with hook and razor represented the traces left by the crocodile spirit in swallowing the candidate: this aspect of the death and resurrection theme was matched by regurgitation or obstetric rituals at the end of the poro session. Candidates who died during the school were said to have remained in the belly of the spirit, and no public mourning could be held for them. Other aspects of the death and resurrection theme included a kind of "baptism" by immersion, the granting of new names, the loss of certain responsibilities incurred in the uninitiated state, and a pretended failure to recognize relatives on first emerging from the poro and returning to the village.

The discipline in the poro is said to have been rigorous, if not brutal. It was sometimes accompanied by a number of human sacrifices, usually of

slave boys. (Cannibal sacrifices—some say, of the eldest son of the candidate—were apparently required for the higher grades of initiation in the Poro society itself.) Such offences as peeping into the poro from the outside, revealing secrets, showing disrespect, or attempting to imitate spirit voices, were punishable by death; upon entry boys would be shown trays containing toes, thumbs, and little fingers of offenders. Boys would be roughly treated, woken up in the middle of the night, and punished arbitrarily. Any boy who contracted an infection after scarification might be killed to prevent an epidemic.

During the school period, the boys learned tribal lore, ethics, morals, and religious ritual, and the tasks that any adult tribesman had to know: techniques of war, hunting, agriculture, husbandry, and a number of specialized trades. The inner community was well organized, with its own officers, and replicas of communal courts and councils. Though discipline was harsh in the poro, some aspects of life were pleasant; there was continual feasting on food provided by masked men who would go to the village and beg, borrow, steal, or extort from the boys' parents and other villagers. In this respect, a poro session would prove costly to the community; its education was in no sense free. The poro, being supposed to prepare a boy for marriage, included a sexual education. Boys who were recovering from circumcision would be fed the products of female incision handed over by the women's society (the

A *Kashi*, or senior Poro official, collects a gift of money from a bystander during a procession of initiates in Sierra Leone. The Kashi is responsible for raising funds and for training boys in the bush school. His headdress holds four skulls and four femurs, supposed to be the remains of those executed for breaches of Poro discipline.

Sande), while girls would consume the products of male circumcision. This may be related to the belief, found among the Dogon and Bambara tribes of the Sudan, that every child is born with two souls, male and female, and that one of them has to be excised by circumcision rituals.

Thus a poro or school held by the Poro provided what we might call a pre-university education for all men in the tribe, while the Sande provided an equivalent training for the women. The Poro also provided a higher education and the key to a higher status for a few, in that its officials were recruited from those who had passed out of the bush school. The school appears to have been divided into three classes: commoners, sons of chiefs (who had leadership tasks), and priests. Boys belonging to the latter group might be sons of priests or boys whose temperaments were found by a diviner to warrant the status. Having prior knowledge, they often joined the poro when it was already well under way.

The priests were organized hierarchically and it is thought that the very highest ranks were open only to hereditary members from a very few families. Some sources claim as many as 99 grades of initiation. The highest levels of secret doctrine remain unknown to outsiders; but the higher a man went in the Poro, the further his influence extended beyond the limits of his own social group. A secret language of signs, perhaps similar to that of the Freemasons (p. 155), ensured that he would be received in other Poro groups whenever he chose to travel. Priests, however, paid dearly for their specialized knowledge. They had considerable personal responsibilities to their own "medicines" and magic paraphernalia, having to feed them constantly with sacrifices, and to tend them like veritable alter egos. Their possession of these "medicines" symbolized their access to various magical powers, and qualified them to perform Poro tasks as well as consultant duties outside the Poro proper. In some groups, priests might possess the right to wear the various masks; in other groups, priests and mask-wearers were two distinct categories.

Research in Liberia and Sierra Leone has shown that the Poro had also a political role. The interests of the Poro were defined in terms of the whole community, so that the Poro was in effect a substitute for the highly organized type of government found further east—in Ghana, for example, or in Nigeria. There was mutual reinforcement of the Poro and political authority in that the chief was the Poro's patron in all external affairs, though subject to the authority of Poro officials within the institution. While quarrels of a minor nature were settled publicly by heads of families and town chiefs, private councils of Poro priests, in league with the higher chiefs, deliberated on major quarrels and "foreign affairs." The higher the matter went, the more secret their councils became. At the very top sat a council of old men who were exempt from the call to war and against whom any kind of insult, or even a brush against the shoulder, constituted little less than treason. When such men died, their death was often kept secret, and was sometimes mitigated by the creation of a personal mask that replaced them. In this way, the great old men shaded by stages into the ancestors who were the real rulers of the Poro and of the bush school, and the ultimate bastions of tribal life and ethics. Their secret councils may have been the means by which a basically democratic society hid the autocratic elements necessary to it; through them, it could ascribe responsibility for judgment to ancestors, or ritual mechanisms such as poison ordeals determined by ancestors, rather than to any particular political official in "open court." Such ideas about the rule of ancestors over their descendants, of the dead over the living, are a common feature of many secret societies. Indeed, in all traditionally inclined societies, ethics ultimately derive from the dead who created and maintained the group in question.

Thus the Poro and similar institutions in this area of Africa can be described as "arbiters of culture" or "controllers of morals." Unlike those independent medicine men, witch doctors, and diviners who work for individuals and are often selfishly motivated, the official wielders of the most powerful "medicines" in such societies work essentially for, and in the interests of, the community at large. The Poro, which works like an ancestor cult, and other societies such as the *Humui*, the *Njayei*, and the Sande, which work through "medicines," monopolize much of cultural life by laying down codes of behavior in the field of activity with which they are concerned. They also control punishments for infringements of those codes and, finally, grant "forgiveness" to offenders. Such forgiveness often includes initiation into the society in question, which ensures that the secret knowledge will spread no further. It is significant that while the Sande society has allowed its candidates to take courses in modern hygiene and mothercraft, the Poro, though severely curtailed by the inroads of modernization, still forbids candidates to take any non-African object with them into the bush. The Poro may die, but it refuses to modernize, and an understanding of its role in regulating social life (which extends to the organization of local trades and industries in parts of northwestern Liberia) may show us why such "core" institutions among underdeveloped peoples should be tampered with as little as possible.

Among the societies of the world, few are more pervaded by ritual activity than the Pueblo Indians of Arizona and New Mexico. Secrecy, too, pervades the whole of their life, though this has come about largely as a reaction to the white man, his missions, and his politics. Another reason for Pueblo secrecy may be the fact that most war magic and ritual—of which there was much in Amerindian life—is, of necessity, secret. Among the Zuni Indians, one reason for keeping out non-initiates was that everyone had to concentrate hard on the matter in hand if a ceremony was to be successful and ignorant people, of course, could not do so. Above all—and this illustrates the disciplinary nature of secrecy—the Zuni often claimed that "power told is power lost": talk and idle gossip about secrets was quite literally believed to lead to loss of the power involved, both for individuals and for their community. The preservation of that power was of the utmost importance, because they believed that the rituals of their priests kept the world and society in being.

The Hopi of the Western Pueblos initiate all boys and girls in the tribe into the *kacina* cult. The ritual is largely undertaken by men. This is a cult of the dead, of the ancestors (*kacinas*) who give clouds and rain, and hence crop fertility, in exchange for ritual attention. The most important kacinas, who appear in the village as masked figures, are the ancestors of the various clans. The initiations take place in *kivas*, underground chambers that represent the places from which the ancestors of the tribe first emerged on earth. Here, as in other initiations, the candidates discover the power of the ancestors, but they also discover that the ancestors are themselves: a myth relates the kacinas to contemporary children by revealing that they were originally children of the first men and women who were lost in a primeval flood. Cutting across this tribal initiation there is another affiliation of each man into one of four societies: the *Wuwutcim* and *Tao* (concerned with fertility), the *Ahl* and *Kwan* (concerned with war). Their initiations also take place in kivas, and are controlled by different clans. In addition to these there are other societies associated with war, rain, curing, and ceremonial clowning, with smaller memberships and lesser roles in the ceremonial organization. The chief concerns of the major Hopi societies are rain bringing and community welfare; they also have the power to afflict offenders with disorders, and to cure them.

There used to be many seasonal ceremonies, and each ceremony existed as a unit, being performed for the benefit of the whole society by a society

Map shows areas of Arizona and New Mexico inhabited by Hopi and Zuni Indians. Top, view of Taos, a Hopi village, showing the palisaded entrance to an underground *kiva* (in foreground). Right, the altar inside an *Ahl* society kiva in Mishongnovi, photographed on the eighth day of a fertility rite performed by the "Antelope" and "Snake" societies. The sand mosaic depicts lightning, clouds, and rain; the two rows of sticks represent the Antelope warriors and their ancestors.

Antelope priests watch Snake priests making a ritual circuit of the village square on the ninth and last day of the fertility rite in Mishongnovi. They carry snake whips, used in their final dance.

whose membership cut across the kinship groups or clans. It was kept alive and transmitted by the "owning" clan, which furnished the meeting place, main officers, and ritual paraphernalia. Certain other clans provided other officers and performed particular parts of the rite. As we move from the Hopi toward the Eastern Pueblos the importance of clans diminishes, the priests exercise a greater degree of central control, and ritual life becomes simpler. Curing societies, with recruitment by trespass and vow-taking during illness, replace societies in which kin considerations are primary in membership selection. Curing takes precedence over rain bringing, perhaps because the East, being partially irrigated by streams, is less dependent on rainfall than the West. Among other Amerindians, the famous medicine lodges of the Algonquin, Ojibwas, and other Lake tribes also lay great stress on curing. Their mythology, however, shows the same preoccupations with war and fertility, while initiations constantly stress the theme that the living are the future dead, the dead are the ex-living, and wisdom consists in becoming used to the idea of one's own death. Ritual divisions into different groups representing such ideas as War and Peace, Summer and Winter, Sky and Earth, are frequently found in Amerindian life. Among them, one often finds so strong an interaction of dead and living, or spirits and men, that the dead ancestors are actually represented on earth in the social life.

Among the Kwakiutl of the northwest Pacific coast, the winter season was traditionally taken up with various dance-dramas arranged in a hierarchical series, each series belonging to a particular dance house or "secret society." The candidate would encounter a guardian spirit who would kidnap him, keep him away from the village for a while, teach him his secrets and then return him to the village. On his return he was so imbued with spirit that he was in a state of frenzy. (In the highest grades of the *Shaman's* society this state often led to ritual cannibalism.) The candidate was then "de-spirited" in a ritual that stressed the death and rebirth aspect of initiation. In the course of this he demonstrated the powers granted him: some sleight-of-hand trick, the impersonation or actual summoning of a spirit. The Kwakiutl were masters of the art of stage effects: changeable masks with movable parts, tunnels, trap doors, hidden speaking tubes, and flying puppets were all used as props in the display. Dances were hereditary, so that no initiate would meet spirits other than those of his own kinship group. The membership of these societies was limited, in that each ancestor-spirit could have only one representative at a time; younger relatives of the initiate were "captured" by lesser spirits of the same cycle. Dance rights could be acquired by neighboring chiefs through marriage dowry or through capture of the dance regalia in war. Here again it is easy to see that no account of secret societies is possible without reference to the social life of the group as a whole.

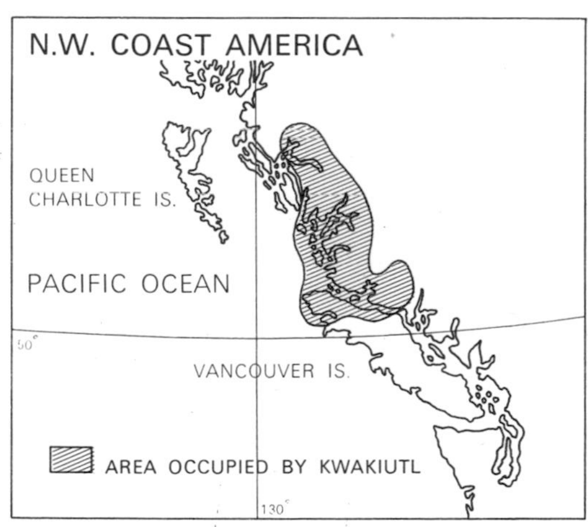

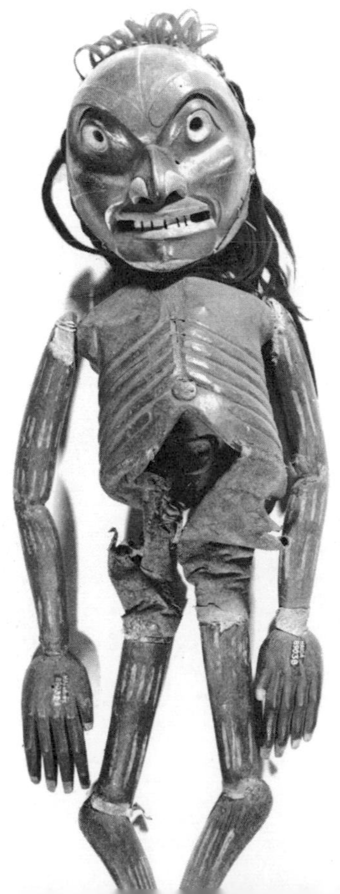

Map of the northwest Pacific coast shows the area occupied by the Kwakiutl. Right, a jointed Kwakiutl puppet that represents the spirit presiding over the Shamans' society ceremonial. Strung on a rope, it flew between the chief and his guests to symbolize the beginning of a performance.

Above, members of a Southern Kwakiutl Shamans' society in ceremonial dress. The crouching figures with elongated masks represent a huge man-eating bird that was supposed to inspire the cannibal dancer. Left, a Kwakiutl cannibal dancer—a shaman of the highest rank. He pretended to bite spectators and to feed on corpses, as if possessed by the cannibal spirit.

A considerable number of new secret organizations has arisen in the less developed parts of the world in the last century or two under the pressures of colonization and modernization. In them one often finds traditional elements, reshaped or reoriented to suit new stimuli. (One such society—Mau Mau—is the subject of our next chapter.) The abolition of the poison ordeal for witches in Africa left a vacuum that has been filled by new, partially secret anti-sorcery cults that achieve the same purpose. Anti-white cults based on the old spirit-revelations of American Indians arose in the late 19th century among the Plains Indians in the shape of the terrible Ghost-Dance religions, associated with the great Sioux uprising of 1890–1. In Melanesia, nativistic secret societies have arisen to explain why the white man's dispensation in the political and spiritual realms has not brought an equal dispensation in the economic realm—the "cargo" of modern goods so highly valued by the white man, and "withheld" by him from the native. Research in Burma has revealed curious cults based on perversions of folk-Buddhist ideas about messianic kings and future Buddhas, which were already known among Chinese rebels in classical times (p. 219) and now have a strong anti-British element. Most of these new secret or semi-secret organizations represent anti-power groups within the society rather than groups working hand in hand with lay power for the benefit of the whole society. They are to be seen in the context of emergent nationalism, as some kind of embryonic political force, though the traditional element in their makeup cannot be overlooked.

Rather than attempt a catalog of primitive secret societies throughout the world we have preferred to examine the notion of secrecy in general and to show that in traditional simple societies, secrecy is used mainly as an instrument of discipline in the acquisition of wisdom. This is true of most tribal initiations, which stress the age-old knowledge of the tribe, handed down by the ancestors and maintained through respect for the dead whom each individual is soon to join. Secrecy can also be an instrument of power through which the governing group ensures that it will remain the governing group. (This is equally true in the arts and crafts, where some mechanism is needed to ensure orderly recruitment and performance, as well as the careers of reigning artists and craftsmen, in each particular field.) Since in some populations that have no secret societies, all men in the tribe are given one initiation, we may regard secret societies not so much as originating out of tribal initiations but rather as representing the specialization of initiation, particularly in cases where the specialized field must be kept clear of competitors.

We have tried to show in this chapter that the concept of the primitive "secret society" as such can no longer remain. We have also tried to destroy the conception of the "primitive" as a devotee of savage rituals. The truth lies in looking at the primitive as a man very similar to ourselves, though living on a smaller scale, in a far more restricted environment, and with less liberty from the pressures of his fellows in every aspect of his life.

2 Mau Mau

In September 1948, the government of the British colony of Kenya received the first official report of a "new movement" among the one-and-a-quarter-million-strong Kikuyu tribe. The movement was Mau Mau, the focus of Kikuyu protests (hitherto ineffective) against the presence of white farmer-settlers on their land. Between 1952 and 1956, Mau Mau was to cost the British and Kenyan governments over $154 million, to tie down 11 infantry battalions and over 21,000 police. Yet its secrecy was so well preserved that until 1950 the police could obtain virtually no evidence of the many initiation ceremonies that were taking place.

By the 1950s, these secret ceremonies engaged the candidate to kill any opponent of Mau Mau, from a European farmer to his own father or mother, on command. They were not tribal initiations, though they did contain some traditional elements. For the emergence of Mau Mau as a secret society with some 12,000 militant members had been preceded by a prolonged breakdown of Kikuyu tribal life under European influence. While the white farmers, with government support, imposed an alien system of land tenure on the Kikuyu, the missionaries imposed on them a Christianity cluttered with over 1800 years of European accretions. They accelerated the process of detribalization by condemning the traditional initiations in which boys and girls had been instructed in their responsibilities to the tribe.

A group of Kikuyu, carrying the corpse of a companion, are arrested as Mau-Mau suspects by forces of the British Kenya Regiment (Karatina, Nyeri Province, February 1954). The men's guard is a member of their own tribe, which was split apart by the violence and "black magic" of the Mau-Mau resistance movement.

Kikuyu legend traces the origin of the tribe to a woman called Muumbi and her husband Gikuyu, who lived in the Fort Hall district some seven or eight hundred years ago. Ngai, the god of the Kikuyu, gave Muumbi nine children; her children gave their names to the nine Kikuyu clans.

By the late 16th century, the tribe had expanded southward across the Chania River to what is now called the Kiambu district and northward to Nyeri at the foot of Mount Kenya. The forest south of the Chania River belonged to the Wanderobo, a smaller tribe that lived by hunting and gathering roots. Each Wanderobo family held a vast area, sometimes as much as 40 square miles, as private property. Though the Kikuyu were powerful enough to have obtained this land by conquest, this would have offended their religious beliefs and legal customs. So a Kikuyu who wanted land would offer a Wanderobo family a payment of goats, sheep, or other goods in exchange. Before the deal was made, the Kikuyu proposed a ceremony of "mutual adoption." This ceremony regularized the religious ceremonies that formed part of his negotiations, which would not be valid unless both parties were Kikuyu or adopted Kikuyu.

A Kikuyu who bought land in this way became a *mbari* or founder of a sub-clan—a social unit comprising all his male descendants and also those of his brothers and male first cousins. Each member of the sub-clan was given a share in the sub-clan estate, or *githaka*, and was subject to the authority of the mbari (or his elected successor) in all matters relating to the sub-clan.

By the late 19th century, the Kikuyu had spread throughout Nyeri, Muranga (Fort Hall), and the Kiambu district. Kiambu was wholly inhabited by Kikuyu mbaris and their tenants. According to Dr. L. S. B. Leakey's *Mau Mau and the Kikuyu* (to which we are indebted for this account): "There can be very little doubt that, had the start of white settlement in Kenya come at this particular time instead of later, very little (if any) land in Kiambu, Kabete and Limuru would have been alienated to white farmers, for the land was carrying a big native population and no government would have tried to dispossess them for the sake of European farming."

Unfortunately, the country was stricken by a series of disasters: an epidemic of smallpox, a major outbreak of rinderpest, and a severe drought, followed by famine and a plague of locusts. Between 20 per cent and 50 per cent of the population died. Kiambu was particularly badly affected. Most of the Kikuyu who had recently bought land there survived only by abandoning the district temporarily and moving back into Nyeri and Fort Hall. To the Kikuyu, this withdrawal did not imply any abandonment of property rights. But by 1902 many flourishing Kikuyu farms had reverted to bush. It was in that year that the Kenya-Uganda railway (begun in 1896) reached the Kikuyu territory, opening up potentially rich farm lands, on which during the next five years the first farmers from Britain settled, under the impression that it was virgin land. In certain cases, where there remained some member of the land-owning sub-clan or his Kikuyu tenant, a payment was made to him by the farmer-settler, who believed in good faith that he had purchased the land. This purchase was in fact contrary to Kikuyu law and custom, which demanded, as we have seen, that any matter relating to the sub-clan as a whole should be referred to the titular head, and that dealings with outsiders should be preceded by a ceremony of mutual adoption. From the Kikuyu point of view, none of the rights acquired by white settlers in Kikuyu lands were valid.

The British government, on the other hand, assumed that by proclaiming a protectorate over East Africa in 1895, it had acquired sovereign rights over all the land. According to Leakey, "It was a widely held belief among the British—one might almost say universally held—that amongst the Bantu, land was not held as property. . . . The idea that there was any part of Africa where land was privately owned, where in fact it had actually been purchased, was unthought of." All the uncultivated land was designated as "Crown Land," with the exception of certain areas that were set aside as "Reserves" for the native population. Quite large areas in the Kiambu district were allocated to European farmer-settlers. The few Kikuyu who remained were told that they could either stay and work for the white farmer or move elsewhere. In practically every case payment was offered either in "purchase" or as "compensation for disturbance." It was a genuine misunderstanding, committed perhaps through imperial overconfidence. At this time the British knew nothing of Kikuyu laws and customs. Nor had they any conception of the extent to which Kikuyu tribal life was organized.

Photograph of 1900 shows European settlers and missionaries riding on the Kenya-Uganda railway, which opened up Kenya's rich farm land—and Kikuyu territory—for settlement.

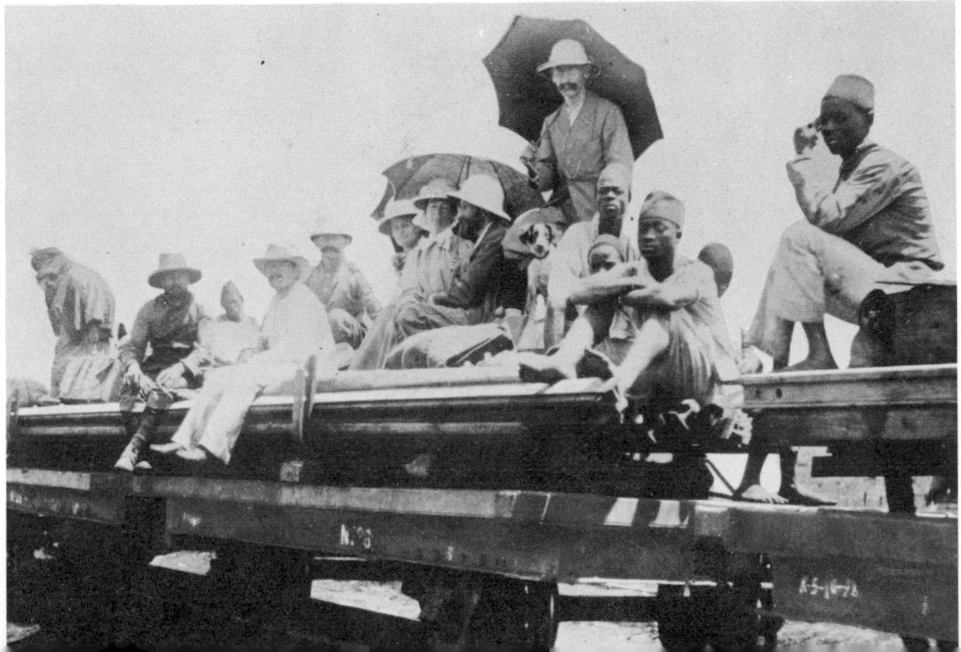

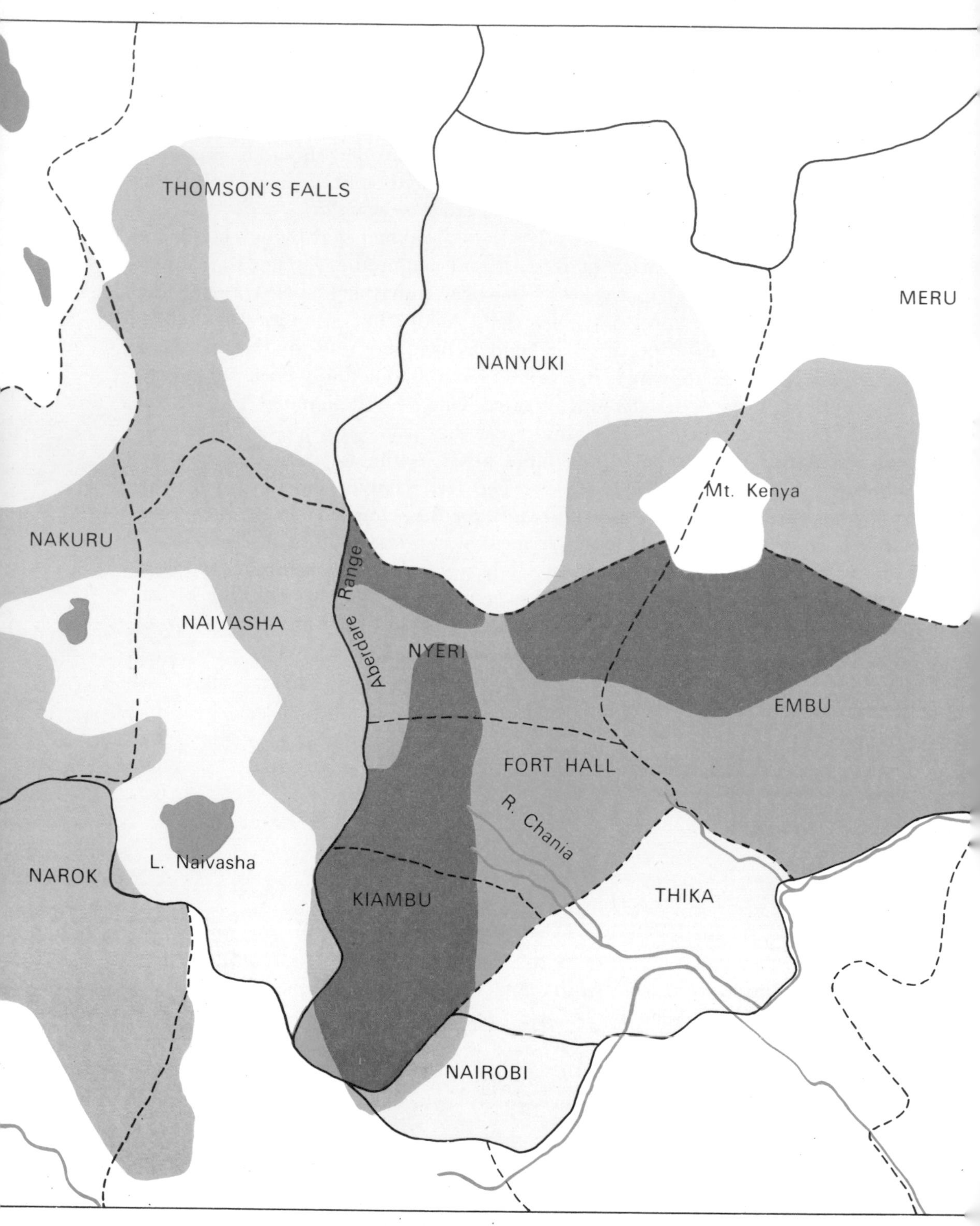

THOMSON'S FALLS
MERU
NANYUKI
Mt. Kenya
NAKURU
Aberdare Range
NAIVASHA
NYERI
EMBU
FORT HALL
R. Chania
NAROK
L. Naivasha
KIAMBU
THIKA
NAIROBI

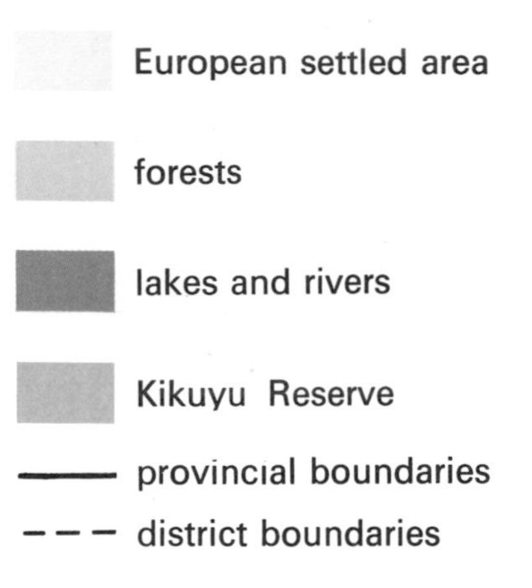

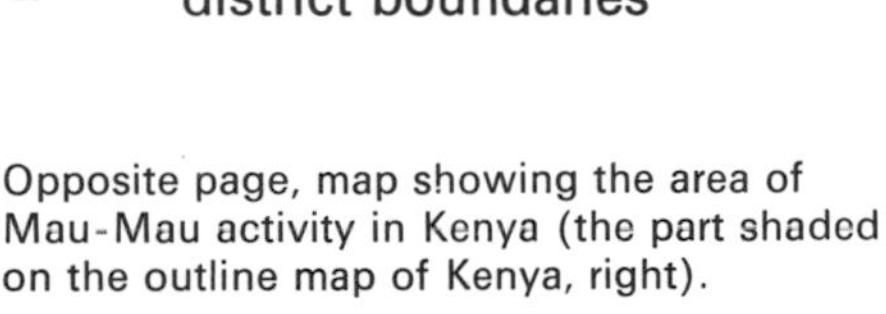

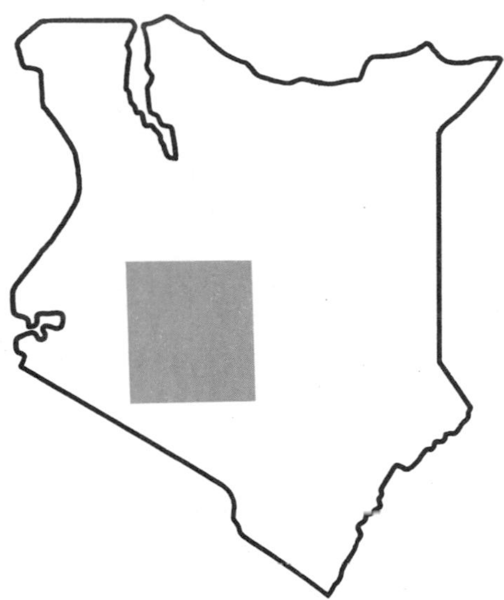

Opposite page, map showing the area of Mau-Mau activity in Kenya (the part shaded on the outline map of Kenya, right).

Among the most honored members of the Kikuyu tribe were the medicine men, or *mundu mugo*, who combined the roles of doctor, diviner, and exorcizer. Some specialized in herbal remedies, others in protective magic, and others in the curing of illness by ceremonial purification. Membership of the group was traditionally confined to men who had undergone a long period of training and earned a high reputation for wisdom. Staunch guardians of Kikuyu law and custom, the medicine men diagnosed illness, mental or physical, as the result of breaking a taboo. For example, a Kikuyu who had touched any substance that was regarded as unclean would go to the medicine man to be cleansed of his guilt by a special ceremony involving the sacrifice of an animal. The medicine men, who worked openly for the benefit of the whole tribe, used protective magic to counteract the spells of the dreaded *murogi*, or black-magic workers, who worked in secret for individuals, and were believed to have the power to kill by witchcraft.

Oaths were an important feature of tribal life, not only in the sealing of any compact but also in the trial of legal cases, when the council of elders had failed to reach a satisfactory verdict. Such oaths were not taken lightly, for the *githathi* stone on which they were sworn had the magical property of bringing death to the false swearer or to a member of his family. These tribal oaths differed from those of the Mau Mau in that they were hallowed by custom, taken voluntarily with the approval of the rest of the family, and administered in daylight before a host of witnesses. Oaths like those of the Mau Mau, administered by force and in secret, were the weapons of black-magic workers. Such oaths were feared by the rest of the community because they violated tribal customs and taboos; they were believed to cause spiritual uncleanness, which could be cured only by the medicine man.

Above, a Kikuyu initiation ceremony for girls opens with a ritual dance. Such ceremonies conferred adult status on a child who had reached puberty. They were the means by which tribal lore was handed down from one generation to another.

Above right, a Kikuyu medicine man holds the 150-year-old *thenge* stone he has inherited from an ancestor. Used like the *githathi* stone, as the guarantee of a legal oath, it was supposed to bring death to the perjurer and to defeat black magic.

It was the medicine man who had the important task of purifying the two separate sites on which all the boys and girls in the tribe who had reached puberty would be initiated into adult life. Until he had been ceremonially initiated, no Kikuyu could be considered a full member of the tribe. The ceremony was preceded by a long period of preparation, during which the elders of the tribe instructed the candidates in Kikuyu laws and customs. The rites themselves began with feasting, dancing, and libations of beer, and culminated in circumcision—the "outward and visible sign" of adulthood. One of the most solemn features of the ceremony was the passing of the candidate through an arch of sugar-cane stems and banana leaves, which symbolized his rebirth. The girls' initiation ceremony was preceded by a race to a sacred tree; the girl who won became the most sought-after bride. Since women outnumbered men, the girls who failed to find husbands were encouraged to become second or third wives in polygamous families. Husbands often took second wives at the request of their first. Each wife had a hut of her own, and the husband had his hut, which he used for entertainment but in which none of his wives slept.

Bewilderingly to the Kikuyu, the missionaries who established stations and schools at Thogoto, Kabete, and St. Austin's in the 1890s and 1900s showed no disapproval of male circumcision, but were appalled at its female equivalent, clitoridectomy. They forbade converts to perform it, or to allow their daughters to undergo the operation. They taught that polygamy was incompatible with Christianity, and that such tribal ceremonies as oathings and cleansings were heathen sacrifices that every Christian convert should abjure. Since many such ceremonies were considered invalid unless all the male

Right, an Anglican missionary sells Bibles to East Africans in the early 1900s. The missionaries struck at the foundations of Kikuyu tribal life by condemning the circumcision of girls at initiation and the sacrifice of animals in oath-taking.

members of the family were present, fathers justifiably resented the wish of their sons to join mission schools. Though sons who did so were often disowned, many young Kikuyu became mission-school pupils and genuine Christian converts at the turn of the century. But later, the advantages of schooling were paid for by lip service to Christianity. During World War I a new generation grew up that wanted to combine European knowledge with African tradition. This generation, uneasily moving between the native Reserve and the growing cities, had only a perfunctory knowledge of religious beliefs and practices—either Kikuyu or Christian. At the same time, the initiations that had always bound the young Kikuyu to their tribe were gradually being reduced to the hasty performance of the circumcision rite.

These uprooted Kikuyu first sought an economic outlet, the sort of jobs that would favor their educational development and bring them financial security. But the search was in vain. Those who went to Nairobi could not earn enough to buy houses and settle down. The educated Kikuyu was an uneasy commuter between the town and the Reserve, where he had to keep a patch of ground to which he could retire. Failing economic satisfaction, he sought political redress. The injustice of the higher standard of living enjoyed in his land by the European interlopers was the more intolerable because it was apparently designed for perpetuation long beyond his lifetime.

Perhaps most infuriating of all was the Kenya Civil Service, composed of government officers of the highest integrity and the best intentions, determined to stand up for the African against all settler demands, but equally determined to fight the Africans' battles for them rather than teach them to fight those battles for themselves. In 1923, in response to agitation from

European and Indian settlers for greater representation of their interests in the legislative council, the British government stated: "The interests of the African natives must be paramount. If, and when, those interests, and the interests of the immigrant races (European and Asiatic) should conflict, the former should prevail." Ten thousand Europeans were given 11 seats, over 23,000 Indians five seats, and the Arab community one. The Africans were represented by one member (not African until 1944) and an overall majority of European civil servants *ex officio*. Though these civil servants might genuinely put African native interests first, African nationalists did not think so.

Service in the British forces during World War I deepened the rift between the old and new generations of Kenyan Africans in culture, education, and environment. Immediately after the war, many Kikuyu attempted to return to Kiambu, and discovered for the first time that their lands had been taken over by Europeans. In 1922, the Kikuyu Central Association, or K.C.A., was started, with a hard core of ex-servicemen and ex-mission-school students. Its rallying cry was the same as that of the future Mau Mau, the recovery of the "lost lands" of the Kikuyu. This platform appealed to Kikuyu of all sorts: not only those living as squatters on European farms that had formerly belonged to them, but also those who had lost no land yet sympathized with the growing numbers of landless Kikuyu.

The K.C.A.'s formation followed immediately on the arrest of Harry Thuku, president of the short-lived Young Kikuyu Association, which had led a protest campaign against the government's threat of reduced wages for African laborers. In March 1922 his followers staged a demonstration during which some Kikuyu were shot and killed by the Colonial police. This incident reinforced Kikuyu resentment of the government; and the K.C.A., convinced that its aims could not be achieved by appeals to the legislative council or by lawsuits, pursued its activities underground.

In 1928, Jomo Kenyatta, who was later to be convicted of "managing" Mau Mau, became K.C.A.'s general secretary. In 1929, at his own suggestion, the association sent him to England to present a petition to the Colonial Secretary, listing Kikuyu land grievances and demanding African representation in the legislative council. Kenyatta was unsuccessful. But he returned to England on behalf of K.C.A. in 1930, and prolonged his visit for 16 years.

Jomo Kenyatta, or Johnstone Kamau, was born in the Kiambu district in or about 1889. He attended a Church of Scotland mission school, then worked as a clerk and meter-reader in Nairobi. He entered African politics in 1922, when he joined Harry Thuku's Young Kikuyu Association. While in England, he joined the Communist party and several anti-colonial associations. He took a Diploma in Anthropology. He married an English girl, Edna Grace Clarke. During Kenyatta's absence, the insistence by some Kenyan missionary societies that Christian Kikuyu girls should not undergo clitoridectomy led to the formation of two independent African Churches: the Kikuyu African Orthodox Church (1935) and the Kikuyu Independent Pentecostal Church (1938). These preached an African Christianity to square Bible teaching with tribal custom. They countered the missionaries' arguments with such texts as St. Paul's "Circumcision is nothing; uncircumcision is nothing."

These independent churches immediately started schools to supersede the European mission and other schools. To prevent supervision, government grants-in-aid were refused. History was taught from an African nationalist point of view. (In 1953, 136 of these schools were closed on the grounds that they were spreading Mau-Mau propaganda and being used for oath-taking ceremonies.) A Kenya Teachers' College was started in Githunguri to train teachers for new schools among the Kikuyu and other East African tribes.

In 1940, the K.C.A. was banned by the government on the grounds that it had established a treasonable relationship with Italian agents in Ethiopia. But four years later, Eliud Mathu (who had just been nominated as the first African member of the legislative council) founded another political party, the Kenyan African Union, or K.A.U., which had the same objectives as K.C.A. Into the new party poured all the old members of K.C.A., together with a host of young men with ideals, grievances, or both.

Kenyatta returned to Kenya in 1946, and became principal of the Teachers' College at Githunguri. But when he presented himself to the governor, Sir Philip Mitchell, in Nairobi, and offered his services in the legislative council, Sir Philip suggested that before entering the national arena Kenyatta should

Jomo Kenyatta presiding over the first Pan-African Congress, held in Manchester in 1945. Though Kenyatta came to England to air Kikuyu grievances, his political interests soon extended beyond Kenya, and he represented Ethiopia at the League of Nations during World War II. Returning to Kenya, he became president of the Kenyan African Union (alleged by the government to be a front organization for Mau Mau). Convicted of "managing" Mau Mau, he was imprisoned and detained from 1952 to 1961.

Kikuyu rebels of the Forty Group, arrested in November 1952 on suspicion of recruiting for Mau Mau, await police interrogation.

reacquaint himself with the Kenyan scene by a period of service in local government. Kenyatta began to recruit actively for K.A.U., of which he became president in the following year. The Kenya Teachers' College became, not unnaturally, a training ground for K.A.U. propagandists.

The K.A.U. under Kenyatta did not represent all shades of opinion even among the Kikuyu. Some believed that their interests could best be served by using Kenya government officials as a shield against the settlers, who were now demanding independence with European supremacy. Those Kikuyu who were convinced Christians in the missionary tradition and those who still preserved the tribal pattern were equally distrustful of K.A.U.

Furthermore, though the largest tribe in Kenya, the Kikuyu made up only one fifth of the total African population. Other tribes distrusted them for their cleverness and their ability to learn. But for this distrust the government might have alleviated the land problem by settling some of the landless Kikuyu on the less intensively cultivated lands of other tribes. The recovery of the "lost lands" remained the main aim of K.A.U. but others, such as resistance to terracing, were added. In the Kikuyu Reserves, the government's insistence on terracing and contour plowing had caused resentment among the laborers, who did not appreciate the importance of soil conservation. Resistance to terracing later became one of the aims of Mau Mau.

Kenyatta was well aware of the importance of soil conservation; but in 1949 he was not prepared to denounce the Mau-Mau policy openly. He denied that he himself had tried to stop terracing in the Fort Hall district, and attributed the order to the Forty Group (an anti-government group that recruited for Mau Mau and was named after the generation that came of age in 1940). It is probable that at this time Kenyatta had not the authority to play the statesman. He could remain at the head of his followers only if he went in the directions they decided. The Forty Group acknowledged Kenyatta as leader provided he did not condemn what they said and did. Though, in October 1950, Kenyatta came out in support of terracing, this was at a meeting in a native Reserve where he was being asked to condemn Mau Mau. All he did was to emphasize that Mau Mau and K.A.U. were separate bodies. This was probably true, though the official *Historical Survey of the Origins and Growth of Mau Mau* (1960) declares that initially "the propagation of Mau Mau and the conduct of the oath campaign was the function of those district branches of K.A.U. officered by Kikuyu. . . ." Many K.A.U. organizers had taken Mau-Mau oaths and Kenyatta knew it. We may conclude that far from leading Mau Mau, Kenyatta was pushed by it.

The first prosecution for oath-administration, which took place in March 1948, failed through a clerical blunder. It was there that the word "Mau Mau" was first heard. It was a nonsense word, made from "*Umu, Umu*" (Out! Out!), given as warning of the approach of police. It was later adopted by the movement to describe the initiatory oath.

Josiah Mwangi Kariuki, author of "*Mau Mau*" *Detainee*, took his first oath in December 1953. The reader may judge for himself whether it was, as Kariuki contends, just like the Freemason's oath of secrecy (p. 155). One evening, a friend who had been with Kariuki at an independent school asked him to come to his house for a cup of tea. When it was dark they went for a walk. After going some 300 yards along a narrow path to the fields, Kariuki saw some men and women sitting in the maize on his left, and on his right an arch about seven feet high, made from two banana stems joined at the top and plaited with bean stalks. It was an almost exact replica of the arch used in the traditional tribal initiations.

At this point, Kariuki realized that though there had been no open invitation, he was going to be oathed. He was told to join three other people, all of whom he knew. They were ordered to remove their shoes, watches, and any other metal things they had with them. Kariuki's friend explained that Kariuki was a student who had been actively recruiting for K.A.U. So he would be a good candidate for the Oath of Unity, *Ndemwa Ithatu*.

They passed through the arch seven times in single file, then lined up in front of the oath administrator Biniathi, a 40-year-old Kikuyu in European dress. Biniathi took the lungs of a goat in his right hand and in his left another piece of goat's meat. They bowed as he circled their heads with the meat seven times, counting in Kikuyu. He gave the lungs to each in turn and told them to bite them. Then they had to repeat this oath slowly after him:

I speak the truth and vow before God
And before this movement,
The movement of Unity,
The Unity which is put to the test
The Unity that is mocked with the name of "Mau Mau,"
That I shall go forward to fight for the land,
The lands of Kiringaya that we cultivated,
The lands which were taken by the Europeans
And if I fail to do this
May this oath kill me,
May this seven kill me,
May this meat kill me.
I speak the truth that I shall be working together
With the forces of the movement of Unity
And I shall help it with any contribution for which I am asked,
I am going to pay sixty-two shillings and fifty cents and a ram for the movement
If I do not have them now I shall pay in the future,
And if I fail to do this
May this oath kill me,
May this seven kill me,
May this meat kill me.

Biniathi anointed each one on the forehead with the blood of the goat, to remind them that they were now fighting for their land and must never think of selling their country. (In some oathing ceremonies, the sign of the cross was made, "In the name of our Lord Jesus Christ.") Then Biniathi made three scratches on the left wrist of each initiate, holding the goat's flesh so that the human blood fell on it. Finally he gave each the meat to bite (a feature of the traditional oath ceremonies), saying, "The act of eating this meat with the blood of each of you on it shows that you are now united one to the other and with us." Then they each paid the oathing fee of 5 shillings (70 U.S. cents) and joined the other people in the maize.

"My emotions during the ceremony had been a mixture of fear and elation," Kariuki wrote. "Afterwards in the maize I felt exalted with a new spirit of power and strength. All my previous life seemed empty and meaningless. Even my education, of which I was so proud, appeared trivial beside this splendid and terrible force that had been given me. I had been born again and I sensed once more the feeling of opportunity and adventure that I had had on the first day my mother started teaching me to read and write. The other three in the maize were all silent and were clearly undergoing the same spiritual rebirth as myself."

Kariuki and the other initiates were told that they must not sleep with a woman for seven days and were warned to keep their membership secret. If they wanted to know whether someone they met had taken the oath, they should ask, "Where were you circumcised?" An initiate would reply, "I was circumcised at Karimania's with Karimania." There were many subsequent oaths, and each one was said to represent a grade.

The first oath was comparatively harmless. The only precise commitment was the payment of money to the organization's funds. Later oaths, which were freely improvised by forest leaders, were the most bestial elaborations on another standard oath, the *Batuni* or Platoon oath, which called on the initiate to kill. When Kariuki took the Batuni oath, he had to squat before Biniathi stark naked. "He told me to take the thorax of the goat which had been skinned, to put my penis through a hole that had been made in it and to hold the rest of it in my left hand in front of me." There were seven vows, taken before Ngai, and sealed by the same curse in the event of betrayal:

(1) "If I am called on to kill for our soil, if I am called on to shed my blood for it I shall obey and I shall never surrender." (2) "I shall never betray our country or anybody of this movement to the enemy, whether the enemy be European or African." (3) "If I am called during the night or the day to burn the store of a European who is our enemy, I shall go forth without fear and I shall never surrender." (4) "If I am called to go to fight the enemy or to kill the enemy—I shall go even if the enemy be my father or mother, my brother or sister." (5) "If the people of the movement come to me by day or by night and if they ask me to hide them I shall do so and I shall help them." (6) "I shall never take away the woman of another man, never walk with prostitutes, never steal anything belonging to another person in the movement, nor shall I hate any other member for his action." (7) "I shall never sell my country for money or any other thing, I shall abide until my death by all the promises that I have made this day, I shall never disclose our secrets to our enemy nor to anybody who does not belong to the movement and if I transgress against any of the vows that I have thus consciously made, I shall agree to any punishment that the movement shall decide to give me and if I fail to do these things, may this oath kill me."

F. D. Corfield, author of the official survey of Mau Mau, contends that by 1952 K.A.U. was little more than a cover for Mau Mau. Mau Mau worked through the well-developed K.A.U. machinery, from its central committee in Nairobi, through its district committees, to its local cells. This organization became what the government called the "Passive Wing" of the Mau-Mau movement, sending orders and supplies to the "Activists" or forest fighters, who had their main bodies (the "Land Freedom Armies") in the regions of Mount Kenya and the Aberdares.

This machinery, so discernible by 1960, was not detected in the early days of Mau Mau. The official reason for the failure is that the intelligence forces were too small to make a correct assessment. But the possibility remains that isolated events, a strike here, a protest march there, a K.A.U. meeting somewhere else, were not connected with one another, at first, except as symptoms of Kikuyu unrest and the growth of African nationalism.

The aims of Mau Mau, as listed by Dr. Leakey in his *Defeating Mau Mau*, were seven: (1) recover the lost lands; (2) obtain self government; (3) destroy Christianity; (4) restore ancient customs; (5) drive out all foreigners; (6) abolish soil conservation; (7) increase secular education. The first two aims appealed to members of such nationalist organizations as K.A.U., which seemed to be making little progress by peaceful means. The others were simply used to draw as many people as possible into the movement, enlisting tribal emotions on behalf of an African rebirth. Though Kenyatta became the movement's symbolic messiah, the role he had chosen was Moses. He wanted to avoid crucifixion and lead his saner followers into the promised land.

The initiation fees and dues meant that Mau-Mau stalwarts, many of them unemployed, would have money on which to live. But this system of payment had already begun to break down before the declaration of the Emergency on October 21, 1952. Candidates for the Mau-Mau oath could not be approached openly. If the candidate would not swear voluntarily, he had to be forced to swear. There was the case of the Catholic Kikuyu woman who was hauled to the oathing hut. When she refused to swear, she was stripped and flogged and told she would be killed and her blood drunk by her persecutors. She still refused, so she was flogged again and hung from a rope until she lost consciousness. As she came round, a bottle of blood was pressed to her lips and she was made to complete the oath. Many Kikuyu would have felt bound by this oath, even though it was involuntary, but she reported it to the police.

A Kikuyu medicine man performs the traditional *thenge* stone ceremony at the request of the government, to release members of Mau Mau from their vows. Left, he prepares for the ceremony by smearing one leg and one side of his face with white chalk and castor oil. Right, after taking the *thenge* stone out of its basket, he places it in a support of twigs taken from the sacred bush. Far right, he stands upright to intone the oath, holding a twig. With the final words—"Let the man who denies this oath fall to the ground and die"—he thrusts the twig through the hole in the stone to demonstrate the fate of perjurers.

Other Kikuyu, less certain in their faith, were successfully brought into Mau Mau against their will. They were torn between fear of evil and the desire for a quiet life. Mau Mau had been planned to unite the Kikuyu against the foreign interlopers, but it began to divide them. There was an outbreak of arson. In Nyeri, Mau Mau shut loyal Kikuyu families into their huts and set them on fire. But no lives were lost. This was in late January and early February, 1952. And on the night of February 6, two European farms in Nanyuki lost crops valued at $3640 through arson.

The arson outbreak was doubly significant. For Mau Mau, it marked the failure to secure the adherence of the Kikuyu by peaceful means; for the government, it meant the possibility of taking more active steps against what had previously been merely the menace of unrest and secret oathings.

In April, the government started a de-oathing campaign to release members of Mau Mau from their vows. "Cleansing" ceremonies were held by the medicine men, who were prepared to purify those who had broken the old taboos by taking the Mau-Mau oaths. This campaign, which was to be continued throughout the Emergency, began in Nyeri, where the medicine men decided to use the "dog-oath"—a solemn oath that had last been used some 40 years earlier to counter an outbreak of black magic. At later de-oathing ceremonies, in Kiambu and Fort Hall, they made use of the *githathi* stone (p. 43). The Mau-Mau countermeasure to this was further recourse to black magic: they sacrificed an animal near the de-oathing center the previous night, with a threat invoking death on all who attended the ceremony or helped the government. Membership of Mau Mau continued to grow.

At about the same time, loyal Kikuyu chiefs and headmen received threatening letters and the first assassinations began. On May 15, 1952, two Kikuyu were found shot in the Kirichwa River, near Nairobi. One had informed against Mau Mau a few weeks before. Six people were committed for trial

for these murders. The man who reported the discovery of the bodies was himself later found assassinated.

Political murder had become the idiom of the day and Kenyatta realized on what a knife-edge he was poised. "If Jomo Kenyatta is arrested by our enemy, I will die if I do not follow him wherever he is, and free him," became the Mau-Mau oath in June. But if he wasn't arrested and shut securely away from the savagery of his people, he knew he would never be able to emerge as the "Light of Kenya." He was playing a dangerous game, which he could win only if the government placed him in the asylum of detention, while they wrestled with the violence that he had done nothing to assuage.

In March 1952, Sir Philip Mitchell had been reported as saying that the general political feeling in Kenya was better than he had ever known it for many years. On June 21, he relinquished office as governor. During the three months that had to elapse before a new governor took office, the acting governor rejected the legislative council's pleas for emergency legislation with the statement, "I categorically deny that there is a state of Emergency." Nevertheless, 59 loyal Africans had been murdered in the previous six months.

The difficulties facing the government must be appreciated. The powers necessary for the suppression of subversive forces (in which K.A.U. and associated bodies were included) could be taken only if a State of Emergency was declared. If it was declared, it must be seen to have been declared not merely as the result of European pressure on government policy, but at the request, and for the protection, of loyal Kikuyu. Sir Philip and the acting governor

The smoking ruins of Lari, a Kikuyu village that defied Mau Mau and was burned to the ground with its inhabitants by local members of the movement on March 26, 1953.

were prepared to incur the charge of complacency because they knew that the declaration of a State of Emergency would aggravate the emergency. If in the intervening months they could have persuaded Kenyatta unequivocally to condemn Mau Mau, it would have been possible to take emergency measures against Mau Mau without the risk of driving more K.A.U. supporters to join the extremists.

Everybody knew that the situation would change with the arrival of the new governor, Sir Evelyn Baring. But in the meantime, motorized Mau-Mau oathing teams were driving out from Nairobi to the Reserve to speed up forced recruitment. There were rumors of oathing assemblies numbering 800 at a time. During 10 days in mid-September, 14 Kikuyu were murdered on suspicion of being informers. On the night of September 25, three gangs, each about fifteen strong, set fire to buildings on five farms at Timau, between Nanyuki and Meru. They killed or mortally maimed 120 cattle valued at $2700, wounded 26 cattle, killed 240 sheep, and wounded 140 more. The livestock were not killed outright, but disemboweled or otherwise mutilated.

Sir Evelyn Baring arrived in Nairobi on September 29, 1952. Ten days later, after a rapid tour of the disaffected areas (during which Senior Chief Waruhiu was assassinated in daylight on an open road), the new governor cabled London recommending the declaration of a State of Emergency as soon as precautionary measures could be arranged. "Most criminal action is planned in, and instructions are sent from Nairobi. This was borne out very clearly by two small towns on two parallel ridges in Fort Hall. The first had many Mau-Mau crimes: the second has had none. The first has a bus service: the second has not—We are facing a planned revolutionary movement. If the movement cannot be stopped, there will be an administrative breakdown, followed by bloodshed amounting to civil war."

On October 21, 1952, the governor announced a State of Emergency. But the operation had begun the night before with the arrival of 12 R.A.F. troop carriers bringing a reinforcement of the Lancashire Fusiliers from the Canal Zone, followed by the arrest of 83 Mau-Mau suspects—including Jomo Kenyatta, whose trial was set for January 1953.

On the second day of the Emergency, Senior Chief Nderi was hacked to pieces, when with two tribal police he ordered an oathing crowd to disperse. A few days later, Eric Bowyer, an elderly European farmer, and his two house-boys were murdered. There was no ostensible reason why Bowyer should have been murdered—or for that matter, Commander Meiklejohn, a retired naval officer living in Thomson's Falls. The indiscriminate illogic of these attacks was meant to spread terror among the European settlers. November 26 saw the murder of Nairobi City Councillor Tom Mbotela, a Luo tribesman, and former vice-president of K.A.U., who had denounced Mau Mau. Two attempts had been made on his life in 1950 and it was known that he was to give evidence for the prosecution in the Kenyatta trial.

In the Reserve and on the European farms, a Kikuyu Home Guard was organized, armed only with native weapons, but working with the African tribal police. Their numbers grew from 5000 to 10,000 by mid-January 1953. In consequence, in the first two weeks of January, Mau Mau murdered 35 Africans. Though the number of European deaths from Mau Mau throughout the Emergency was only 32—fewer than those caused by traffic accidents in Nairobi—they were of such savagery and senselessness (such as the butchery of the six-year-old Michael Ruck) that they provoked in Europeans a cold hatred that was sometimes as difficult to control as Mau Mau's hatred of Europeans. But from the beginning the struggle was primarily between those Kikuyu sworn to achieve independence by force and those who considered it must not be won at the cost of law and order.

Whether or not the declaration of the Emergency had anticipated an armed rising planned for some later date is uncertain. What is sure is that during the early phases neither side had any clear strategy. There was a build-up of government forces, both from outside and within—recruitment of police, home guards, and intelligence. But instead of there being any clear-cut combat area, there was a series of isolated incidents and a dispersion of government forces in defensive positions. In this situation the majority of Kikuyu, who wanted a quiet life, found it diplomatic to collaborate with both sides. When the Home Guard wanted a defensive ditch, they dug it; when the Mau Mau wanted food, they gave it.

But on the night of March 26, 1953, there occurred two incidents that initiated a new phase. At about 9.30 P.M., 80 Mau Mau with a truck attacked the police station at Naivasha in the Rift Valley, killed the watchtower sentry and the charge-room clerk, captured 18 automatic weapons and 29 rifles and as much ammunition as they could carry, and escaped unharmed.

Half an hour later, at Lari, 30 miles away, a force nearly a thousand strong attacked the families of men in the Kikuyu Home Guard. Huts were bound with cable so that the doors could not be opened, then they were soaked in gasoline and set alight. Those escaping from the huts were hacked to pieces. Chief Luka, who had opposed Mau Mau, was killed and mutilated, together with his eight wives. One of these saw his body split in two halves before it was flung in her face. One woman who escaped with her arm cut off at the joint had seen her baby decapitated and its blood drunk by her attackers. She was able to give the names of 50 whom she recognized as her neighbors and local men. In the Lari massacre, 84 people were killed, two thirds of them women and children; 31 survived, but mutilated and scarred for life. Two hundred huts were burned down, 1000 cattle maimed, and an unknown number of charred relics represented the unidentified dead.

The Naivasha raid convinced the authorities that Mau Mau was militarily more formidable than they had thought. The Lari massacre, like the Nazi obliteration of Lidice, struck the civilized world with horror. If they had planned it deliberately, the Mau Mau could not have scored a double victory surer to secure their ultimate defeat. Though Kariuki, in "*Mau Mau*" *Detainee*, tried to evade the guilt for the Lari massacre, his apology was unsubstantiated. The uncommitted Kikuyu henceforward were prepared to join in defeating Mau Mau. But this was something that would take time.

In April, Kenyatta and five of his associates were convicted of "managing" Mau Mau. Kenyatta (described by the magistrate as "the master mind behind a plan to drive Europeans from Kenya") was sentenced to seven years' imprisonment with hard labor. The phase that followed was probably evolutionarily necessary, even though it was not very effective. In June, General Sir George Erskine was called in as Commander in Chief East Africa to coordinate the activities of the police, the military, and the civil authority. The Kikuyu Home Guard was finally issued with some firearms to replace its *pangas*, or double-edged knives. To the 420 European conscripts raised from the 45,000-strong European community was added a contingent of 7000 Asians (from 150,000, mostly Indians). European prejudice had hitherto resisted the demand of Asians to be conscripted.

There had been significant migrations of Kikuyu meanwhile. From the European farms in the Rift Valley went a large number of Kikuyu, some evicted by the government from Mau-Mau-dominated areas, some dismissed by apprehensive farmers, and others anxious to avoid the new and more stringent identity-card system that had been imposed on Kikuyu living outside the Reserve. The already crowded Reserve was forced to accommodate these 60,000 newcomers. Many of these, given a bleak welcome, went on to swell

Nairobi Africans detained in April 1954, when mass arrests by government forces crippled Mau Mau's urban organization.

the Mau-Mau forces in the forests of Mount Kenya or the Aberdares. Dedan Kimathi and other forest "generals" found the invasion of what Kimathi called this "uninvited rabble" an embarrassment. Some were fanatics, some believed that Kenyatta—whose appeal against conviction dragged on for a year and a quarter—had won the day, some were frightened by the increasing control of the Reserve by police and military, and others felt that even if they had taken the oath unwillingly, they were involved with Mau Mau.

Military operations in the forests during 1953 had shown such limited returns that the government decided to launch an attack on the Passive Wing in Nairobi in 1954. To do this, it would be necessary to withdraw most troops from the front line. Operation Anvil, the massive screening of some 60,000 city Kikuyu, was planned for April 24. But before that, in a routine skirmish on Mount Kenya, an important prisoner was taken, Waruhiu Itote. In 1942, at the age of 20, Itote had joined the King's African Rifles and risen to the rank of battalion Signals Corporal in the Pacific. Demobbed, he became a fireman on the East African Railway. Under compulsion he took the Mau-Mau oath in 1951, voluntarily he undertook duties with K.A.U. at public meetings or private executions. On Mount Kenya, he promoted himself to the rank of "General China."

Up to this point, there had been no personal intelligence between the government forces and those of Mau Mau. Kenyan-born, 27-year-old Ian Henderson, then an assistant superintendent of police, talked to Itote for three days. Born and brought up with Kikuyu, Henderson knew every idiom of the Kikuyu mind. He persuaded Itote to go back and try to arrange the surrender of some 5000 Mau Mau on Mount Kenya.

The operation failed through a series of mistakes. The Mau-Mau leaders, suspecting that the proposed surrender-talks were a trap, failed to appear at the final forest rendezvous, fixed for April 10. The attempt was abandoned, and the waiting troops were transferred to Operation Anvil in Nairobi.

In the first fortnight of the operation, each sector of the city was cordoned off in turn, and its African inhabitants were screened. Ex-Mau Mau disguised in long hooded robes helped to identify their former associates. Those whose passes were not in order, or who could give no satisfactory explanation of their presence in Nairobi, were transported in lorries to a reception camp at Latanga for further questioning. By May 8, about 30,000 Africans had been screened, and 16,538 of these had been sent to detention camps. Waruhiu Itote was put in the same camp as Jomo Kenyatta, who tried to educate him so that he could become the head of his bodyguard. (This post-Independence aim has not been realized at the time of writing. Signals Corporal Itote, "General China," is a 2nd Lieutenant in the Kenyan Army.) Throughout the rest of the year, a battalion was kept permanently in Nairobi, and intelligence teams made surprise raids in districts where Mau Mau were thought to persist. At the end of the year, Mau-Mau detainees totaled about 77,000.

In destroying the Passive Wing in Nairobi, this operation cut off the forest fighters' supplies. The government turned its attention to the Mau Mau in the forests of Mount Kenya and the Aberdares, who were now isolated.

In January 1955, an operation was organized in the Aberdares to drive Mau Mau out of their hideouts. This operation, which accounted for only 161 Mau Mau, was followed in March by another, which accounted for 277. These enormously costly and unrewarding "grouse drives," the bombings that wounded far more elephants, rhinos, and buffaloes than men, and the sealing off of the Reserve reduced the Mau Mau to a state of dehumanization without parallel in modern times. But it was the Kikuyu themselves, rather than European troops, who were to provide the final solution to the Emergency. In May, five special teams, each composed of ten ex-Mau Mau, were attached to the police at Nyeri. In three months, these teams had discovered and killed 24 of the 51 major Mau-Mau leaders. Of those that remained, Dedan Kimathi was by far the most formidable.

Kimathi was the most pathetic victim and monstrous creation of the movement that swept Kenyatta into power, a psychopath with delusions of grandeur and paranoiac obsessions worse than any Caesar chronicled by Suetonius, but already designated, at least by J. M. Kariuki, for the role of "the greatest hero of us all," the Robin Hood of later Kenyan myth-history. Kimathi was born illegitimately in the Tetu location, on October 31, 1920. When he was 11, his grandmother on her deathbed gave him her blessing. This he came to believe was Ngai's promise that he would become leader of all the Kikuyu. He was clever and was taught at both mission and independent schools. Devoid of gratitude, he stole from the old man who paid for his schooling and, after being driven away, repaid the old man by having him murdered by Mau Mau. He stayed nowhere very long. Undisciplined and

Waruhiu Itote, leader of Mau-Mau forces on Mount Kenya and self-styled "General China," stands trial at Nyeri in 1954. Itote's life was spared in return for his efforts to secure the surrender of other Mau-Mau "generals."

unprincipled, he won a certain admiration for his wildness and evasion of punishment. He was attracted to K.A.U. and, while acting as muscleman at mass meetings, he imbibed its heady doctrines. In 1952, having taken the Mau-Mau oath twice, he became leading oath-administrator in the Ol'Kalou and Thomson's Falls area, as well as branch secretary of K.A.U. He took the aims of Mau Mau in deadly earnest and explored the Aberdare forests as the scene of his future operations. He organized the mass oathing at which Senior Chief Nderi was hacked to death (p. 55). After the murder, Kimathi was captured and imprisoned. But one of the guards belonged to Mau Mau, and Kimathi bought liberty with his bicycle. He fled to the Aberdare forests with his Bible in Kikuyu. This Bible revealed his divine mission: he was Abraham, Moses, the Messiah, Ngai's chosen instrument. This conviction won him leadership over the Mau Mau in the Aberdares; religious awe held them, even later when Kimathi was insane.

In the early stages, he had a clear plan of organization. He enrolled his men in military formations on British Army lines. The ultimate objective was to take over European farms. He had two main councils, the first to formulate policy and appoint leaders, the second to train the rank and file in forest warfare and to break down all links with civilization. All those who refused to cooperate were to be killed, whatever their color. The Passive Wing in Nairobi was useful for supplies. But Kimathi made his position plain when at a jungle ceremony he proclaimed himself "Prime Minister Sir Dedan Kimathi, K.C.A.E., by God Knight Commander of the African Empire."

Kimathi was not a brave man, nor an ascetic. Given the best of everything as of right, he became the prey of Caesarism. As leaders emerged who might challenge his position, he demoted them and sent them to distant posts. If they protested or returned, they were strangled and left to the hyenas. Kimathi's "Land Freedom Army" split into groups, some acknowledging his overlordship, other carrying on the struggle for survival alone.

Mau Mau became for these forest fighters an animal way of life. Supplies from the Passive Wing dwindled, then vanished. The forest had to supply everything. They made snares of wire from crashed airplanes to trap animals for food and clothing. They gathered wild fruit, roots, and honey. With hair plaited to make the removal of lice easier, they came to look on their old lives as remote, even frightening. The struggle for existence was the only reality.

In his classic story *The Hunt for Kimathi*, Henderson tells how he gradually won over the forest fighters, individually and in groups, and then sent them back into the forest, armed, to bring in, or to kill, their former comrades. After a six-month search, Henderson and his men found Kimathi and drove him to the forest fringe. They captured him on October 22, 1956. In the following five months, Kimathi was tried, sentenced to death, and executed.

Kimathi's capture, which came almost exactly four years after the declaration of the Emergency, was thought to mark the end of the militant Mau

Elusive Mau-Mau commander Dedan Kimathi, captured only after a six-month search by special police in the jungle of the Aberdares.

Mau. In all, 10,527 Mau Mau had been killed—4686 of them by the Kikuyu Home Guard and the tribal police. By January 1960, when the new governor, Sir Patrick Renison, formally proclaimed the end of the Emergency, Mau Mau appeared to persist only in a few forest groups. In fact (though vastly reduced) it survived in all but name.

Mau Mau had been officered by men who saw themselves as national freedom fighters, and were not prepared to release their hold on the rank and file until their purpose had been fulfilled. In late 1960, settlers once more heard rumors of secret oath-taking ceremonies, reputedly organized by members of the new Kenya African National Union—the political party that was to bring Jomo Kenyatta into power. In the period immediately preceding Kenya's independence, men like Mau-Mau "Field Marshal" Mwariama—whose 300 followers terrorized the Meru area—trained new initiates in the forests, collected arms and ammunition, and awaited an opportunity to drive out those European settlers who remained.

In 1963, when Kenya became independent, Jomo Kenyatta was appointed prime minister. Men who had been avowed members of Mau Mau won seats in the new Kenya National Assembly. On November 6, an amnesty was proclaimed for all "persons still hiding in the forests," but the response was so small that the amnesty had to be extended. Groups left the forest, received their pardons, and returned to the forest immediately after. On December 16, by agreement with the government, several Mau-Mau "generals" led the remnants of their armies out of the forest to surrender, and heard a speech in which Kenyatta expressed the hope that they would settle peacefully on land allocated to them by the government. Though hundreds of Mau Mau surrendered, the fact that Kenyatta had to declare yet another amnesty in 1964 points to the failure of this rehabilitation scheme. In Timau, where 45 plots of land had been made available, only one man had taken occupation of his allotted farm. The evidence suggests that Mau Mau will survive—perhaps as a protection racket in the remote villages, and as an anti-government group within Kenyan politics.

Above, Jomo Kenyatta is sworn in as prime minister of Kenya in the presence of members of his cabinet and the Rt. Hon. Malcolm Macdonald, the governor-general. The ceremony took place in June 1963, two years after Kenyatta's release from detention. Mau-Mau members lingered on in the forests long after Kenya's independence, though several hundred responded to the series of amnesties Kenyatta declared. Left and right, Mau-Mau "generals" as they emerged from the forest to surrender after Kenya's official independence day, December 12, 1963.

3 Thuggee

Shortly after Lord Cornwallis's capture of Seringapatam, capital of Mysore, in 1799, Mysore and several of the neighboring kingdoms in southern India came under British control. It was then that the scattered British soldiers and administrators began to discover that gangs of stranglers infested the roads of southern India in the winter season of travel: about a hundred of these stranglers were caught near Bangalore. But they also seemed to operate in the north; in 1810, the bodies of 30 travelers, ritually dismembered, were found in wells between the Ganges and the Jumna. Travelers were frequently murdered in various parts of the vast subcontinent. Authority was weak, and many bands of robbers lay in wait for villagers or townsmen stupid enough to wander abroad out of their own areas. There was nothing to prove that these murders were in any way connected until, in 1816, Richard Sherwood, a surgeon at Fort St. George in Madras, managed to find informers among the ritual killers who terrorized the Indian roads. It was his account of the sect that eventually led to its investigation and suppression; rarely has one brilliant academic article prompted such effective political action.

Dr. Sherwood entitled his article *Of The Murderers Called Phansigars*. "The *Phansigars*, or stranglers, are thus designated from the Hindustani word *Phansi*, a noose. In the more northern parts of India, these murderers are called *Thugs*, signifying deceivers." The sect was often protected by local rulers,

Kali, Hindu goddess of destruction. Probably a pre-Aryan war deity and mother goddess, she is revered as the "divine mother" and as a consort of the god Shiva. The Thugs claimed her as a tribal ancestor and worshiped her with human sacrifices until the mid-19th century. (Detail from a North Indian bazaar painting, about 1830).

with whom it shared the loot seized from murdered travelers, and its members lived as ordinary peasants. The killers never attacked Europeans, for fear of retribution; and they operated a good hundred miles from their homes against fellow travelers on the roads. "*Phansigars* never commit robbery unaccompanied by murder, their practice being first to strangle and then to rifle their victims. It is also a principle with them to allow no one to escape of a party, however numerous, which they assail, that there may be no witnesses of their atrocities. The only admitted exception to this rule is in the instance of boys of very tender age, who are spared; adopted by the *Phansigars*; and, on attaining the requisite age, initiated into their horrible mysteries."

They operated, according to Dr. Sherwood, in gangs of 10 to 50 men. They were mainly Muslims, yet they did have Hindus among them and they worshiped Hindu deities. Their advance intelligence was excellent. They sent ahead scouts to investigate and win the confidence of wealthy travelers. Later, the main body of the Phansigars joined their companions as strangers. Scouts were placed in front and behind the victim or victims, in case these should escape. "Two *Phansigars* are considered to be indispensably necessary to effect the murder of one man, and commonly three are engaged. . . . While travelling along, one of the *Phansigars* suddenly puts the cloth round the neck of the person they mean to kill, and retains hold of one end, while the other end is seized by an accomplice; the instrument crossed behind the neck is drawn tight, the two *Phansigars* pressing the head forwards; at the same time the third villain, in readiness behind the traveller, seizes his legs, and he is thrown forward upon the ground. In this situation he can make little resistance. The man holding the legs of the miserable sufferer, now kicks him in those parts of the body endowed with most sensibility, and he is quickly despatched."

The murderers' weapon was the *rumal* or handkerchief they wore knotted around their waists. If other travelers came up before the body was buried, the gang would wail over it, as if one of their own number had died, and they would often feast or camp on the grave of their victims to destroy traces of newly dug earth. The bodies of victims were mangled, both to prevent identification and to satisfy the ritual demands of the cult. The legs were disjointed, the face was disfigured, and body was gashed and gutted "to expedite its dissolution, as well as to prevent its inflation," for jackals might detect and dig up an inflated corpse. Each band of Phansigars had a special ritual butcher to attend to the corpses.

Dr. Sherwood was very much a superior European of the Age of Reason; thus he observes of the cult of the Phansigars that "the frequent association of the most abject superstition, with the deepest guilt, has often been noticed." The sect worshiped Kali or Bhowani, the Hindu goddess of Death. Before a marauding expedition, a sheep was sacrificed in front of an image of the goddess, a black-skinned vampire-like figure, smeared with dried gore.

An English artist's impression of a captured Thug leader (engraving from *The Illustrated London News*, February 18, 1843). He carries a pickax, a knife, and a rope noose (a superfluous detail, since Thugs used waistcloths for strangling).

Beside her were images of the lizard and the snake and the emblems of murder—the noose, the knife, and the pickax (so sacred a tool that it was supposed to fly automatically into the hand of its user). Flowers were scattered about, and fruit, cakes, and spirits offered to the goddess. "The head of the sheep being cut off, it is placed, with a burning lamp upon it and the right fore foot in the mouth, before the image . . . and the goddess is entreated to reveal to them whether she approves of the expedition they are meditating. Her consent is supposed to be declared, should certain tremulous or convulsive movements be observed, during the invocation, in the mouth and nostrils, while some fluid is poured upon those parts."

The religious tradition of the sect had it that in the golden days of mythology Kali helped her followers by devouring the dead bodies of their victims. On one occasion, however, a novice looked back and saw the goddess in the act of eating a corpse; as a punishment, she refused to continue gobbling down the evidence. Yet she liked her devotees well enough to present them with one of her teeth for a pickax, a rib for a knife, and the hem of her sari for a noose. She ordered her followers in future to cut up and bury their prey, and she also told them that they should favor the colors of yellow and white, even in their nooses.

The Phansigars were highly superstitious on their expeditions. Some signs of good luck were thought to be a lizard chirping, a crow cawing on a living tree on the left side of the road, a partridge calling on the right side of the road, and the sight of a tiger. Bad signs were a hare or a snake crossing the road, a crow cawing on an animal's back, a screeching owlet, a sitting ass that brayed, the howl of a single jackal, and a dog shaking its head.

Four mid-19th-century paintings show the parts played in a ritual murder by Thugs of different grades. Above left, two *sothas* or deceivers divert a traveler's attention to help the *bhartote* or strangler behind him. Above, a bhartote tightens the noose, while his accomplices hold the victim's feet and hands. Left, Thugs carry corpses away from the murder site. Below, a group of *lughas* mutilate the bodies at a well.

Kali was a woman, and protected certain crafts; her followers tended to spare women, gold and iron and brassworkers, smiths, carpenters, and stonecutters. "Washermen, potmakers, pariahs, chucklers [shoemakers], lepers, the blind and mutilated, a man driving a cow or a female goat" were also spared. Many parties were protected on the roads by containing some of these categories of people, for the ritual murderers had to slay all or none to destroy witnesses. Later the sect degenerated and began killing indiscriminately for money; but in their beginnings the Thugs meticulously observed their taboos. The tradition was that one gang had murdered a woman and had never prospered afterwards, eventually being wiped out.

Like most efficient secret societies, the Phansigars had a vocabulary of secret signs and a secret language. Dr. Sherwood described these. Certain marks on the road showed that a victim had been prepared, and pointed the way taken by the scouts. "Drawing the back of the hand along the chin, from the throat outwards, implies that caution is requisite—that some stranger is approaching. Putting the open hand over the mouth and drawing it gently down implies that there is no longer cause for alarm." There were special terms for pickax and knife—*mahi* and *cathini*. A phrase meaning "Sweep the place" meant "See that no one is near"; "Bring firewood" meant "Take up your positions"; "Eat betel" meant "Kill him"; "Look after the straw" meant "Take care of the corpse, bury it and keep watch"; and "Descendants of Bhowani?" meant "Are you also Phansigars?" Intermarriage helped to preserve the Phansigars' secrecy. Indian families in their own villages keep very much to themselves, and the Phansigar women knew that any disclosure of the secrets of their menfolk would mean the destruction of them all.

Initiation into the order was by birth, though some captured male children were also initiated. Boys of 10 or more were allowed to accompany the murder bands, with a near relative as a tutor. The tutor forced the child to be absolutely obedient and to carry his bundle and his food. Slowly, he taught the boy to understand the mystery of Kali and to be wholly silent to strangers. "He is instructed to consider his interest as opposed to that of society in general; and to deprive a human being of life, is represented as an act merely analogous and equivalent to that of killing a fowl or a sheep." At first, the boys were only allowed to watch the murders at a distance; but soon they took part in the operation as scouts, and eventually, after the age of about 18, as murderers themselves. Sometimes the young murderers used hemp and other drugs to nerve themselves for an attack; but most of the older Phansigars used no drugs in their trade.

At the height of the sect's activity, tens of thousands of travelers were killed annually; one source puts the number of its victims over the years at more than a million. One Thug alone at his trial claimed to have been a witness to so many ritual murders that he had "stopped counting when he reached the thousand." The Phansigars inspired such terror that they had operated for centuries without much retribution, for no one would inform against them. Yet the Indian authorities, when they caught a band, walled each one up alive in a pillar or cut off his hands and nose.

What shocked Dr. Sherwood most about the sect was that it murdered without guilt. "What constitutes the most odious feature in the character of these murderers, is, that prodigal as they are of human life, they can rarely claim the benefit of even the palliating circumstance of strong pecuniary temptation. They are equally strangers to compassion and remorse—they are never restrained from the commission of crimes by commiseration for the unfortunate traveller—and they are exempted from the compunctious visitings of conscience, which usually follow, sooner or later, the steps of guilt. '*Phansigari*,' they observe, with cold indifference blended with a degree of surprise, when questioned on this subject, 'is their *business*'; which, with reference to the tenets of fatalism, they conceive themselves to have been pre-ordained to follow." Fatalism also led them to compare themselves to tigers; for they claimed that just as the tiger fulfilled the designs of nature by preying on other animals, so they simply fulfilled their own destiny in preying on men. Everyone's fate was written on his forehead; the servants of Kali were merely agents of the goddess, not the cause of men's deaths. So ended Dr. Sherwood's account of the Phansigars, who were known from then onward by their northern name of Thugs.

One of the first people to read Sherwood's paper was William Sleeman, a young officer in the Bengal army who already had a strong interest in native affairs and had learned four Indian languages. Sleeman became absorbed in the problem of Thuggee, and it was this as much as anything that prompted him to apply for transfer to the civil service in 1818. In 1822, as soon as he was given charge of a whole district in the Nerbudda valley, he began to investigate Thug activities within his territory. His discoveries there created a sensation because they suggested that Thuggee was a nation-wide organization. As a result, Sleeman was empowered to investigate Thuggee over a much wider area in 1826, and in 1830 the governor-general, Lord William Bentinck, officially appointed him to suppress Thuggee over the whole of central India.

Sleeman found a situation of particular difficulty. The Thugs were nearly impossible to distinguish from the Dacoits and other bandits along the roads; they were protected by villagers, out of fear, and by local rulers, whom they bribed. As the bodies of dead travelers were rarely found, no one knew whether missing relatives had fled, been eaten by beasts, died of natural causes, or fallen to the marauding armies of the native princes, which extorted plunder from all and sundry. There were no police outside the British possessions in India, and so Sleeman had to found his own force. Because the Thugs' activities were so widespread, he also had to obtain permission for local courts to try crimes committed in other districts.

Sleeman, who had learned the Thugs' language, *Ramasi*, from Sherwood's paper, was able to build up a network of informers among them. He also mapped out the usual scenes of their crimes, plotted their habits, and cataloged their methods of choosing and disposing of their victims. His new body of armed helpers was sent after the Thugs wherever he found them, despite protests from some of the native rulers and the British administrators of some neighboring states. And in studying his Thugs as carefully as Sherlock Holmes studied Moriarty, Sleeman became their historian.

According to Sleeman, the Thugs may originally have been Persian light horsemen from the pastoral tribe of the Sagartii, whom Herodotus describes as fighting with only a dagger and a noose of twisted leather. They came to India, perhaps, with the Muslim invaders. The Thugs themselves boasted that the eighth-century carvings in the caves of Ellora showed Thugs already engaged in ritual murder. "In one place," a Thug leader, Feringheea, testified, "you see men strangling; in another burying the bodies: in another carrying them off to the graves. There is not an operation in Thuggee that is not exhibited in the caves of Ellora." A Persian historian tells of 1000 Thugs captured at Delhi about 1290 and released, in a mistaken act of clemency, to terrorize Bengal. In the 16th century, the emperor Akbar captured another 500 Thugs, while the French traveler Thevenot talks of the "cunningest robbers in the world" strangling travelers on the road from Delhi to Agra in the 1680s.

The Thugs themselves explained their origin in terms of the Hindu tradition that a demon had devoured mankind as each human was created. The

Two captured Thugs holding their *rumals*. Both turned informers, and their confessions are on record. (Paintings by an Indian court artist, about 1842.)

demon was so large that the depths of the sea covered him only to the waist. Then Kali came to the rescue and cut the demon down; but from every drop of his blood, another demon sprang up. When she killed these demons, each drop of their blood produced still more demons. But while orthodox Hindus maintained that Kali solved the problem of the multiplying demons by licking the blood from their wounds, the Thugs claimed that Kali grew tired and made two men from the sweat on her arms. She gave these two original Thugs handkerchiefs and told them to kill all the demons without shedding a drop of blood. The Thugs immediately obliged and then offered to return the handkerchiefs. But Kali made them keep the handkerchiefs to serve as a memorial and to provide a holy and profitable way of life for them and their descendants. The two men were not only permitted to strangle men like demons, but were commanded to do so. A Thug born into the trade could not escape his duty of religious murder.

Between the Thugs and Sleeman there developed a strange kind of understanding. Sleeman felt himself very much the instrument of God and destiny, as did the Thugs. A popular historian of the Thugs commented that one of their replies to Sleeman might have come from the mouth of an ancient Hebrew defending the record of his conquering and chosen people. "From the time that the omens have been favourable," the Thug declared, "we consider travellers as victims thrown into our hands by the deity to be killed, and that we are the mere instrument in her hands to destroy them: that if we do not kill them, she will never be again propitious to us, and we and our

Major-General Sir William Sleeman (1788-1856), head of the government department for the suppression of Thuggee. (Portrait by George Duncan Beechey, 1851.)

Map of Thug murder sites in the Kingdom of Oudh (now in Uttar Pradesh, North India), based on the lithograph made by Sleeman's assistants at Lucknow Residency in 1858. Information from captured Thugs helped them to locate the *beles* or murder sites, which totaled 274 along 1406 miles of road —an average of one about every 5 miles.

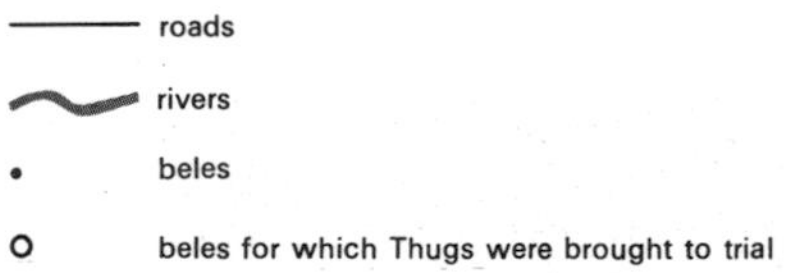

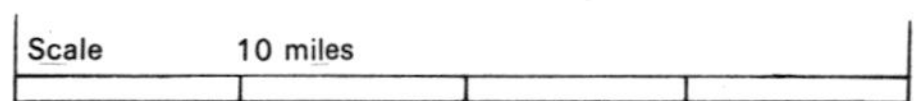

families will be involved in misery and want." The Thugs thought they were no longer being protected by Kali from the British because they had murdered outside their tabooed categories. "I have a hundred times heard my father and other old and wise men say," the Thug Nasir confessed to Sleeman, "when we had killed a sweeper and otherwise infringed their rules, that we should be some day punished for it; that the European rulers would be made the instruments to chastise us for our disregard of omens and neglect of the rules laid down for our guidance." Killing travelers was not wrong; killing the wrong sort of traveler, in the wrong way, was fatal.

Though Sleeman interrogated captured Thugs at length, he (like Sherwood) failed to discover why, being dedicated to a Hindu deity, they should include many Muslims. (When he taxed one Muslim Thug with disloyalty to his religion, the Thug tried to justify his worship of Kali by declaring that she was identical with Fatima, the daughter of Mohammed.) But Sleeman added

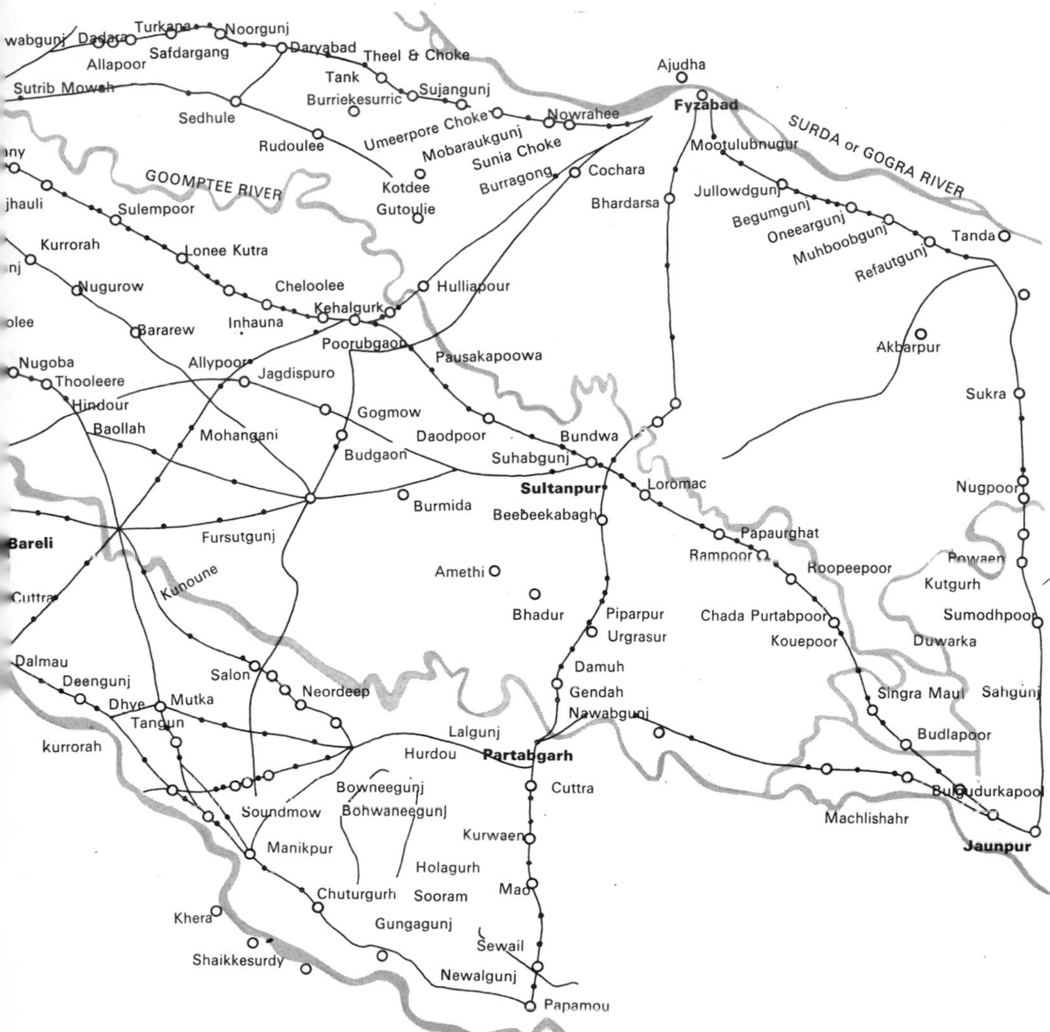

enormously to Dr. Sherwood's account of the mysteries and ceremonies of the Thugs, and revealed them as a religious cult with a sense of communion with each other and with their goddess and a dedication to their way of life that have rarely been equaled in the history of secret societies.

The symbol of the sacred pickax was as important to the Thugs as the symbol of the Cross was to the Templars. It was consecrated in an elaborate ceremony, being passed through fire seven times. It was used, like the Cross, as the guarantee of an oath. A perjurer was meant to die a terrible death six days after swearing by the pickax, his head gradually turning round until his face stood over his shoulder. If the sacred pickax fell from the hands of its bearer in the gang, his death or the dissolution of the gang was certain within a year. "Do we not worship it," a Thug said to Sleeman of the pickax, "every seventh day? . . . Is its sound ever heard when digging the grave by any but a Thug? And can any man even swear to a falsehood upon it?"

Sleeman wrote a detailed description of the ritual feast or *Tuponee* that took place after every murder, sometimes upon the grave of the victim. The *goor* or coarse sugar took the place of the Christian communion bread and wine. It was placed on a blanket or sheet, spread on clean ground. Near it was placed the consecrated pickax and a piece of silver as an offering. The leader of the gang sat on the cloth, facing west; ranged around him was an even number of the most distinguished stranglers. The rest of the Thugs of inferior grades sat around the cloth on the ground. The leading Thug poured a little of the goor into a hole in the ground and prayed: "Great goddess, as you vouchsafed one lakh and sixty-two thousand rupees to Joora Naig and Koduck Bunwari in their need, so we pray thee, fulfill our desires." Such an honest prayer for gain has rarely been uttered, even by a gambler. The other Thugs repeated the prayer, while the leader sprinkled holy water on the pit and the pickax and put a little goor on the hands of the Thugs who sat on the blanket. The signal for a symbolic strangling was given and the Thugs ate the goor from their hands in solemn silence. The remainder of

In an early operation against Thuggee, a British officer and his detachment of sepoys ambush a gang of Thugs gathered around a camp fire (from a drawing by a European artist, about 1825).

the goor was then distributed to the surrounding Thugs. It was eaten only by those who had actually committed a murder; any goor that fell on the ground was buried in the pit. If, by chance a novice ate some of the goor, he was forced to go out and do his strangling at once. Because of the need for secrecy, curtains were always carried to erect a tent in which the Tuponee murder feast could be performed.

Feringheea spoke of the extraordinary impact this ceremony made: "We all feel pity sometimes, but the goor of the Tuponee changes our nature. It would change the nature of a horse. Let any man once taste of that goor, and he will be a Thug though he know all the trades and have all the wealth in the world. I never wanted food; my mother's family was opulent, her relations high in office. I have been high in office myself, and become so great a favourite wherever I went, that I was sure of promotion: yet I was always miserable while absent from my gang, and obliged to return to Thuggee. My father made me taste of that fatal goor when I was yet a mere boy; and, if I were to live a thousand years I should never be able to follow any other trade."

Aging Thugs, jailed for 35 years at Jubbulpore, entertain the visiting Prince of Wales with a demonstration of their strangling technique (engraving from *The Prince of Wales' Tour of India*, 1877).

Sleeman declared that among the Thugs he had rarely discovered "*wanton cruelty*; that is, pain inflicted beyond what was necessary to deprive the person of life—pain either to the mind or body. The murder of women is a violation of their rules to which they attribute much of our success against the system . . . but no Thug was ever known to offer insult either in act or in speech to the woman they were to murder. No gang would ever dare to murder a woman with whom one of its members should be suspected of having had criminal intercourse."

The Thugs were dedicated to killing for Kali; but outside their profession, they were pillars of family morality. One of Sleeman's assistants, indeed, paid the Thug Makeen Lodhi the compliment of being one of the best men he had ever known, to be trusted "in any relation of life save that between a Thug who has taken the *auspices* and a traveller with something worth taking upon him. They all look upon travellers as a sportsman looks upon hares and pheasants; and they recollect their best sporting grounds, and talk of them, when they can, with the same kind of glee!"

Sleeman's intelligence from Thug informants, called approvers, was so good that he could forecast the movement of Thug gangs in the winter killing season. The government of the British in India printed his genealogical tables of Thug families and maps of Thug crimes. Meanwhile, his European assistants, sepoys, troopers, and armed irregulars rounded up the gangs of Thugs, whose pride in their past achievements began to work against them. The Thugs had always been proud of being perfect deceivers, capable of gulling any traveler about their true identity; now they fell like pigeons into Sleeman's net. The Thugs had been confidence men for so long in order to make friends with prospective victims that they eventually became the victims of overconfidence.

The size of the Thug gangs had grown by Sleeman's time, particularly in the north of India. They now moved about in groups of 20 or 30 and could combine quickly into gangs of 150—an assembly large enough to murder up to 30 travelers at a time. Greed had brought more Thugs out on to the roads and they had begun to kill indiscriminately for profit, selling off girl children to prostitutes and leaving too many live witnesses and unburied corpses behind them. When Feringheea himself was caught in January 1831, he had just returned from an expedition on which he had been present at the murder of 100 men and five women. Yet Sleeman did support Feringheea enough to secure a pardon for him, despite the reluctance of the British administration to spare such a notorious killer. And Feringheea, in return, provided valuable information.

The incredible persistence of the Thugs is well documented in the volumes of evidence that Sleeman collected against them. The Thugs tracked one Muslim prince for days. He was mounted on a horse and carried a pair of pistols, a bow, and a quiver full of arrows. The Thugs, posing as Hindu pilgrims, approached him as friendly protectors; but he was suspicious of strangers and would have nothing to do with them. On the next day, the prince overtook another group of pilgrims, who were also Thugs; they asked for his company and protection, but he again refused. On the third day, the growing band of Thugs struck up a relationship with the servants of the prince, his butler and groom, who begged their master to accompany such respectable and holy men. The prince again refused. On the fourth day, in the middle of a solitary plain, the prince encountered a party of five Muslim sepoys weeping by the side of a dead companion; these were actually another gang of Thugs with a victim whom they had just killed. They said that their companion had died of fatigue and that they were too ignorant to repeat the burial service from the Koran over his body. The prince could hardly refuse to perform the last rites for his fellow Muslims. He dismounted, removed his weapons for the burial service, washed ritually, and knelt to begin the service. At this moment, the Thugs strangled him and his servants and buried them in graves already prepared for the occasion.

Sleeman was helped in his suppression of the Thugs in the 1830s by the kangaroo courts he used to try them. Though many Thugs were sentenced to death or imprisoned, those who turned approvers were pardoned, and Sleeman actually founded schools to teach their sons another craft. The parents

The interior of a temple of Kali frequented by Thugs, from a sketch made in 1840 by Mrs. Fanny Parks. An enthusiastic student of Thuggee, she was disappointed in the statue of Kali, which looked "more like a child's toy than a redoubtable goddess."

found such an idea degrading; but, in the end, they themselves joined the schools to learn brickmaking, building, and weaving. Their carpets became so famous that Queen Victoria, whose agents had eliminated the Thugs as a threat to the *Pax Britannica*, commissioned a carpet for Windsor Castle. So Sleeman's Thugs, turning their talents for knotting waistcloths to the problem of threading carpets, produced a two-ton carpet measuring 80 feet by 40 feet for their new queen to walk upon.

Details of the hangings of Thugs have been preserved by travelers of the time. Mrs. Fanny Parks (a friend of Sleeman who visited a temple of Kali that was frequented by Thugs) wrote of the execution of 25 Thugs in 1831: "It would be impossible to find in any country a set of men who meet death with more indifference than these wretches; and, had it been in a better cause, they would have excited universal sympathy. As it was, there was something dreadful in the thought that men, who had so often imbrued their hands in blood, should meet their death with such carelessness. I believe that they had previously requested to be allowed to fasten the cord about their necks with their own hands; certain it is that each individual as soon as he had adjusted the noose, jumped off the beam, and launched himself into eternity; and those who first mounted the ladder selected their ropes, rejecting such as did not please them. One of them, who had leaped off the beam, and had been hanging for more than three seconds, put his hand up and pulled his cap over his face."

Such bravery in the face of death proved attractive to the British proconsuls. They could not despise the Thugs; they felt that they had met worthy, if misguided, adversaries. They liked the sense of honor of these men, who

Below, Thugs at Jubbulpore, turned from crime to carpet-weaving, pose with one of their products in 1874. Right, the carpet woven by Thugs for Queen Victoria, now in the Waterloo Chamber at Windsor Castle.

could not endure to be hanged by the hands of a mere *chamar* or skin-curer. Indeed, British justice seems to have chosen its categories of retribution as carefully as a good Thug himself. Of the 3689 Thugs tried before 1840, only 466 died by hanging; most of the remainder were transported or imprisoned for life, while 56 were pardoned as approvers. Another 651 Thugs were tried in the next eight years and, except for isolated outbreaks, the cult of Thuggee came to an end.

Thuggee may have been a rigorous cult in its early days before the coming of the British; but when it was exposed it had already become a degenerate form of secret society—the Thugs' looting and murder for the sake of religion could hardly be distinguished from plain criminality. Religion was important to them, but capable of evasion. Throughout the long religious wars between Hindus and Muslims in India, there was complete religious tolerance among the Thugs. Muslim Thugs adopted Hindu beliefs and Hindu Thugs did not despise the Koran or the idea of Paradise. Most interestingly, the Thugs never played the role of a resistance movement to the British. Their compromise of Hindu and Muslim differences allowed them to accept any form of political authority, as long as they could ply their trade. They never touched a European, for fear they should be discovered and punished; their itch for concealment was stronger than their itch for profit, for Europeans were known to carry much money with them on their travels.

If the Thugs had any political effect, it was negative and divisive. In the chaos and anarchy that the British found in India, the British could easily apply their principle of "Divide and Rule" and use the troops of one petty state to conquer those of another. The Thugs helped to add to the general

feeling of insecurity and terror in the subcontinent, so that the peasants often welcomed the British as their only guarantee of justice. The elimination of the Thugs by Sleeman and his assistants was the most graphic proof the peasants could have had; the villagers saw for the first time in Indian history the possibility of safe travel, guaranteed by troops and police that were not venal. In a society dominated by caste, the addition of another caste of conquerors hardly mattered; what did matter was the establishment of a strong central government that could end the extortion and murder practiced by local rulers and groups of bandits.

As a secret society, the Thugs became too well known. Their vanity was greater than their discretion. Their testimony in front of Sleeman was full of pride in their trade; but astonishingly, Thug approvers were almost as vain about serving the great East India Company as they had been about serving Kali. In the old days, one Thug approver said, "a man who peached was either killed by his old associates, or by *Davey* [Kali]. They were only rare and solitary instances; now we do not fear, as we are many and become servants of Government." Sleeman won the confidence of the Thugs to such a remarkable extent that they believed he owed his success against them to Kali's support. The Thugs again and again repeated that if they had observed their rules and omens, they would have been inviolate for all time. "We were often admonished but we did not take warning," one Thug said, "and we deserve our fates." The Thugs were thoroughly convinced that the killing of women or people from prohibited trades and the ignoring of omens would lead to their destruction. In fact, they admitted that killing outside the accepted ways was murder. "No man's family ever survives a murder," another Thug declared; "it becomes extinct. A Thug who murders in this way loses the children he has, and is never blessed with more."

So the Thugs wished death upon themselves. Their fatalism and their religion allowed them to act out the urge toward murder and suicide in a way not permitted to civilized men outside the state of war. When the Thugs became degenerate, they almost willed their own suppression, as many secret societies do when they are conscious of backsliding. The Ku Klux Klan, for instance, in its third and most degenerate form, was to be as guilty about its tarnished image and as riddled with government spies as the Thugs in their decline. Yet the Klan was always something of a Southern resistance movement against the North of the United States and the Negro, while only in recent times has Thuggee been associated with Indian nationalism.

In an interesting letter, John Masters, who used Thuggee as the theme of his novel *The Deceivers*, tells of 10 years of thuggery in the Gwalior area after Indian independence. "There was a lot more than kidnapping—there were several murders, with or without robbery at the same time. There was a single Robin Hood type of figure, who was obviously being helped by the villagers, partly through fear and partly through some claim on his behalf, or by him, to be a modern Thug . . . thinking for one thing that it would be a nice patriotic Indian sort of murder/robbery." With the rise of nationalism in India, bandits are bound to use the Thugs as a justification for their crimes, though, as Masters points out, modern communications really prevent a revival of Thuggee. "It was essential for Thuggee to flourish that men should set out on six-month journeys through lands infested with cholera, cobras, flooded rivers, and ordinary bandits—so that when the travelers didn't return, no one worried for two years; then it was too late to find out; and the cobras got blamed again. . . ."

The Thugs in India could exist only in chaos and ignorance; the British suppressed them more effectively by the railway and the telegraph than by the rope noose they used against their enemies' rumal. A modern industrial nation cannot tolerate any threat to its travelers or its lines of communication. Efficient modern Thugs, such as the American Mafia or Cosa Nostra, find it more profitable to control some of the lines of communication than to plunder them. After all, it is easier to rob a traveler by making him pay a toll for the services he needs than to strangle him for his wallet. You can only strangle a man once, while you may make him pay tribute all his life.

Engraving of 1855 shows crowds arriving on foot and by elephant for the opening of the East Indian railway linking Delhi and Calcutta. By the turn of the century, modern communications were superseding the elephant and the roadside camp site, making an anachronism of organized Thuggee.

4 The Mysteries

The ancient world of the Mediterranean had a rich fabric of religious cults, and notable among these were the "mysteries," such as those at Eleusis and those of Isis and Mithra. These mystery cults were a means of expressing and satisfying the individual's need for a personal and dramatized faith that could give him the assurance of immortality. The type of religious experience provided by their rituals added an extra dimension to the official state cults and to the ordinary piety of agricultural and domestic shrines; it also reflected the cosmopolitanism and urbanization that had made such traditional religious practices less meaningful. Aristotle rightly remarked that the point of participation in a mystery was not to learn, but to experience a change. This change was not just a matter of spiritual elevation or ecstasy, but was also conceived as a rebirth. It was effected through the performance of a sacramental drama, in which the initiate was by turns spectator and participant. Thus the idea of a sacred performance was central to the mystery cults.

The secrecy surrounding some of these cults was essentially a reflection of their religious and initiatory nature. Their members may have prized secrecy as a way of being exclusive; but the cults were not primarily, if at all, secret societies pursuing some social or political aim. Indeed, though the initiate might be reticent about the details of the ceremonies, there is a surprising amount of information available to the historian.

An Attic votive tablet of the fourth century B.C. depicts two scenes of initiation into the Eleusinian mysteries. Both show the *kernophoria*, a preliminary rite in which the candidate approached the throne of the "corn-mother" Demeter with a *kernos* (a sacred cult vessel containing offerings of seeds) on her head.

Before we look at the history of these cults, however, we should appreciate some of the confusing changes of meaning that have come over the word "mystery." The Greek word *musterion* signified a rite that was performed in the presence of initiates only. The Latin form of the word had the same meaning, but Cicero also used it in an extended sense, meaning "a secret." In the New Testament, the plural "mysteries" typically refers to the revelatory acts of God, though we can detect the beginnings of the process by which it came to mean something beyond comprehension. This change gives the wrong impression that mysteries are mysterious truths to which we have not as yet penetrated and therefore that the mystery cults essentially involved secret doctrines. In fact they were more concerned with the enactment of sacred dramas and the display of holy objects. It was only the rule that these should be reserved for initiates that made them esoteric. Thus a breach of the rule of secrecy essentially meant doing anything that would make open or unlicensed performances of the mysteries possible.

A study of the history of these cults must begin with an understanding of the needs they met. In Greece in the sixth century B.C. official religion was multifarious in its manifestations. The life of the city-states was interwoven with a whole series of religious festivals, and official functions (such as the reception of foreign embassies) coincided with sacred feast-days. In town and country, local cults were an important part of daily living. In addition, Panhellenic festivals (such as the Olympic Games) and Panhellenic institutions (such as the Delphic oracle) helped to foster a sense of cultural solidarity between the city-states. The Homeric writings performed a similar function. Nevertheless, the need for a personal religion—concerned with hopes of communion with the gods and of immortal life—was not wholly met by the traditional complex of observances. It was at least partly met by the spread of the cults of Dionysus and of Orphism, and by the development of the Eleusinian ceremonial beyond its origin as a local agricultural festival.

The mythology lying behind the mysteries at *Eleusis* concerns Demeter (the "corn-mother"), and finds its first literary form in the Homeric hymn to Demeter, which probably dates from the latter part of the seventh century B.C. The myth describes how Hades enticed Demeter's daughter Persephone (or Kore) into his kingdom beneath the earth. The situation was serious enough for Zeus to intervene. But it was a rule that no one could return from the underworld once he had eaten anything there. As Hades had tricked Persephone into eating some pomegranate seeds (symbolic of marriage), Zeus could not unconditionally demand her return to earth. Instead, by a compromise, Persephone was permitted to dwell on earth for eight months of the year, but required to live below with her grim consort for the remaining four.

This myth expresses a synthesis between agricultural rites and concerns about the afterlife. Like the corn-maiden who sends up shoots from beneath the earth in spring to announce her return from Hades, the initiate may be

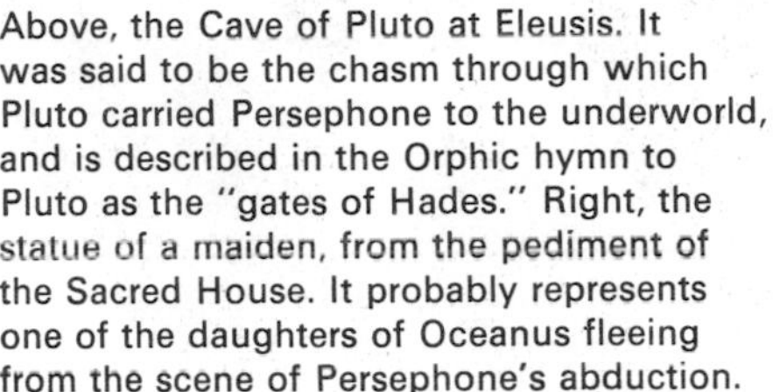

Above, the Cave of Pluto at Eleusis. It was said to be the chasm through which Pluto carried Persephone to the underworld, and is described in the Orphic hymn to Pluto as the "gates of Hades." Right, the statue of a maiden, from the pediment of the Sacred House. It probably represents one of the daughters of Oceanus fleeing from the scene of Persephone's abduction.

born again. This concern was reinforced by the incorporation of Dionysus into the Eleusinian myth and ritual. Dionysus was both a vegetation deity and the god of wine; he became the focus of an ecstatic cult (immortalized in Euripides' tragedy *The Bacchae*) in which the devotee sought communion with him. Consequently, the significance of the Eleusinian festivals, which was originally agricultural, could be coupled with a sense of identification with a perpetually dying and rising god.

The main rituals, or Greater Mysteries, took place in autumn. They involved a procession of the initiates (*mustai*) from Athens, followed by the performance of the initiatory rites, which lasted for several days. These included a sacred pageant, and culminated in a display of sacred cult-objects in a dramatic blaze of light within the *Telesterion* or hall of initiation—the principal edifice in the complex of sacred buildings. The Lesser Mysteries, originally held only in February, were regarded as a necessary preliminary to the Greater. But with the growing influence of the cult, which attracted prospective initiates from a wide area, the Lesser Mysteries came to be held twice a year, to give those who were unable to be present in February the chance to qualify for the September celebrations. The tendency of Eleusis to

Above, an Attic vase painting of the fifth century B.C. shows Dionysus (who became identified with Orpheus) playing his lyre. The god of wine, he was worshiped with orgiastic rites, and was usually depicted with a wine cup or grapes in his hand.

Right, Orpheus, at the gates of Hades, looks back to claim his dead wife Eurydice and loses her (third-century Roman wall painting). Like Orpheus, who had tamed the beasts and gods of the underworld with the music of his lyre, the Orphics sought to tame the bestial or Titanic side of their nature; they practiced austere disciplines to obtain release from the "sorrowful weary wheel" of death and rebirth. In earlier versions of this myth (which resemble that of Dionysus's descent to Hades) Orpheus succeeds in bringing Eurydice back to life—a sign of his power to immortalize his initiates.

attract people from beyond the Athenian city-state had already become apparent before the Persian Wars, and by the late fifth century B.C. the city was a recognized center of pilgrimage for the whole Hellenic world. The absorption of Greece into the Roman sphere of influence gave the cult an even wider clientele, including, later on, a number of Roman emperors. Cicero, himself an initiate, wrote: "Among the many and excellent gifts of Athens to the life of mankind, none is better than those mysteries by which we are drawn from savagery into civilization."

Though the rites at Eleusis conveyed no doctrine, no special metaphysical, ethical, or social message, they returned the individual to his daily life with a sense of serenity and of assurance in the face of death. Initiation, however, created no community apart: there was no Eleusinian "church." This was partly because the original community aspect of the festivals was conceived—and could only be conceived—as local and agricultural.

Orphism, which flourished in the sixth century B.C., had a more developed theology and a body of sacred writings. This movement also owed something to the cult of Dionysus, which penetrated into the Greek peninsula from Phrygia and Thrace. Orphic asceticism contrasted markedly with the orgiastic practices of the early Dionysian brotherhoods and sisterhoods. Nevertheless, Orphism made important use of the Dionysian mythology and gave it a strong doctrinal interpretation, while moderating the wildness and fervor of the cult.

According to the central legend, Zagreus (identified with Dionysus) was destined by his father Zeus to be the ruler of the world. Zeus's plan, however, met with the fierce opposition of those formidable giant deities, the Titans. (This appears to be a mythological reflection of rivalry between Olympic and earlier forms of religion.) The Titans succeeded in slaughtering the child Zagreus, and proceeded to eat him. Zeus, in sorrow and anger, burned them

The passion of Dionysus-Zagreus, revered by the Orphics as the redeemer who suffered, and attained everlasting life. (Wall painting in the villa of the Dionysiac mysteries at Pompeii.)

up with his shafts of lightning. The ashes of the Titans were the material out of which the human race was fashioned. Yet Zagreus was not for ever dead. His heart was rescued from the ashes by the goddess Athene, and after it had been swallowed by Zeus, Zagreus was reborn as the son of Semele, an earth-goddess. This legend, unedifying at first sight, had a double significance for the Orphics. First, it meant that the human race contained elements of both good and evil—Titanic evil and the flesh of the divine Zagreus, particles of which were, of course, present in the Titanic ashes. Secondly, the divine Zagreus was, after all, reborn, so that the initiate, through communion with him, might also experience rebirth and entry into a higher life.

The first aspect of the myth was the most important in Orphic theology. The body was conceived as a hindrance to the spiritual life—hence the famous motto *soma sema*, "the body a tomb." Initiation into the Orphic path set the devotee on the way to release. Only through the exercise of ritual and ascetic practices, including abstinence from meat, could his immortal soul be liberated. This notion was coupled with a belief in reincarnation. Thus the idea of initiation was extended; it became a way of life rather than simply a ritual drama. However, Orphism never became a sect within Greek religion. It was, rather, a movement, whose boundaries were by no means fixed, for allegiance to Orphic doctrines was not incompatible with other religious observances.

The diffusion of Orphism was not the work of any central organization. Yet Orphic cult associations grew up here and there in the Greek-speaking world. Insofar as there was any central allegiance, it was to the mythological figure of Orpheus and to a body of sacred literature. The importance of Orpheus lay partly in the fact that he represented a substitute for the cult-heroes who validated local and official cults in the traditional religion of the city-state. This function of Orpheus was important because Orphism, like the Eleusinian mysteries, was not confined in membership to any particular locality and because, unlike them, it was not centered on a particular sacred shrine. The figure of Orpheus provided a mythological focus to a movement that had no geographical focus.

Because Orphism had a developed theology and a clearly defined goal (the raising of the soul to divine status through the acquisition of everlasting life, and escape from the round of transmigration), the details of its mythology were allegorized. This perception that the myths point beyond themselves was used by Plato, for instance in the *Phaedo*, in the Orphic-influenced myth describing the future life. But such allegorizing was not strictly the expression of a "secret knowledge" available only to initiates. For this development we have to turn to *Pythagoreanism*.

There was a notable overlap between Orphism and the teachings of Pythagoras, who flourished about 530 B.C. His brotherhood was much more in the nature of a secret society committed to certain esoteric doctrines. An echo of this intellectualization of initiation is heard in the words Plato is reported to have inscribed over the entrance to the Academy: "Let no one who is ignorant of geometry enter here." For Pythagoras, the life of the intellect had a sacred significance.

He was a teacher in transition between two worlds. It was not merely that he left his native Samos, possibly to escape the rule of the tyrant Polycrates, and founded a brotherhood in the "new world" of southern Italy, at Croton. More importantly, he was a blend between a charismatic seer and a speculative philosopher. He put mathematics to work both as an element in his metaphysics and as an activity to be pursued by the religious sect he gathered around him. But still more vitally, Pythagoras conceived the ascetic rules and food taboos he inherited in part from Orphism as an aid toward the full attainment of higher knowledge. This knowledge was expressed in his metaphysical system. The fact that asceticism was a preparation for an understanding of reality indicates that to him intellectual inquiry was not just "science" but a means of salvation. Consequently, the secrets of the Pythagorean community came to differ in character from those of the Eleusinian mysteries. Now *doctrines* were central to the revelation the initiate could expect to receive, and he was required to keep them secret.

We have seen that the impact of the mysteries in Greece was partly due to the fact that neither the official or local agricultural ceremonial, nor the Olympian religion, was fully adapted to meet the need for a personal and dramatized faith. A similar observation may be made in regard to Roman religion. Though the spirit of ancient Roman religion was graver and darker than that of Greek polytheism, it also was open to the challenge of orgiastic and personal forms of faith, precisely because it was tied up in the same way with agricultural and domestic cults on the one hand, and with official transactions with deity on the other. While Rome was, through many vicissitudes, in process of imposing her rule on Italy and extending it toward Carthage and Greece, such official transactions became even more important to her. The support of the gods and the whole apparatus of divinations and auguries seemed essential once she had embarked on a career demanding military and political success. These rites had a communal significance. But in a time of increased cosmopolitanism they needed supplementing by more dynamic and ecstatic forms of religious life. The enlargement of the Roman Empire, too, changed the character of the city's population. When Rome contained a large number of immigrants, traditional and official cults could hardly remain meaningful to all her inhabitants.

An early sign of the impact of ecstatic cults was the wave of Dionysian practices that swept Italy early in the second century B.C.; these were suppressed in 186 B.C., because of the excesses involved. Because of her increasingly mixed population, Rome was a center for the introduction of various oriental cults, notably that of the Phrygian *Cybele*, the *Magna Mater* or "great mother." Cybele was one expression of a religious factor strong in the ancient Middle East: the worship of the mother goddess. Under various names, as Ishtar, Astarte, Isis, and Rhea, she was associated with fertility rites that, like those of Eleusis, could carry a promise of individual rebirth and salvation.

Cybele's cult was associated with Mount Ida in Asia Minor. It was introduced into Rome in 205 B.C., when Hannibal was still on Italian soil, as a result of a Sibylline oracle stating that a foreign foe could be defeated with the help of the Idaean mother. Part of the legend surrounding Cybele concerned the god Attis; his self-castration, death, and rebirth became a symbol of the salvation awaiting the initiate, who became identified with him in ritual ecstasy. The wild and bloody nature of the rites, administered by castrated priests, did not accord easily with Roman ideas of religious propriety. But despite opposition, the worship of Cybele made headway, and enjoyed a long career in Rome. As late as the fourth century A.D., one defender of paganism (then being revived through the efforts of the emperor Julian the Apostate) could assign spiritual importance to her rituals as an allegorical expression of the career of the human soul. The cult included rites of a sacramental nature, such as a sacred meal, and the immolation of a bull (the *taurobolium*, which was also a feature of Mithraism). Similar to Cybele-worship was the

Above, an ancient Roman sculpture shows a high priest of Cybele, the "great mother," with his ritual paraphernalia. It includes a whip decorated with human heads (with which the priest flagellated himself) and a tambourine, flutes, and cymbals (played to accompany his frenzied dances). The medallion on his chest represents the god Attis, whose story was reenacted in Cybele's rites. Cybele was said to have chosen Attis as her priest, and to have driven him to madness and self-castration when he broke his vow of chastity. Right, a statuette of Baubo, another mother goddess, from Priene in Asia Minor (fifth century B.C.). Similar figures were found in the sanctuary of Demeter at Eleusis.

cult of Ma, a Cappadocian deity who was identified with the Roman goddess of war, Bellona. Ma was introduced to Rome in about 85 B.C. by Sulla, and the taurobolium of the cult of Cybele was probably taken from that of Ma-Bellona. But of the various forms of worship introduced into Rome from the East, the most important were the mysteries of Isis and Mithra.

The worship of *Isis*, coupled with that of Osiris or of the syncretistic god Serapis, was the result of an interplay between ancient Egyptian and Hellenistic religion. Though the Isis cult was a development of a liturgy and a mythology having deep roots in Egypt's past, it claimed to have a relevance wider than that of a local or national cult.

Ancient Egypt had its "mysteries," in the sense of sacred dramatic rituals, and these incorporated the mythology of Osiris, a dying and rising god who came to be especially concerned with men's destinies in a future life. According to the myth, Osiris was murdered by his brother Seth, a weather god, and his body was launched in a coffin on the waters of the Nile. According to another phase of the myth, Seth later found the coffin and succeeded in dismembering and scattering Osiris's corpse. The various pieces were eventually collected by the sorrowing Isis, his consort, and Osiris was restored to life by Horus, their son. The notion that Osiris's coffin was launched on the waters of the Nile is connected with the fact that he was also identified with the Nile, whose life-giving waters were the cause of fertility. Osiris was regarded as judge of the dead and (in common with deities in much Egyptian and other mythology) was merged with the sun-god, who had played an important role in earlier Egyptian mythology. The agricultural aspect of Osiris made his mysteries an essential part of the social fabric of Egypt.

That social fabric was woven around the figure of the pharaoh, who was not simply monarch, but also a representative of divinity. It was only through him that society and agriculture could prosper, for he mediated the benefits of the cosmic order to the terrestrial kingdom over which he ruled. The resurrection of Osiris, as expressed and ensured by dramatic ritual, was a symbol of the continuance of social cohesion and agricultural fertility: the pharaoh himself was regarded as a descendant and embodiment of Horus, and in this role he could reenact the restoration of the dead god. The concern for the immortality of the pharaoh, expressed in an astonishing and spectacular succession of pyramids, was itself of communal significance, though the practice of mummification (a costly business) slowly spread beyond the royal family. This gradual democratization of the funerary rites gave Osiris, as god of the underworld, a greater relevance to individuals. This is reflected in the Egyptian *Book of the Dead*, a guide to the future judgment of the individual and to the afterlife awaiting him.

The work of modern scholars has produced an impressive understanding of the complexities of ancient Egyptian myths and rituals. Nevertheless, many details of the religion and of the funerary cults remain obscure. There have been many attempts, especially among the Rosicrucians, to assign an occult significance to the Egyptian mysteries and to the pyramids (in particular the Great Pyramid). For example, one such group argues by numerological speculation (depending on the dimensions of the internal galleries and other features of the Great Pyramid) that the pyramid builders had an occult and prophetic knowledge of human history. As we shall see in a later chapter of this book, such speculation is connected with the notion of deep truths known to the ancient Egyptians but since lost, or distorted by the Christian Church. No doubt the antiquity and the numinous quality of these silent monuments of the Egyptian desert are felt to give authority to such ideas, especially where there is a sense of revolt against Christian orthodoxy. Their advocates generally allow no rational refutation of their speculations because they suspect scientific historians of a biased attempt to conceal the esoteric truth.

It was against the general background of ancient Egyptian mythology that the cult of Serapis was promulgated by Ptolemy I, who reigned from 323 B.C. to 283 B.C. and founded the dynasty that ruled Egypt after the death of Alexander the Great. He succeeded in establishing the cult in Memphis and Alexandria. Serapis was a composite figure, a combination of Osiris and the sacred bull Apis, together with some Greek features. No doubt Ptolemy hoped that the worship of Serapis would be, among other things, a means of cementing solidarity between his Greek and Egyptian subjects. In any event, this cult was a factor in spreading the cult of Isis still more widely in the Hellenistic and Roman worlds.

The Egyptian gods were not destined, as it happened, to have too easy a time in Rome itself. There were periodic attempts, in the latter part of the first century B.C. and in the reign of Tiberius, to suppress their cult. In A.D. 19, for instance, the priests of Isis were crucified after a sexual scandal in which they were thought to have been involved. Nevertheless, the growth of this form of piety was not to be denied, and the emperor Caligula went so far as to establish a temple of Isis in the Campus Martius. This almost amounted to a trespass on the sacred territory belonging to the ancient gods of the city. The fervor and secrecy of the Isis rituals, together with xenophobia, account for the hostility shown toward them by the more orthodox Roman authorities. Here, as elsewhere, there were frequent accusations of license among Isis's followers. However, it is clear that the worship of Isis had a deep spiritual significance, which is brought out in the famous account of initiation contained in the *Metamorphoses* or *Golden Ass* of Lucius Apuleius (second century A.D.).

This tale, partly autobiographical and partly allegorical, indicates how Apuleius is saved from his lower and bestial self, represented by the ass into which he is magically transformed. In the mysteries he is brought to the threshold of Proserpine—that is, he virtually dies; then he is shown the "sun at midnight" and is enthroned with Isis. Here is repeated the common theme of the mystery religions—the rebirth and deification of the individual.

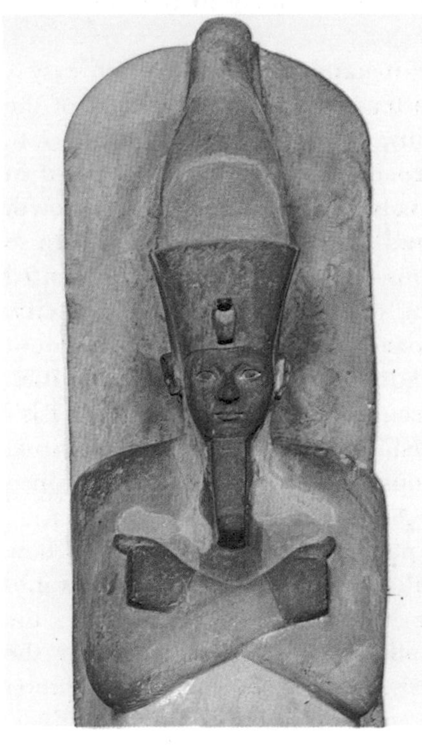

Above, a detail from an ancient Egyptian papyrus illustrating embalmment and burial —rites that were modeled on the legend of Osiris's death and resurrection. The two mourners watching over the embalmed body represent Nephthys, Osiris's sister, and Isis, his sister-wife. The goddesses were said to have preserved Osiris's body until his son Horus restored it to life. The resurrected Osiris is represented by the upright *djed* column with its human head. After seven days of mourning, the mummy also was raised upright; priests then performed the rite known as "opening the mouth" (the act by which Horus was said to have revived Osiris) so that the dead man's soul could return. Left, a statue of Amenhotep I in the attitude of an Osiris. Embalmment, and identification with Osiris, were originally prerogatives of the pharaohs. Opposite page, a rite in the Roman mysteries of Isis, the mother goddess of many names. An initiate, "purged of his mortality" and "filled with divine power," appears on the dais. The worshipers kneel, while priests shake the cult rattles, and incense rises from the altar. (Painting in the Temple of Isis, Pompeii.)

Important too in Apuleius's account is the essentially syncretistic nature of the worship of Isis. Isis is identified explicitly with Ceres or Demeter, with Venus, with Minerva, with Bellona and others. She is all these goddesses, though her true name remains Isis. In this way the cult could claim all the devotion poured upon all the mother goddesses in the Mediterranean world; it could also claim to contain the essence of all the mystery religions. This syncretism turned Isis into a universal figure, though her real blessings could be fully experienced only by initiates who pledged devotion to her.

There is no mistaking, from Apuleius's account and from the other information available to us, that the cult of Isis, with its attendant ascetic practices, could be a genuine vehicle of conversion. To prepare himself for the complex and continuing rites, the devotee abstained from sexual intercourse, from wine, bread, and meat. His head was shaved as a symbol of renunciation. As a votary of the goddess he believed that he was given the grace and strength to lead a pure and joyous life. We see here once again the theme noticed in the Eleusinian mysteries: the aim is the sacramental change of the devotee, not inculcation of a creed. The secrets of Isis could not be divulged to the profane because they lay in the experience of initiation. They involved no doctrine, except insofar as the rites implied a belief in rebirth and salvation.

A common feature of the mystery cults of the Roman Empire, with the exception of that of Eleusis, was their oriental origins. The other main mystery, *Mithraism*, stemmed ultimately from Iran. Mithra (or Mithras) was originally an Iranian sun-god; but the reforms of Zoroaster, which gave birth to Zoroastrianism, involved the temporary eclipse of the earlier polytheism, and Mithra shared in this eclipse. In the course of the evolution of Zoroastrianism, however, the older myths were reintroduced and adapted. Thus Mithra came to be regarded as the eye of Ahura Mazda, the supreme being—an understandable conception, since the sun travels over the earth and seems to look down on the doings of men. When Mithraism emerged as a separate cult, Mithra himself became the supreme lord. Thus, in accordance with Zoroastrian teaching, he was regarded as the source and representative of good, locked in a struggle (destined to be successful) with the forces of evil and disruption. Unlike early Zoroastrianism, but like the other mystery cults, Mithraism laid great stress on sacramental ritual.

It was believed that a main instrument of Mithra's victory over evil was the sacrifice of a sacred bull. This primeval bull was the prototype of all living things, including vegetation. The heavenly drama of Mithra's sacrifice was reenacted on earth in the taurobolium, a ceremony like that found in the cults of Cybele and Ma-Bellona, and perhaps borrowed from them. Once again we notice that the mystery had its roots in an agricultural fertility rite. The sacred bull, as it died, was supposed to bring forth corn and vines and other living things from its flanks. All this was reflected in the ceremonies of initiation. The initiate was baptized in the blood of the dying bull, and took part in a

Mithra as sun god (from a fourth-century cult vessel). Mithraic initiates believed that their god brought not only fertility, but also light. As *sol invictus*, he was identified with the supreme sun god, who was said to have shared his divine banquet, and to have ascended with him to heaven.

sacred meal of the elements of bread and wine. The divine banquet corresponded to the banquet that Mithra celebrated after sacrificing the bull.

However, the liturgy of Mithraism was a highly complex one, and we are uncertain as to all its details. There were seven grades of initiation, bringing men ultimately to the highest stage of heavenly life. The details of these grades remain obscure, but it can be inferred that they involved tests of courage and endurance. Each grade corresponded to one of the seven spheres through which Mithra himself was believed to have ascended to heaven. This scheme was adapted from the astrological belief that the soul had to pass through the spheres of the seven planets on its way to heaven; the stars were regarded as immortal souls. Nevertheless, the initiate was not identified with the god, since it was the life-giving bull, rather than Mithra himself, that died and by its death liberated the forces that culminate in immortality. In this respect the Mithraic legend differs from those of Osiris and other dying gods.

The elaborate scheme of the Mithraic initiations was well adapted to the milieu in which the faith made most of its converts—the Roman army. Each stage was called, significantly, a *sacramentum*, a term primarily used for the oath of loyalty taken by soldiers upon their entry into the legions. What is more, the ethic inculcated by Mithraism corresponded to the virtues expected of soldiers. The men's sense of solidarity with Mithra in his transcendental struggle against the forces of evil strengthened their loyalty in the battles they fought against the enemies of the empire. The assurance of immortality fostered courage. The flavor of Zoroastrian uprightness and probity still attached to the mystery religion, enhancing the old Roman virtues that now had to be shared by an army that was racially and culturally very mixed. This aspect of Mithraism partly accounts for its masculine, and especially military, nature. If women played a role in the faith, it was a minor one.

The spread of the cult is attested by the discovery of Mithraic shrines as far apart as Syria and the borders of Scotland. It was greatly helped by imperial encouragement, and a number of emperors themselves adopted the title of *invictus*. Mithra, as *sol invictus* ("the unconquerable sun"), was thus in some degree identified with the emperor. This new adaptation of emperor-worship was no doubt designed to cement the loyalty of the numerous legionaries who belonged to the Mithraic confraternities.

It may be seen from this survey of the main mystery cults of the ancient Mediterranean world that they shared certain features. First, they all had their basis in fertility and vegetation rites: in them, the dying god or goddess generated life through death. But in the mysteries, these rites were no longer regarded in the light of their original agricultural function. This is not surprising, since they catered for a population that was not of necessity tied to the land, and was, in the case of Rome, thoroughly urbanized. The fertility aspect accounts for the outer indecorousness of many of the rituals. The castration of Attis, the pinetree carried in procession to symbolize him, the bloody sacrifices, all these had their natural habitat in fertility magic. It was largely because the myths and rituals were allegorized that they acquired a personal meaning for the urban population and for sophisticated cosmopolitans like Apuleius. As a result, the discretion and secrecy that were a necessary corollary of the concept of sacred initiation gained a new dimension: only the initiate could understand fully the inner, spiritual meaning of the rites. But this itself reflects a fundamental aspect of the mysteries referred to earlier—that what counted was the experience of the initiate, rather than the acquisition of esoteric knowledge.

A second important feature of the mysteries was that they were not confined in membership to any particular local or national group. In this sense they were universal, though this universality was restricted in Mithraism, with its emphasis on masculine virtues. As part of the tendency to universalism, there was some syncretism, particularly in the mysteries of Isis. In any event, the gods of these cults were not exclusive. Apuleius, for instance, could participate in religious rituals other than those of Isis, even if they could not have the same profound personal meaning for him.

The decline of the mysteries was in part due to the growing impact of Christianity. The latter faith had features that, to the Greco-Roman mind, assimilated it to the mysteries, and this partly accounted for its appeal. The eucharist was a sacred meal seemingly analogous to that found in Mithraism, and baptism had a strong sacramental significance that made it a rival to the idea of rebirth in the mysteries. Likewise, Christ was a dying and rising god—though without the fertility connotations of an Osiris or a

Above, the sacred meal of the Mithraic initiates. Masked servers provide wine and loaves of bread for the two participants. (Sculpture from Konjica, Yugoslavia.)

Below, an early Christian love feast, with eucharistic associations. It consisted of wine with bread or fish—symbols of Christ. (Third-century Roman catacomb painting.)

Dionysus. The ethical content of the faith attracted those who, like Apuleius, saw in the mysteries more than a form of ritualism. At the same time, Christianity, in the course of its penetration into the Greco-Roman world, was able to make use of Platonism, and thus wedded philosophy to personal faith in a way the mysteries did not. It provided a comprehensive view of the world as well as a ritual. And its jealous God prevented it from becoming entangled in the multiplicities of contemporary mythology, which did not always appeal to the sophisticated elite.

Nevertheless, it is useful to probe more deeply into the likenesses between early Christianity and the mystery cults. The impression of similarity is reinforced by the fact that reticence and secrecy began to surround the eucharist. This development probably dates from about the middle of the second century A.D., though some have argued that it began much earlier, before the time when St. John's gospel was written (toward the end of the first century). It happens that *John* contains no account of the institution of the eucharist by Christ, such as is found in the other three gospels and in St. Paul's *I Corinthians*. This may indicate that the author of *John* wished to keep the details of the eucharistic liturgy out of a document that was to be in rather general circulation. But in any event, the practice of secrecy in this

Left, Christ as Orpheus, or the good shepherd (third-century painting from the Roman catacombs). The earliest portraits of Christ depict him as a young man surrounded by sheep and goats; in many, it is uncertain whether he is charming the animals, or watching over his flock. Right, a Christian, with hands bound, awaits his martyrdom. Though Christianity was not illegal, Christians were sometimes ordered to make an offering to the emperor, and executed when they refused. (Detail from a fourth-century Roman wall painting.)

matter is attested by Tertullian (*c.* A.D. 160–230), St. John Chrysostom (*c.* A.D. 345–407) and St. Augustine (A.D. 354–430). Tertullian declares that that which is holy should not be cast to the dogs, and that "it is a universal custom in religious initiation to keep the profane aloof and to beware of witnesses." This is a conscious comparison with the mystery cults.

The secrecy surrounding the eucharist involved the exclusion even of catechumens, or those who were being prepared for full membership of the community, from the celebration. They were allowed a place in the church building during the first part of the service, but with the start of the eucharistic liturgy proper they were dismissed. Thus the full meaning and central expression of the Christian faith were not available to them until they graduated by partaking in their first communion at Easter.

The growth of such sacred reticence may have owed something to the sporadic persecutions inflicted on the early Church; it was, no doubt, desirable to exclude hostile informers. On the other hand, secrecy itself led to the spreading of wild rumors about Christian rites, including the charges that child-sacrifices and cannibalism were features of the eucharist. Clearly the language of the Lord's Supper—"This is my body. . . . This is my blood"—could generate a literal interpretation of the sacrament among outsiders.

But though there was secrecy about the eucharist, as a protection of its solemnity, there was little reticence about the teachings. St. Paul's discourse in Athens, on the hill of Areopagus, was a prototype not just of the public preaching through which Christianity penetrated the synagogues and the Greco-Roman world, but also of the attempt to seek within pagan culture a religious and intellectual basis on which the essential teachings of the Christian revelation could be built. It is true that there were some, like Tertullian, who resisted the attempt, on the ground that Greek philosophical and other ideas might obscure and distort, rather than enhance, the Christian message. "What," he asked, "has Athens to do with Jerusalem?" Yet the main trend, culminating in the work of St. Augustine, was toward adapting pagan doctrines to Christianity. Thus Christianity was able to present publicly a coherent and uniform view of the world. As we have seen, the mysteries were less secret teachings than secret rituals. Though Christianity may occasionally have conformed to the latter idea, it was committed to open teachings and preachings.

The control exercised by the Christian Church over its initiates, and the relative uniformity of belief between local congregations scattered across the empire, checked the development of the religious eclecticism characteristic of the world of the mysteries. This was in line with the anti-idolatrous and exclusive features of the Judaism from which the new religion sprang. The mysteries, on the other hand, lacked social coherence, because it was possible for a person to be initiated in more than one. Moreover, and indeed as a result of this situation, the mysteries tended to cater for the more affluent. Those who could pay the fees could enter; and the fees for the initiations of Isis, for example, were quite high. Christianity, by contrast, absorbed people from the lower orders, including slaves. Though from the earliest times members of the upper classes adhered to the faith, its main success was among artisans and the lower classes in general. Christianity had two distinct advantages: first, it was (literally) cheap; secondly, it was not socially exclusive. Admittedly, the Mithraic cult might claim the first of these advantages, and it was largely confined to a profession comprising people of different ranks. But it made its appeal to that particular group, and could not be socially universal. Moreover, it was not adapted to the metaphysical beliefs of the intellectual and religious elite.

Though Christianity was not socially exclusive, it was religiously so. The Jewish heritage made it hostile to idolatry, including emperor-worship. This resistance to the state cult was an explosive issue, and gave Christians the reputation of being subversive. Christians were dubbed *atheoi* (literally "atheists," but a better translation would be "gods-less ones"). Their rejection of the surrounding religion, and the fact that they were inclined to proselytize, caused them to be looked upon as socially dangerous people, even as revolutionaries. This, from the point of view of those outside the Church, gave Christianity something of the character of a secret society threatening the established order.

A representation of the rite of baptism in the early Church (detail from a Roman catacomb painting of the fourth century). Because baptism meant rebirth into the life of the spirit, a person who was baptized was called *infans* ("newborn child") and was depicted as a child. He stood naked in the baptismal water, which flowed from above—as if from the mouth of the dove of the spirit—into the font. After the rite he put on white robes, was welcomed as a "new lamb" of the shepherd, and admitted to the eucharist for the first time.

Yet while Christianity differed from the mysteries, it was able to draw upon the religious concerns that gave the latter their life. It was able to preach immortality, a resurrected God, renewal of life in baptism, and a eucharistic mystery. It therefore conformed to the feelings of many folk in the Greco-Roman world into which it went. Persecution gave it a strong solidarity. Its doctrines and its repudiation of polytheism provided a solution to the problems of the upper-class intellectual, while its belief in a future life and the efficacy of sacraments had a strong emotional appeal.

The secret and exclusive aspects of Christianity were perhaps incidental to its development, for it did not see itself as merely a sect of initiation nor as a religious club. Indeed, they began to disappear with the enfranchisement of the faith under and after Constantine. By this time its homogeneity, though imperiled by movements such as Arianism (condemned as a heresy), was guaranteed by a unified structure, which gave it a strong advantage over its rivals. The fact that Christianity had an analogy to the mystery cults, without being one, explains in part its success. Its differences from the mystery cults—its exclusiveness, its doctrinal concerns, its social solidarity—help us to understand the nature of those cults, and to avoid thinking of them in terms of the religion we know today.

5 The Assassins and the Knights Templar

Since the Middle Ages, legend has obscured the history of the Assassins, the secret society that began in 11th-century Persia as a religious order. One of the earliest stories to reach Europe was brought back by Marco Polo, who traveled through Persia on his way to China in 1273. In a fortified valley between two mountains, says Polo, the Sheik or "Old Man" of the Assassins had planted a beautiful garden that grew every fruit in the world. The garden was watered with streams of wine, milk, and honey. Like the prophet Mohammed's paradise, on which it was modeled, it held gilded palaces, *houris*, dancers, musicians, and singers. And it was seen only by those who were to be made Assassins. Young men who had been trained in arms at the Old Man's court were drugged, taken to the hidden garden, and initiated into its delights. They lived there in luxury for a few days, convinced that their leader had transported them to paradise. When they were suddenly drugged again, and taken back to his court, they were eager to risk their lives for him in order to return. "Away they went," concluded Polo, "and did all that they were commanded. Thus it happened that no man ever escaped when the Sheik of the Mountain desired his death."

This romantic story is true in at least one respect: there is little doubt that the Assassins were drug-takers, for their name is derived from the Arabic word *Hashshishin*, meaning "users of hashish." The tale of the garden paradise

A painting from a 13th-century Spanish manuscript shows a Crusader playing chess with a Saracen, suggesting the impact made by Islamic culture on the Christian armies, and especially on the Knights Templar, who played an ambivalent role in the contest for the Kingdom of Jerusalem.

possibly has its origin in the hallucinations produced by the drug. But oriental legend had already created an Eden out of the fertile valley near the chief Assassin stronghold at Alamut, south of the Caspian Sea. Stories about the Assassins may have been confused with this tradition and with the legend of King Shedad, who tried to equal Allah's paradise by building his own.

The Assassins sprang up like dragons' teeth in the cracks of the Arab caliphates. On the prophet Mohammed's death (A.D. 632), a struggle for the succession had broken out. The Sunnis, or orthodox Muslims, held that the elected caliphs of Baghdad were the rightful leaders of Islam. Against this Sunni majority the Shia sects rebelled. They upheld a strict social order based on absolute obedience to their priest-kings, the *imams*, who were the direct or spiritual descendants of Mohammed through his daughter Fatima and his son-in-law Ali. They believed in the approaching millennium, when one of the past imams would return to earth as the *Mahdi*, or "guided one," and establish the rule of justice. A discipline of secrecy and a belief in the value of suffering for religion's sake helped the Shias to survive Sunni persecution. Their example of the Passion was the martyrdom of Ali's younger son Husain, killed while trying to regain his birthright, the caliphate.

In the eighth century, after the death of the sixth imam, Jafar as-Sadiq, the Shia sects themselves splintered apart. The majority, called the Twelvers, supported the succession of his son Musa, and his descendants, believing that the millennium would come with the return of the twelfth imam in that line. The Ismailis, or Seveners, supported the succession of Musa's elder brother Ismail; they held that his son Mohammed, who had disappeared in A.D. 770, was the seventh and last imam, and that the millennium would come with his return to earth as Mahdi. Ismaili missionaries or *da'is* traveled through the rest of the Arab world preaching this subversive doctrine. So successful were they in Tunisia that the Ismailis were able to establish a rival caliphate there in A.D. 909. It was known as the Fatimid caliphate because the first caliph, Ubaydullah, claimed to be a direct successor of Fatima and Ali through the prophet Ismail, and to be the Mahdi. During the 10th century, while the Fatimid caliphate extended its boundaries to Sicily, Egypt, Cairo, and North Africa, the Ismailis elsewhere remained a secret society working to overthrow the Sunni caliphs of Baghdad.

Missionaries trained in the Grand Lodge of the Ismailis in Cairo continued to travel, preaching a doctrine that negated most of the orthodox Islamic beliefs. They held that Muslim law and scriptures contained an inner meaning that was known only to the imams. They taught that there were only seven prophets: Adam, Noah, Abraham, Moses, Jesus, Mohammed, and Ismail. In the order of creation, the prophets stood at the level of Universal Reason, second only to God. After the prophets came the "Prophet's companion," Ali (level of Universal Soul), the seven imams (level of Primal Matter), the chief da'i or Grand Master (level of Space), and the da'i (level of Time).

Last in this sevenfold chain of creation stood man. Though God himself was unknowable, a man could work through these grades as far as Universal Reason, and a new aspect of the teaching would be revealed to him at each level. Because such views were heretical, every Ismaili initiate was required to conceal his beliefs in accordance with the Shia discipline of secrecy and to conform, outwardly, with the state religion.

In Ismaili writings, there is usually a frenzied wanderer who seeks truth through trial and suffering until he is at last accepted into the faith by an imam, who reveals to him the true meaning of Muslim law and scriptures. Such a search is described by Hasan-i Sabbah, founder and first Grand Master of the Assassins, in his memoirs.

Hasan came from a Twelver Shia family in western Persia. According to a famous Ismaili story, he was at school with the poet Omar Khayyam and the great Sunni statesman Nizam al-Mulk, who became the Assassins' first victim. Though the story is historically inaccurate, the change of the three schoolfriends into rebel, poet, and statesman is a useful allegory of the opportunities and the rivalries of the time. Hasan himself tells us that he searched enthusiastically, as a youth, for the secrets of science and religion. He writes of his conversion to Ismailism after a period of spiritual doubt: "In the midst of this a severe and dangerous illness occurred. God desired that my flesh and bones become something different—'God changed his flesh to better than his flesh and his blood to better than his blood' applied to me." Purged and spiritually reborn, Hasan went to Cairo in 1078 to ask the eighth Fatimid caliph for permission to spread the Ismaili gospel in Persia (then in the hands of the Seljuk Turks). The caliph agreed, on condition that Hasan would support the claims of the caliph's eldest son, Nizar, to be the ninth Fatimid. Thus the sect of the *Nizaris*, or Assassins, was born.

Legends about Hasan's early travels of missionary subversion tell of his release from prison because of the terror caused by the collapse of a high tower near his cell, and of his quelling a storm at sea with the words "Our Lord has promised that no evil shall befall me." In fact, Hasan wandered in Iran and picked as a strategic center the fortress of Alamut ("Eagle's Teaching" or "Eagle's Nest"), perched high up in the northern mountains.

In the absence of large artillery, castles on rocks usually fell only to starvation, thirst, disease, or subversion. The garrison of Alamut soon expelled its Sunni chieftain and accepted Hasan in his place. Legend tells of the Sunni chieftain taking a bribe and falling for Dido's old cowhide trick—he promised Hasan as much land as a cowhide would include and then had to cede him the whole fortress when Hasan girdled it with strips of cut leather.

Hasan, who pursued spiritual power through political power, changed the role of the Ismaili initiate to the role of assassin. At the same time, he modified the grades of initiation. The only descriptions of these grades, and of the "mysteries" revealed to initiates, date from the 19th century. They

Photographs show some of the remaining evidence of Assassin occupation at the sites of their castles. Left, a short bronze dagger dating from the time of the Assassins, recently found at Alamut. Below, a glazed bowl from the castle of Samiran (one of the few surviving examples of Assassin pottery). Right, a 200-yard-long cistern cut out at the foot of the rock of Alamut—part of the water system constructed in the 12th century by Hasan-i Sabbah. It stored water for use in the castle and in the valley below, where Hasan planted fruit trees. Far right, a narrow slit in the rock of Alamut that gives access to a green enclosure with a spring—conceivably the site of Hasan's fabled garden. Below right, probable layout of Alamut Castle. Though largely destroyed, it still has a vine, and the cisterns used for storing rainwater.

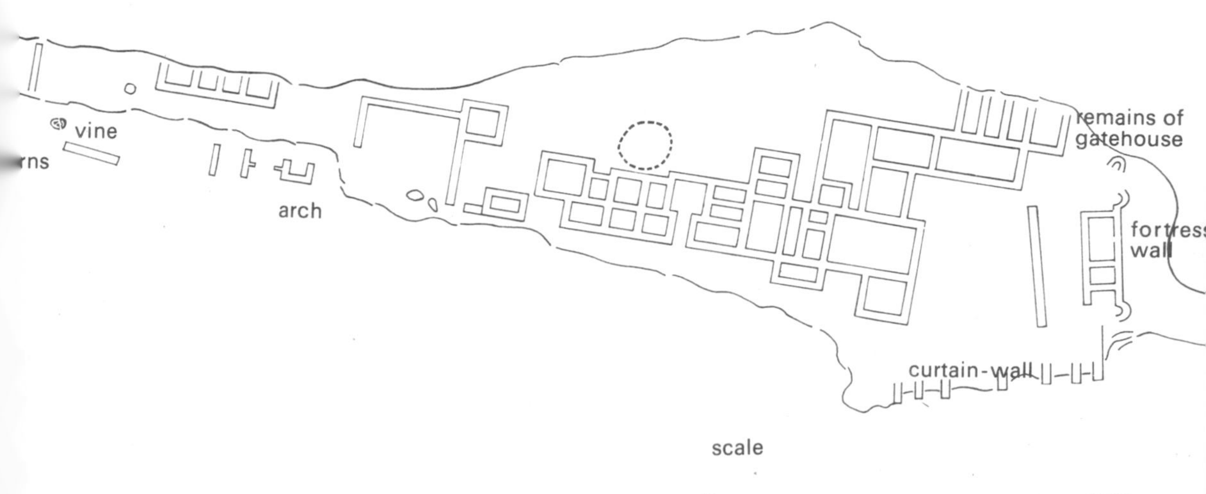
vine
rns
arch
remains of gatehouse
fortress wall
curtain-wall
scale
0
200
feet

were written by European scholars who saw the Ismaili hierarchy itself as a mere brainwashing system. According to their accounts, the teaching given at each level negated everything that had been taught before. The innermost secret of the Assassins was that heaven and hell were the same, all actions were indifferent, and there was no good or evil except the virtue of obeying the imam. We know nothing of the Assassins' secrets, because their books of doctrine and ritual were burned in 1256 with their library at Alamut. We know that Hasan emphasized the Shia doctrine of obedience to the imam, but we do not know exactly what changes he made in the Ismaili hierarchy. Persian tradition has it that below Hasan, the chief da'i or Grand Master, came the senior da'is, the ordinary da'is, the *rafiqs* or companions, the *lasiqs* or laymen, and the *fidais* (devotees) who did the murders.

In his asceticism and singleness of purpose, Hasan was an ideal revolutionary leader and conspirator. He is said to have remained continuously within his home in the fortress for more than thirty years, only going out twice and appearing twice more on his roof. His invisibility increased his power. From his seclusion he strengthened the defenses of Alamut, purged the ranks of his followers (even putting to death two of his own sons), and continued with his strategy of seizing hill fortresses as centers of local subversion. He elevated his authority to tyranny over life and soul. The will of the Old Man was the will of his imam, the caliph, and thus the will of God.

After the caliph's death in 1094, and the failure of Nizar's claim to the succession, Hasan broke away from the Egyptian Fatimids and set himself up as an independent prince. By winning over garrisons and assassinating local governors he occupied strongpoints and terrorized the Sunnis, Persians and Turks alike. The conspiracy of the determined few, as usual, was hardly opposed by the fearful many. On the model of Mohammed himself, who had fled to Medina to rally support and reconquer Mecca and all Arabia, Hasan hoped to take over the whole caliphate of Baghdad.

By the authority of his rank and by the use of drugs, Hasan trained bodies of Nizaris in such blind obedience that, like the Japanese suicide pilots of World War II, they welcomed death during an attempt at assassination. They preferred the dagger as a weapon, and the court or the mosque as a place of execution; they scorned the use of poison and backstairs intrigue, for their code was more that of soldiers than of harem murderers. Legend tells of one fidai's mother who rejoiced when she heard that her son had died in an attempt on a ruler's life, then put on mourning when he returned alive. Similar legends grew up around other loyal fidais who stabbed themselves or dashed out their brains on the rocks below the battlements to prove their obedience to the Old Man's command.

The Assassins, rather like the Mafia of later times, operated from their strongholds a protection racket under threat of death; their techniques helped to undermine the Seljuk empire and to fragment even more the fragmented

Hasan conducts his fabled initiations at Alamut, which began with the distribution of drugged wine. (A 14th-century French painting for *The Travels of Marco Polo*.)

An illustration to an 11th-century Shia treatise portrays the prophet Mohammed proclaiming his son-in-law Ali his successor. The historical Assassins had their origins in the Shia sect, who were supporters of Ali in the succession quarrel that broke out after Mohammed's death.

Arab world. Suspicion ran riot, and murder was a normal method of princely government. Thus the Crusaders, coming to the Holy Land, found only a divided enemy, disorganized by the Assassins. In fact, Hasan had spread the sect to Syria, where the Prince of Emessa was struck down in 1102 on his way to fight the Crusaders. Hasan may not have intended to aid the Christian invaders; but he did help the Crusaders to entrench themselves in the Levant.

By their success in terrifying powerful Arab rulers, the Assassins brought retribution down on the Ismailis in Sunni territory. The Seljuk sultans and local Sunni populations retaliated by wiping out many Ismaili settlements in the Levant and Persia. After about 1105, though the Assassins remained powerful in local fortresses, they were no longer a serious military threat.

Hasan-i Sabbah died in 1124. His two immediate successors continued his policy; but the fourth Old Man, Hasan II (1162-1166) claimed that he was the Mahdi, whose coming marked the end of the Shia discipline of secrecy. He seceded from the religion of Islam to found his own religion and opened the secrets of the sect to all, thus driving away many of the more orthodox Nizaris. He preached liberation from the letter of Muslim law, especially the bans on wine-drinking and pork-eating. He held that the enemies of the Assassins, by choosing to live outside the new faith, had surely chosen death, though their bodies might still walk and talk. "Having failed to choose Life when he had the opportunity," Hasan II said, when he refused to pardon a Sunni leader, "he does not now exist to be revived."

Hasan II was too daring for his followers; he wanted a spiritual revolution as well as a political one. He was murdered by his brother-in-law, and the Persian Assassins, though remaining politically independent, returned to a more orthodox faith, actually adopting a Sunni version of Muslim law. The Syrian branch of the Assassins, led by the wily Rashid Ad-Din Sinan (1162-1192), became independent of the Persian Old Man and began to kill for cash rather than for political control or religion. Sinan became a local Syrian hero, accommodating himself to the surrounding powers or terrorizing them in order to keep his followers independent. He became particularly famous for his intrigues against Saladin and the Crusaders.

Already the Crusaders occupied great fortresses in southern Syria, such as the Krak des Chevaliers, and Sinan, fearful of Sunni attack, agreed to pay a yearly tribute of two thousand pieces of gold to the Templars to avoid being caught between them and the Sunnis to the north. When Saladin rose to power in Aleppo, however, the fearful Sinan sent out his Assassins twice to kill this formidable threat. The Assassins failed and Saladin replied by ravaging Ismaili territory. Legend has it that Saladin stopped persecuting the Ismailis because he woke up to find a poisoned dagger by his pillow, placed there as a warning by the Assassins. More probably, Sinan and Saladin decided not to waste their strength upon each other, but to unite, at least temporarily, against the Crusaders. Saladin was certainly helped in 1192 when two murderers, probably sent by Sinan, struck down Conrad of Montferrat, Prince of Tyre and King of Jerusalem. According to the 12th-century *Chronicle of Ambroise:*

> . . . two youths lightly clad, who wore
> No cloaks, and each a dagger bore,
> Made straight for him, and with one bound,
> Smote him and bore him to the ground,
> And each one stabbed him with his blade,
> The wretches, who thus wise betrayed
> Him, were of the Assassin's men. . . .

Sinan had been bribed to send out the killers, either by Saladin (according to Arab sources) or by Richard Coeur de Lion (according to French sources). Fear of the Assassins had become so widespread that both Richard and Philip Augustus of France were later to be accused of training up their own picked youths to murder each other.

The fame of the Assassins bred and multiplied until no European chronicler could leave them out of his mixture of history and romance. Louis IX of France, in Joinville's 13th-century chronicle, resists many attempts on his life by the Assassins. In 1250 he receives a visit from three Assassin envoys who claim that they receive tribute from the emperor of Germany, the king of Hungary, and the sultan of Babylon—"because," the chief envoy says, "all these realize that they can live no longer than it shall please my Lord." Louis replies by threatening the Old Man, who then decides to ally himself with the French king and sends him a ring and a shirt of brotherhood, though he still appears in Alamut attended by an ax-bearer crying in front of him, "Bow all of you before the one who carries the death of kings in his hands." So piety in Joinville allies itself with political murder, for both rulers are concerned with the same things, the possession of castles in the Near East and the slaughter of their enemies.

Thus the Assassins entered into mythology, until any attack on a ruler's life was ascribed to them and the word "assassin" became part of the English and French languages. Even in 1271, after the Mongols had destroyed the Persian and Syrian Assassins, an attempt on the life of Prince Edward at Acre was laid at their door. The Assassins were loathed and feared throughout the Arab and European world, though they merely systematized the Muslim practice of assassination. Yet they had little choice; as a small minority, they had to attack mass strength by stealth.

The Assassins, like the rest of the eastern Arab world, showed little resistance to the Mongol advance in the mid-13th century. Though branches of the sect reached India, its resources were scattered and its discipline sapped. The fear inspired by the Assassins was nothing to the horror used by the Mongols to break their enemies' morale. Yet the Mongol general Hulagu, who had made rivers run with blood, piled up pyramids of skulls, and turned

gardens into deserts, began by failing ridiculously in front of the walls of Alamut and other Assassin fortresses. But the Assassin terrorists were themselves out-terrorized. They decided to parley rather than resist the grandson of Genghis Khan, who was later to be beaten by the Egyptian Mamelukes and never knew how to conduct a proper siege.

The Assassin fortresses were surrendered and razed one by one, though Alamut was so strong that it almost defeated the enemy's efforts to destroy it; its stores of food and water were so great that Hulagu himself wondered at his good fortune in capturing such a stronghold without a fight. The Mongols, as soon as they had taken over the Assassin fortresses, massacred the Persian Ismailis, while the Syrian Assassins were reduced by the Sultan Baybars, the scourge of the Mongols, into hired killers at the Egyptian court.

Though the Assassins were destroyed at this time as a political power, leaving the Sunnis dominant in the shrunken Muslim world, their Christian imitators survived for a few decades longer. There is little question that Hugues de Payens, the Burgundian knight who founded the Order of the Temple in 1118 with eight other knights and "poor fellow-soldiers of Christ," modeled his organization on that of the Assassins. The two organizations certainly knew each other in Syria before 1128, when the Templar Rule was written. The division of the Templars, under their Grand Master, into grand priors, priors, knights, esquires, and lay brothers closely follows the traditional hierarchy of the Assassins (p. 112). Even the colors worn by the knights, red crosses on a white ground, were the same as those of the Assassin *rafiqs*, who wore red caps and belts and white tunics. Some claim that the Templars only adopted the Assassins' "hues of innocence and blood, and of pure devotion and murder" because the rival Knights Hospitaler wore black. However that may be, the function of the Templars was virtually the same as that of the Assassins—to serve as an independent power on the side of their religious faith.

By 1152, when the Assassins murdered the Count of Tripoli, the Templars had forced the Syrian branch to pay them a yearly tribute (p. 114). William of Tyre claims that later in the century Sinan offered to turn his Assassins into Christians, if the Templars stopped exacting their yearly ransom; but that the Templars greedy for their money, killed the Assassin envoy and prevented this remarkable conversion. Fanciful as the story seems, it may have some basis in fact, for it refers to the period of Hasan II, whose reforms at Alamut may have alienated Sinan and prompted him to make overtures of some kind to the Christians.

Hulagu's siege of Alamut in 1256 (painting from a French translation of the Persian *History of the World Conqueror,* 1437).

A page from a 12th-century manuscript of the Rule of the Temple. Reminding the " revered brothers " that they have renounced worldly pleasures, it commands them to serve " the king on high " with horses and arms, and to be "diligent in hearing mattins and every devotion in its entirety, from a pure and pious inclination." It also urges them to be humble and to despise the sufferings of the body, promising that after holy Mass they will be "nourished by the food of God and sanctified, learned, and fortified in the Lord's commandments; none shall be faint-hearted at the fight, but shall be prepared for his crown."

From the beginning the Templars, who were sworn to poverty and obedience and chastity, attracted a remarkable band of cavalrymen to their banners. They particularly sought out excommunicated knights, who had nothing to lose. Somewhat in the manner of the Foreign Legion, they used discipline and war to purge the sins of the "rogues and impious men, robbers and committers of sacrilege, murderers, perjurers, and adulterers" whom St. Bernard of Clairvaux declared were swarming to the Holy Land. St. Bernard, however, so approved of the Templar's methods of saving the lost that he wrote a glowing letter in praise of the new order to Hugues de Payens. Armed with this letter, Hugues attended the Council of Troyes in 1128 and won for the Templars papal sanction and exemption from excommunication.

Thus a band of holy ex-sinners was created—a Salvation Army with a two-handed broadsword in its hand. "You see them never combed," St. Bernard wrote, contrasting them favorably with rich knights, "rarely washed, their beards bushy, sweaty and dusty, stained by their harness and the heat." In an age when the king of France only changed his clothes three times a year, the Templars were proud that their mantles remained on their backs until they rotted off or were slashed apart by enemy swords. They even slept with their clothes on, in lighted dormitories. After all, lice and dirt were easier to bear than a hair shirt or a belt of nails.

The first avowed aim of Hugues de Payens and his knights was simply to protect the pilgrim routes to Jerusalem and the other holy places. But the Crusader kings of Jerusalem, realizing that the knights might provide a regular standing army to beat off sudden Muslim incursions, encouraged them to take part in military campaigns. Though the Templars were independent of the authority of kings, owing allegiance only to the pope, they soon made themselves invaluable in the defense of Crusader gains in the Levant.

In the disastrous Second Crusade (1146-1150), when the Muslims thrashed the knights of Europe, the Templars prevented total catastrophe. The secretary of Louis VII declared that their discipline and obedience to their Grand

Master inspired the whole army: "All, rich and poor, gave the word that they would not flee the field, and that they would obey in everything the Master who was given to them." Later in the campaign, Louis acknowledged how much he relied on the Templars' support. "We could not imagine," he wrote back to Europe, "how We could have lasted a moment in this country without their aid and assistance. Their help was available from the first day of Our arrival until the moment We send this letter."

The Middle Ages was a time of generous giving to religion. Many estates in England, Spain, and France were bequeathed to the Templars by returned Crusaders grateful for their lives, or by Christians who thought that their own road to heaven was defended by the guardians of the Jerusalem road. The "poor fellow-soldiers of Christ" rapidly grew rich, and became that most dangerous of things for themselves, an envied institution of independent moneylenders. Because of their vows of honesty and their papal immunity from civil jurisdiction, they became the bankers of the Levant, and later of the courts of Europe. Louis VII accepted a large loan from the order, noting that the money must be repaid quickly, "lest their House be defamed and destroyed." Even the Muslims banked with the Templars, in case the fortunes of war should force them to ally themselves with the Christians. Though usury was forbidden to Christians in the Middle Ages, the Templars added to the money they banked or transported by paying back an agreed sum less than the original amount, while a debtor returned more than his debt. The Paris Temple became the center of the world's money-market.

The Templars, like most religious sects, had their own ceremonies of initiation and their own regulations—the so-called "Rule of the Temple." These were to provide the key to their destruction, though the Templars could hardly have existed as a proud and efficient military caste without special ceremonies to distinguish them from other orders such as the Hospitalers and the Teutonic Knights. The investitures were secret, being held under cover of darkness in the guarded chapter house. The Rule was secret in so far as it was known in its entirety to only the highest officers of the Temple. We know it only in copies, which simply describe the constitution of the order, and the duties and ceremonies of each rank. But because of this element of secrecy, and because the original manuscript of the Rule has not survived, opponents of the Templars have always postulated the existence of a separate, secret Rule that would endorse blasphemy and sexual license. The final prosecutors of the Templars were to accuse them of forcing their initiates to spit on the Cross and to become homosexuals; in fact, the Templars were more likely to make a novice tremble in front of the Cross and the knights of the order than to make him despise both.

An unbiased account of their initiation ritual gives the following details. The Master of the Temple asked the assembled knights three times if there was any objection to a particular novice being admitted to the order; the

novice himself was shown "the great hardships of the House, and the commandments of charity that existed." He was also asked if he had a wife or betrothed, debts or hidden disease, other vows or other master. If the novice answered these questions satisfactorily, he knelt in front of the Master and asked to become "the serf and slave of the House." The Master replied that many things were required of him and that the Templars' beautiful horses and costume were no more than the "outer shell" of their life. "You do not know the hard commandments that are within; because it is a hard thing for you, who are master of yourself, to make yourself the serf of another. For you will hardly ever do what you want; if you wish to be on this side of the sea, you will be sent to the other side; or if you wish to be in Acre, you will be sent to the land of Tripoli or Antioch or Armenia, or you will be sent to Apulia or Sicily or Lombardy or France or Burgundy or England or to many other lands where we have Houses and possessions. And if you wish to sleep, you will be made to stay awake; and if you sometimes wish to stay awake, you will be ordered to go and rest in your bed."

Then the novice was warned that he must not enter the order for his own advantage, but to forsake the sins of the world, to serve our Lord, to be poor, to do penitence and to save his soul. He swore that he would obey the Master of the Temple in everything, live all his life without private possessions, follow the customs of the House, help in the conquest of the Holy Land, stay for the

Far left, St. Bernard (1091-1153), Abbot of Clairvaux, founder of the Cistercian Order, and first patron of the Knights Templar (painting from Jean Fouquet's *Heures d'Etienne Chevalier*, about 1450). Left, the medieval city of Jerusalem (detail from a 15th-century French painting). Above, a 13th-century seal of the Templars that depicts two knights on one horse—symbolic perhaps of poverty.

rest of his life in the order "both in strength and in weakness, for better or for worse," and never allow a Christian to be robbed of his goods. Once the novice had sworn by God and the Virgin Mary to observe all these rules, the Master accepted him into the order, putting the mantle on him and promising him "bread and water and the dress of the poor and much suffering and travail." The chaplain then recited the psalm *Ecce quam bonum* and the knights repeated the Lord's Prayer. The novice could have no illusion, after a ceremony of this sort, that he was not engaged in an order that demanded total obedience to the end of his days.

Guiot de Provins, the 12th-century monk who belonged to many holy orders and condemned his own time as "vile and filthy," testified to the Templars' integrity, praising them above all other religious orders. He found them dedicated unto death, supermen whom his shrinking flesh could admire and refuse to join.

Better far be cowardly and alive,
Than dead, the most famous of them all.
The Order of the Templars, I know well,
Is beautiful and excellent and sure—
But keeping healthy keeps me far from war.

Yet those brought up from birth to be knights, who had no hope of marrying or inheriting lands of their own, might well prefer to rise to the command of a Templar castle in the Levant than to subsist on a feudal lord's charity in Europe. Merit in battle and organization meant promotion in the order; rarely was feudal rank important in the election of the Grand Master of the Templars, though the increasing wealth and power of the order tended to attract more ambitious and greedy men to try and gain its leadership.

The first three Grand Masters were good commanders and organizers and diplomats; also, above all, they were men of faith. Their banners bore the device: *Non nobis, Domine, non nobis, sed nomini tuo da gloriam* ("Not to ourselves, Lord, not to ourselves, but to Thy name give the glory"). But, at the siege of Ascalon in 1153, the fourth Grand Master, Bernard de Tremelai, actually ordered his men to beat back their Christian allies so that the Templars might gain all the credit for capturing the town. The seventh Grand Master, Philip de Milly—who had once been a great feudal baron himself—began to intrigue in the political squabbles that split Jerusalem apart.

The eighth Grand Master, Odo de Saint-Amand (1170-1179), followed his example; William of Tyre said that "his nostrils swelled with the breath of fury" and that "he did not fear God nor respect any man." He broke the king of Jerusalem's treaty with Saladin by which no new fortresses were to be built on the frontier; his excuse was that the Templars, being independent, could be bound by no treaty. The fortress he built soon fell into the hands of Saladin, and the Templar garrison was massacred. Odo himself died in prison in 1180, refusing to be ransomed with the proud declaration of poverty: "A Templar can only offer as a ransom his belt and his sword."

His aged successor soon died and in 1184 a young and ambitious Grand Master, Gerard de Ridfort, was elected. Ridfort was to play a large part in the destruction of the Kingdom of Jerusalem. In the succession quarrel after the death of the boy-king Baldwin V (1186), he gave the Templars' support to the unpopular Guy de Lusignan and had him crowned king of Jerusalem instead of the regent, Raymond III of Tripoli, who was backed by the Hospitalers. The divisions among the Crusaders were exploited by Saladin, whose treaty of peace with the Crusader kingdom had just been broken by the treacherous Reynald de Chatillon, Prince of Antioch. Saladin, with the connivance of Raymond, marched on Jerusalem in 1187. Ridfort, with only 150 knights, attempted to stop the army of 7000 Muslims outside Nazareth. The Templars were massacred, and Ridfort himself made his escape to Nazareth with only three of his men.

Raymond, seeing the Crusader kingdom menaced with total destruction, abandoned Saladin and allied himself with Guy de Lusignan and his fellow Christians. The Templars gave Guy de Lusignan money to equip an army to oppose the conquering Saladin. Though Raymond wanted to fight a delaying campaign, Ridfort persuaded the vacillating Guy de Lusignan to take the offensive against the Muslims. In the baking heat of July, the Crusaders left their supplies of water and advanced across the desert to attack Saladin, who had just taken Tiberias. They came to a halt at nightfall on the parched hill of the Horns of Hattin. The Muslim army surrounded them and, when day came, they drove the Crusaders up the slope. Ravaged by thirst, the Crusaders charged again and again towards the waters of the Lake of Tiberias. Raymond and his knights broke out of the tightening noose; but the rest of the Crusaders were all slaughtered or captured, and the scarlet tent of Guy de Lusignan was trampled to the ground.

Saladin did not spare the surviving Templars and Hospitalers; they had fought him so desperately and so long that he had them all beheaded—except for Ridfort. Aggressive in liberty, Ridfort became a coward in captivity. Like the last of the Old Men of the Assassins, who surrendered his fortresses to the Mongols, he lost his nerve. Ridfort ordered the garrisons of the remaining Templar strongholds to yield to Saladin; and Jerusalem fell to the Muslims in October 1187. A hundred years later, when the order was under trial, one high officer of the Temple said that the wicked Ridfort had introduced the custom of spitting on the Cross into the ritual of initiation as the price of his release by Saladin. Whether this was true or false, Ridfort's role in ruining the Kingdom of Jerusalem was the equivalent of reviling his faith.

The Templars never fully recovered from Ridfort's disastrous rule. Though they grew wealthy and powerful again, even in the Levant, they had lost their reputation for pure religious devotion. They became politicians of the Christian faith, more ready to accommodate themselves to Muslim rulers and customs for the sake of their own interests than to attack with the sword every evidence of Islam. This policy, combined with the facts that they spoke Arabic and (unlike other Christian orders) wore long beards in the Muslim fashion, played into the hands of their detractors. Opponents of the Temple did not forget that their first home had been a mosque, built on the site of Solomon's Temple in Jerusalem. A visiting Muslim envoy had been allowed to say his prayers to Allah there, facing Mecca, though the mosque had been converted into a Christian church. The Templars themselves often pointed out that the Virgin Mary, to whom they were dedicated, had her place in the Koran. They knew of the esoteric doctrines of the East; their discipline of prayer, fasting, and scourging for sins was severe enough to satisfy the most rigorous Muslim; and they knew that their position in the Levant was tenable only as long as they had Arab allies and the Arab world remained divided. When the Templars were accused of worshiping a phallic idol called Baphomet, they were really being accused of dealing with the worshipers of Mohammed.

After Ridfort, a series of more cautious Grand Masters restored something of the position of the Templars in the Holy Land. They played their part in the great siege of Acre and, when the city was captured in 1191, they made it their new headquarters. They backed Richard Coeur de Lion in the Third Crusade (1191-2); when Richard failed to take Jerusalem, he slipped away from the Holy Land in a Templar disguise and a Templar galley. Their

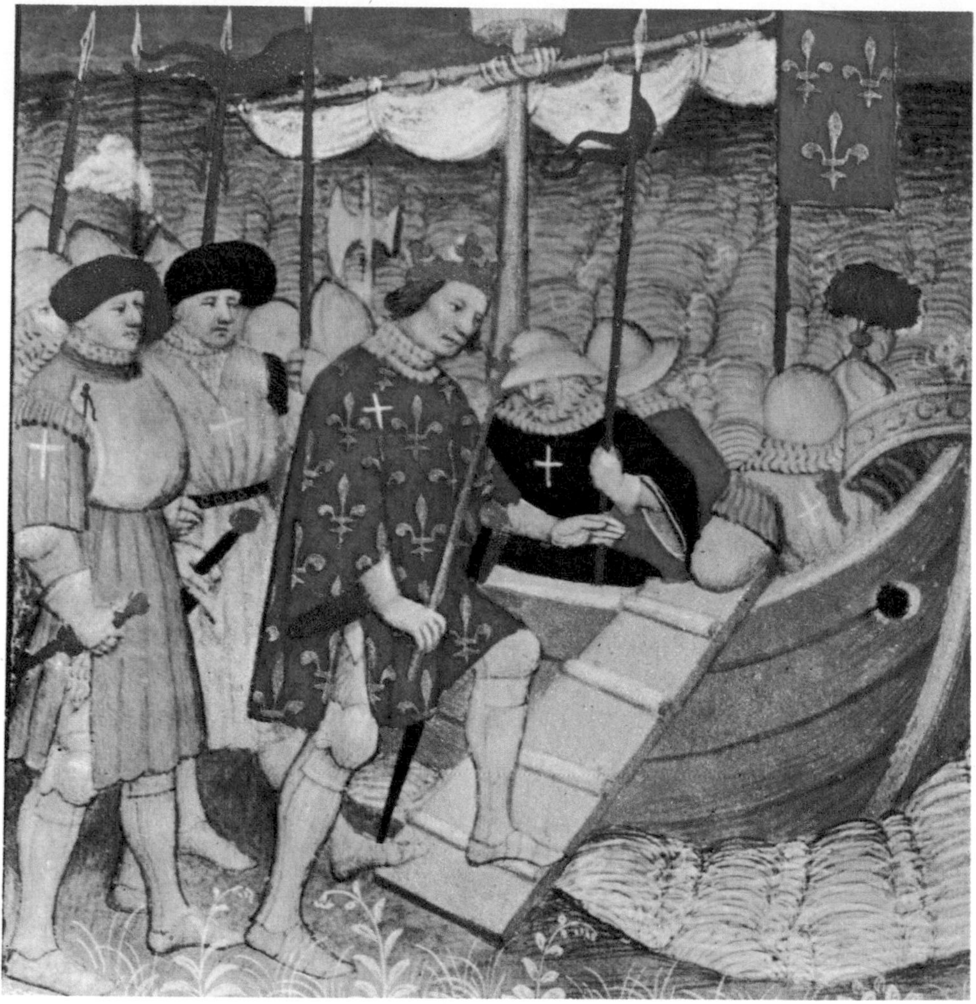

Left, detail from an early painting of the battle of Krak, a Crusader victory of 1163. A Templar rides in front of two knights with banners, probably the French commanders Hugues de Lusignan and Geoffrey Martel. (Mural in the Templar chapel of Cressac, western France, 1170-80.)

Below left, Louis IX of France (1226-70) embarking on his crusade of 1248, which ended with his capture at Mansura (painting from a 15th-century French book of hours). Right, Holy Roman Emperor Frederick II (1215-50), patron of the Teutonic Knights and leader of the sixth crusade.

great Castle Pilgrim near Acre, moated on all sides except the east by the sea, was the starting point of the Fifth Crusade (1218-21). Its initial success at the siege of Damietta in Egypt was mainly a Templar success. In action after action during the Crusades, the Templars and the Hospitalers provided the core of Christian resistance, for they alone had the long experience needed to beat the Arabs on their own ground.

Yet the rising power of the Templars again went to their leaders' heads. They became more concerned with their own independent power than with Christian unity. In 1228, they refused to help the excommunicated Frederick II on his crusade—but not without good reason, as Frederick was even more ready to deal with the Muslims than they were. They attacked the Hospitalers, who wanted to conclude peace with the sultan of Egypt; and, when Frederick II confiscated their property in Apulia, they drove his Teutonic Knights out of Acre. In 1232, they opened negotiations with the sultans of Damascus and Kerak, in order to regain control of the city of Jerusalem. By 1244, they had won back most of the holy places by diplomacy instead of direct assault. "After a silence of fifty-six years," wrote their Grand Master, "the divine mysteries would once more be celebrated in the Holy City."

In the same year, however, the advancing Mongols brought catastrophe on the reviving Crusader Kingdom. The Christians' hope that Genghis Khan would annihilate the Muslims in alliance with them was dashed when the savage Khwarizmian Turks, displaced by the Mongols, bypassed the new Templar fortress at Safed and sacked the Holy City. Baybars, the future sultan of Egypt, led the Khwarizmians and the Egyptians against the Templars and their allies at Gaza, and wiped them out; the Grand Master and 300 knights perished. The second phase of the order ended like the first, with military slaughter and the loss of Jerusalem.

The third and final effort of the Templars began in 1248 with the crusade of Louis IX of France, later St. Louis. Acre was still the base of Crusader operations; Damietta was again taken, but Louis's advance into Egypt, undertaken against the Templars' advice, ended in defeat at the battle of Mansura in 1250. Louis, who began by refusing to negotiate alliances with Arab rulers, was eventually beaten by the swamps and plagues of Egypt, and all the individual bravery of the Templars could not bring him success. However, he depended heavily enough on the financing of the Templars to urge the nomination of Amaury de la Roche, a trusted servant, as Master of the Temple in France. In 1263, the pope himself wrote to the Grand Master of the order, urging him to accept Louis's nominee. "If you consider," the pope wrote, "with what care the King of France defends your Order and its rights; with what protection he surrounds you; how much he esteems you, you and all your professed—you would immediately grant him all he asks, especially as your compliance will be repaid by future favours." If the king of France needed the Templars as bankers and Crusaders, the Templars needed the king of France to protect them from envious rivals. As long as their interests coincided, the Temple was safe and the money-changers within it.

Yet, in the Levant, the Templars lost their remaining fortresses. Caught between the Mongols, and the Egyptians under Baybars, they lost stronghold after stronghold. No more effective help came from Europe, which used its knights increasingly in its own quarrels; the Kingdom of Jerusalem was considered lost after the failure of so many Crusades. The pope himself wanted to recruit Crusaders in the Levant to help him against the Germans. The troubadour Oliver the Templar despaired in 1265: "Crazed is the man who wants to fight the Turks, since Jesus Christ is no longer fighting them. They have conquered—they will conquer, that lies heavy on me—French and Tartars, Armenians and Persians. They know that every day they will humiliate us, for God sleeps."

In 1291 Tripoli fell, and Acre was assaulted by the Egyptian armies. After a desperate siege, which united at last the rival Frankish lords and the

A medieval French representation of Baphomet, the "devil" or foreign god the Templars were accused of worshiping. His name derives from medieval Christian forms of the name Mohammed, which became *Mafomat* in Spanish, *Bafomet* in Provençal. (Sculpture at Saint-Merri church, Paris.)

military orders, Acre fell when Muslims forced its walls by the Accursed Tower. The last Templar stronghold was mined, and the city razed to the ground. The population was slaughtered or sold into slavery; the price of a girl in the Damascus slave-market fell to one drachma. The Templars fled to Cyprus with the remnants of their fleet, losing their last castle on the island of Ruad off the mainland in 1303. They had lost their function as the police of the routes of the Holy Land, for there was no Holy Land left to police. Not until 1917 would another Christian army enter Jerusalem, and then the tombs of the Templars in London would be crowned with laurel.

The Templars, however, were not finished by defeat at the hands of the Arabs. They still had 20,000 members of their order and the riches of their European holdings, and hoped to use Cyprus as a base from which to reconquer the Holy Land. Philip IV of France, who had begun by trying to curb the independent power of the Temple within France, switched to borrowing heavily from the order in return for his protection of it. In 1303 when he broke with Pope Boniface VIII, Philip signed a formal treaty of alliance with the French Templars and put them in charge of the state finances; in 1305, when the Paris mob attacked him, he took refuge in the Temple.

Yet Philip was to destroy the Temple for one reason alone, its wealth. Wealth is sometimes forgiven by governments, if they can exploit it; wealth with independence is unforgivable. In 1305, Philip's chance came. An ex-Templar, Esquiu de Florian, came to him with a lurid denunciation of the order. A new pope, Clement V, was elected; Clement, a sick man, was in the pocket of France. At Philip's request, Clement asked the Grand Master of the Temple, Jacques de Molay, to consider plans for the projected Crusade and for the amalgamation of the Templars and Hospitalers under the leadership of a prince of France (an old project that would have confined the Templars to the East and deprived them of their possessions in Europe). When de Molay rejected the proposal, Philip used popular rumor and the secrecy of the Templars' rite to break the order. He had debased the coinage, expelled the Jews and the Lombard bankers; he had to find another golden goose to pluck. After appointing 12 spies to enter the order and discover its iniquitous secrets, Philip denounced the Templars to the Inquisition on a charge of heresy. On October 13th, 1307, he suddenly arrested Jacques de Molay and every Templar in France.

Few Templars were strong enough to hold out against the racks and screws and whips of Philip's torturers; like Jacques de Molay, most of them confessed what the torturers wished them to confess. Yes, the Templars were homosexuals, forced to kiss the mouth, navel, and anus of their initiator. Yes, novices were made to spit on the Cross. Yes, the Templars had worshiped the devil Baphomet, which was a jewelled skull or a wooden phallus; they also worshiped the devil in the form of a cat, in the presence of young virgins and female devils. Thirty-six of the Paris Templars died under torture within

Above, one of the Templars arrested in 1307 kneels at the feet of Pope Clement V and Philip IV. Above right, Jacques de Molay is burned at the stake with Geoffrey de Charney, head of the Templar house in Normandy, March 14, 1314. (Paintings from *Les Chroniques de France*, about 1388.)

Below left, Philip attends the execution. Tradition has it that de Molay cursed him from the stake, prophesying that he would die within the year. Below, supposed manner of Philip's death, November 1314. (Paintings, 1470-83, for Boccaccio's *De casibus illustrium virorum et feminarum*.)

a few days of their arrest, and the remainder were only confessing to a hotchpotch of the diabolical and sexual fantasies of their age. Above all, the Templars were made the scapegoat for the loss of the Holy Land; they were accused of selling to the Muslims what they had fought to hold.

Obscene and ridiculous as most of the charges against the Templars were, the order was open to attack by the secular state for its pride, its independence, and its secrecy. Homosexuality, and the coarse gesture of spitting on the Cross, may possibly have existed in some Temples. Yet, on the whole, the Templars suffered because the kings of Europe wanted to centralize their states. The Kingdom of Jerusalem and the Templars were the victims of the revolutionary kings who turned their attention to their own countries rather than to uniting Christendom. The Templars had estates all over the world, and an annual income of some $90 million in Europe alone. When, in November 1307, the pope ordered the kings of Europe to arrest every Templar in their territories, all except Denys of Portugal took the opportunity of plundering such wealth. Though the goods of the Templars were finally made over to the Hospitalers, precious little slipped out of the hands of the kings; and the Hospitalers were careful to refuse such possessions as might lead them into conflict with the secular power.

Jacques de Molay, who, like Ridfort and the last Old Man of the Assassins, had ruined his sect by ordering it to surrender and confess, ended by retracting his confessions and denying all the evil he had spoken of his order. In 1314, when he was brought out onto a scaffold in front of Notre Dame to receive his sentence, he declared: "I confess that I am indeed guilty of the greatest infamy. But the infamy is that I have lied. I have lied in admitting the disgusting charges laid against my Order. I declare, and I must declare, that the Order is innocent. Its purity and saintliness have never been defiled. In truth, I had testified otherwise, but I did so from fear of horrible tortures." He was burned alive the following day.

So ended the Templars, the victims of the greed of kings and of their own pride and wealth. The Assassins, curiously enough, survive to this day in India as part of the Ismaili sect whose spiritual head is the Aga Khan. But the Templars have gone the way of all secret societies whose power seems to constitute a threat to the state. As a 14th-century poet asked:

> The brethren, the Masters of the Temple,
> Who were well-stocked and ample
> With gold and silver and riches,
> Where are they? How have they done?
> They had such power once that none
> Dared take from them, none was so bold;
> Forever they bought and never sold. . . .

Until they were sold to satisfy the greed of kings, in whom the state was sovereign and indivisible.

6 The Rosicrucians

In August 1623 a number of extraordinary notices appeared in the streets of Paris. They proclaimed: "We, deputies of the principal College of the Brethren of the Rosy Cross, are staying visibly and invisibly in this town by the Grace of the Most High, to whom the heart of the Just turns. We show and teach without books or masks how to speak the language of every country where we wish to be, to bring our fellow men out of the error of death." According to one contemporary account, the first response to this announcement came from a lawyer who was heavily in debt, and wanted to learn how to make himself invisible to his creditors. He succeeded in finding the mysterious Rosicrucians, who agreed to teach him their secrets. But they wined and dined him so well beforehand, that when they initiated him by immersing him in the river, he drowned.

This story, though obviously satirical in intention, indicates something of the controversy and the obscurity that surround the early history of the Rosicrucians; their nickname, the "Invisibles," refers as much to their elusiveness as to their claims to supernatural powers. The word *Rosicrucian* itself gives us a further idea of the difficulty that attends any factual study. It is generally supposed to be derived from the Latin *rosa* (rose) and *crux* (cross); and certainly the rose and the cross have always been the symbols of Rosicrucian societies. The same symbols occur on the seal used by Martin Luther, and in

A painting from a 16th-century manuscript that describes the regeneration of the soul in terms of medieval alchemy. In this form of symbolism, which became synonymous with Rosicrucianism, the soul is compared to base metal that is to be transmuted into gold. An Ethiopian emerging from the mire represents the soul after the first, or "blackening," stage of transformation; the substance that revives and whitens it is personified as a queen.

the family arms of the Lutheran deacon Johann Andreä, who (as we shall see) may or may not have been the originator of Rosicrucianism. The Christian significance of the cross, and of the rose stained with Christ's blood, might appear to answer all questions. But the cross may not be a Christian cross at all. Both rose and cross are found, with numerous meanings, in the symbolism of the Jewish Cabala. For the alchemists the cross denoted the four elements; for Hindus it is the symbol of creation; for some medieval writers it was a code for "light." The rose is identified with the sun, the central element in Zoroastrian worship. It is the Egyptian symbol of rebirth. It is connected with Lakshmi, the Hindu goddess of love and creation. The Rosalia was a Dionysian festival, and the mysteries at Eleusis were associated with Dionysus. In the 13th-century *Roman de la Rose*, the rose may be a symbol of illumination, reminding us of the troubadours' connection with the Albigensians, a disguised survival of pre-Christian religion. In fact, the rose is also a symbol of secrecy; in this sense, Cupid used it to cover illicit *amours*, and the expression *sub rosa* derives from the rose hung in late medieval times above the council table to show that all present were sworn to secrecy. The largest and most active of modern Rosicrucian societies tells us that the rose at the center of the cross represents "the physical body of man, with arms outstretched to the sun in the East, which depicts the Greater Light." And, as though this were not confusion enough, there is another school of thought that derives the first syllable of "Rosicrucian" not from *rosa* at all, but from *ros*, the Latin word for dew (dew being considered by the alchemists to be a powerful solvent). But this is only to scratch the surface of the subject; it is discussed for 27 pages by A. E. Waite in his book *The Brotherhood of the Rosy Cross*.

If we are to describe Rosicrucianism in the terms customary among historians, only one course appears possible. This is to take as a point of departure its first incontestable document, the *Fama Fraternatis of the Meritorious Order of the Rosy Cross*, published in Germany in 1614; to examine it in relation to the social and intellectual atmosphere of that time and place; and finally, to trace the overt record of Rosicrucianism, shadowy and broken as it is, to the present day.

Germany in the early 17th century presented a scene of doubt and confusion. The conflicts and strivings of the preceding epoch had led neither to unity, nor to good government, nor to much improvement in the conditions of life. A prey to the selfish rivalries of its own petty princelings and of its more powerful neighbors, the country felt the threats that were soon to become realities in the misery and chaos of the Thirty Years' War. Protestants especially had cause for depression. The Catholic Church, far from collapsing as they had hoped, had launched the Counter-Reformation and had regained a great deal of lost ground. Thinking men were in search of an intellectual and spiritual equipment more profound and potent than the ideals they had inherited from Martin Luther.

Somewhere, they believed, there was a hidden wisdom. Its character, gropingly apprehended, was in part mystical, in part scientific. The aim pursued was to probe the secrets (in the language of the period, the "mysteries") of the natural world, and so to gain a new degree of power over it. Any clues might be worth following up, whether they came from the great civilizations of the past, from the culture of the East, or from speculative minds whose pioneering efforts had been dismissed by their contemporaries. Naturally, in the still undeveloped state of scientific method, it was almost impossible to distinguish between fact, fantasy, and sheer charlatanism. Alchemy, for instance, might be a process symbolic of spiritual development or merely an unsuccessful conjuring trick with the mundane purpose of making gold on the cheap. Yet some of the ideas of the alchemists showed flashes of insight that strangely foreshadowed modern conceptions of the structure of nature and of chemistry based on the analysis of elements, validated centuries later by science. A modern parallel—in that we cannot be sure where wishful fantasy ends and investigation into another order of reality begins—is in the field of telepathy and extrasensory perception.

Left, the seal of Luther (1483-1546). Like the Rosicrucian emblem, it is based on a rose and cross motif. Below, a detail from *Fishing for Souls* (1618), by A. P. van der Venne. The painting shows Catholics and Protestants competing for converts, illustrating the confusion that reigned after Luther's break with Rome.

Of the great civilizations to which scholars of the period looked back, the most awe-inspiring was the civilization of ancient Egypt. Tradition had it that the Egyptian mysteries were a key to a complete knowledge of the universe and of man; this knowledge had been preserved in a number of books, called the *Hermetic* writings because they were attributed to a legendary Egyptian prophet known as Hermes Trismegistus ("Thrice Greatest Hermes") and identified with Thoth, the Egyptian god of wisdom. The Hermetic books fall into two groups: on the one hand, works dealing with astrology, alchemy, and magic, and on the other, dialogues describing the soul's regeneration in terms of a journey upward through higher spheres. The Hermetic books, first printed in the late 15th century, had had an immense influence on Renaissance thinkers. They were universally accepted as authentic until the early 17th century, when it was proved that they had actually been written as late as the second and third centuries A.D. by a succession of anonymous Greeks living in Egypt. Though their emphasis on ecstasy and illumination seemed to confirm their association with the ancient Egyptian mystery cults, what they actually reflected was the relatively new gnosticism (from the Greek *gnosis* or knowledge) that had flourished in the early Christian era, and had an admixture of such Greek schools of thought as Platonism and Neoplatonism.

The first of the Hermetic books to be circulated were the *Pimander*, or *On the Power and Wisdom of God*, a gnostic creation story in which Hermes Trismegistus played the part of an Egyptian Moses, and the *Asclepius*, or *Perfect Word*, which ascribed to the Egyptians the art of bringing statues to life, and was a major factor in the Renaissance revival of magic. The second important factor in that revival, and in the climate that generated Rosicrucianism, was the study of the Cabala—a form of Jewish mysticism that developed in France and Spain in the 12th and 13th centuries.

The word *Cabala* is Hebrew and means "received tradition"; its philosophy was supposed to have been handed down orally from Moses himself. It was said to be contained in the prophetic books of the Old Testament; it was expounded in the *Sepher Yetsirah* or "Book of Creation" (probably composed between A.D. 300 and 600) and in a text called the *Zohar* or "Brightness" (first circulated in the 13th century, in Spain). The Cabala conceives God as an infinite light, from which the whole of creation emanates through ten successive spheres called the *Sephiroth*. The Sephiroth themselves represent attributes of God: first supremacy, then wisdom, intelligence, love, power, compassion, eternity, majesty, foundation, and glory. Though sin has separated man from the Sephiroth, their divine attributes remain active in him, and he may, through them, return to the source of light. Students of the Cabala maintained that this might be achieved by a system of meditation on the names of God and on the 22 letters of the Hebrew alphabet. They provoked the antagonism of the orthodox rabbis both by their claim to possess hidden knowledge and by their emphasis on revelation and ecstasy.

Hermes Trismegistus, the legendary Egyptian sage and magician. He was acclaimed by Renaissance philosophers as a prophet of Christianity, and as the author of "all mysterious doctrines." (Painting from a 16th-century alchemical manuscript.)

In the early Middle Ages, Cabalists studied in secret. In the 15th and 16th centuries, however, influential Gentiles took up the Cabala. It was expounded (as a system of practical magic) by Cornelius Agrippa in Germany and (as a mystical experience) by Pico della Mirandola in Italy. Pico della Mirandola and other Renaissance humanists found many correspondences between the Cabala and the newly translated Hermetic writings. In their eyes, Cabalist magic corroborated Hermetic magic, and the two philosophies, far from conflicting with Christianity, actually seemed to verify it. In them, they saw the promise of a renewal of piety and morality and a general reformation of mankind. This form of religious syncretism, so essential to the development of Rosicrucianism, had an astonishingly wide influence in the 15th and 16th centuries. In the 17th century, when the Hermetic writings were dated, its influence waned; but the Hermetic-Cabalist tradition lingered on. As the historian Frances Yates shows in her book *Giordano Bruno and the Hermetic Tradition*, it went underground and became the special preoccupation of minority groups and such secret societies as the Rosicrucians and Freemasons, who both preserved and elaborated it.

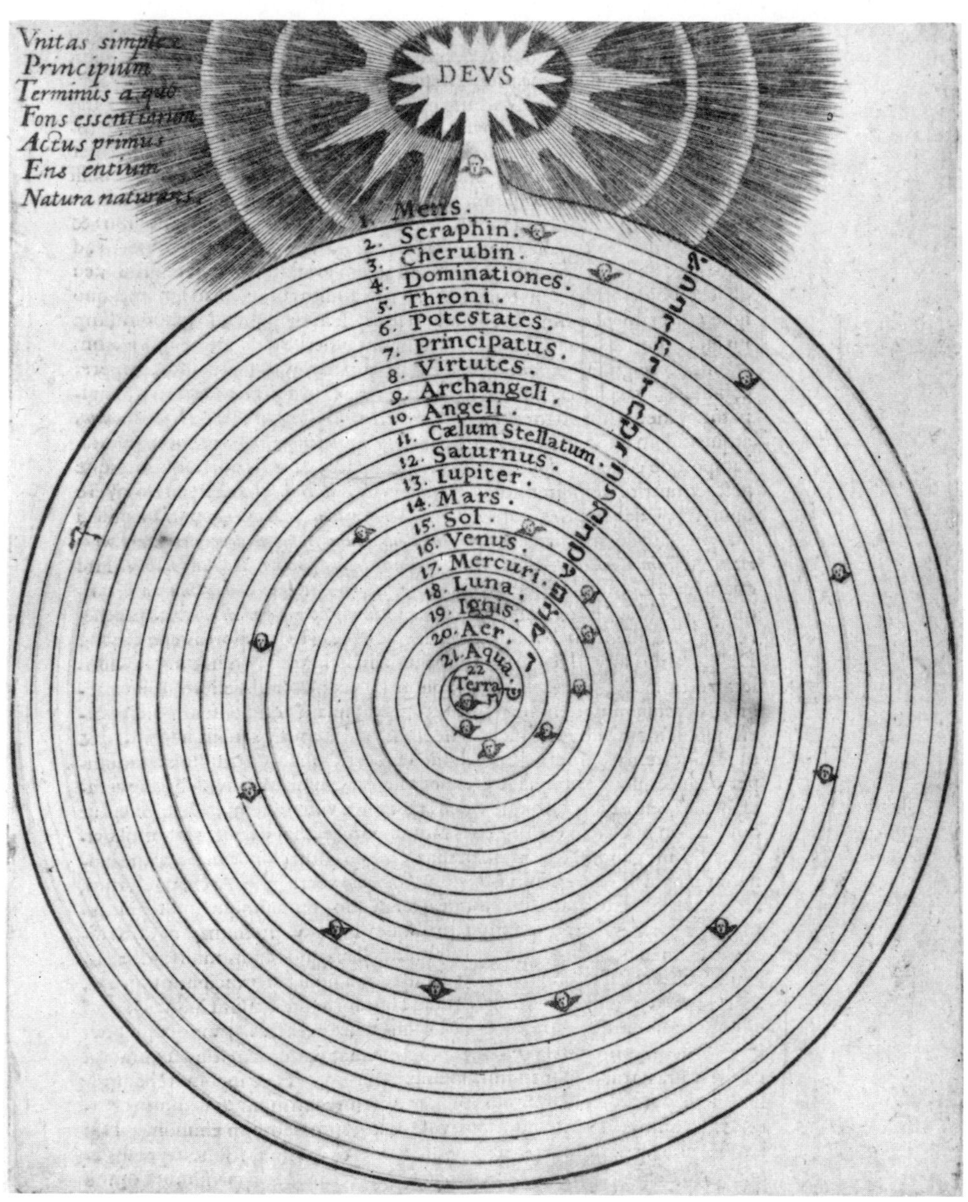

Diagram illustrating the Hermetic-Cabalist view of man in the universe, from a work by Rosicrucian apologist Robert Fludd (1619). The soul of man moves in an outward spiral from earth (at center), through the spheres and angelic hierarchies, toward God. The spheres and the hierarchies are correlated with the 22 letters of the Hebrew alphabet.

The Hermetic-Cabalist view of the universe, and especially the belief in man's power to draw down and manipulate natural forces from higher spheres, is strongly marked in the work of the Swiss alchemist and physician Paracelsus (1493–1541), who provides a link between the Renaissance and the first period of Rosicrucianism. His intellectual ambitions were boundless; born Theophrastus Bombast von Hohenheim, he chose a name that was intended to show his superiority to Celsus, a Neoplatonist whose ideas had been revived and enjoyed much prestige. His central idea was that a new understanding of nature might be gained by identifying the "vital properties" of rocks and plants. These, he urged, would provide a better antidote to disease than the remedies of Galen and of the accepted medical authorities. Whether by luck or by intuition, he achieved a number of unexpected cures during his term as town physician of Basel. Lecturing and writing ceaselessly, he was an enthusiast both for the Hermetic tradition and for the Cabala. As one account of his career suggests, "it is a problem how to reconcile his ignorance, his erroneous observations, his ridiculous influence and theories, with his grasp of method, his lofty views of the true scope of medicine, his lucid statements."

The same words might well be applied to the first document of Rosicrucianism, the *Fama Fraternatis* of 1614. It was this document that first announced the existence of a Rosicrucian order, and invited "the learned and great of Europe," to whom it was addressed, to make their sympathies publicly known; they were assured that if they did so, they would hear from the fraternity. Readers were promised that if they would desert their false teachers (the Pope, Galen, and Aristotle) and join the order, they would attain a deeper knowledge of nature and a share in bringing about a general reformation of the world. Though the authors promised their followers "more gold than both the Indies bring to the king of Spain," they condemned the gold-making of the alchemists as "ungodly and accursed," implying that the riches they themselves valued were spiritual, not material. The main part of the *Fama* related the life and death of Christian Rosenkreuz ("Rosy Cross"), a mythical figure described as the founder of the order. According to the *Fama*, Rosenkreuz was born in 1378, of a noble family in poor circumstances. At the age of four, he was placed in a monastery. When still "in his growing years," he set out with a monk on a pilgrimage to Jerusalem; but the monk died in Cyprus, and Rosenkreuz stayed in Damascus, where he became well known for his medical skill. Then he went to "Damcar" (a city stated to be in Arabia, but apparently mythical), which was the home of wise men "to whom Nature was discovered." The wise men, who had been expecting him, taught him Arabic, physics, and mathematics, and introduced him to the *Book M*, which contained the secrets of the universe, and which he translated into Latin. Having studied botany and zoology in Egypt, and magic and the Cabala at Fez, he was equipped to teach the learned of Europe how to "order all their studies on those sure and sound foundations." As he was not made welcome in Spain, he

Allgemeine vnd General
REFORMATION,
der gantzen weiten Welt.
Beneben der
FAMA FRA-
TERNITATIS,
Deß Löblichen Ordens des
Rosenkreutzes / an alle Gelehrte
vnd Häupter Europæ geschrie-
ben:
Auch einer kurtzen RESPONSION,
von dem Herrn Haselmeyer gestellet / welcher
deßwegen von den Jesuitern ist gefänglich ein-
gezogen / vnd auff eine Galleren ge-
schmiedet:
Itzo öffentlich in Druck verfertiget /
vnd allen trewen Hertzen communiciret
worden.

Gedruckt zu Cassel / durch Wilhelm Wessell /
ANNO M. DC. XIV.

Above, the title page to the first edition of the *Fama Fraternatis* (Cassel, 1614). Left, a Rosicrucian woodcut from *Secret Symbols* (Altona, 1785). It contains the date 1604, and represents the tomb of Rosenkreuz as the "philosophers' mountain" —an alchemical symbol of regeneration.

returned to Germany and began work on a book containing "whatsoever can be desired or hoped for by man." In this work he was assisted by seven monks from the monastery where he had grown up. When they had completed their book, the eight decided to form the Fraternity of the Rosy Cross, and to live in different countries where they might influence learned men. Before dispersing, they agreed to profess nothing but to cure the sick, without payment; not to distinguish themselves by any particular costume; to meet annually in Germany; to nominate their successors before dying; to adopt the initials R.C. as their seal; and to keep their fraternity secret for 100 years.

The *Fama* also declared that Rosenkreuz had died in 1484 (at the age of 106), and had been buried in a hidden tomb. In 1604, this tomb had been discovered by the authors of the *Fama*; it lay behind a concealed door bearing the words "I shall open after 120 years." Inside was a seven-sided vault lit by a mysterious luminary set in the roof. In the center stood an altar, beneath which they found the body of Rosenkreuz "whole and unconsumed." The tomb also contained a chest of mirrors "of divers virtues," a parchment entitled the *Book T*, and described as "our greatest treasure next to the Bible," and a dictionary (not otherwise known) compiled by Paracelsus. The *Fama* gave no hint as to the whereabouts of the tomb. It ended as enigmatically as it had begun, with the assertion that true philosophers would see the heavens open and angels ascending and descending, and would have their names written in the Book of Life.

The authors gave no clues to their identity, beyond the assurance that they were Lutherans. But in spite of this, and in spite of its obscure symbolism, the *Fama* was received by intellectuals with something of the excitement that might mark the publication of a revolutionary political manifesto today. It was read not only in Germany, but also in other European countries; in three years it ran into nine different editions, as well as several translations into Latin and Dutch. The *Fama* was soon followed by two other books, the *Confessio Fraternatis Rosae Crucis* (1615) and the *Chemical Wedding of Christian Rosenkreuz* (1616). The *Confessio* gave further details regarding admission to the order, stressing that it was open to men of any social class, and that its only aim was the pursuit of true wisdom, and adding (as a matter of interest) that it possessed more gold and silver than the rest of the world.

The *Chemical Wedding* is a more puzzling work, an elaborate allegorical romance in which a mythical king and queen are married with a great deal of weird ceremonial. The book opens with an account of Rosenkreuz's deliverance from the "dungeon of ignorance" and his journey to the wedding, at which he appears (after many ordeals) as the guest of honor. The title of the book indicates that its symbolism is that of alchemy; the text suggests that this alchemy is not the transmutation of base metals into gold, but the regeneration of the soul. Nevertheless, some scholars regard the book as a purely imaginative work of earlier date, having little to do with the Rosicrucians. Others see it as a destructive satire designed to exaggerate, and thus to discredit, Rosicrucian mysticism. But in one respect, that of authorship, more is known about the *Chemical Wedding* than about the *Fama* or the *Confessio*. It was written by the Lutheran Johann Valentin Andreä (1586–1654), as he himself revealed in his autobiography.

As a young man, Andreä ran the intellectual gamut of his age. He studied astronomy, mathematics, optics, and philosophy at Tübingen, and during his studies was attracted to millenarian and visionary forms of religion, in defiance of the Lutheran Church. However, he became a Lutheran deacon in 1614, at the age of 28, and apparently remained a staunch upholder of Lutheranism for the rest of his life. Three considerations have inclined historians to place Andreä as the author of the *Fama* and the originator of Rosicrucianism. He certainly wrote the *Chemical Wedding*; and in the years leading up to 1614, he was an enthusiastic advocate of various unorthodox plans for Christian union, including one in the form of an ideal republic to be called the City of the Sun. As the French writer Paul Arnold shows in his recent history of the Rosicrucians, Andreä's circle of friends at Tübingen was deeply interested in Hermetism,

Cabalism, and Christian mysticism. The probability is that the *Fama* was produced jointly by the members of this circle, chief among them being Andreä, Wilhelm Wense (who played an active part in the Christian union project) and the Hebrew and Greek scholar Christoph Besold (who later became a Catholic). One apparent objection to this argument is that in the books Andreä later wrote as an orthodox Lutheran he made repeated attacks on the Rosicrucians. But, as Arnold points out, all Andreä's condemnations of the Rosicrucians are carefully qualified. In his *Turris Babel* (1619) he observed "in all their writings there is something useful to be found"; and in his will of 1634 he wrote: "Though I now leave the Fraternity itself, I shall never leave the true Christian fraternity, which, beneath the Cross, smells of the rose, and is quite apart from the filth of this century."

The probability that the *Fama* was produced jointly by several minds has a bearing on the most important question to be considered, which is not so much who wrote the *Fama* as whether the Rosicrucian order was in fact founded in 1614. There are four possibilities. It may be that there was no such order when the *Fama* appeared, and that the book was an attempt to start one. This attempt may have represented a serious scheme, a dream devoid of organizational plan, or (at a pinch) an intellectual joke. Or one may believe—but only the devoted Rosicrucian would—that the story of Rosenkreuz is an allegory describing the rediscovery of wisdom and the order's emergence in 1614 from one of its ordained periods of "silent activity" or secrecy, supposed to occur every 108 years. A third theory is that the order had in fact been in existence for some years, and that the *Fama* was designed to increase its influence. There are records of an extreme Protestant sect called the Militia Crucifera Evangelica, founded by a German scholar called Simon Studion in 1586. Studion's book *Naometria* is a mystical work that makes use of the symbols of the rose and the cross, but most scholars do not regard it as essentially or necessarily Rosicrucian. We are thus left with the probability that Andreä and his friends, identifying themselves allegorically with Rosenkreuz and his seven monks, formed the order in about 1614, when they published the *Fama* as its manifesto.

Many people tried to join the order by writing and publishing sympathetic replies, the method suggested in the *Fama*. The library at Göttingen contains a collection of these open letters. But no further communication emanated from the fraternity other than its supplementary publications, the *Confessio* and (if it is so regarded) the *Chemical Wedding*. So far as we know, all the would-be members were disappointed. Descartes, who was living at Frankfurt in 1619, vainly tried to get in touch, and decided that the fraternity did not exist. At the end of the century, the famous German philosopher and mathematician Gottfried von Leibniz wrote, "I suspect that the Brethren of the Rosy Cross are a fiction."

Perhaps the order never had existed. Perhaps some recruits were admitted in a secrecy that was never broken; of this we have no evidence. Perhaps none

Above, Johann Andreä (1586-1654), supposed author of Rosicrucian manifestos. Right, the first page of a letter applying for admission to the "fraternity," written by the English antiquary Elias Ashmole (1617-92).

were considered worthy, though a number of the letter-writers stated their credentials as experts in alchemy or the Cabala. The founders may well have rejected applicants who were interested only in making gold, and failed to appreciate their higher aspirations. But it is far more likely that the founding group soon fell apart, Andreä turning to regular Lutheran doctrine and Besold to the Catholic Church.

In this vacuum, it was not surprising that the word Rosicrucian should have taken on the broader and vaguer meaning of *magus*, nor that it should have become a synonym for charlatan. False prophets, and even outright swindlers, came forward with the claim that they were the true Rosicrucians; most of these did not identify themselves, but gave reasons why the order must be secret and difficult to contact, and invited applications in the manner of the *Fama*. One German applicant, Ludovicus Orvius, complained that in 1622 he had paid 1000 Netherlands dollars to an alleged representative of the fraternity, who then expelled him without revealing any worthwhile secrets; Voltaire, a century later, told how the Duc de Bouillon had suffered from a similar confidence trick.

On a more serious level, the decade after 1614 saw an intense public debate, chiefly in Germany, reflected in scores of pamphlets that are still in the libraries, and doubtless more that have not survived. Whether the fraternity existed as an organization or not, its hopes and promises were a vital preoccupation for intellectuals of the age. While some attacked them as dangerous heresy or as delusive nonsense, others embraced them as assurances of spiritual renewal; others again extended a qualified welcome. The German naturalist and physician Andreas Libau, for instance, advised the Rosicrucians to concentrate on the moral improvement of individuals and give up the idea of reforming the world. Many elements in the controversy remain obscure and self-contradictory. A typical mystery is the case of Irenaeus Agnostus. He claimed that he was a member of the order and that his book, the *Epitimia Fraternatis Rosae Crucis* (1619), was published by its authority; yet in it he condemned all other Rosicrucians as magicians, charlatans, and Jesuit agents.

The most elaborate and weighty defense of the elusive fraternity was the *Themis Aurea* (1618), by the German physician and philosopher Michael Maier (1568–1622). He explained that it was the successor to a series of secret groups, including a college of magi in Persia and a college of Brahmins in India. It must be judged, he insisted, by its few true adepts, and not by the unsuccessful students and impostors who inevitably gathered around it. He declared that true adepts possessed a wisdom consisting of a mastery of religion; of medicine; of "natural magic"; of the "perfection of all arts"; of alchemy; and of the "anatomy and idea of the whole universe" expounded in Rosenkreuz's *Book M*. Thus equipped, they held the secret of three kinds of healing: of body, soul, and spirit. Their ultimate secret was that of "incredible virtue," which ensured that piety, justice, and truth prevailed in their characters and that the contrary vices were dispelled. Though there is a good deal that Maier does not discuss—in particular, the actual content of Rosicrucian medicine, "arts," religion, and so forth—the *Themis Aurea* is the nearest we can get to an exposition of early Rosicrucian beliefs, and a guide to what the whole business is about. But even this cannot be regarded as authoritative, for Maier was not himself a member of the fraternity, as he scrupulously informed his readers.

In England, the most prominent defender of Rosicrucianism was the physician Robert Fludd (1574–1637). Fludd, in his early writings, declared himself a disciple of Rosicrucianism. But he implied that there was no order in the sense of an organization, and that the acquisition of the essential wisdom was the sole qualification. "I affirm," he wrote, "that every Theologus of the Church Mystical is a real Brother of the Rosy Cross." Fludd had been a student of the Hermetic writings, of the Cabala, of alchemy, and of the medical theories of Paracelsus; he understood alchemy in its symbolic sense, and in his writings, as Waite says, "celestial treasure is contrasted with the metallic gold which is sought after by errant and false alchemists." He became acquainted with

Rosicrucian ideas either on his own travels in Germany or during a visit to England by Maier, or both. He wrote several works defending the Rosicrucians, including one entitled *A Compendious Apology for the Fraternity of the Rosy Cross, pelted with the Mire of Suspicion and Infamy, but now Cleansed and Purged as by the Waters of Truth* (1616).

For Fludd, Rosicrucian wisdom meant in the first place a new system of natural philosophy, derived partly from Paracelsus and partly from the observation of nature and of the stars. He held that the visible universe was full of mystical characters; initiates in true wisdom could recognize them and attain a perfect knowledge of all things in heaven and earth. The power of understanding, as visualized by Fludd, was granted by the spirit of God to chosen individuals who were pure in heart, unrecognized by ordinary men, possessed of heavenly riches, but poor in the sight of the world. The gifts of the spirit, he concluded, were prophecy, miracles, tongues, and healing.

But in its homeland, Germany, the fraternity was already discredited. As Arnold says tersely: "The Rosy Cross was a laughing-stock"; and Waite

Rosicrucian symbolism in the frontispiece to Robert Fludd's *Summum Bonum* (1629). The bees around the rose represent believers receiving divine nourishment.

observes that by 1630 "the subject was dead and done with." There follows in the history of Rosicrucianism a gap of nearly a hundred years. Modern Rosicrucians, undeterred by the lack of evidence, describe this as another of those periods of "silent activity," during which, they claim, only "descendants of active members are initiated into the order." However this may be, the next period of Rosicrucianism was the 18th century. This period saw the elaboration of rituals, oaths, and grades of initiation. Two detailed sets of rules were published, one in 1710 and another in 1777, in Germany; the order existed in France and in England, where it influenced the development of Freemasonry; it also existed in Russia, until its suppression by Catherine the Great. The activities and aims of this order, as stated in contemporary sources, were a matter of superstition and ceremonial, bearing little trace of the ideals that had inspired the early Rosicrucian manifestos. During this period occultists began to fabricate evidence of the antiquity of organized Rosicrucianism, a tendency that reached its climax during the 19th century and is still evident today.

During the latter part of the 19th century a tremendous impetus to esoteric studies came from two sources. In France, the cabalistic writings of the Abbé Constant, better known as Eliphas Lévi, prepared the ground for proliferation of so-called Rosicrucian societies under the leadership of the Marquis Stanislas de Guiata and the eccentric Joseph Péladan. The influence of Lévi's *Dogme et Rituel de la Haute Magie* (1861), was reinforced in the English-speaking world by the publication of Madame Blavatsky's *Isis Unveiled* and *Secret Doctrine*, after the foundation of the Theosophical Society in 1875.

The appeal of the Theosophical movement, and that of the Rosicrucian societies of the period, can be partly explained by the powerful combination of paradoxes inherent in their teachings. While they rejected atheism, they were also anticlerical, thereby providing a channel for the religious aspirations of people who were dissatisfied with orthodox church teachings. They protested against the gross materialism of modern science, though they themselves were at pains to employ "scientific" language. To a generation shaken in its faith by the facts of natural evolution, they held out the hope of a spiritual evolution—a hope formerly held only by small minorities in the West. The first of the modern Rosicrucian societies was the *Societas Rosicruciana in Anglia*, established in 1865. This society was an offshoot of Freemasonry, and its membership was confined to Master Masons; its stated aims were "to afford mutual aid and encouragement in working out the great problems of life, and in discovering the secrets of nature; to facilitate the study of the systems of philosophy founded upon the Kaballah and the doctrines of Hermes Trismegistus." Members were also "concerned in the study and administration of medicines, and in their manufacture upon old lines." They taught and practiced "the curative effects of coloured light," and cultivated "mental processes . . . believed to induce spiritual enlightenment and extended powers

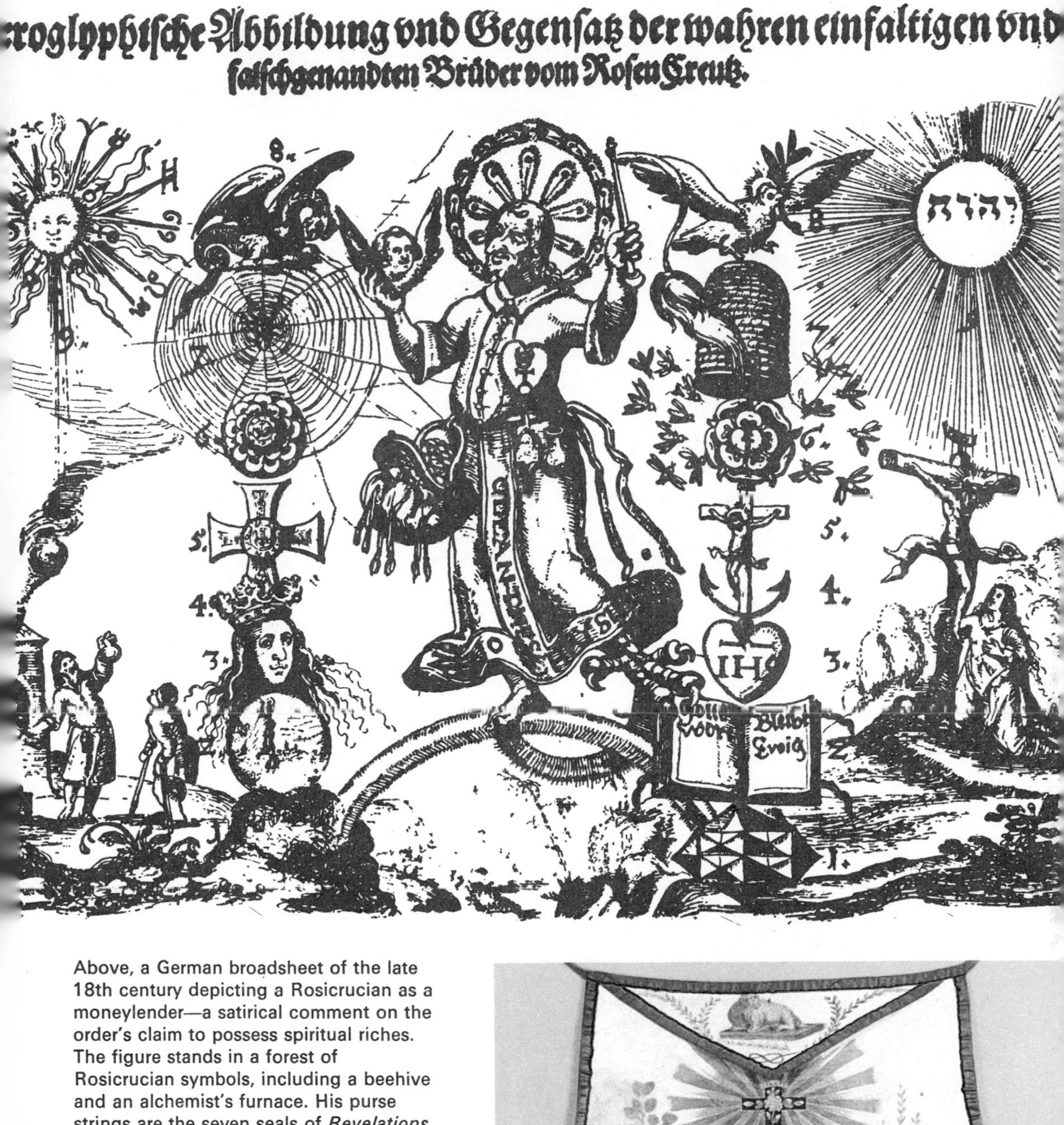
roglyphische Abbildung vnd Gegensatz der wahren einfaltigen vnd
falschgenandten Brüder vom RosenCreutz.
יהוה
Gottes Wort Bleibt Ewig

Above, a German broadsheet of the late 18th century depicting a Rosicrucian as a moneylender—a satirical comment on the order's claim to possess spiritual riches. The figure stands in a forest of Rosicrucian symbols, including a beehive and an alchemist's furnace. His purse strings are the seven seals of *Revelations* and one of his feet is replaced by a bird's claw—a medieval "mark of the devil." Though the highly organized Rosicrucian societies of the 18th century provoked some ridicule, Rosicrucian degrees were firmly established within Freemasonry. Right, Rosicrucian symbols on a Masonic apron of the Grand Orient de France, seventh degree (about 1850).

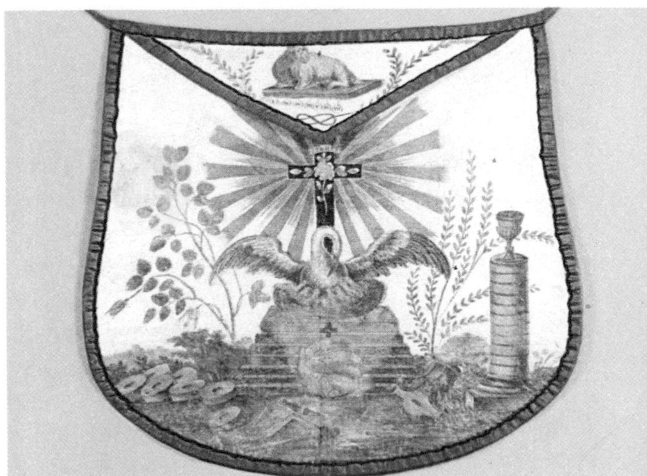

of the human senses, especially in the directions of clairvoyance and clair-audience." Among the society's leading members were the London coroner Dr. Wynn Wescott, who became its third Supreme Magus in 1891, and the museum curator Macgregor Mathers, who was a translator of the *Zohar*.

In 1887 Wescott came across some papers containing instructions on magic rites and cabalist doctrine. To pursue these studies, he opened a "Temple of Isis Urania," and founded a new society, the *Hermetic Order of the Golden Dawn*. The Golden Dawn had no relation to Freemasonry, and was open to men and women. It had connections, and some overlap of membership, with the Theosophical Society. In fact, Madame Blavatsky drew on the same sources of ancient wisdom as the Rosicrucians, while Mrs. Annie Besant, her pupil, believed Francis Bacon and the Comte de Saint-Germain to be reincarnations of Christian Rosenkreuz. The point at variance was the study of magic, of which the Theosophists disapproved. The Golden Dawn made a considerable appeal to artists and poets, especially to the Irish; its members included the poet W. B. Yeats (expelled from the Theosophical Society for "magical practises"), George Russell (the writer "AE"), the Irish patriot Maud Gonne, the theatre manager Annie Horniman, and the novelist Algernon Blackwood. The bond with the Irish was forged by Mathers, who was an enthusiast for Celtic tradition and adopted the title of Count of Glenstrae.

The root of the Golden Dawn's teaching was the Cabala. The Neophyte passed through the grades of Zelator, Theoricus, Practicus, and Philosophus to the Portal grade, which prepared him for the "reception of Light"; beyond this was the grade of Adeptus Minor, which connected the candidate with his "Higher Genius." This initiation, which took place in a seven-sided chamber modeled on the mythical tomb of Christian Rosenkreuz (p. 138), completed the training of the "Outer Order"; the adept then advanced to the Inner Order, and to a series of higher honorific titles. Members took many oaths of secrecy, but some idea of the magical ceremonies and experiments performed at the temple leaked out to the public; in 1897, Dr. Wescott had to resign because such activities were deemed incompatible with his position as coroner. Mathers then appointed himself Supreme Magus of the order, in obedience (he claimed) to instructions given by his "Secret Chiefs," three spirits who appeared to him at midnight in the Bois de Boulogne. He aroused the resentment of the other members by demanding a signed oath of allegiance, and expelled those who did not comply—somewhat rashly, since one of these was Miss Horniman, who had been providing him with an income.

Another conflict arose over a prospective member called Aleister Crowley, who was to become notorious as the self-styled "Baphomet" or "Great Beast." Mathers introduced Crowley to the order and quickly promoted him to the exalted grade of Adeptus Minor, despite the opposition of other members. After another dispute, the order took a vote and expelled Mathers, who took refuge in Paris and retaliated by sending Aleister Crowley to London to take over the temple. This led to an open schism, and then a dispute between Mathers and Crowley, who engaged in magical warfare. Mathers called on the services of a vampire to destroy his former protégé; but Crowley triumphantly relates that he "smote her with her own current of evil."

In its early years, the order had engaged in serious philosophical study as well as the practice of magic. But magical extravagances came to predominate, and disputes weakened the order. Its decline was accelerated by the trial in 1901 of Mrs. Rose Horos, one of Mathers's discoveries, who was convicted of immoral activities and jailed for seven years. The intellectuals left the order one by one; Yeats, however, remained a member until 1909.

Meanwhile, another Rosicrucian society had been formed by Eliphas Lévi, a figure revered by the Golden Dawn, and a strong influence on Mathers in his Paris period. This was the *Kabbalistic Order of the Rosy Cross*, founded in 1889. The society was essentially a revolt against Freemasonry, which in its view had lost all spiritual and philosophical meaning and was dominated by Anglo-Saxon Protestants. Disregarding their Lutheran origins, Rosicrucian societies had long admitted Catholics to membership, as the rules of 1710 show; Lévi and his friends now asserted that the order must be exclusively Catholic. The history of the French order, however, followed much the same course as that of the British. The study of Hermetism and Cabalism was submerged in personal rivalries and public scandals. Then came a split into two rival orders, and expulsions ordered by Joseph Péladan, one of the founder-members and evidently a French Mathers. Arnold records that a fragment of the order was still in existence at the outbreak of World War II.

It was from this branch of the ancient tree, however, that Rosicrucianism was transplanted to America (or, one might say, revived, for Rosicrucian groups had been known there in the 18th century). H. Spencer Lewis, a New York advertising man and clearly an outstanding organizer, joined Péladan's order in France in 1909. In 1915, he founded an order in the United States—the *Ancient Mystical Order Rosae Crucis* (AMORC), which today claims the right to call itself the "true, authorized Rosicrucian organization." Its headquarters and Supreme Temple are located at San Jose, California, in an extensive group of buildings that includes an "Oriental, Egyptian" museum and art gallery, a Rose-Croix university, a science museum and planetarium, and a research library.

The idea of a small select membership has been abandoned; AMORC has 60,000 members in America alone, as well as divisions in Britain, France, Germany, Switzerland, and Africa. Its publications are marked by a shallowness typical of many American bodies devoted to self-improvement and to simplified brands of religion and philosophy. They are secret only in the sense that they are not offered for consideration and criticism, of which outsiders are deemed incapable. AMORC recruits through advertising in the press; those who answer its advertisements receive a pamphlet called *Mastery of Life*.

Above, early members of the Societas Rosicruciana in Anglia photographed on an outing in the 1890s. In the foreground sits Dr. Wynn Wescott, the society's third Supreme Magus, and founder of the Hermetic Order of the Golden Dawn. Left, Aleister Crowley, the Golden Dawn's most notorious member, in the regalia of an Adeptus Minor (photograph of 1907). Crowley declared himself master of the society's highest order, the *Argentinum Astrum*, or "Silver Star." Below, Crowley's seal as a Magus. It bears the name of the Egyptian priest Ankh-f-n-khonsu whose stele—exhibit no. 666 in the Cairo Museum—was "discovered" there by Crowley's wife Rose.

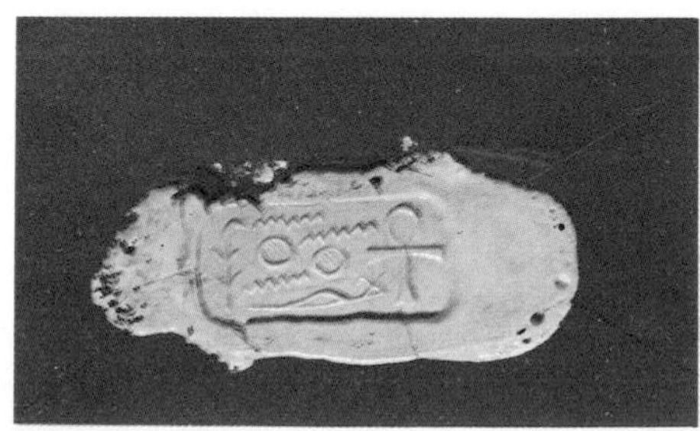

Below, an example of the magical insignia worn by Golden Dawn members who had been initiated into the Inner Order *Rosae rubis et aureae crucis* ("of the red rose and the golden cross"). Symbolically colored, it combines a cross covered with magical symbols, and a rose whose petals are inscribed with the letters of the Hebrew alphabet. Initiates into this order were instructed in a system of magic derived from the cabalistic works of the 19th-century French occultist Eliphas Lévi. They learned how to consecrate talismans, and performed ceremonies that were supposed to conjure up spirits.

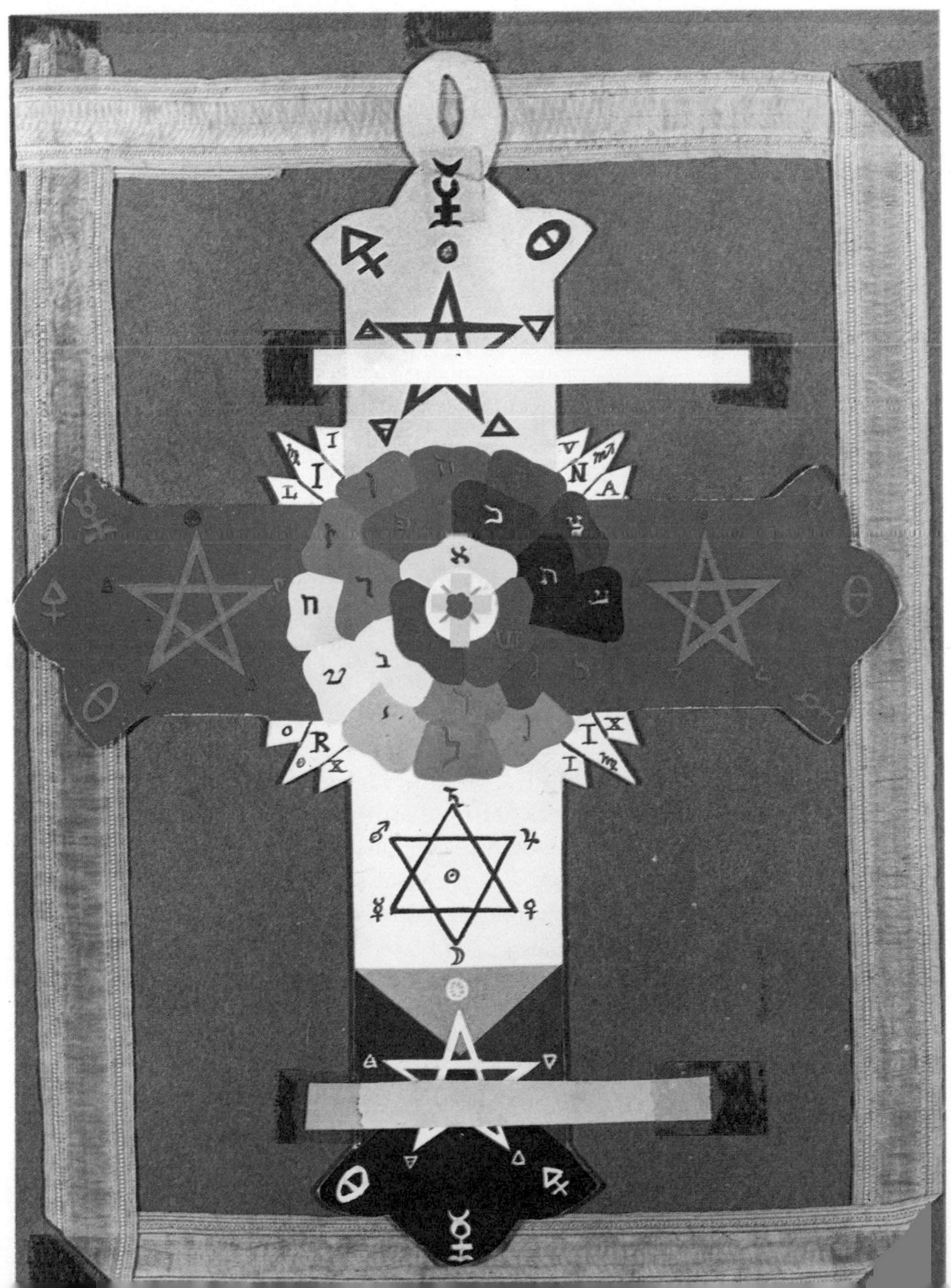

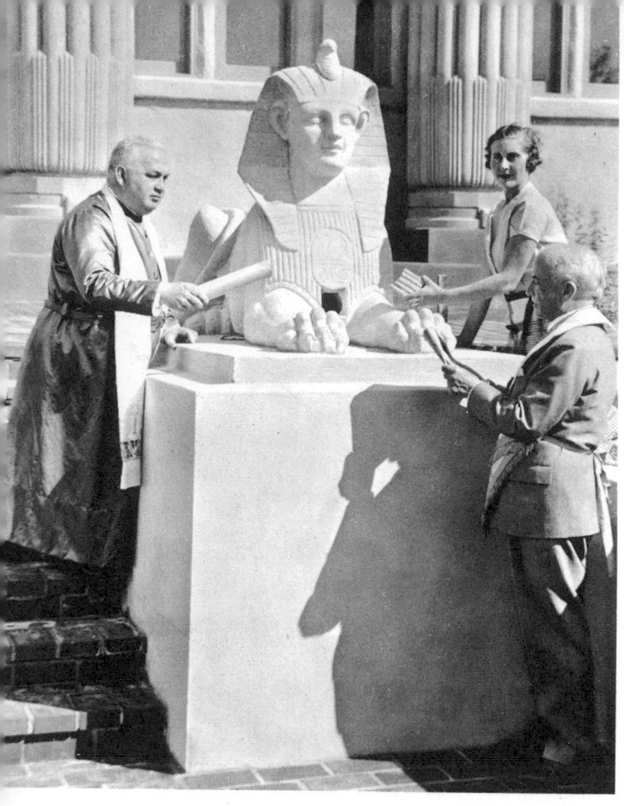

The teachings of Rosicrucian societies today represent an uneasy compromise between 19th-century occultism and 20th-century science. Left, H. Spencer Lewis, founder and first Imperator of the *Ancient Mystical Order Rosae Crucis*, deposits a scroll recording the society's principles "for posterity" between the paws of a sphinx (San Jose, California, July 1934). Right, in the society's chemistry laboratory at San Jose, members are lectured on the "structure of matter."

This introductory pamphlet is intended (in the words of its concluding note) "for careful and discreet distribution only to those who seem worthy of admission to the Order." Designed, in fact, to reach people who have expressed an interest and taken the initiative to secure it, the pamphlet is not on sale at bookstalls or shops. Its tone is confidential and personal, its appeal not to "the learned and the great," but to the common man with (it is suggested) an hour or so a week to devote to Rosicrucianism. The reader is promised the opportunity to reshape his life, and invited to become a student member by sending a fee to his regional office. He is assured that the teachings are within the grasp of "anyone able to read and understand his daily newspaper"—a far cry from the rarified wisdom of which the *Fama Fraternatis* spoke. The object of these teachings is not the reformation of the world so much as efficient functioning in the world as it is. In one leaflet, a salesman testifies that the application of Rosicrucian principles has enabled him to "knock the 't' out of can't."

Applicants must declare their belief in a supreme being or mind, but need not declare themselves to be Christians. They are encouraged to attend lodge meetings, but may confine themselves to private study of the lessons, through which they can progress by degrees from Neophyte to Adept. The ritual of the first degree, as one might expect in view of its 18th- or 19th-century source, is "very similar indeed to the third (or Master Mason's) degree of Freemasonry." The lessons themselves include such topics as "the mysteries of time and space; the human consciousness; the nature of matter; perfecting the physical body; the effect of light, color, and sound upon the mind and body; the ancient

philosophies; development of will; human emotions and instincts; and the phenomena of intuition." These topics are clearly related to the interests of the 19th-century Rosicrucian societies (p. 144); their relation to the ideas behind the original Rosicrucian manifestos is more difficult to find, unless it lies in the paradoxical combination of magic and mysticism that characterizes Rosicrucianism. Alchemy, for instance, is understood in its symbolic sense, as a model for spiritual development; yet in June 1916, Dr. Spencer Lewis gave a public demonstration of practical alchemy in New York and (according to Rosicrucian reports) transmuted a piece of zinc into gold, after 16 minutes during which he "concentrated a little known power of mind."

As we have seen, the broken history of Rosicrucianism does not matter to the Rosicrucian, who is taught that interruptions are inevitable. He might also argue, more convincingly, that the real history is not that of an institution but of a body of knowledge. The outside observer finds the history of Rosicrucianism obscure and discontinuous, difficult to place in the development of human thought and action. Its appeal has seldom been great; only twice has it attracted any of the outstanding minds of the time: at its presumed origin in Germany, and when Yeats and his circle joined the Golden Dawn. Its effect on social and political events has been even slighter, and the world has scarcely been influenced, much less reformed, by its existence. Whether its students have imbibed more knowledge or nonsense is an open question. At least it can be said that, compared with many secret societies, the Order of the Rosy Cross has not done much harm.

7 Freemasonry

Freemasonry as an institution first appeared in the 17th century, in England. In the 18th and 19th centuries it attained a surprisingly wide influence in Europe and in the United States, and its structure became the model for that of many secret groups. Though Freemasonry was by no means the oldest of ritual brotherhoods, it became the classic example of that kind of association. It was (and still is) generally regarded as a continuation of the English stone-masons' guilds of the Middle Ages. Later in this chapter we shall look at the evidence that can be brought in support of this view. But the first and most remarkable fact about Freemasonry is not so much its claim to antiquity (a claim common among secret groups) as its enormous appeal today. In the past hundred years, with the rapid development of technology and the rise of scientific rationalism, many ritual brotherhoods have disappeared from Western society. Yet Freemasonry, with all its myth and ritual, still flourishes; there are some 750,000 Freemasons in Britain, over 4,000,000 in the U.S.A., and over a million more in the rest of the world. We are bound to ask what features of this particular group have enabled it to survive and to maintain its attraction. To answer this question we must consider the nature of the secrets Freemasonry claims to possess; but first, we must determine to what extent Freemasonry remains secret, bearing in mind that its mass appeal may depend largely on secrecy itself.

God, the supreme architect or geometer, creates the universe with a turn of his compasses. A 14th-century painting foreshadows the Freemason's conception of God as the "world's Great Architect" whose compasses have defined the limits of good and evil. (Illustration from an Anglo-French biblical history.)

Freemasonry—conceived as a "secret science"—has many characteristics of the secret society: an oath of secrecy that imposes death on the betrayer, secret passwords and signs, and rituals that relate a mythical history of its origins and include a mimed ordeal of death and rebirth. But while its secrecy tends to arouse the curiosity of most outsiders, its method of recruitment is likely to deter those who are merely idly inquisitive. No one can become a Mason unless he is sponsored by two people who are Masons already. Yet Masons are bound neither to reveal their membership to outsiders, nor to try and persuade anyone to become a Mason. Even when the prospective member has found sponsors and made his application, he may have to wait several months before he is contacted by a lodge; it may be several months more before he is interviewed by the officers of the lodge and asked the prescribed question "Why do you want to become a Mason?" If his application is to proceed it must be approved by all the officers he has seen. A further, and even longer, period of waiting may follow before he is actually initiated into Masonry, for the initiation ceremony is an elaborate one, and most lodges hold only a limited number each year.

The candidate soon learns that Freemasonry is (in its own words) "a peculiar system of morality, veiled in allegory and illustrated by symbols." These symbols are taken chiefly from the actual craft of the stonemason, and they play a vital part in Masonic ritual and teaching. Since Freemasons are not working stonemasons, such tasks as smoothing and shaping the stone are interpreted as metaphors. As the Master of the lodge explains when he ceremonially presents the candidate with a stonemason's tools, "We apply these tools to our morals." The typical initiation ceremony combines many archaic features. Immediately before it, the candidate is divested of his jacket and his collar and tie, and also of any money or metal articles he may have about him (the ritual explains that this is done so that he will remember, if ever he meets a fellow-Mason in "distressed circumstances," the moment when he himself was received into Masonry "poor and penniless"). His left trouser-leg is rolled up above the knee, his shirt is opened to expose his left breast, and his right shoe is removed and replaced by a slipper (the ritual itself gives no explanation for these practices). He is also blindfolded (in Masonic parlance, "hoodwinked") to demonstrate his "state of darkness," and a running noose, or "cable-tow," is placed around his neck. After the lodge has been formally opened, he is led to the outer door by the Tyler or doorkeeper. At the threshold, he is confronted by the Inner Guard, who holds the point of a dagger to his bared breast, barring his way. He is then led before the Worshipful Master, the chief officer of the lodge. The Worshipful Master recites a prayer to the "Almighty Father and Supreme Governor of the Universe," and puts a series of ritual questions to the candidate, who is required to answer according to a prescribed formula and without a slip of the tongue. Kneeling in front of the Worshipful Master's pedestal, with his right foot "formed in a square," and the point of a pair of compasses touching his breast, the candidate then swears not to reveal, write, indite, carve, mark, engrave, or otherwise delineate any part of the secrets in Masonry. Should he do so, he accepts the penalties of "having my throat cut across, my tongue torn out by the root, and buried in the sand of the sea at low water mark, or a cable's length from the shore, where the tide regularly ebbs and flows twice in twenty-four hours, or the more effective punishment of being branded as a wilfully perjured individual, void of all moral worth, and totally unfit to be received into this worshipful Lodge. . . ."

The Worshipful Master then gives orders for the blindfold and noose to be removed, and explains to the initiate the significance of the trials he has just experienced. He gives him the step, the sign, the grip, and the word of an Entered Apprentice Freemason: a short pace with the left foot, bringing the right heel into its hollow; a hand drawn rapidly across the throat (the "penal" sign); a pressure of the thumb on the joint of a man's first finger, while shaking hands; and the word *Boaz*, to which he ascribes the meaning "in strength." The candidate then receives the apron that identifies him, within the lodge, as an Entered Apprentice. He learns that, as such, he symbolizes the "first foundation stone" of a building, on which he may raise "a superstructure perfect in all its parts and honorable to the builder." He is also presented with the "working tools" of the first degree—a 24-inch gauge, representing the 24 hours of the day (part to be spent in prayer, part in labor and refreshment, and part in serving a friend or fellow-Mason); a gavel, representing the force of conscience; and a chisel, representing the advantages of education. There follows an exhortation to obedience—not only to the precepts of Freemasonry but also to those of the Bible, and to the laws of the State. Then the Worshipful Master gives an explanation of the tracing board of the first degree, one of the three symbolical pictures that are displayed to initiates. When the ceremony is over, the candidate is said to have "worked the first degree"; within a few months he may attain the other two "Craft" degrees, those of Fellow-Craft and Master Mason.

Many Freemasons stop at this point, but a further ceremony, called the Royal Arch, admits enthusiasts to a great variety of higher degrees, derived from many different sources. Some are called Cryptic Degrees; some are revived orders of chivalry, such as the Knights Templar and the Knights of Constantinople. The Ancient and Accepted Rite, a system of 33 higher degrees, includes a legacy of Rosicrucianism, the degree of Knight of the Pelican and Eagle, the Sovereign Prince Rose Croix of Heredom—the ritual of which is based on the crucifixion of Christ. Other initiations in the same system confer on the Mason such titles as Perfect Master, Prince of Jerusalem, Grand Pontiff, Chief of the Tabernacle, Commander of the Temple, Grand Elected Knight Kadosh, Grand Inspector Inquisitor Commander, and Sublime Prince of the Royal Secret.

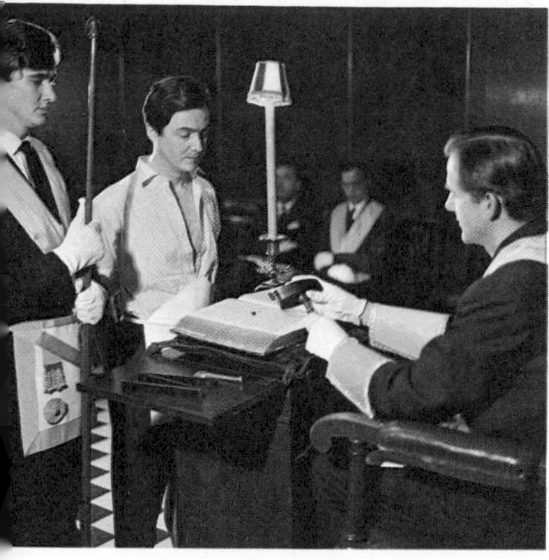

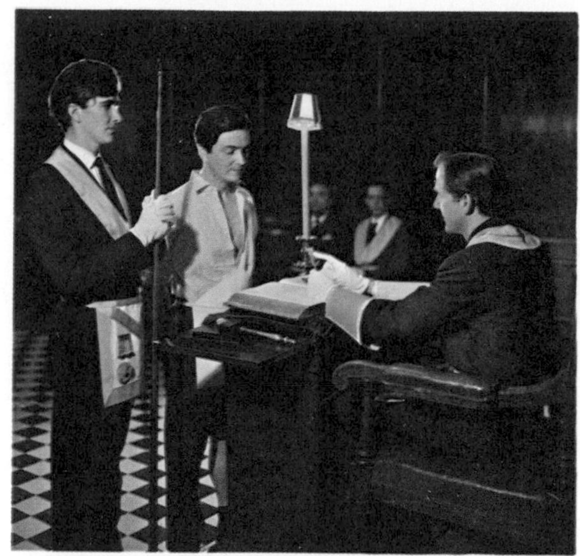

Left, the interior of an English lodge. Above left and above, four scenes from a reconstruction of a Masonic initiation ceremony, photographed in the same lodge. (Left to right) : the candidate is halted at the door by an Inner Guard, who holds the point of a dagger to his bared breast. To take the oath, he kneels in front of the Worshipful Master—pictured here with the "working tools" of the first degree. After giving the initiate the signs and the apron of an Entered Apprentice, the Worshipful Master presents him with the gauge (representing the "24 hours of the day") ; the gavel (the "force of conscience") ; and the chisel (the "advantages of education"). The ceremony ends with an explanation of the first-degree tracing board.

Right, John Harris's design for the first-degree tracing board (1815). Its symbols include the three pillars of Freemasonry; the rough ashlar and the perfect ashlar; and a ladder to heaven, with rungs that represent moral virtues. The ritual explains: "The Universe is the Temple of the Deity whom we serve; Wisdom Strength and Beauty are about His throne as pillars of His works, for His Wisdom is infinite, His Strength omnipotent, and Beauty shines through the whole of the creation in symmetry and order. The Heavens He has stretched forth as a canopy; the earth He has planted as a footstool; He crowns His Temple with Stars as with a Diadem, and with His hand He extends the Power and the Glory . . . ."

If most of these titles are 18th- or 19th-century creations, the word *freemason* itself dates back at least as far as the 14th century; it may have been coined as an abbreviation of "freestone mason," freestone being the malleable type of stone used in fine carving and for such details as arches and windows. A freestone mason, therefore, was far more of a skilled craftsman than a "rough-mason," who merely shaped rough stone into blocks. But the name of freemason also had another significance: that those who possessed it were free men, under the control neither of a feudal overlord nor of a municipal corporation. Most medieval workers had to belong to craft guilds that regulated their duties and conditions. The guilds (like the early trade unions) were not national; each one was limited to a borough or city, whose mayor and council gave it a charter and ultimately controlled it. Its members included employers as well as wage earners (masters and journeymen). In London, where masons were continually employed on big projects such as London Bridge, they belonged to an organization of this type, the London Mason's Company. But elsewhere, their work often took them outside the towns. Most houses were built of wood, and the worker in stone was chiefly in demand for the construction of cathedrals, monasteries, and castles. Unlike tailors or tanners, who worked in small domestic units consisting of one master and a handful of journeymen, the masons were employed in large groups. However, what distinguished the masons from most other medieval workers was the fact that they were migratory: they had to find out what projects were in hand, and make their own way to work on them. All freemasons apparently belonged to a national assembly, though records of when it met and how it functioned are scanty. On a local scale, they organized themselves in lodges. The lodge was a building such as one finds at a modern construction site, in which the workmen took their meals and rested. The word came to mean the center in which they planned their work, and thus became a collective word for a body of masons.

According to the London Masons' Regulations of 1356, the medieval mason had to begin his career with seven years under instruction. He was then regarded as trained, and entered on the rolls as a member of the lodge, but still classified only as an entered apprentice. Seven years later, he attained the status of fellow of craft. The man in charge of a building project was called a master mason. These terms, as we have seen, are used to describe the three "Craft" degrees in modern Freemasonry (the "of" in "fellow of craft" has somehow disappeared). The master mason had considerable importance and dignity, primarily because the profession of architecture did not exist. The design of a building was the responsibility of the clerk of the works, in the case of Church buildings a cleric, and in the case of castles and halls, a royal or feudal official. The clerk of the works was an educated man—the post was held for instance by the poet Chaucer. However, records indicate that the master mason often had a free hand. He was qualified in geometry, then classed as one of the seven liberal arts. He also kept the building accounts.

The rules of the masons' assembly—known as the *Old Charges*—are preserved in at least 115 documents, the earliest of which are two manuscripts written in about 1390 and 1425. In the fuller version, that of 1425, a preamble names Euclid as the founder of masonry, and traces the history of the craft from the building of the Tower of Babel and of Solomon's Temple. It claims that masonry was introduced into France by King Charles Martel (himself, it was said, a mason) and then into England, where the first charter was obtained with the help of St. Alban and the first assembly summoned by King Athelstan. The *Old Charges* also contain moral obligations regarding honesty, sobriety, piety, and loyalty to the king, which masons were bound to observe for the sake of their collective reputation. These documents are the source of some of the mythical history and the moral precepts of modern Freemasonry. But though they laid stress on the moral obligations of masons, the *Old Charges* were essentially guild rules, as the following excerpts suggest:

"You shall be true to one another, that is to say to every Master and Fellow of the Craft . . . and do to them as you would they should do to you.

"That no Master take upon him any lord's work nor other work but that he know himself able of cunning [skill] to perform the same.

"That the Master honestly and truly pay his Fellows their pay as the manner of the Craft doth require.

"That no Master nor Fellow supplant other of their work. . . . You shall not put him out unless he be unable of cunning to end the work.

"That every mason shall receive and cherish strange masons when they come over the country. . . . He shall set him a fortnight on work at the least and give him his hire, and if there be no stones for him then to refresh him with some money to bring him to the next lodge."

All medieval craft guilds and brotherhoods had their "secrets"—that is to say, methods of work they concealed from outsiders in order to keep some kind of copyright in their crafts. This system was devised partly by craftsmen in order to keep the limited amount of work in qualified hands, and partly by the municipal authorities in order to prevent runaway serfs and other strangers from exchanging the bondage of the feudal countryside for the relative freedom of the towns. The exclusiveness of the guilds and brotherhoods was ensured by secret passwords and initiation ceremonies. Many such rituals survived in the 19th century after the beginning of the industrial revolution (they are satirized by Charles Dickens in *Barnaby Rudge*), and abbreviated or mock initiation ceremonies were still acted out in some trades in recent years, for example, among coopers. Medieval stonemasons, working in the countryside and often joined by strangers, ran special risks of being fooled by impostors. By the late 16th or early 17th century, Scottish masons had apparently invented various signs of recognition, including special grips and a "mason's word," and these signs have their counterparts in modern Freemasonry. Similar masons' fraternities grew up in several parts of medieval Europe. In

Above, the Cooke manuscript of the *Old Charges*, about 1425. Right, a detail from a 15th-century painting showing masons building the Tower of Babel. Tradition has it that the mason's word is "as old as Babel, when they could not understand one another, and they conversed by signs."

Germany, the *Steinmetzen* had their rules, their lodges ("Bauhütten"), and their secret grip. In France, the *compagnonnages* had an elaborate organization divided into three branches, with rituals of initiation. The compagnonnages survived into the 19th century, by which time they had been influenced by modern Freemasonry and had absorbed the Masonic legend of Solomon's Temple into their mythology. But they remained a craft guild run on exclusive trade-union lines. There was a considerable gulf between the medieval craft guilds and brotherhoods and the form of Freemasonry that appeared in England in the 17th century. Freemasons distinguish between the two by describing the first as "operative" and the second as "speculative" masonry.

The origins of the 17th-century organization are obscure, and though its founders clearly had a knowledge of the stonemasons' regulations and practices, there is no evidence that they were themselves working masons. On the contrary, it seems that in this period separate lodges were founded for (and perhaps by) men who were not masons by trade. In Scotland, such people may have been admitted into the regular lodges as honorary members; the admission of one honorary member into the Edinburgh Lodge was recorded as early as 1600. Both these practices spread rapidly, and by 1670 the Aberdeen Lodge consisted of 4 noblemen, 3 gentlemen, 15 tradesmen other than masons, and only 10 working masons. However, the first real landmark in the history of modern Freemasonry was the foundation, by the London Masons' Company, of a parallel body called the "Acception" in about 1619. This organization was set up for the admission of men who were not masons by trade; they were known as "accepted Masons" or "gentlemen Masons" and they did not belong to the company proper, though they paid double the regular initiation fee, and doubtless helped to build up the funds.

The motives that spurred non-masons to join associations modeled on the stonemasons' lodges are far from clear, though we may hazard a guess that secrecy itself was a major attraction. Many may have been motivated by a spirit similar to that which generated Rosicrucianism (p. 133), the conviction that they might obtain access to a hidden wisdom. This was the avowed motive of one Welsh poet, Goronwy Owen, and also of the antiquary Dr. William Stukeley, who admitted that curiosity led him "to be initiated into the mysteries of Masonry, suspecting it to be the remains of the mysteries of the ancients." Another factor (indicated by Douglas Knoop and G. P. Jones in their book *Genesis of Freemasonry*) was probably the growing interest of amateurs in architecture and in antiquity; this taste developed among those wealthy enough to make the Grand Tour of Europe, and many gentlemen travelers returned with a passion for Palladian architecture and an urge to have their own designs executed. These motives are typified in the case of Elias Ashmole (1617–92), the founder of the Ashmolean Museum at Oxford, who became a Freemason in 1646. As an antiquary, Ashmole had a strong interest in medieval architecture, and he collected material for a work on Windsor Castle. He had delved into alchemy and the Cabala (p. 134), and he was deeply interested in Rosicrucianism. This has led some scholars to suppose that he was responsible for the introduction of Rosicrucian symbolism, and the Rose Croix degree, into Freemasonry, though lodge records indicate that he was an infrequent attender.

At the same time, the architectural profession was coming into formal existence, and later in the century many architects also became Freemasons, following the lead of Sir Christopher Wren (1632–1723). But by 1735, modern or "speculative" Freemasonry was in full flower, and members connected with architecture and building must have been heavily outnumbered. A *Pocket Companion for Freemasons* laid down: "No man ought to attain to any dignity in Masonry who has not, at least, a competent knowledge in geometry and architecture; and if the sciences were more followed in the Lodges, what is unhappily substituted in their place would not prevail as it does." The reproving phrase suggests that many of the newcomers had joined simply because the lodge was a good club. Nevertheless, much of their time must have been spent in earnest "speculative" discussion, for it was in the years leading up to this time that the symbolism of Freemasonry first developed and that the tools and methods used in the building trade were endowed with a precise moral significance. Thus the unhewn stone, or rough ashlar, that is part of the furniture of every Masonic lodge, is said to represent "man in his infant or primitive state, rough and unpolished"; the polished stone, or perfect ashlar, represents man "in the decline of years, after a regular well-spent life in acts of piety and virtue, which can no otherwise be tried and approved than by the Square of God's word and the Compass of his own self-convincing conscience." Taking the comparison even further (and by analogy with Christ's words "Know ye not that ye are the temple of God . . . ?"), Solomon's Temple is taken to represent perfected man. A book by John Bunyan, *Solomon's Temple Spiritualized* (1688), drew a similar allegory, also using the procedures of building to illustrate the process of spiritual development.

If this form of symbolism had a biblical flavor, it was not exclusively Christian. After the religious passions of the preceding century, the mood favored a rejection of dogma and a tolerance of any personal belief that did not exclude the idea of a supreme being. Deism—a syncretistic belief in God distinct from theological doctrine—was widespread among the educated people and the wealthier classes from which Freemasonry drew its members, until a more orthodox Christian faith became socially necessary in the 19th century. This religious tolerance was reflected in the first Masonic *Book of Constitutions* (1722–23), which laid down that Masons might belong to any religious sect, but that they could not be atheists. "It is thought more expedient only to oblige them to that religion in which all men agree, leaving their particular opinions to themselves." The *Constitutions*, which included an elaborated version of the *Old Charges*, were drawn up by a minister of the Church of Scotland, Dr. James Anderson (1684–1739). They are the documents

THE

CONSTITUTIONS

OF THE

FREE-MASONS.

CONTAINING THE

Hiſtory, Charges, Regulations, &c.
of that moſt Ancient and Right
Worſhipful *FRATERNITY.*

For the Uſe of the LODGES.

LONDON:

Printed by WILLIAM HUNTER, for JOHN SENEX at the *Globe*, and JOHN HOOKE at the *Flower-de-luce* over-againſt *St. Dunſtan's Church*, in *Fleet-ſtreet*.

In the Year of Maſonry —— 5723
Anno Domini —— —— 1723

The title page to Anderson's *Constitutions* and the frontispiece, which includes a diagram of Euclid's 47th proposition. It had enabled stonemasons to find a simple method of checking right angles, and was represented here as a secret of the craft.

that first formulated the patterns of Masonic ritual and symbolism. They were prepared at the request of the new United Grand Lodge, which had been formed in 1717 by the union of four London lodges, and which found "fault with all the Copies of the *old Gothic Constitutions.*" The authority of the United Grand Lodge soon extended throughout England (Scotland and Ireland had their own Grand Lodges), and even to lodges in the colonies. Its formation, and the publication of Anderson's *Constitutions*, mark the beginning of modern Freemasonry. Both the Masonic legend of Hiram Abiff (described as King Solomon's master builder), and the hierarchy of Freemasonry, with a Grand Master at the top of the pyramid and Provincial Grand Masters in various districts, date from about this time.

Anderson's *Constitutions*, however, met with bitter opposition from some of the existing lodges, whose members objected to the rules and ceremonies in their revised form. In 1751, these dissenting members (known as the "Ancients") formed a rival Grand Lodge, with its own Grand Master, "under the old institutions." The Ancients were not recognized in England, but they were both recognized and favored by the Grand Lodges of Scotland and Ireland. Reunion was not achieved until 1813, through an agreement between the rival Grand Masters, the Duke of Sussex and the Duke of Kent, who were brothers of George IV. (The points at issue were to have been settled by a professor of "the Art and Mystery of Speculative Freemasonry," but the two princes never appointed a professor.) In spite of this dissension, the 18th century saw an enormous growth of Freemasonry. As the Duke of Montague (Grand Master in 1721) wrote in his autobiography: "It became a public fashion." It was indeed very much more public than secret; for a time, it was the custom for Freemasons to parade the streets of London once a year in their aprons. Because it drew most of its members from the wealthy middle classes, Freemasonry was—and in most Protestant countries still is—eminently respectable. The first three Grand Masters in England were a gentleman, a civil servant, and a scientist; but the fourth was a duke. Since then, the Grand Master has often been a member of the royal family, the most highly placed being the Prince of Wales (King Edward VII) and the Duke of York (King George VI).

As the precepts of Freemasonry required, the English lodges held aloof from religious and political controversy, and supported the orthodoxy of the age: the Hanoverian monarchy, the parliamentary constitution, and religious toleration under the passive aegis of the Church of England. On the continent of Europe the history of Freemasonry was far more turbulent, controversial, and complicated. "Speculative" Freemasonry crossed the Channel soon after its establishment in 1717; a lodge was founded in 1725 by a group of English noblemen and gentry who were staying in Paris. But in the eyes of the Bourbons, and other absolute monarchs, the essential Masonic idea of tolerance was by definition subversive and dangerous. In 1737, Louis XV issued an edict forbidding all loyal subjects to have anything to do with Freemasonry. In the ensuing decades repression was intermittent; lodges often met freely, but at intervals they were raided by the police, and Freemasons were imprisoned. Freemasonry met similar opposition in Spain, in the Kingdom of Naples, and elsewhere. In Germany and Austria, however, there were monarchs who sympathized with the spirit of tolerance and philosophical inquiry, and looked

Four early representations of the ceremony of raising to the third degree. The rite is a reenactment of the murder of Hiram Abiff, Solomon's mythical master builder. Above left, a guard retires to admit a candidate. Above, the candidate enters.

with favor on the growing lodges. Frederick the Great (1740–86) was largely responsible for introducing Freemasonry into Prussia and was himself Grand Master, while the rulers of various other German states, and the emperor Francis I of Austria, were also Freemasons. It has been suggested that Mozart (who was an ardent Freemason) alluded to this state of affairs in his opera *The Magic Flute* (1791), particularly to the protection of the Freemasons by the liberal emperor Joseph II and the hostility of the empress Maria Theresa.

The story of Freemasonry in the 18th century is confused by the fact that several schools of thought, and several religious and political forces, influenced and infiltrated the lodges. The greatest stir was caused by a succession of mystics, among whom it is hard to distinguish the men of genuine faith and learning, the cranks and neurotics, and finally the charlatans and swindlers. By this time Freemasonry had absorbed something of the Hermetic-Cabalist tradition (p. 135), and had begun to relate itself to the ancient Egyptian mystery cults. Its reverence for the "good religion" of the Egyptians finds full expression in Mozart's *Magic Flute*, in which the Masonic tradition is identified with the Egyptian tradition, and souls make their way to salvation through the mysteries of Isis and Osiris. While some lodges adopted Rosicrucian mysticism, and studied the Cabala, others adopted Rosicrucian magic and devoted themselves to practical alchemy, following Johann Schrepfer of Nuremberg, who claimed that he could make gold and exorcise spirits. In Germany, in Russia, and especially in France, considerable success was gained by the extraordinary Count Cagliostro (1743–95), whose claims were unlimited: he offered the ability to make gold, effect miraculous cures, prolong sexual powers, dominate the world of spirits, and extend life to a span of 5557 years. Cagliostro, who dominated the Lyon Lodge, created his own brand of "Egyptian Masonry," which included women's lodges presided over by a "Queen of Sheba."

Above, the candidate lies in a mock grave to be "stabbed to death." Above right, he is raised on the five symbolic "points of fellowship" : hand to hand, foot to foot, knee to knee, breast to breast, and hand over back (French engravings, about 1750).

The innovation brought about by all these influences was the addition of the higher degrees, which did not exist in medieval masonry or in Anderson's *Constitutions*. These degrees, as we have mentioned, included the Rose Croix, degrees recalling the ancient mystery cults, and revived orders of chivalry. They were the cause of disputes and schisms among Freemasons, especially in France where there were two rival centers of authority: the Grand Orient, which favored the higher degrees, and the Grand Lodge, which did not. An uneasy reunion was effected in 1773 under the Grand Mastership of the Duc d'Orléans (1747–93), who later renounced his title and played a major role in the French Revolution under the name of Philippe-Égalité. An important influence in various French lodges was that of Scottish Jacobites living in exile in France, and particularly of a Scotsman called Michael Ramsay (the Chevalier Ramsay, as he called himself). His aim was evidently to get sympathy and money from Freemasons for the restoration of the Stuart dynasty; his method was to form groups within Freemasonry by recruiting to the Scottish Rites, of which he was perhaps the inventor. Ramsay himself came from Kilwinning, and he claimed that the Kilwinning Lodge was the oldest in Masonic history and that it had always been connected with the Knights of Malta. Though this was a fantasy and though the new system of degrees gained few adherents in Scotland, it became popular in Europe.

The Jacobite cause was supported by the Vatican, and eagerly assisted in particular by Jesuits. This brought about an alliance—how extensive or how official, we cannot be certain—between Jesuits and Freemasons, or at least "Scottish" Freemasons. However James Stuart, the Old Pretender, disowned Ramsay, whom he described in a letter as a madman. Lodges at Rome and Florence, apparently consisting of exiled Jacobites, were found to contain agents of London, as well as Italian freethinkers, Jansenists, and some morally disreputable characters. In 1738, Pope Clement XII issued a bull that forbade Catholics to join or support Freemasonry on pain of excommunication. The main argument he employed was that Masons must have something to hide because they were bound to keep secrets, even from the Church. "If they were not doing evil," he wrote, "they would not have so great a hatred of the light." He drew the conclusion that they were "depraved and perverted," dangerous to "the well-being of souls," and consequently "most suspect of heresy." Other phrases in the bull, however, were in a more mundane tone: Freemasonry was "against public security," and it disturbed "the peace of the temporal State"; there was a reference to "other just and reasonable motives known to Us." Since the popes at that period seem to have been more concerned with earthly than with spiritual authority, there are reasons for thinking that the bull was primarily a political move.

It was an open question whether it was intended to apply universally. Cardinal Corsini, one of its chief sponsors, informed the Grand Duke of Tuscany that Freemasonry "was formed in England as an amusement or decent diversion but . . . has degenerated in Italy, and has become a school of ungodliness." Clement's bull was received in Spain and Portugal, where Freemasons were tried, tortured, and imprisoned by the Inquisition, and in Poland. Elsewhere it was largely ignored, as was a reaffirming bull by the next pope, Benedict XIV. In 1751, Benedict wrote: "The King of the Two Sicilies . . . seems to want to do something about them [the Freemasons], but his ministers, who are members of the sect, will add their indolence to that prince's normal half-heartedness."

We have seen that free inquiry and tolerance were the hallmarks of "speculative" Freemasonry. We have seen also that an association of this character was inevitably suspect to authority in countries such as France, where people were encouraged to think only along lines approved by the monarch and by the established Church. As soon as men became Freemasons, they seemed to place themselves in opposition to both Church and State. In the first place, Freemasons devoted themselves to the spread of knowledge in its broadest sense, and to discussions that tested official dogma in the light of that knowledge. They were confident that understanding and tolerance would gain ascendancy in men's minds and that dogma would correspondingly be undermined and finally rejected. Logic led them to the realization that their aims could be pursued only when free debate and the spread of knowledge were guaranteed, and when the barriers erected by authority were lowered or overthrown—only, that is, in a changed social system. The preconditions for the triumph of knowledge were freedom of association, of speech, and of the press; the abolition of censorship by State or Church; freedom of worship; the rule of law in society, though not in the realm of ideas; freedom from arbitrary arrest and imprisonment without trial; the right for every man to choose his type of employment and place of residence, which meant the abolition of feudal serfdom; and a government whose power was controlled by public opinion and subject to a representative parliament. All this amounted to a program for fundamental change, and to demands that authority would not concede unless it was forced to. Consequently, even if Freemasonry as an institution and the lodges as organized groups remained neutral in politics, Masons as individuals were bound to take up the position of reformers, and in case of need, of revolutionaries.

The political battle was to come later; the first offensive was launched in the sector of knowledge—of enlightenment, to use the term adopted by those committed to it. As the outcome of an abortive plan to translate *Chambers's Encyclopaedia* into French, the scheme of a French encyclopedia was set on foot under the editorship of Denis Diderot (1713–84). Diderot was a rationalist in philosophical outlook, a radical in politics, and in religion a Deist and an opponent of the Church. He was also a Freemason, and so were a number of his celebrated colleagues in the task (though in several cases the fact is doubtful). Diderot wrote large sections of the *Encyclopedia* himself, and

A procession of mock Masons in London, April 27, 1742. Until this time, English Masons paraded openly in their regalia, exciting the curiosity—and the derision—of the public; exposures of Freemasonry were best sellers. (Engraving of 1742.)

others were contributed by the men who are called the philosophers of the Enlightenment: Voltaire, Rousseau, Montesquieu, d'Holbach, and d'Alembert. The *Encyclopedia*, like Freemasonry itself, was the expression of the new humanitarianism, cosmopolitanism, and rationalism (though that very rationalism, combined as it often was with faith in a "religion of Reason," appears irrational today). Parts of the work were highly controversial. It laid down the doctrine that the duty of government was the well-being of the people; it challenged all beliefs that could not be justified by human reason; and it also cast doubt by historical method on certain Christian teachings and traditions. From 1751, when the first of the 28 volumes appeared, the *Encyclopedia* was itself a battlefield. It was banned both by the royal council and by the clergy; copies were seized, Diderot and others concerned were imprisoned, and at one period the printers sabotaged it by cutting sections out and burning the manuscript. But the *Encyclopedia*—sold sometimes openly and sometimes secretly—had an enormous influence on thinking people.

The role of Freemasonry in the lively intellectual climate of the Enlightenment gained new adherents for it; it was luckily, if rather surprisingly, free from serious persecution in the ensuing decades. Voltaire, the idol of all Frenchmen opposed to established authority, was doubtless a sympathizer (and almost certainly a secret Freemason) through his friendship with Frederick the Great. It was not in France, however, but in America that the ideas of the Enlightenment were first translated into action and made the foundation for

a system of government—as the Declaration of Independence and the Constitution clearly show. From 1730 onward, Masonic lodges had been formed in several American towns, but they were politically neutral in the English tradition. Outstanding individuals, however, make a definite link between Freemasonry, the new political ideas, and the struggle for independence. Benjamin Franklin, whose American Philosophical Society upheld the rationalist outlook, became a Freemason in 1731 and was soon Grand Master of Pennsylvania. Other famous American Freemasons of the period include George Washington (who was Charter Master of the Alexandria Lodge), Alexander Hamilton, and such revolutionary heroes as Paul Revere and Admiral John Paul Jones. Lafayette, also a Freemason, provided an added link with the France of the Enlightenment.

At this time some reformers and Freemasons in Europe had the idea of organizing a selectively recruited body to spread knowledge and to serve the cause of freedom. Mirabeau (who may or may not have been a Freemason) put on paper a scheme for such an "intimate association," to be modeled organizationally on the Society of Jesus. "We have quite contrary views," he wrote, "those of enlightening men, of making them free and happy, but . . . who should prevent us doing for good what the Jesuits have done for evil?" The plan was eventually put into effect in Bavaria, where Adam Weishaupt (1748–1830) a professor of canon law at the University of Ingolstadt, founded the secret society of the *Illuminati*—that is, the Enlightened—in 1776.

Its aims, the foundation members decided, were "to make the perfecting of the reasoning powers interesting to mankind, to spread the knowledge of sentiments both humane and social, to check wicked inclinations, to stand up for suffering and oppressed virtue . . . to facilitate the acquirement of knowledge and science." Weishaupt's own writings opened wider perspectives. "Princes and nations," he forecast, "will disappear without violence from the earth, the human race will become one family and the world the abode of reasonable men. Morality alone will bring about this change imperceptibly." And he asked: "Why should it be impossible that the human race should attain to its highest perfection, the capacity to guide itself?"

Weishaupt was not a Freemason when he founded the Illuminati, but he became one in the next year; his conscious plan was to infiltrate and, where possible, to dominate the lodges, in order to select the "enlightened" from among the more promising Freemasons. Together with Baron von Knigge, a bookseller named Johann Bode, and other associates, he had for a time some success. The Masonic lodges at Munich and Eichstadt became seminaries of the Illuminati, and their influence was exerted in others. But the Jesuits of devoutly Catholic Bavaria mounted an attack on the new society and made use of personal scandals (for example, the fact that Weishaupt had an illegitimate child) to discredit it. In March 1785 the elector of Bavaria specifically outlawed both Freemasons and Illuminati. Weishaupt, dismissed from his university post, fled to Gotha in fear of arrest. No further authentic record of the Illuminati remains.

In 1789, the fuse laid by men like Diderot and Voltaire set off the explosion of the French Revolution. A vast number of books and pamphlets has been written to prove and disprove the supposed connection between the Revolution and Freemasonry. First in the field, in 1798 and 1799, were the Abbé Barruel, a French émigré in England (and former Freemason), and a Scottish writer called John Robison, who claimed that the whole Revolution was secretly planned and directed by Freemasons. A later addition to the theory was that the real hidden hand was that of the Illuminati, who had transferred their secret center and their operations from Bavaria to France. If so, they must have diverged greatly from the ideas of Weishaupt, who, as we have seen, expected monarchy to "disappear without violence" under the imperceptible influence of morality.

No serious historian today believes that the French Revolution was caused by a conspiracy involving (according to Cadet de Gassicourt) only 27 "true initiates," while all the others involved were cast as "dupes." J. J. Mounier, refuting Barruel in 1801, commented coolly: "Very complicated causes were replaced by simple causes within the grasp of the most idle and most superficial minds." That Freemasonry was one of the contributory forces in causing the downfall of the *ancien régime* is a far more serious proposition, and one to which many French Freemasons have assented with pride. Here, as in the American

Revolution, the evidence leads us to conclude that Freemasonry as an organization played little or no part, but that Freemasons filled some important roles.

They were probably associated for the most part with the moderate groups that shaped the course of the Revolution until 1791, and were crushed or swept aside as it mounted to its climax. The Duc d'Orléans, who was Grand Master on the eve of the Revolution, stood for constitutional monarchy, and was guillotined in 1793. Lafayette was a figure of the same type. What is certain is that in 1792, when the Jacobins were in power, Freemasonry was outlawed and the lodges were dissolved. This seems to argue either that the Jacobins equated the Freemasons with the moderates whom they regarded as enemies, or at least that they considered the lodges a likely hiding place for counter-revolutionary plotters. Both hypotheses rule out the idea that Jacobins and Freemasons were hand in glove, to say nothing of the notion that the Revolution was still following a course charted by Freemasonry. The question is complicated by the fact that all the Jacobin leaders—Marat, Danton, and Robespierre among others—have been named as Freemasons. But the evidence in every case is doubtful; and, even if it is accepted, the possibility remains that these men, by the time they came to power, had abandoned or turned against Freemasonry.

Title page design from the first edition of Diderot's *Encyclopedia* (1751-72) includes Masonic symbols, the square and compasses.

Freemasonry began to function legally again in France in 1798. When Napoleon became emperor, he informed the Freemasons that "their highly moral aim and purpose were worthy of his favour and protection." This took the form of vigilant control, with the emperor's brother Joseph installed as Grand Master, though he was never initiated into Freemasonry. The Freemasons evidently drew the lesson that safety lay in being loyal to whoever was in power; the Grand Orient welcomed the Bourbons in 1814, Napoleon during the Hundred Days, and the king once more after Waterloo. For some, however, Freemasonry was indissolubly connected with the struggle for freedom. Its presence, or at least the presence of Freemasons, was detected in the "Conspiracy of Equals" of 1796, a last despairing attempt to put France back on the road of pure revolution; in the United Irishmen, who rebelled against British rule in 1798; in the Philhellenic movement devoted to the liberation of Greece; and in the Decembrist revolt of 1825 against tzarism. The facts regarding each of these episodes are obscure, but there is no ground for supposing the existence of any centrally directed Masonic campaign against authority. In one country, however, it is legitimate to say that the lodges as a whole were deeply involved in politics. This country was Italy, where democratic and forward-looking elements aimed at the goal of national unity, finally achieved in 1860.

Their instrument was a secret society whose members took the name of *Carbonari* (p. 195). Their lodges were not identical with the Masonic lodges, but membership overlapped to a great extent; it is fairly certain that most Freemasons were Carbonari, and most Carbonari—including leading figures such as Garibaldi—were Freemasons. A similarity of outlook, too, was shown by the clause in the rules of the Carbonari providing for freedom of conscience but enjoining worship of a supreme being. Both this society and Freemasonry were proscribed throughout Italy, with the exception of Piedmont, the base of operations in the campaign for nation unity. The lodges began to meet openly again only after Italy was united, when Garibaldi became Grand Master.

An important consequence of the alliance with the Carbonari was that it ranged the Freemasons of Italy in militant opposition to the Vatican. While the country was divided into many small units, all of them under absolute rule and without democratic rights, a considerable territory in central Italy was governed by the pope in the capacity of a temporal sovereign. The popes of the period, to retain their dominions, set themselves against national unity and allied themselves with neighboring kings and grand dukes. Carbonari and Freemasons naturally maintained that the flag of a secular Italy should fly over the whole country and that the pope should be content with his spiritual empire. Often they went further, and made it clear that in a united Italy the authority of the Church would be limited and priests would be deprived of the power to tell people what to read or what to believe. Grand Master Lemmi declared: "We have applied the Chisel to the last refuge of superstition, and the Vatican will fall beneath our vivifying Mallet." Masons, he urged, should work "to scatter the stones of the Vatican, so as to build with them the Temple of the Emancipated Nation."

The Vatican replied in kind. Between 1821 and 1902, the popes issued 10 encyclicals to denounce Freemasonry and to renew the ban first pronounced by Clement XII. Though the actual cause of hostility was limited to Italy and was at least in part political, the ban this time was enjoined on Catholics everywhere. In France, after a period of tactful conciliation toward the Bourbon monarchy, Freemasonry again showed strong democratic sympathies. The revolution of 1830, which deposed Charles X and installed a constitutional monarchy under Louis Philippe, was celebrated by a Masonic festival. In 1848, when he in turn was overthrown and France became a republic, Freemasons again rejoiced. An address to the new government by the Grand Orient asserted that Masonic banners had always borne the words "Liberty, Equality, Fraternity," and expressed pleasure in "the grand national and social movement that has just taken place."

The Republic was short-lived; a *coup d'état* in 1851 brought another Napoleon to power. His prefect of police ordered Freemasons to dissolve their lodges, and the Grand Orient complied. Soon afterward, however, Napoleon III decided to adopt the tactics of the first emperor, and told the Freemasons that they were welcome to reassemble with his nephew, Prince Lucien Murat, as Grand Master. Murat imposed on them a new constitution of an authoritarian kind. As a Masonic historian put it, "the independent spirit of French Freemasonry was quenched," and they were expected to display "inactive and blind submission." In 1860 Murat made a speech in sympathy with the pope; the Masonic journal demanded his resignation, but it was suppressed and several lodge masters were suspended. After a couple of years of disputes, the emperor gave ground, modified the constitution, and replaced Murat. But his abdication in 1870 was greeted with delight by Freemasons.

The next year saw armed conflict between the new Republican government, socially conservative in policy, and the Paris Commune, which had socialists at its head. There was by now a distinctly socialist trend of thought in Freemasonry; Louis Blanc, who had raised the slogan of *la république sociale* in the 1848 revolution, and Pierre Joseph Proudhon, the best-known French socialist thinker, were both Freemasons. The Parisian lodges tried to mediate between the government and the Commune, but the government rebuffed their efforts. They then decided to display their banners on the walls of Paris, and to join the Commune if the banners were touched by a single bullet. "Several thousand Masons," Jellinek writes in his history of the Commune, "proceeded down the boulevards amid enormous enthusiasm. . . . The marchers were gay with symbolic ribbons, blue, green, white, red, and black, with gold and silver spangles, triangles, suns, and trowels." Bullets not only hit the banners but wounded a Mason, and the lodges resolved to defend the Commune in arms.

Despite this episode, Freemasonry was to flourish under the Third Republic. The central political issue for many years—an issue still not entirely dormant in France—had been the antagonism between State and Church. Catholic hostility to Freemasonry was unabated, and Freemasons supported governments that imposed restrictions on religious orders and refused financial aid to Church schools. The France of the Third Republic had two rival Establishments, each powerful in its own sphere; regular attendance at Mass led to promotion in the army, while anticlerical views made it likely in the universities and the civil service. Where their outlook was favored, Freemasons often rose to high positions.

Anathematized by the Vatican, and still forbidden and persecuted in Spain, Freemasonry was the target of fierce verbal attacks almost everywhere. Even in Britain, despite its obvious respectability, it had its enemies. In America, a sensation was caused by the murder—allegedly by Masons—of William Morgan, who had published an "exposure" of Freemasonry in 1826. Lodges were attacked by mobs, many of them had to close down, and the issue was drawn into the political arena by "anti-masonic" candidates for election. It was not until the second half of the century that American Freemasonry recovered from these blows. Today it is firmly established and regarded as above reproach socially and politically; its membership is made up chiefly of businessmen. The United States is in fact the chief stronghold of Freemasonry today.

Below, a satirical American view of the conflict between Freemasonry and the Roman Catholic Church, which reached its climax in 1884 with the promulgation of the last anti-Masonic encyclical, *Humanum genus.* (Cartoon from *Puck* magazine, May 7, 1884.)

Right, the title pages of two fictitious "exposures" of Freemasonry by the French hoaxer Leo Taxil (1854-1907). Taxil's fantasies—translated into four languages—were widely accepted as evidence of Masonic devil-worship and debauchery.

As might be expected, all attacks on Freemasonry have exploited the secrecy of Masonic ritual, the oath quoted at the beginning of this chapter, and the privacy of lodge meetings. Its opponents have reiterated the argument of Clement XII, that what is secret must be sinister, and have even revived the Abbé Barruel's theory about the role of Freemasonry in the French Revolution. Some have tried to trace a chain of events through Masonic links with the Carbonari and Masonic support of the Left in France, in order to prove that the Freemasons (with the Illuminati, alleged to be still secretly functioning, as the directing center) were weaving ceaseless plots to disrupt the established social order and plunge the world into anarchy. The Russian Revolution of 1917 has been represented as a Masonic achievement and Freemasonry has been denounced as the ally or inspirer of Communism, despite the fact that it is forbidden in Communist countries. Masons have been blamed for the assassination of the Archduke Franz Ferdinand, which sparked off World War I, for the ruinous German inflation of 1924, and for the Spanish civil war.

Very often, and notably during the Dreyfus affair in France, anti-Masonry has gone hand in hand with anti-Semitism. Freemasons and Jews have been bracketed as evil international conspirators bent on undermining patriotism and destroying the security of plain honest folk—somehow, they have been depicted as ruthless capitalists and Communists at the same time. In Europe, the attacks mounted to a climax with the ascendancy of Fascism and Nazism.

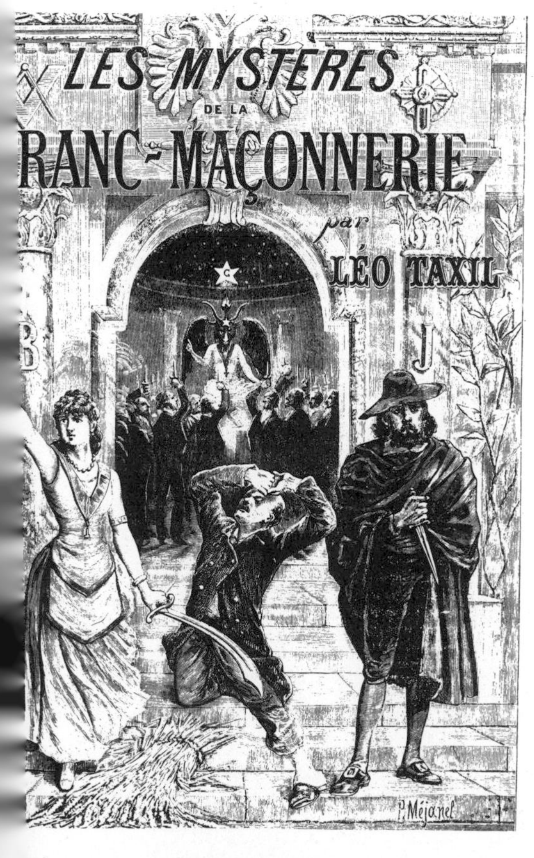

Mussolini dissolved the Italian lodges, and many Freemasons were imprisoned or exiled. Hitler acted yet more ruthlessly in Germany and in the countries he conquered; Freemasons in considerable numbers ended their lives in concentration camps. In France, and elsewhere, Freemasons and devout Catholics—as well as men of the Left and conservative-minded patriots—worked together in the resistance movement, and suffered together in Gestapo jails and concentration camps.

Since the end of World War II, the warfare between the Church and Freemasonry has been largely a thing of the past, though its echoes are still heard from time to time. In England, where high dignitaries of the established Church are Freemasons, some people still argue that the religious syncretism of Freemasonry makes it incompatible with any Christian orthodoxy, and allege, for example, that some of the Masonic passwords have a pagan and therefore satanic derivation. The archaic oath of secrecy, with its gruesome penalty, has also been the subject of much controversy, though (needless to say) it has never been enforced. Indeed, many people who take the oath today would be hard put to it to define what they are supposed to keep secret, unless it is simply the ritual steps, signs, and passwords. These have long been accessible to any outsider who cares to do a little research in a good library, for Freemasonry has a vast literature. There are at least 100,000 published works on the subject, though many are no more than anti-Masonic and pro-Masonic fantasies.

In some respects, Freemasonry represents a development analogous to Rosicrucianism, though it has been far more influential. Conceived in an age that was deeply concerned with the nature of the universe and of man, it

In the U.S.A. today, there are over 9000 "Scottish Rite" Freemasons, and thousands more belonging to other rites, or to such quasi-masonic groups as the Shriners. These groups are primarily social or philanthropic in their functions; their secrecy is minimal, and their rituals are highly dramatized. Left, the Daughters of the Nile, a "philosophical" society composed of Shriners' wives, parade at the coronation of their new "queen" (Omaha, Nebraska, 1956). Right, regular Freemasons in Lexington, Massachusetts, take part in their annual church parade.

received its impetus from a sincere spirit of inquiry, and could thus be a genuine source of "enlightenment," whether intellectual or moral. Today, though it no longer has the same impetus, Freemasonry still seems to have something to offer its members. For most of them, it may be little more than a social club with the added attraction of secrecy; many, no doubt, also enjoy the enactment of the rituals. Some believe that the Masonic teaching embodies an "ancient wisdom, which has been passed, like a golden thread, from civilization to civilization"; and some understand it as a system of self-development. Nevertheless, many people are drawn to the organization by the belief that membership will bring them material benefits, whether through the practice of Masonic principles in the business world (one of the spheres in which Masonic handshakes and code questions are still widely used as a means of recognition) or through Masonic charity, which raises large sums of money each year for the endowment of Masonic schools, orphanages, hospitals and old-age homes.

In today's highly industrialized societies, Freemasonry seems to be becoming more and more like an unofficial "guild" of businessmen—if only because it does require mutual aid and "square dealing" among its members. There is no reason to suppose that outsiders are necessarily denied such treatment, nor that such practices must be detrimental to the business world as a whole. As far as most of its members are concerned, Freemasonry is today a lively and efficacious mutual-aid society, whose ritual is consecrated, not invalidated, by age, and is no less relevant to modern life than the rituals of the law-courts, the universities, or any public body.

8 Nationalist secret societies

Alien or minority rule, imposed by conquest, is the most common of the conditions that tend to produce the nationalist secret society. Irish nationalist societies emerged in the 18th century, when an Anglo-Irish Protestant minority consolidated its rule over the Catholic majority; Italian nationalist societies developed in the early 19th century, after 250 years of Spanish and Austrian domination. Opposition to such rule usually begins in the form of an open cultural society, set up as a club for the leaders of the oppressed majority. This club progresses from considerations of culture to demands for reform from the occupying power. When these are resisted, the club either splits into moderates and extremists, or goes underground. At this point the nationalist secret society is formed. Its aim is insurrection, its organization military.

The Irish nationalist societies serve as a model. The condition of Irish Catholics in the 18th century was desperate; a severe penal code denied them all civil rights and left them at the mercy of Protestants, while the very words "Irish landlord" meant extortion and oppression. In the South, the great peasant mass had no remedy for despair and a potato diet except to drink and plot against the English rulers and their regiments. But the peasants in Ulster, in the North, were dissenters, immigrants from Scotland who hated the Papists even more than they hated their own landlords. Like the poor whites in the Southern States of America, who tolerated the planter because he made them

The assassination of the French president Sadi Carnot by an Italian anarchist, June 24, 1894. Like the anarchists, many political conspirators have been inspired by hopes of world revolution; few of them have failed to invoke nationalism, or to work along nationalistic lines. (Detail from a painting by Flavio Constantini.)

RF
RF
RF

feel superior to the Negro, the Ulstermen tolerated the landlord because he made them feel superior to the Catholic.

While the English administration of Ireland was distinguished by its toughness and ruthlessness, Irish Catholic resistance was distinguished by its tenacity. John Mitchel's patriotic *History of Ireland* well sums up the situation in the late 18th century: "In Ireland they found themselves face to face, not two classes, but two nations; of which the one had substantially the power of life and death over the other. When we add to this that one of these two nations had despoiled the other of those very lands which the plundered race were now glad to cultivate as rackrented tenants; and also that the dominant nation felt bound to hate the other, both as 'rebels' who needed only the opportunity to rise and cut their masters' throats, and as Papists who clung to the 'damnable idolatry' of the mass, we can easily understand the difficulty of the 'landlord and tenant question' in Ireland."

The Irish have always shown a talent for clandestine organization, particularly at the village or ward level; Irish immigrants to the United States were to make the Tammany political machine in New York the model of urban boss politics. By the 1780s, when the American Revolution set the example for the successful overthrow of British rule, both Northern and Southern Ireland had had experience of organized resistance outside the law. In the North, the Oakboys and Steelboys had sworn oaths of secrecy, slaughtered cattle, carried arms, and burned houses in defiance of compulsory road-building and rent increases. In the South, the Whiteboys had attacked landlords, armed with scythes, clubs, and swords.

"England's difficulty is Ireland's opportunity" has long been a political maxim. In 1778, when France entered the American War of Independence and England was fully engaged in trying to suppress that revolt, the Protestant Irish had raised a militia called the Volunteers, a force of 80,000 men who were well-armed and officered by the Protestant gentry. The British government, alarmed by the possibility of an Irish revolt and by the Protestant colonials' demands for something suspiciously similar to "No taxation without representation," granted a form of home rule to the Irish parliament in 1782. Yet this concession merely meant that a million Protestants now ruled three million unrepresented Catholics in Ireland; the historian W. E. H. Lecky described the system as government through rotten boroughs (whose members of parliament were elected by a handful of voters) "by the gentlemen of Ireland, and especially by its landlord class." As Theobald Wolfe Tone, the leader of the first nationalist secret society in Ireland, later wrote: "It was a

A proclamation issued in 1712 by the Lord Justices of Ireland illustrates the extreme severity of the penal laws, which denied civil rights to all Roman Catholics.

BY THE

Lords Juſtices and Council

OF

IRELAND,

A

PROCLAMATION.

Con. Phipps. Canc. *Jo. Tuam.*

HEREAS *Bryan Mc. Hugh*, a Popiſh Prieſt, ſtands Convict of Celebrating a Marriage between a Proteſtant and a Papiſt, contrary to an Act of Parliament lately made in this Kingdom, and has thereby Incurred the Pains, Penalties and Forfeitures of a Popiſh Regular. And whereas the ſaid *Bryan Mc. Hugh*, having been Tranſmitted to the City of *Dublin*, in Order to be Tranſported beyond the Seas, purſuant to the Directions in the ſaid Act, made his Eſcape, and Returning to the County of *Longford*, hath as We are Informed Publiſhed ſome Forged and Counterfeit Order, pretended by him to have been Signed by *Joſhua Dawſon* Eſq; Deputy Clerk of the Council; by Colour whereof, the ſaid *Bryan Mc. Hugh* Endeavoured to Shelter himſelf from Juſtice. And whereas the ſaid *Bryan Mc. Hugh* in Purſuance of the Lords Juſtices Orders, was lately Apprehended in the County of *Longford*, and has again made his Eſcape: And foraſmuch as We are Deſirous that ſo Notorious a Malefactor may be ſpeedily brought to Condign Puniſhment,

We do therefore by this Our Proclamation, Publiſh and Declare, That if any Perſon or Perſons ſhall Apprehend and Take the ſaid *Bryan Mc. Hugh*, and cauſe him to be Committed to the next County Goal, to be Proceeded againſt according to Law, ſuch Perſon and Perſons, ſhall Have, Receive, and be Paid, the Sum of Twenty Pounds *Sterling*, within Twenty Days next after the ſaid *Bryan Mc. Hugh* ſhall be ſo Apprehended and Taken.

And We do hereby Strictly Charge and Command all Juſtices of the Peace, and Chief Magiſtrates of Cities and Towns Corporate, and all Sheriffs, Bayliffs, and other Her Majeſty's Officers, to Uſe their utmoſt Endeavour to Apprehend and Take the ſaid *Bryan Mc. Hugh*, in Order to bring him to ſpeedy Juſtice.

Given at the *Council-Chamber* in *Dublin-Caſtle*, the 11th Day of *July*, 1712.

Abercorn, W. Meath, W. Kildare, Cha. Feilding, P. Savage, Rich. Cox. Rob. Doyne, Cha. Dering, Donat. Brien, Wm. Steuart. Sam. Dopping.

God Save the Queen.

Dublin: Printed by *Andrew Crooke*, Printer to the Queen's Moſt Excellent Majeſty, in *Copper-Alley*, 1712.

The Dublin Volunteers, commanded by the Duke of Leinster, hold their annual parade under the statue of William III in College Green (1779). In 1792 their loyalties shifted from the House of Orange to the Irish peasants; they refused to parade in William's honor, and exchanged their orange cockades for Irish green. (Engraving after Francis Wheatley, 1784.)

Revolution which, while at one stroke it doubled the value of every borough-monger in the kingdom, left three-quarters of our countrymen slaves . . . and the Government of Ireland in the base and wicked and contemptible hands, who had spent their lives in degrading and plundering her."

In this shadow of independence, the Volunteers began to enlist working-class Catholic recruits and gradually disintegrated. In 1785 Henry Grattan, the Protestant leader in the Irish parliament, protested: "The old, the original Volunteers had become respectable because they represented the property of the nation, but attempts had been made to arm the poverty of the kingdom. They had originally been the armed property; were they to become the armed beggary?" Here, as in the United States, independence was not to mean social revolution. The Volunteers broke up into groups of armed men, including the Protestant Peep o' Day Boys and the Catholic Defenders.

In the 1790s the creed and example of the French Revolution gave fresh inspiration to the Irish Catholics. They found a leader in the young barrister and pamphleteer Wolfe Tone, who declared: "To subvert the tyranny of our execrable Government, to break the connection with England, . . . and to assert the independence of my country—these were my objects. To unite the whole people of Ireland, . . . to substitute the common name of Irishman, in place of the denominations of Protestant, Catholic, and Dissenter—these were my means." Thus Tone formulated the method by which nationalism might be used to win independence for an oppressed and divided country. In Belfast in 1791 he drafted the resolutions for the founding of the *Society of United Irishmen*, which demanded Catholic emancipation in a united Ireland ruled by a reformed parliament. To the Belfast declaration, the Dublin branch of the society added a pledge to press for a reformed parliament through "a brotherhood of affection, an identity of interests, a communion of rights, and a union of power among Irishmen of all religious persuasions. . . ."

In 1793 England entered the war against revolutionary France, with the Irish parliament's support, and the leaders of the Dublin United Irishmen were jailed. The society then dropped its ideas of constitutional reform in favor of treasonable and revolutionary action; it built up a resistance movement that could assist a French invasion. By 1795 the officers of the United Irishmen at village, county, and provincial levels had become field officers in a guerrilla movement, so that there was (in the words of the historian Philip Harwood), "a sort of pyramidical hierarchy of sedition, with an infinite number of small local societies for the base, and gradually towering up, through the nicely fitted gradations of baronial, county, and provincial committees, to the apex of a national executive directory." Having adopted subversion as its method, the society became secret. There was a minimum of time-wasting ritual; at initiation, a new member simply swore an oath of secrecy on the New Testament. The password was merely, "I know U," to which the reply was, "I know N," and so on through all the letters of the words "United Irishmen."

Two engravings from the *Irish Magazine* of 1810 depict scenes in the suppression of the 1798 rebellion. Above left, a rebel is executed on the traveling gallows. Above, another is capped with blazing pitch. According to the historian Sir Jonah Barrington, similar atrocities took place before the rebellion. "Slow tortures were inflicted, under the pretence of forcing confessions; the people were goaded and driven to madness." Left, the badge of the United Irishmen. It combines the Irish harp with the French cap of liberty. Opposite page, the rebel camp at Vinegar Hill, County Wexford. The main rebel army was defeated there on June 21 by 20,000 regular troops. In Barrington's words: "The troops advanced gradually but steadily up the hill; the peasantry kept up their fire, and maintained their ground; their cannon was nearly useless, their powder deficient, but they died fighting at their post." (Engraving from a painting by George Cruikshank, 1845.)

Members were armed and drilled, and by 1796 the society was ready for revolt. But its supporters, armed only with pikes, needed French regular troops to engage the English army with its cannon and muskets. Wolfe Tone and the Anglo-Irish revolutionary leader Lord Edward Fitzgerald, who now allied himself with the United Irishmen, made many trips to France, trying to persuade successive French governments to invade Ireland; the French navy actually made invasion attempts in 1796, 1797, and 1798. The first was defeated by storms, the second (from Holland) was intercepted, and the third ended in quick disaster, for the French troops were slaughtered soon after landing by those of Lord Cornwallis, then viceroy. The United Irishmen failed to coordinate their rising with any of these invasions. They made one attempt in May 1798, but the organizers, including Lord Edward Fitzgerald, were arrested before the event, and the rebel army of 20,000 was defeated by British troops. Ulster did not rise in support of the society, which had become an overwhelmingly Catholic organization; in fact, Ulster threw up a counter-organization, the Orangemen, to resist attacks from Catholic guerrillas. Armed landlords, the yeomanry, and the Orangemen joined with the British troops in suppressing the Catholic rebellion. Fitzgerald died of wounds in jail during the rising; Tone (who was arrested in the same year on board a French ship) received the death sentence in November and committed suicide. The United Irishmen ceased to be an active revolutionary force.

Left, Theobald Wolfe Tone (1763–98), founder of the United Irishmen. In a statement prepared for his court-martial he wrote, "I have laboured to create a people in Ireland by raising three millions of my countrymen to the rank of citizen."

Opposite page, an engraving showing the eviction of Irish peasants during the great famine of the 1840s. (*Illustrated London News*, December 16, 1848.)

The Fenians, who emerged some 50 years later, were the heirs of the United Irishmen; but they were revolutionaries with a different purpose, for circumstances in Ireland had changed. In 1800 the English government had passed an Act of Union to incorporate Ireland into the parliament at Westminster. In 1829 the Catholic Emancipation Act had been passed through the pressure of the Irish barrister Daniel O'Connell and his Catholic Association, whose officers had acquired more real power in the South than the official administration. The aim of the Fenians was complete independence, an Irish Republic separate from the British Crown. And though Catholic emancipation had removed one popular grievance, the great famine of the late 1840s gave the Fenians a vast fund of hate to use in their search for recruits.

The failure of successive potato crops led to a sharp reduction in Ireland's population; between 1845 and 1851 it fell from 8½ million to 6½ million. (It has been estimated that a million died of famine, and another million emigrated to the United States.) Embittered by the failure of the parliament in Westminster to send relief, and by the Anglo-Irish landlords who had evicted tenants from their plots in order to apply new farming techniques, the Irish-Americans planned revenge. They saw the great famine as a plot devised by the British government to break the spirit of the Irish people and to reduce their numbers. In Mitchel's words, the policy of Anglo-Irish landlords and British governments had led to a system "by which a beautiful and fertile island, producing noble and superabundant harvests year after year, became gradually poorer and poorer,—was reduced to buy its bread,—reduced, at length, to utter starvation, and, finally, to cannibalism." The English commercial system of Free Trade and the repeal of the Corn Laws in 1846 had

indeed beggared Ireland; but the problem had been aggravated by Ireland's enormous increase in population in the early 19th century. Nevertheless, it was easy to lay the fault on "Irish landlordism . . . grown so rotten and hideous a thing that only its strict alliance, offensive and defensive, with British oligarchy, saves it from going down to sudden perdition."

In 1848 Irish Catholics who opposed O'Connell's cautious policy attempted to organize an armed rising. But the government, informed of the plan, deported some of the leaders; three others—John O'Mahony, Michael Doheny, and James Stephens—fled to the United States. On the soil of America, where there was cheap land for the asking and no system of rack renting or tithe paying, they founded the *Fenian Brotherhood* (also known as the Irish Republican Brotherhood, or I.R.B.). In the same year (1858) they sent funds to Ireland for the formation of an Irish wing. The Fenians were organized on the continental revolutionary model of cells of 10, whose members were theoretically unknown to other members. The oath they adopted was frankly revolutionary; it paid no lip service to reform. The Irish version ran: "I, X, do solemnly swear, in the presence of Almighty God, that I will do my utmost, at any risk, while life lasts, to make Ireland an independent democratic Republic; that I will yield implicit obedience, in all things not contrary to the law of God, to the commands of my superior officers; and that I shall preserve inviolable secrecy regarding all the transactions of this secret society that may be confided to me. So help me God! Amen." In spite of the form of the oath, the Catholic priesthood in Ireland proved hostile. As early as 1858, a Catholic priest informed on a group of Fenians in Ireland, who were brought to trial. The oath was then amended to exclude the vow of secrecy; it was replaced by a vow of allegiance to the Irish Republic, which stated that the republic was "already virtually established," and thus turned rebellion into a form of patriotic resistance.

The American Civil War (1861–65) provided the revolutionary Irish-Americans with a training in military tactics and in the use of arms. It also gave the Fenians the hope that the English government's sympathy with the Confederate South would lead her into the war and thus create an opportunity for a successful rebellion in Ireland. The Fenians were able to operate in security on American soil because the Irish vote was an important factor in American politics. Feeling safe from persecution, they dropped most of their efforts at secrecy and held a public convention in Chicago in 1863. There, they called for the establishment of an Irish Republic; but this was only to be achieved after the invasion of Canada, and the establishment of an independent Canadian Republic. Three attempts were made by the Fenians to raise a revolt in Canada, the first in 1866; on each occasion, they were quickly dispersed. In 1867 they made attempts to take over military supplies held at Chester Castle in England and to start a rebellion in Ireland itself; but the risings were put down with ridiculous ease. The Fenians' activities ceased a few years later. Apart from the murder of a policeman and a few civilians, and the successful engineering of one prison escape, they had achieved nothing.

By operating publicly, the Fenians had lost all the advantages of secrecy. Any expatriate Irish-American who landed on Irish soil was an obvious target for British police. Both the United Irishmen and the Fenians recruited indiscriminately and were riddled with British informers, so that the British authorities were warned of most of their planned attempts at insurrection. From the point of view of a successful insurrection, a hard core of well-armed, expert revolutionaries, such as the Bolsheviks were to have, would have been more useful than a milling mass of emotional adherents, armed only with pikes and liable to melt away at the first charge of the militia or the police.

Each failure of a nationalist secret society tends to provoke the elimination of its moderate elements by the ruthless, on the grounds that measures have not been extreme enough. On the ashes of the Fenians in America rose the *Clan-na-Gael*, a secret organization with plans to assassinate Queen Victoria, sink British shipping with submarines, and blow up the House of Commons with nitroglycerin manufactured in a hidden factory near Birmingham. In the 1880s explosions actually occurred in the House of Commons and the Tower of London, and at London Bridge, but the terrorists injured nobody except themselves—a fate similar to that of the anarchist who attempted to blow up Greenwich Observatory in 1894.

The Clan-na-Gael's use of naked terror in England itself alienated many English supporters of Irish home rule. Parnell, the parliamentary leader of the Irish Home Rule party, refused to recognize terrorism, and the more moderate of the old Fenian supporters in Ireland joined him in his campaign for land reform through the Land League. The Irish bloc in the English

Right, the American Fenians under the leadership of William Roberts invade Canada (May 1866). A thousand men crossed the border and captured St. Armand, before being beaten back by Canadian troops. (Drawing from *Harper's Weekly*, 1866.)

Below, armed Fenians rescue two of their leaders, Colonel Kelly and Captain Deasey, from a prison van in Manchester (September 18, 1867). Arrested for his part in the abortive Irish rising, Kelly had already laid plans for the formation of the Clan-na-Gael. The rescue provoked severe reprisals, and three of the men involved were sentenced to death. (*Illustrated London News*, September 28, 1867.)

parliament helped to secure the disestablishment of the Anglican Church in Ireland (1869) and a Land Act to protect tenants (1881). Perhaps every open movement for political freedom needs its hidden militants to terrorize the powers-that-be, though its leaders must officially condemn the violence of those militants. In the opinion of one Irish historian, P. S. O'Hegarty, "in the last analysis it was the Whiteboys and the Ribbonmen and Captain Moonlight who made possible the respectable superstructure above them which condemned them."

In 1882, a group of ex-Fenian terrorists called the Invincibles murdered Lord Frederick Cavendish, the chief secretary for Ireland, and Thomas Burke, the undersecretary, in Phoenix Park, Dublin. Their action was particularly embarrassing to the Irish cause, because the Liberal party in England was then planning to introduce reforms in Ireland, and it seemed that independence might be gained by political means. Only when attempts to pass home rule bills for Ireland failed did the impetus again pass to the revolutionaries; an attempt to stem the rising tide of English culture by reviving the national language, Gaelic, culminated in the formation of the political revolutionary movement *Sinn Fein* (1905). In this case, as in the case of so many other 19th-century movements, attempts to preserve an eroding culture led to a new revolution.

It was Arthur Griffith (like Wolfe Tone, a pamphleteer and journalist) who turned the Gaelic League into a political movement. Sinn Fein meant "We Ourselves"; it called for Irish independence through action in Ireland by Irishmen. It sought to make the Irish conscious of their own traditions, their own language, culture, and separateness. The folly of the English House of Lords in delaying the third Home Rule Bill for Ireland in 1912 led to a surge of support for the Irish revolutionaries as against the Irish constitutionalists. It also gave the Protestants of Ulster, fearful of future Catholic domination, time to organize and arm. They found a determined leader in Sir Edward Carson, who declared in 1914: "I am not sorry for the armed drilling of those who are opposed to me in Ireland. I certainly have no right to complain of it; I started that with my own friends."

After the declaration of war in 1914, the Home Rule Bill was suspended for the duration. On Easter Monday 1916, the revived I.R.B. and two other revolutionary groups seized the General Post Office and other strategic points in Dublin, and held them for a week. They issued a proclamation declaring "the right of the people of Ireland to the ownership of Ireland, and to the unfettered control of Irish destinies, to be sovereign and indefeasible." Thus the movement for Irish independence was asserted in blood; this confirmed the

One of the many patriotic posters that were issued after the execution of the revolutionary leaders. It is entitled "The Birth of the Irish Republic, 1916."

Above, the ruins of the Dublin Post Office after the Easter Rising. Seized by 150 men under the I.R.B.'s commander-in-chief, Padhraic Henry Pearse, it became the rebel headquarters, and was gutted by fire.

Opposite page, six years later, after the signing of the Anglo-Irish treaty, a British officer hands over Dublin Castle to an officer of the Irish Free State Army and his band of recruits (January 1922).

Irish revolutionaries as the leaders of the Irish Catholics and strengthened their claims in the peace settlement after the war. The execution of 16 of the captured revolutionary leaders provided the movement with martyrs—the last ingredient necessary to end moderation and invoke a full-scale civil war. In a poem entitled *Sixteen Dead Men*, W. B. Yeats wrote:

O but we talked at large before
The sixteen men were shot,
But who can talk of give and take,
What should be and what not
While those dead men are loitering there
To stir the boiling pot?

After World War I, when the Treaty of Versailles failed to deal with Irish independence, a guerrilla war broke out in Ireland. This rapidly grew into a full-scale insurrection, for its Catholic leaders had widespread popular support. In 1921 the British prime minister Lloyd George recognized the Irish revolutionary cabinet, which held effective control of large areas in Southern Ireland. A treaty was signed to give Southern Ireland the status of a dominion and the name of the Irish Free State; Ulster was excluded, however, for the Irish Catholic guerrilla army had not established its control in the North. Ireland was split, as India was to be after World War II.

The Irish secret societies were in many ways a reflection of the other nationalist secret societies of the period. They began by pressing for constitutional reform within the laws of England; they ended by taking revolutionary action against the British army. They splintered apart into squabbling groups during the negotiations with England and after independence was won. (The Sinn Fein leader, de Valera, refused to recognize the treaty with England for many years, though he later became prime minister of Ireland.) They learned through many bitter failures the lessons of security, and learned them so successfully

that the role of the revived I.R.B. in the Easter Rising was not recognized for many years. And they succeeded in their long-term object—what Arthur Griffith defined as "making England take one hand away from Ireland's throat and the other out of Ireland's pocket."

The Irish societies, like the continental nationalist societies, had middle-class, educated leaders who capitalized on a tradition of agrarian lawlessness. But there was one important respect in which they did not follow the continental pattern: they never succeeded in influencing the city mob, which was usually hostile to them, if not in sympathy with the English. The nationalist secret societies of Europe, which fomented many insurrections in the 19th century, often relied on mass urban revolt. The British historian Sir Lewis Namier, in his acute examination of the causes of the European revolutions of 1848, found that the revolutionaries were almost exclusively middle-class intellectuals who capitalized on popular outbursts, many of which originated in the crowded slums of capital cities.

It was the French Revolution that set the pattern of the urban revolts. In the capital of France, conspirators plotted, rose to power, and were overthrown; as Paris went, so went the nation. The French revolutions before the time of Bonaparte proved that a small and determined body of men, such as the Jacobins, could seize power and hold on to it briefly by using their agents and armies to put down opposition at home and abroad. The so-called "Conspiracy of Equals," François Babeuf's failed rising on behalf of the *sansculottes* in 1796, ushered in the age of the professional revolutionary—of men like Filippo Buonarroti (1761–1837) and Auguste Blanqui (1805–1881). These men, in love with revolution, its preparation, and its ritual, made the small secret society an instrument of nationalism.

The policy of the urban revolutionary was clear-cut. He aimed to form a group of militants, to cause unease by terrorist activity, and to use the support of army officers of liberal sympathies. He would wait until famine or depression made the urban mob restive, then foment a riot, seize the strategic points of a

Three Frenchmen who made the secret society an instrument of national revolution. Far left, François "Gracchus" Babeuf (1760–97). Founder of the Society of Equals, he claimed that the French Revolution had failed. He organized the "Conspiracy of Equals" in 1796, but was arrested before the event and condemned to death. Left, Filippo Buonarroti (1761–1837). Exiled for his part in the Conspiracy of Equals, he recorded it in a book that became the bible of 19th-century revolutionaries. He was associated with Carbonarism, Freemasonry, and Mazzini's Young Italy. Right, Louis Auguste Blanqui (1805–81). Inspired by Babeuf, he founded the Society of the Seasons and a series of similar groups; he developed the technique of insurrection in the revolutions of 1839, 1848, and 1871.

city (such as parliament, palace, and newspaper offices), declare his group of revolutionaries to be the provisional government, and suppress any attempt at counter-revolution. The beauty of the method was that it needed few militants and little, if any, mass support. The professional revolutionaries generally regarded government as a sort of conspiracy of the rich against the people, who were supposed to be ignorant or passive. As self-appointed plotters for the poor, they sought to supplant the clique of the rich. After the revolution they would educate the people to understand that they, the revolutionaries, were indeed their leaders. It was Blanqui who coined the term "the dictatorship of the proletariat," in an attempt to justify the period following a successful revolution, when the professional revolutionaries, not yet having won the support of the nation, would dictate to the nation. The first of the Blanquists' failures as revolutionaries, in 1837, occurred because they assumed that they had the mass support of the French workers, though they had done little to secure it. They plotted in a void, and Blanqui himself was silly enough to divide his society of fellow conspirators into Years, Seasons, Months, Weeks, and Days, led by a man called Sunday.

Though its ritual was often ludicrous, the nationalist secret society was probably the most important agent of political change in the early 19th century; its effectiveness was unquestionable in times of disorder. In various countries, particularly Italy, the Masonic lodges had become the instruments of the political awakening of the middle classes. The most famous of the nationalist secret societies on the continent of Europe, that of the *Carbonari* of the early 19th century, was heavily influenced and penetrated by Freemasons. But the Carbonari, though they adopted much of the ritual of the older brotherhoods, were essentially a political organization dating from the period of Napoleonic rule in Italy. Their first lodges were founded in Capua between 1802 and 1810 by a group of republican officers in the French army who were hostile to the development of Bonapartism. The function of these early lodges was to stir up political opposition to the French, and to press for constitutional

guarantees; they made many recruits among Italian army officers, landowners, and officials. The Carbonari borrowed their name, and much of their ritual, from the mutual-aid societies of charcoal-burners that had flourished since the Middle Ages, and had been influenced by Freemasonry in the 18th century.

The initiation ceremony of the Carbonari was a hotchpotch of traditional rituals, with ordeals by blindfold and fire, confrontation by Cross and ax. Their oath of initiation was modeled on that of the Freemasons; with his hand resting on an ax, the initiate swore "upon this steel, the avenging instrument of the perjured, scrupulously to keep the secret of Carbonarism; and neither to write, engrave, or paint anything concerning it, without having obtained a written permission. I swear to help my Good Cousins in case of need, as much as in me lies, and not to attempt anything against the honour of their families. I consent, and wish, if I perjure myself, that my body may be cut in pieces, then burnt, and my ashes scattered to the wind, in order that my name be held up to the execration of the Good Cousins throughout the earth. . . ."

The oath of the Carbonari was not overtly political; it contained "not a word of the purpose," as Mazzini noted "with surprise and suspicion" when he was initiated into the society in 1827. But the Carbonari, being recruited from the ambitious middle classes, wanted political advancement for that social group. Their lodges spread from France to Spain, Italy, Greece, and even Russia; everywhere they represented the cause of liberalism against the Holy

Left, armed Carbonari on patrol (illustration from *Memoirs of the Secret Societies of the South of Italy*, 1821). Recruited largely among army officers and the police, the Carbonari raised revolts in Naples in 1820 and in Piedmont in 1821. In 1831 Metternich intervened to crush their attempt to seize the Papal States. Right, the arrest of two Carbonari in Lombardy (19th-century Italian painting).

Alliance set up to control Europe after the defeat of Napoleon in 1815. In a series of insurrections in 1820 and 1821, the Carbonari won constitutions in Spain and some of the Italian States, and independence for Greece. They were most effective where they recruited to their cause young army officers who were popular enough with the troops to be able to incite them to rebellion. The reactionary powers of Europe, however, soon put down the new constitutional governments, and, with the collapse of the last coup inspired by the Carbonari, the Decembrist rising against Nicholas I of Russia in 1825, the heyday of the middle-class, quasi-masonic secret society was over.

The social model of the Carbonari had been the constitutional regimes of England and the United States; though international in organization, they were nationalist in their aims. They never attracted mass support. But they did show that conspiracies of the rising middle classes against the old regimes of Europe could force concessions from reactionaries, if the army was disaffected. A successful pattern of conspiracy had been set, and it was imitated; in the revolutions of 1830, when mass support was forthcoming for risings in Paris, Belgium, Poland, Spain, and various parts of Germany, Italy, and Switzerland, the secret societies were no longer isolated groups of conspirators. Those who plotted to win concessions for the middle classes found themselves, almost willy-nilly, the leaders of nationalistic agitation. They became the leaders of the people, particularly where large areas speaking one language were split

Three early 19th-century paintings record the revolutionary fever of the age. Above, K. I. Kolman's painting of the Decembrist rising on the Senate Square in St. Petersburg, December 14, 1825. In an attempt to force constitutional reform, secret-society members among the troops mutinied, and refused to take the oath of allegiance to the new tsar, Nicholas I. Above right, a painting by Adolph Menzel depicts the funeral of the men who fought for a liberal constitution in the Berlin rising of March 1848. Left, Meissonier's painting *La Barricade* illustrates the fate of Frenchmen who upheld the tradition of 1848 and resisted Louis Napoleon's coup d'état (December 2, 1851).

up into a series of petty principalities, as in Germany and Italy, or where many different language-groups were forced together in an uneasy union, as in the Austro-Hungarian Empire. The result of the revolutions of 1830 was the creation of one new European nation, Belgium, and of several liberal constitutions on the continent of Europe. Perhaps their most significant aftereffect was to split the moderates in certain countries, such as France, from the radicals. Once the middle class of a principality, a nation, or an empire had won a share in the legislative power, it showed as much zeal in suppressing radical secret societies as any aristocratic regime.

In 1848, when revolution spread through Europe like a contagion until hardly a capital was free from mob violence and hardly a suppressed nation failed to revolt, the divergent social aims of the emerging nationalist leaders became only too clear. As in Ireland, those who had plotted for a constitution were suspicious of those who had plotted for separatism, and both were afraid of those who had plotted for a social revolution. In such dangerous and anarchic situations authoritarian regimes can often regain control, because they represent the only known stability. There are usually at least two revolutions in any given revolutionary situation: the first displaces the established regime, the second decides which of the revolutionary groups shall dominate the others and form the new government. The French revolution of 1830 put middle-class

Right, Russian anarchist Mikhail Bakunin (1814–76). A member of the International, he formed his own International Social Democratic Alliance; he inspired anarchists throughout Europe, particularly in Spain. Above, Ben Shahn's portrait of Bartolomeo Vanzetti and Nicola Sacco, the Italo-American anarchists executed for first-degree murder in 1927. Widespread conviction that the men were innocent made them martyrs in the anarchist cause.

liberals in power. Once they held the reins of government they turned on the professional revolutionaries and the Paris workers who had supported them. They withdrew concessions made to the workingmen and in 1834, when these rose in a second rebellion, slaughtered several hundred of them on the barricades. Blanqui, the hero of these new insurrectionaries, was already in jail. In other capitals of Europe, too, urban mobs found that the liberal nationalists they had helped into power turned on their own supporters for fear of a second revolution. In the last resort, the middle classes preferred any stable regime, even an authoritarian one, to a regime that was liberal but weak.

The new leaders of the middle classes came from the constitutional and cultural clubs. Various political clubs rose briefly to power in 1848, but religious divisions, allied with the irrational hatreds of nationalism, brought them into conflict and dissipated their success. Teutonic peoples and Slavs could no more agree than Irish Catholics and Orangemen; the result was that both the Austro-Hungarian Empire and British control of Ireland were able to survive into the 20th century. The early 19th century was the period of the revolutionary middle class, which often had to go underground and form secret societies to win concessions from aristocratic regimes and to gain representation in a parliament. But after 1848, the nationalist secret society in Europe changed its nature. Once the wealthier middle classes were accepted within the framework of aristocratic European government, the secret society became a focus of petty bourgeois or proletarian discontent. Thus conspirators like Blanqui, who spent most of his life plotting or in prison, eventually succeeded in winning the mass support of the Paris workers. Blanqui's League of the Just, and the League of Outlaws (a secret society of German workingmen in Paris), were the forerunners of the Communist League of Marx and Engels, which dropped the ritual paraphernalia of the older brotherhoods—what Marx described as "superstitious authoritarianism."

In some respects, the political secret society after 1848 was more international than national. Marx and Engels, the German-born authors of the *Communist Manifesto*, preached a class war across national frontiers, though every Communist insurrection was actually carried out within the framework of a single nation. The history of the Bolshevik movement, indeed, is a history of *Russian* conspirators, who imitated the Blanquists in their small, close-knit band of trained revolutionaries, the Carbonari in their appeal to officers in the armed forces, the Irish rebels in their exploitation of agrarian disaffection, and the Paris Communes in their use of the urban mob. The Bolsheviks were the most successful national secret society of all time, despite their claim to represent the working classes everywhere. The Communist Revolution failed to spread after the Bolshevik success in Russia only because the Bolsheviks were Russians before they were internationalists. The middle-class conspirators of 1848 had given up international solidarity for national squabbling; the Bolsheviks gave up international revolution for national strength.

The most purely revolutionary of the secret societies of the late 19th century were the *anarchists*. They also were international by declaration, but national by procedure. The anarchists were believers in revolutionary action in the direct tradition of Babeuf, Buonarroti, and Blanqui. As their first objective was the overthrow of governments, they were forced to work on nationalistic lines. The early anarchist philosopher Mikhail Bakunin (1814–76) shared Babeuf's belief that the French Revolution "was only the forerunner of another revolution, greater and more solemn, which would be the last." Neither realized that the French Revolution had loosed nationalism on the world rather than liberty, equality, or fraternity.

The anarchists held that the final revolution would be brought about by a handful of dedicated revolutionaries, who would overthrow governments until all national states withered away. Their method was to be direct action; self-styled anarchists murdered the Tsar Alexander II of Russia in 1881; others murdered President Carnot of France in 1894, King Humbert of Italy in 1900, and the American president William McKinley in 1901, emulating the old Assassins in their dedication to the slaying of rulers. European states, however, did not wither away after the assassination of their leaders as Arab kingdoms had done; instead of dissolving their apparatus of government, they merely replaced their rulers. Before his execution in 1894, one French

The title pages of Czech, French, and Spanish editions of the notorious anti-Semitic forgery, the "Protocols of the Elders of Zion." A prime example of the theory of conspiracy, the work outlines a fantastic scheme for world domination, which it attributes to a secret Jewish "government" supported by Freemasons and liberals. First published in Russia about 1902, the Protocols were introduced into western Europe by émigrés. They were widely credited until 1921, when they were found to be a version of a French satire on Louis Napoleon—Joly's *Dialogues aux enfers entre Machiavel et Montesquieu* (1865). Reissued as Nazi propaganda in the 1930s, the Protocols helped to inflame the anti-Semitism that claimed the lives of six million Jews during World War II. Though discredited, they remain in circulation in many countries and are still being reprinted today.

anarchist, Émile Henry, claimed that anarchism could never be destroyed because "its roots are too deep: it is born at the heart of a corrupt society which is falling to pieces; it is a violent reaction against the established order." But nationalism proved too strong for the anarchists, despite their fanatical secrecy and terror tactics, and anarchism was eventually destroyed as a political force. To be successful, a political secret society must seek to control the established order, not to destroy it. Even the Bolsheviks had to reemploy the old Tsarist bureaucracy because it was the only group with experience in operating the machinery of a large state.

The theory of conspiracy, as the American historian Richard Hofstadter has pointed out, lies at the grass roots of democratic society. The people must always search out villains, real or mythical, to explain their ills, for democracy, by its very nature, can hardly oppress. Conspiracies may be attributed to any secret group, to bankers, armaments manufacturers, Jews, Catholics, Masons, heretics, anarchists, or Communists. Once the group is named, it is believed to have power. When a real conspiracy against the government is named and feared by government supporters, it will win the support of those who regard the government itself as a conspiracy against the people. But it must prove its power by committing acts of terrorism or martyrdom if it is to gain the publicity necessary for segments of the people to accept its leadership

in a future insurrection. (The success of the Bolsheviks, for example, was due to their acceptance as revolutionary leaders by the workers of Moscow and Petrograd after their exploits in the revolution of 1905.) If its insurrection is successful, the revolutionary secret society becomes the government. Only the anarchists, who declare all governments to be secret conspiracies against the people, are consistent in remaining a revolutionary secret society, permanently out of power; for they cannot, by their own declarations, form any national government whatsoever.

The political secret societies of the 20th century in Europe have fed more on hatred and dreams of conquest than on real oppression. In Asia, the Middle East, and Africa, nationalist societies have run through the 19th-century European pattern of a middle-class revolt against imperialism, backed by mass popular support; but in Europe theories of persecution and racism have muddied their drives. The Italian Fascists, who were members of a secret paramilitary conspiracy under Mussolini before they became the rulers of Italy and the agents of Italian imperialism, preached a virulent nationalism that proved attractive to the Italian masses. The Nazis emulated their example; they appealed as an open nationalist group to the dark springs of anti-Semitism and Aryan superiority. Though their leaders were known, their conspiracy to take over the state remained secret.

Left, another example of Nazi propaganda, from a German children's book of the 1930s. Idealized Nazi youths embody the myth of Aryan superiority. (Illustration from *Trust no Fox on the Green Heath and No Jew upon his Oath*, Nuremberg, 1936.)

Opposite page, in November 1937, after the discovery of the Cagoule's arms dump in Paris, police officers confiscate stockpiles of weapons and ammunitions.

Yet the Fascists in both Italy and Germany rose to power openly, through the weakness of the democratic parliamentary system. They used terror tactics, though not to the extent of guerrilla warfare; but they could not have seized power without widespread popular support. The nationalist secret societies that sapped the will of France to resist Fascist attack in 1940 were more traditional in form. The French right wing organized itself on the Italian and German model for the overthrow of the Third Republic, which had the support of a majority of Frenchmen. It played through the classic pattern of the nationalist secret society in the 20th century, which attracts support from traditionalists of all classes who fear an international conspiracy, whether of Jewish capitalists or of proletarian Communists.

The chief propaganda organ of the French right wing was Léon Daudet's *L'Action Française*. From 1908 to 1944, this newspaper concentrated on smearing republican or left-wing politicians and officials in order to sap the French people's faith in democracy as a system. In his columns Daudet denounced government ministers as self-confessed sex maniacs, debauchees of the lowest order, tearful pansies, drawing-room hermaphrodites, syphilitics, prostitutes, and bits of brothel refuse. He accused the police and the civil service of conspiring with politicians to suppress the French right wing. In 1935, under

the filthy smoke screen of Daudet's propaganda against what he called "democrashit," dissident members of *L'Action Française* formed a paramilitary secret organization called the Secret Organization of National Revolutionary Action. This organization was popularly known as *la Cagoule* ("the Hood") because in some of its provincial branches members wore hoods to conceal their identity, like Klansmen.

The Cagoule, which drew much of its support from existing secret societies, and had its own oath of secrecy, was organized on military lines. It aimed to recruit 120,000 members—about the strength of the Bolsheviks in the Russian Revolution. It had execution squads for dealing with traitors and enemies; its intelligence branch was told: "the sense of duty and the realization of the circumstances must be so exalted that every man must consider himself free of every moral and social obligation when engaged in the execution of a mission. He must give himself up to his job without reserve, any idea of pardon for a failure must be ruled out, for a man who enters such a team does not leave it." The Cagoule imported arms, including machine guns and dynamite, from Germany, Belgium, Spain, and Italy. In September 1937, it engineered two explosions in the offices of industrial employers' associations in the Étoile district of Paris, in the hope of driving big business to support the right wing.

But the arrest of the Cagoule's leader, Eugène Deloncle, in October, led to the discovery of its arms dumps, and the confiscation of its weapons and munitions.

The right wing, now effectively disarmed, had to wait until the outbreak of World War II to spread defeatism in the French army, to welcome Hitler and Mussolini, and Pétain with his Vichy government. The rightists, of course, were a power in both northern France and Vichy during the war years, though it was curious that a nationalist group like the Cagoule should have accepted German domination of France. As a satirist in *Le Canard Enchaîné* had commented in 1936: "There are people who are astonished to hear our supernationalists who want, so they say, France for the French, howling: 'Long live Mussolini! Long live Hitler!' This attitude is, however, traditional. The ultra-patriots, for the last century and a half, have always preferred foreign governments to their own."

Conspiracy theories still flourish in France. Perhaps the most interesting and modern of these, which has displaced the forged "Protocols of the Elders of Zion" and the theory of the international conspiracy of Jewish bankers, is the theory that a number of politicians in power belong to a secret society called the *Synarchie*, which aims to take control of France (and eventually, of the world) by manipulating bureaucratic and technocratic levers. The conspiracy began, it is said, in 1931, when an official called Jean Coutrot formed a group called "X-Crise," in order to bring about a "synarchic" order, in which a perfect collective life could be achieved by the smooth exercise of power—a sort of pacific national socialism based on hierarchy and the specialization of function. The supposed conspirators were dubbed "technocrats" because, like Coutrot, all were distinguished ex-students of the *École polytechnique* in Paris. This theory may owe less to fact than to the popular fear of faceless bureaucrats. In this age of automation, it is hardly surprising that technocrats should inspire more fear than anarchists.

The perfect example of a nationalist secret society taking over the reins of government by pacific means and putting its program into action is supplied by the *Afrikaner-Broederbond.* This society grew up among Afrikaners of Dutch descent after they had lost their independence in the Anglo-Boer War (1899–1902), and had become part of a united South Africa. They were, numerically, a minority of the white population; but they believed they might be a majority in the future. The Broederbond was founded in 1918 as an Afrikaans cultural society; by 1934 it had become a nationalist splinter group within the ruling elite. It aimed to break away from the English-speaking South Africans and the Commonwealth. Its declared solution for South Africa's ills was "that the Afrikaner-Broederbond should rule South Africa." Nevertheless, under the leadership of the ex-Boer General Smuts, who was determined to keep South Africa united and to have peace between the English-speaking whites and the Afrikaners, South Africa remained a dominion within the British Commonwealth and fought for Britain in both world wars.

An ox-wagon, symbolic of Afrikaner nationalism, enters Pretoria during the reenactment of the Great Trek in 1938. Backed by the Broederbond, the celebrations rallied the forces of the Afrikaner minority. They inspired Nazi notions of racial supremacy, and threats of revolt against Smuts's government.

In 1938, the Broederbond was a driving force behind the symbolic reenactment of the Great Trek of 1838, by which Cape Afrikaners had moved north and escaped British rule. This centenary celebration inflamed the forces of Afrikaner nationalism, which began to identify themselves with Nazi racism. Dr. Malan (a founder-member of the Broederbond and prime minister from 1948 to 1954) was pushed by the Bond into praising a new paramilitary Afrikaner organization called the *Ossewabrandwag*, which claimed as many as 400,000 adherents—more than the total strength of the South African armed forces. In 1940, when the Nazis appeared to have won the war in Europe, and Britain and its Commonwealth stood alone, the Afrikaner nationalists threatened to rebel with the Ossewabrandwag. But with the entry of the United States into the war against Germany and the German defeats in Africa and Russia, the Broederbond turned against the Ossewabrandwag. It was canny enough to see that its chances of taking over democratically, as a nationalist party, from the aging Smuts were far better than its chances of leading a successful pro-Nazi putsch.

The motives of the Bond were well analyzed by Alan Paton, perhaps its most famous opponent today: "What was the Broederbond? A clique seeking power? Agitators playing on grievances? Afrikaner zealots with one overriding and patriotic purpose? Undoubtedly it was all these. Whatever else it may have been, it drew much of its power from the resentments of the 'Century of Wrong.' Its relation to Afrikaner Nationalism was vital yet obscure. Not every member of the Nationalist Party was a member of the Broederbond, and some Nationalists . . . condemned it root and branch. Of course both the Broederbond and the Nationalist Party kept wounds open and played on grievances of the past, but who can doubt that the grievances were there?"

Smuts thought the Broederbond so subversive that in 1944 he forbade civil servants to join it. He feared its tactics of infiltration and saw that it might well take over the levers of government, both secretly within the bureaucracy and overtly through the Nationalist party at the polls. Smuts's ban, however, did not halt the gradually increasing power of the Bond, and in 1948, when the Nationalist party came to power through the polls with a seemingly permanent majority in favor of its policy of *apartheid*, the Bond achieved its object. Though the Bond remains a secret society, the official policy of extreme nationalism and apartheid is its policy; promotion within the civil service and the judiciary and in the Nationalist party depends largely on faithful membership of the Bond. A one-man commission appointed by the South African government in 1964 to enquire into secret organizations found the Bond "not guilty of any conduct mentioned in the Commission's terms of reference"; these included attempts to dominate the prime minister, treason, nepotism, and subversion of the state and of morals. The commission's report, which put the Bond's membership at 6768, described its organization into 473 local divisions, each of which had between 5 and 50 members. It found that membership was restricted to white Afrikaans-speaking Protestant males over the age of 25; men who were Freemasons were not eligible. At a "simple but dignified" initiation ceremony, the candidate pledged not to divulge his membership or that of others, and not to disclose anything he might learn from the Bond's documents, discussions, decisions, and activities. He was told that the members of the Bond were "mission-conscious Afrikaners who desire to represent and serve the best that is in our nation." In fact, the Afrikaners led by the Broederbond represent one of the most fiercely anti-egalitarian secret societies of all time, though they remain a minority group. They achieved power by peaceful means, but they will fight to the death against any attempt by the black majority to achieve equality with the white nationalist minority.

Many of the techniques of the modern political secret society were formed in the French Revolution, which loosed nationalism on the world. Today, nationalism continues to sweep through the countries of the world, and fuel is added to its fires by the dead wood of racism. Wherever any minority rules a

Negro rebels in Zanzibar salute their leader, Kenyan-born "field marshal" John Okello, after the success of their armed conspiracy against Arab rule (1964).

majority of another race or creed, a nationalist secret society representing that majority plots to gain power. Its means are legal or illegal, depending on the chances of revolution. Thus in 1964 the Negroes in Zanzibar succeeded in ousting their Arab rulers in a nationalist and racist revolt by the majority, sparked off by a secret society trained in revolutionary techniques; but groups with as small a hope of success as the Scottish or Welsh nationalists have done little more than put candidates forward at elections. Whenever a minority fears the oppression of a majority within a given country, it also may plot for independence through secession or partition; both the Kurds of Iraq and the Nagas of India, for example, are led by nationalist secret societies in their respective fights for independence. There is no limit to the demands of any group for self-rule, once it considers itself to be a nation. And any group can be persuaded that it is a nation, separate and indivisible, by the propaganda of a small political society prepared to lead it to independence. In a world split into rival areas of influence—American, Russian, and Chinese, and to a lesser extent, British, French, Egyptian, and Cuban—would-be political conspirators have little difficulty in obtaining supplies of money and arms from foreign powers. Mass disaffection in a particular area or group can be exploited by trained agitators to produce a revolt, and to enable them to seize power. Nationalism is still the cry that rallies the mass of the people to the side of the plotters; until its fires are spent, the political secret society will remain a major instrument of change.

9 Chinese secret societies

In June 1900, the entire foreign community in Peking was under siege. Shocked by the murder of Westerners, and the destruction of their property, more than 3000 people (the foreign ministers, their families, missionaries, and their Chinese converts) had taken refuge in the Western legations from the troops of the imperial Manchu government. The siege had been triggered off by the terror tactics of the Boxers (p. 227)—the name given to an anti-foreign secret society that was at first denounced by the Manchu government, and later incorporated into the imperial army. The Boxer Rising, and the siege at Peking, ended after 55 days with the arrival of British, Russian, American, and French relief forces, and the flight of the Manchu court.

The motives of the Manchu government baffled Western observers at the time, and confirmed their view of China as a chronically unstable country with a maze of criminal organizations and a government that belonged to the Dark Ages. They came to regard the Chinese as sinister "Celestials" with a kind of congenital propensity for organizing secret activities—a view that might have been corrected by a glance at history, and some understanding of traditional Chinese social structure.

The Boxer Rising had been preceded by a long series of aggressions against China by the Western powers. Britain's easy victory in the first Opium War (1842) had sparked off a competitive scramble for territory that included

Kwan-Ti, ancient Chinese god of war, wealth, and literature, and patron deity of oath-taking associations (detail from a Buddhist wall painting of the Ming dynasty, 1368-1644). The embodiment of loyalty and brotherhood, he holds the "sword of righteousness"—a symbol of China's traditional resistance to foreign rule.

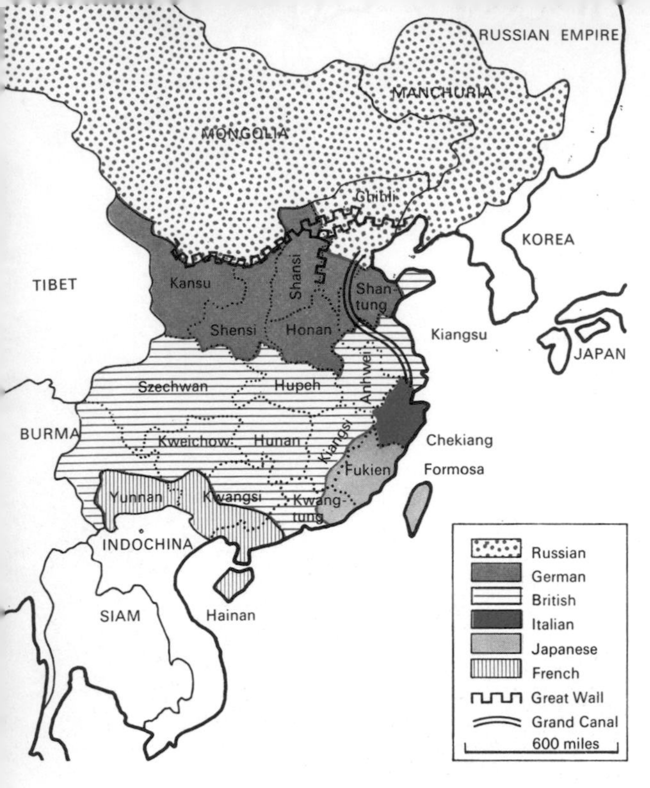

Left, map based on a document of 1900 shows foreign "spheres of interest" in imperial China—areas in which five European powers and Japan had acquired rights to finance the development of mines and railways, in the conviction that China would be formally partitioned between them. Right, a typical European cartoon of the period depicts their armies as lilliputian heroes besieging the Chinese "giant" behind the Great Wall. The situation was dramatically reversed by the Boxers, whose fierce campaign against foreigners culminated in the siege of the Western community in Peking. Far right, British marines behind their barricade in Peking's Mongolian market (photograph of 1900).

the annexation of almost all China's outlying dependencies, the outright seizure of land in China proper, and a succession of so-called treaties under which all the European powers in turn, together with the United States and Japan, had gained special commercial and political privileges. Some of these powers had also exacted privileges for their missionaries, who obtained the right to reside in China and yet remain under the jurisdiction of their countries of origin. One of the latest and most flagrant acts of aggression was that by which the Germans had gained control of the post of Tsingtao in Shantung Province in 1897. The first recorded appearance of the Boxers was in the same province early in the next year.

The Boxers were the first of the modern anti-foreign movements that were to outlast the fall of the imperial system and continue far into the 20th century. But organizationally they represented a much older tradition. The soil of China, and indeed of all places where large numbers of Chinese have settled, has traditionally always been particularly fertile for the development of unofficial associations. The secret societies are but one example of the enormous number of such organizations (benevolent associations, credit and loan associations, trade and craft associations, guild-like associations, "family" associations, recreational and learned associations) that have flourished among the Chinese for the last two thousand years. But there is nothing very strange in this; in Western Europe, too, such matters as trading and manufacturing regulations, road-making, many aspects of public order, education, and social welfare measures were for centuries the province of private, voluntary associations. Indeed, when Europe and China first made contact they still had

much in common, China differing mainly in being far larger than any single Western state, far more populous, and (until the end of the 18th century) considerably more advanced in most forms of technology.

Up to that time, in fact, the Chinese social system was rather more complex than contemporary Western social systems, government more rationalized, and associational development greater. It was only with the Industrial Revolution that Europe began to draw ahead technologically, militarily, and economically, to develop more rational methods of government, and to extend the sphere of official administration into what had hitherto been private fields. Meanwhile China retained her traditional social system and philosophy of government, which became increasingly ineffective in the face of 19th-century change and gave increasing scope to the development of private associations, including secret societies. Thus the period in which the West for the first time began to draw ahead coincided with the period in which China appeared to stagnate or even to go backward—a fact that goes far to explain the mutual misunderstandings and antagonisms that have bedeviled the relations between the two regions. Moreover, the West did not scruple to take political and economic advantage of the material superiority it enjoyed at that particular time.

But recent history alone does not suffice to explain the strength of China's secret societies, whose origins lie far back in time and whose success and survival depended upon the special conditions of China's traditional constitution and social structure, particularly the imperial monarchy, the bureaucracy, and the traditional religious organizations.

Chinese tradition places the beginning of the monarchy in the third millennium B.C., but the imperial system proper dates from the third century B.C. This period saw the first unification of the state under the Ch'in dynasty (255-206 B.C.) and its centralization under the Western Han dynasty (202 B.C.-A.D. 9). In theory, the monarch was an absolute ruler, the sole source of authority, and the only rightful controller of all legislative, executive, and judicial powers. As the "Son of Heaven" he could do no wrong. At the same time, according to the doctrines of Confucius, he was expected to set the people a perfect moral example, and to gain their confidence by his benevolence, righteousness, and virtue. A ruler who failed in these duties was said to forfeit the "mandate of Heaven"; it was the duty of the people to resist and even depose him.

The idea of imperial righteousness was so closely connected with beliefs about the structure of the universe as a whole that natural calamities (such as floods) or portents (such as comets) were held to indicate that the emperor had failed in his duties, and they alone were sometimes regarded as sufficient cause for rebellion. It is hardly surprising that the period that saw the first development of this political theory should also have seen the first recorded uprising of a secret society.

In A.D. 9 the throne of China was seized by an usurper called Wang Mang, who introduced radical reforms in taxation, usury, commerce, and the ownership of land. These policies provoked considerable popular antagonism, and a secret society, called the *Red Eyebrows* after the makeup worn by its members in battle, declared itself entirely devoted to the cause of overthrowing the usurper. The Red Eyebrows, who arose in what is now Shantung Province, seem to have played an important part in the revolt that led to the assassination of Wang Mang, and the foundation of the Eastern, or Later, Han dynasty in A.D. 25. But after this success the Red Eyebrows continued to behave like marauding bandits, and eventually had to be suppressed. This was achieved by a simple trick: the imperial soldiers also painted their eyebrows red, and in the ensuing confusion the real Red Eyebrows were completely routed.

In practice, of course, it was not possible for the emperor to rule so enormous a country as China personally. The two Han dynasties marked the beginning of rule through a nationwide bureaucracy of officials who, though answerable to the emperor, acted mostly on their own initiative. Despite rebellions, periods of governmental breakdown, and various reform movements, the bureaucratic system survived into the 20th century. Two aspects of that system—its method of recruitment and the extent of its control—are particularly relevant to the development of the secret societies.

Civil servants were recruited through a system of public written examinations, which were theoretically open to everyone, regardless of class. Naturally, not everyone who entered the examinations passed, and this meant that there was always a large number of men, well educated in the literary sense, who could not find employment in the civil or military services. In times when the imperial power was weak or corrupt, such men might well be tempted to join the peasants in opposition to the government; secret societies of rebels were also likely to benefit from their leadership.

The bureaucracy did not penetrate to the villages; its lowest offices (the "yamen") were situated in market towns. Indeed, it was believed that the government should not be concerned with the regulation of people's everyday lives. Partly because of this belief, and partly because communications were slow, the greater part of ordinary people's activities, which were centered on the villages, fell outside the central government's control. Here lay the opportunity and the need for the growth of private associations. Here too lay the chance for the successful organization of subversion and crime, in societies that would, of necessity, be secret.

Any organization that defies constituted authority depends for its survival on the loyalty of its members, who are particularly vulnerable to denunciation. The use of ritual is one of the most potent methods of maintaining group solidarity and individual loyalty, for ritual has the capacity of marking participants off from the ordinary world and emphasizing their mutual identification. This function is all the more effective when (as in the case of the best-known

TABLE OF DYNASTIES

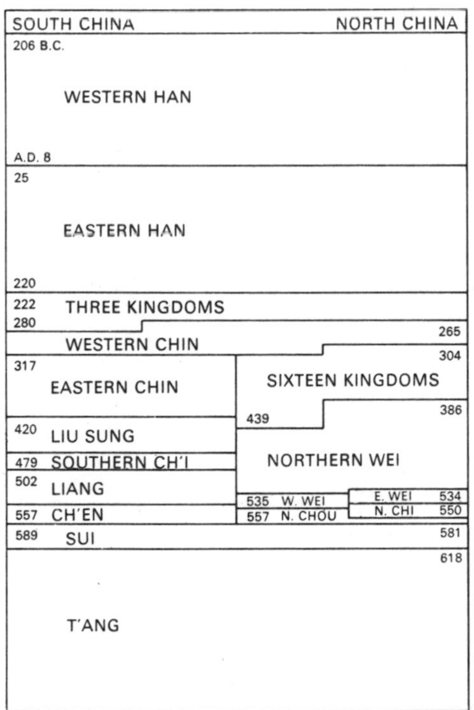

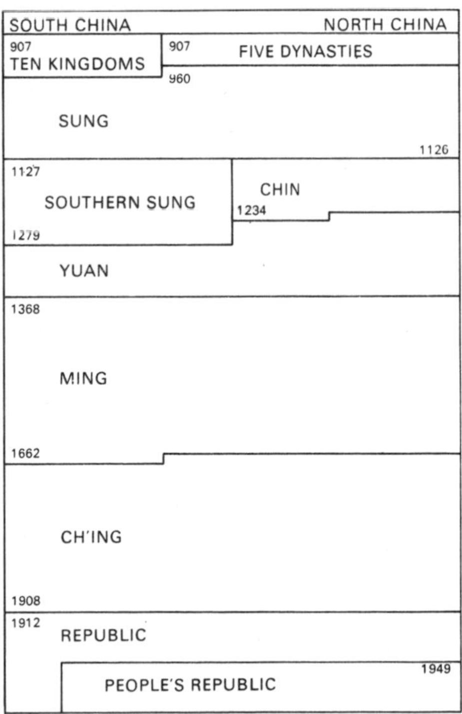

Chinese secret societies) the ceremony takes the form of a fully fledged rite in which the whole of the supernatural world is believed to be involved. The particular forms of ritual that are used by Chinese secret societies depend on two of the three strands of religious thinking that have existed side by side in the society at large: Taoism, Buddhism, and the series of rites and beliefs popularly summed up as Confucianism. The coexistence of these different religious traditions has provided the secret societies with a particularly rich field for symbolism; most of them have drawn on Taoism (a philosophical system founded by Lao-tzu in the 6th century B.C., and associated with alchemy and shamanistic magic) and Buddhism (first introduced into China from India at the close of the Later Han dynasty, but not widely disseminated for several centuries). Confucianism, being the philosophical and ritual basis of the official imperial regime, could hardly provide the ritual foundation for subversion and crime. But both Taoism and Buddhism, from their earliest days, have periodically been forced underground to avoid government persecution. Thus from time to time certain of their sects have had to take on the character of secret societies.

The Later Han rulers had the greatest difficulty in maintaining their supremacy, partly because the older states still clung to their traditional independence. This was a turbulent period, which saw the rise of other groups of rebels such as the Copper Horses and the Iron Shins. These movements may have been associated with Taoism, whose priests were often on bad terms with the government.

About A.D. 170 there arose in northeastern China a leader called Chang Chüeh, who is believed to have been closely related to the hereditary Taoist leaders. Chang Chüeh, whose followers regarded him as a god, claimed supernatural powers and the gift of healing. He rapidly increased his following until, in A.D. 184, it was strong enough for open rebellion. Wearing yellow headbands (which earned them the name of *Yellow Turbans*) an immense number of the rebels, led by no less than 36 "generals," marched and struck so rapidly that in a single month they had subdued most of north China. Both the Red Eyebrows, who helped restore the Han dynasty, and the Yellow Turbans, whose conquests helped to fragment its empire, may be regarded as forerunners of the notorious 19th-century secret societies in their mixture of religion, crime, and political disaffection. That same mixture was to appear over and over again in the long history of imperial China; so also was the pattern according to which the leaders of successful rebellions first made use of, then repudiated, secret society help.

In the gravely unsettled period that followed the Yellow Turban rebellion, there emerged three popular leaders who were to become national heroes. Many of the best loved stories of Chinese tradition, drama, and literature, concern these three leaders—Kwan Yu, Liu Pei, and Chang Fei, who on one occasion swore a famous oath of blood brotherhood in a peach garden. The

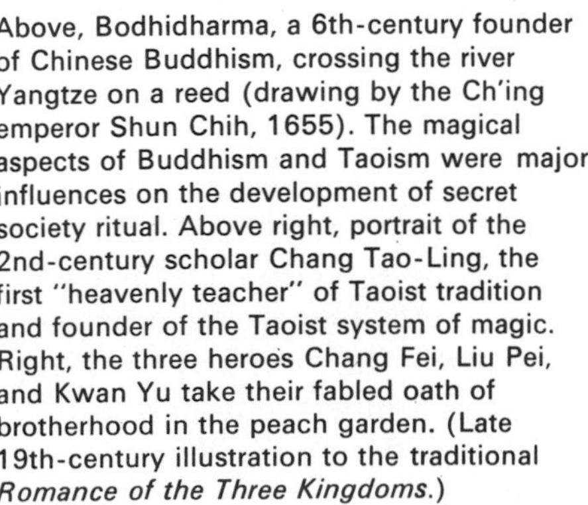

Above, Bodhidharma, a 6th-century founder of Chinese Buddhism, crossing the river Yangtze on a reed (drawing by the Ch'ing emperor Shun Chih, 1655). The magical aspects of Buddhism and Taoism were major influences on the development of secret society ritual. Above right, portrait of the 2nd-century scholar Chang Tao-Ling, the first "heavenly teacher" of Taoist tradition and founder of the Taoist system of magic. Right, the three heroes Chang Fei, Liu Pei, and Kwan Yu take their fabled oath of brotherhood in the peach garden. (Late 19th-century illustration to the traditional *Romance of the Three Kingdoms*.)

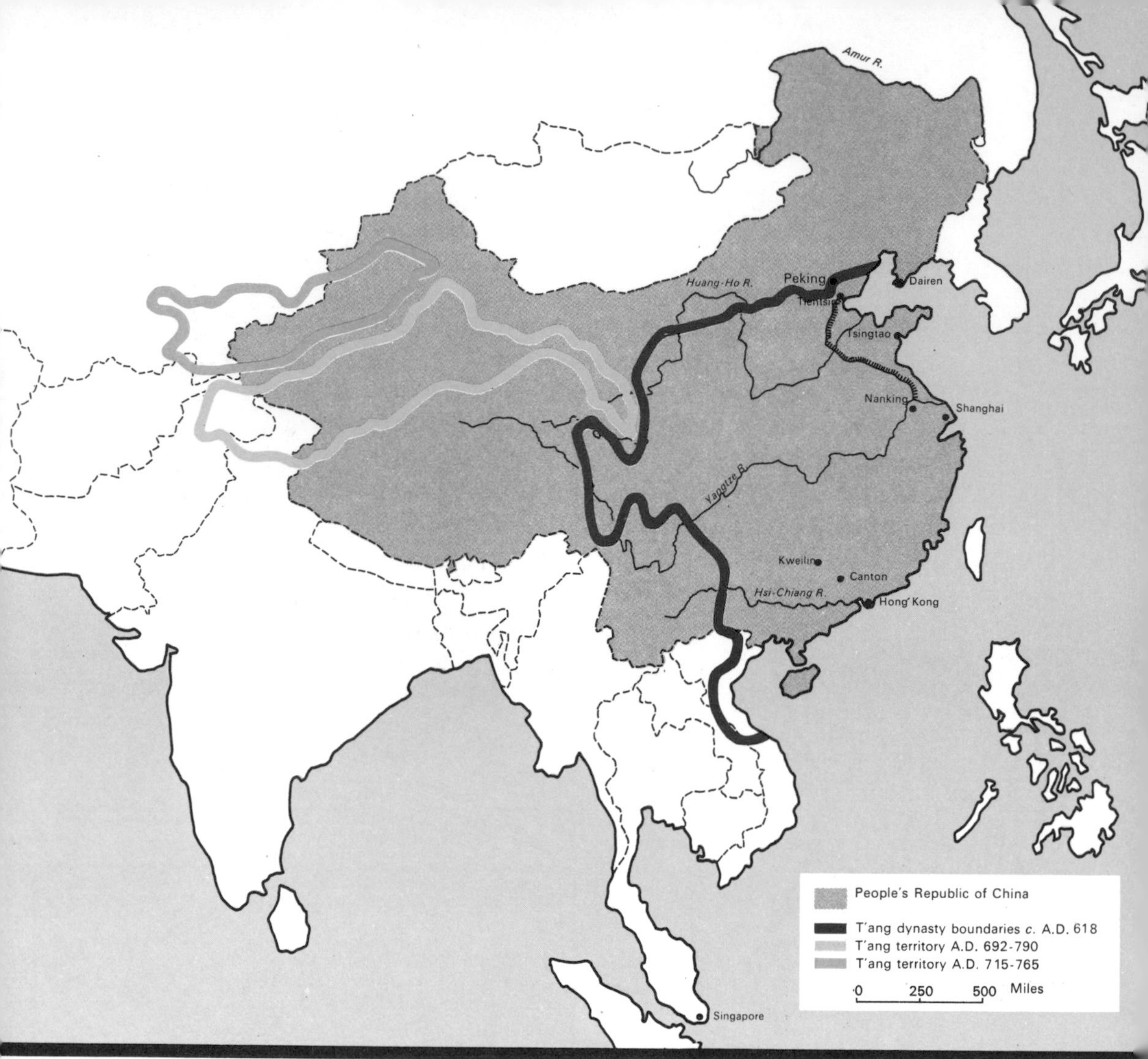

secret societies took these heroes for their own; Kwan Yu, later deified as Kwan Ti, became both the god of war and the patron god of all brotherhoods, while the "peach-garden oath" became an important feature of the initiation rituals of many secret societies.

After the breakdown of the Han empire in A.D. 220, the territory that had once been unified China was split up into the Three Kingdoms of Wei (in the north), Wu (in the southeast), and Shu (in the southwest), founded by Liu Pei, who was of Han descent. The reunification of China under the short-lived Sui dynasty in A.D. 589 was followed by the great T'ang dynasty (A.D. 618-907). In the T'ang period the boundaries of the country were extended to the west, so that China covered an area almost as great as it does today. This period saw the greatest flowering of Chinese Buddhist culture, despite three officially inspired persecutions. It was during these persecutions that Buddhism first developed its own underground organization. Secret religious sects are common features in most kinds of human society, but from this time onward they became particularly prevalent in China. At the same time, the rituals of most Chinese secret societies took on a strong Buddhist flavor, which they have retained to this day.

The three centuries of T'ang rule were followed by the Sung dynasty (A.D. 960-1280), at the close of which China fell completely under foreign domination for the first time. The Sung emperors, who had already lost the territory north of the Yangtze River, were finally overrun by the Mongols under Kublai Khan, who declared himself emperor of all China, and founded the Mongol, or Yüan, dynasty. Chinese revolts were widespread, many of them originating from old Sung strongholds in the south and southeast. At first there was little coordination, simply a series of spontaneous movements against the hated foreigners. One of the most successful was a movement of Buddhist origin known as the *White Lotus Society*, whose leader claimed to be of Sung descent. The members of this society were sometimes known as the Red Turban Rebels, because they wore red headbands in their battles against the Mongols. The White Lotus Society of this period, like the other rebel associations, depended for its success on strong leadership and the unswerving loyalty of its members, and was of necessity secret.

The original White Lotus Society is said to have been founded about A.D. 376 for the purpose of meditating upon and invoking the name of Amitabha Buddha, or the Buddha of the "Pure Land" to which worshipers might obtain entrance by their devotions. Zendo, the founder of one of the chief Buddhist sects of Japan, is said to have adopted the society's doctrine about A.D. 634. The society was severely attacked in the persecutions initiated by some of the T'ang emperors, and this experience may have contributed toward its later emergence as a political movement.

In 1344, a rebel leader called Han Shan-Tung, whose grandfather had been closely associated with the White Lotus, proclaimed the near advent of Maitreya, the "Buddha of the Future," and attracted many followers to the society. His recruiting campaign was greatly helped by the appearance of an omen presaging the downfall of the dynasty—one of the many that have appeared at appropriate moments in Chinese history. At this time, one of the common pastimes among children in the central provinces of Honan and Hupeh was a singing game with the words:

"When stirs the one-eyed man of stone,
This dynasty will be o'erthrown."

In that very year, workmen engaged in the perennial task of repairing the banks of the Yellow River turned up a stone image of a one-eyed man. The incident, or perhaps simply the rumor of it, provoked intense excitement. Multitudes of people joined the White Lotus, including four prominent rebel leaders. Their rebellion spread rapidly through central China, though Han Shan-Tung himself was killed at an early stage. The White Lotus and other rebel groups, greatly helped by the exploits of Fang Kuo-Chen (a famous sea captain) and other privateers, finally combined under the leadership of a former Buddhist monk, Chu Yuan-Chang, and succeeded in driving the Mongols out of China. In 1368, Chu himself took the title of emperor with the name of Hung Wu. Though it was Chu Yuan-Chang who became the new emperor, it was the White Lotus that gave the new dynasty its name, Ming, after two messianic figures, Big and Little Ming Wang, who were thought to have been sent by Buddha Maitreya to restore peace and order to the world.

Whether the early Ming emperors repudiated the secret societies that helped them to power, or whether the politically active members simply dispersed once their object was achieved, the White Lotus Society kept very quiet during the greater part of the Ming period. Only toward the end of the period, when the dynasty became weak and corrupt, and foreign armies again threatened the Chinese borders, did the White Lotus again take part in uprisings, along with other bodies. Nevertheless, the White Lotus does not appear to have been implicated in the final rebellions that destroyed the reality of Ming power and paved the way for the conquest of China by the Manchus. In 1644, China again fell under foreign control, which this time was not so easily shaken off. The rule of the Manchus (known as the Ch'ing dynasty) lasted right up to 1911.

Almost from the beginning, however, the Manchu emperors had troubles to face: first from non-Chinese peoples on their borders, and later from rebellions at home. In this period, sects and societies arose in bewildering number, linked together in a maze of interconnections. Analysis is made the more difficult by the fact that they often changed their names to avoid suppression. The White Lotus Society was at this time also known as the Incense Smelling Sect and the White Yang Sect; it may have been connected with the Eight Diagrams, or Celestial Principles, Sect, and the Nine Mansions Sect, and was almost certainly connected with the important Heaven and Earth Society (which itself has many other names, including the Triad Society, the Hung League, and the Three United Association). The Ch'ing administration also had to contend with the Celestial Bamboo Sect, the Prebirth Sect, and many others, whose leaders had such impressive and high-sounding titles as Great King of Red Heaven, Great King of Red Earth, and Great King of Red Mankind.

By the middle of the 19th century China had experienced nearly a hundred years of political and religious revolt, which had only been aggravated by the Manchus' cruel methods of suppression. In the history of all this political activity, the name of the White Lotus appears and disappears in a somewhat puzzling way. One White Lotus uprising took place in 1774, in the very middle of the reign of the most powerful and glorious Ch'ing emperor, Ch'ien Lung (who was so glorious and powerful that later patriots were at pains to construct the story that he was really of Chinese, not Manchu, descent). After uprisings of the Eight Diagrams and Nine Mansions Sects in 1786-88, and of the Heaven and Earth Society in 1786-89, the White Lotus sparked off the great rebellion of 1794, which spread over nine provinces and took eight years to suppress. Then, in 1814, came another Eight Diagrams uprising, in which the rebels broke into the royal palace (called the Forbidden City) in Peking, and attempted literally to seize the throne. There is little doubt that there was a close connection between all these movements, which had many similarities, and that the White Lotus was one of the most influential.

An account of the rebel attack on the royal palace is given by William Stanton (one of the first Westerners to take a scholarly interest in Chinese secret societies) in his book *The Triad Society, or Heaven and Earth Association*, published in Hong Kong in 1900:

"This insurrection was planned by a man named Li Wan-Cheng, who had a large number of followers in Honan, and Lin Ching, who had followers in Chili and Shantung. These leaders pretended to be able to foretell events by reading the constellations. Lin Ching undertook to bribe the eunuchs within the palace from their allegiance, and obtain their assistance in introducing some of his followers, who were to seize the palace. It was arranged that the party to be admitted and those bribed to assist them, were to wear

Above, portrait of the first Ming emperor Hung Wu (1368-99). A former Buddhist monk, he came to power with the aid of the White Lotus Society, but outlawed it, together with other rebel sects, in 1394. Right, a woodcut from *The Water Margin* or *All Men are Brothers*, a historical romance of the period that reflects the popular sympathy for rebel brotherhoods. A band of outlaws ambush a government official who is leading one of their comrades to execution.

white handkerchiefs on their heads, by which to recognize each other. Their adherents in Honan and Shantung were to rise simultaneously.

"In the meantime the rebels had quietly secreted arms, in wine shops, in the inner city. On the 16th day of the 9th month, three or four hundred of the rebels, dressed like villagers, and carrying baskets of persimmons, under which arms were concealed, assembled around the four gates of the palace and did a good business selling their fruit to the guards and idlers about the gates. After a while, seeing an opportunity when the soldiers were off their guard, they grasped their weapons, dropped their baskets and rushed on and slew the guards, almost without opposition. They then entered the palace, cutting down all without the badge of partisanship. It happened that the eunuchs engaged in their cause, through some mistake, were under the impression that the rising was to take place on the 26th instead of on the 16th of the month, and were consequently unprepared; but nevertheless many of them took prominent part in the rising. In the rush into the palace the insurgents became confused in their movements, and were at a loss how to proceed. This enabled those in the palace who remained loyal, to successfully resist them until assistance came.

"The emperor happened to be away at Moukden, on a visit to the imperial tombs; but his second son, afterwards known as the Emperor Tao-kwang, displayed great energy and bravery in the emergency. Hastily collecting a party of guards and eunuchs, he put himself at their head, and drove the rebels from one part of the palace to another, shooting them as they tried to escape, or to hide themselves on the roofs or amongst the rafters of the buildings. The prince himself shot some of the rebels, and while doing so, discovered he had traitors amongst his own little band. A eunuch, a member of the rebellious society, loaded a musket for him, but omitted the bullet. The prince took a steady aim, and fired at a man on the roof, who carried a white flag, but without hitting him. This raised his suspicion, and he loaded the musket for himself, and, to obviate any magic, tore a silver button from his clothes and rammed it in for a bullet. He fired again and this time the man toppled over. The eunuch was at once seized and afterwards executed. During this melée many of the rebels are said to have been killed by lightning, in a terrible thunderstorm that broke out.

"Lin Ching was not present at this outbreak. He remained at Huang village, some distance from the capital, waiting for tidings of how the plans at the palace had succeeded, and of the expected risings in Honan and Shantung. An intelligent lictor named Chang Ssu, conceived the design of capturing him, and accordingly hurried off in a cart for Huang village. On arrival he went straight to Lin Ching and congratulated him on the success of the enterprise he had planned. He told him the palace was captured and his followers urgently required his presence amongst them before taking further action. Lin Ching believed the story and set out with the lictor for Peking.

A contemptuous British caricature (1832) of Tao-kwang, the prince who displayed "great energy and bravery" in the action against the Eight Diagrams rebels in 1814. He is shown here as a tyrant extorting customs dues from the British, who were soon to defeat him in the first Opium War.

There he soon heard of the failure of his plans and the annihilation of his brave little band, and he was shortly afterwards executed."

This story tells us a good deal about the secret society rebellions of those years. The scale of their operations and the extent of their success demonstrate the unpopularity and the impotence of Manchu rule. They often involved whole provinces (many of which were larger than European states), and tens of thousands of fighting men. At times, they were supported by members of the imperial court, many of whom were Chinese, not Manchu; and more than once they came close to overthrowing the dynasty. All these movements, though clearly political in their aims, also had their religious aspects. They relied strongly on such magical beliefs as those that appear in this story—the reading of the stars, and the suspicion that the rebels might be invulnerable to bullets unless those bullets were made of silver. But above all they were associations of men bound together by the strongest possible ties of mutual loyalty, self-sacrifice, and courage.

During the 19th century, the Manchu imperial court, increasingly hated by its Chinese subjects, and unable to control the commercial, political, and intellectual incursions of the newly industrializing Western powers, took refuge in an ever more backward-looking philosophy and increasingly repressive legislation, which it could not properly enforce. When the day finally came for the last Manchu emperor to leave his throne (he is still alive, an ordinary citizen in People's China today), China had seen more than a century of civil war, misrule, and misery. This period saw a huge increase in secret society activity, as people took to banditry, turned to religion for help the state was unable to provide, or organized attempts to overthrow a government that was now seen to be not only foreign, but useless.

All this makes it strange that since the middle of the 19th century little has been recorded of the White Lotus Society. It seems likely that many of its members, together with its political aims and much of its ritual, have been transferred to other associations, particularly the Heaven and Earth, or Triad, Society, which is sometimes regarded as its successor. On the other hand, the White Lotus may simply have changed its name. One of the many White Lotus ramifications, the Unity Sect, reappeared as a nationwide movement in the long Japanese occupation of China before and during World War II. Today not a few Chinese, both prominent and humble people, owe their lives to this society, whose excellent organization enabled it to smuggle them through the Japanese lines to safety. In recent years, the People's Government has been pursuing an active campaign against a number of politico-religious societies, the Unity Sect probably amongst them.

The White Lotus, as we have seen, was primarily a religious body; it took on the characteristics of a rebellious faction in times of religious persecution and political disaffection. A Chinese imperial decree written in 1813 summed up the situation neatly and accurately: "In normal times the society was engaged in daily worship . . . and reading scripture, claiming thereby to make its members invulnerable to weapons, fire or drowning; but in times of famine and disorder they might plot for the Great Enterprise" (the founding of a new dynasty). This pattern was widespread; and all the later secret societies—Triads, Red Spears, Big Swords, Small Daggers, Yellow Beards, Single Hearted Celestial Principles, Dragon Flower Sacred Religions, to name but a few—were heirs to the White Lotus in this respect.

Yet there were differences of emphasis, and sometimes even of content and aim. The Taiping movement, whose rebellion in the mid-19th century drew in almost every other movement of the time and came within an inch of success, began as a kind of Christianity.

The *Taiping Tien Kuo*, or "Heavenly Kingdom of Universal Peace," was the name chosen for a new (and, of course, Chinese) dynasty by its would-be founder, a one-time village schoolmaster called Hung Hsiu-Ch'uan. Hung Hsiu-Ch'uan was born about 1812, some 30 miles from Canton. He was sent to school at the age of seven and studied hard in the hope of improving the family fortunes by obtaining an official post. He failed the crucial examinations —possibly because the Manchu system of selection was heavily weighted against southern candidates—and conceived a violent hatred for the Manchus. In 1837 he fell ill, and during this illness had a series of visions in which he saw himself purified of all evil by a venerable old man with a long golden beard, and receiving instruction from a friendly middle-aged man who told him how to conduct himself and assisted him in the work of exterminating demons.

A few years later, Hung Hsiu-Ch'uan, now working as a village schoolmaster near his home, came across some Christian missionary tracts in Chinese. To his astonishment, they enabled him at last to interpret his visions. The venerable old man was clearly God the Father, and the friendly, middle-aged one Jesus the Saviour; the demons were the idols of the old Chinese faiths. Hung Hsiu-Ch'uan and one of his friends, convinced that they had found the way to everlasting life, baptized themselves and at once began preaching to others. By 1834 Hung had no doubt that God had spoken to him in person, just as he had spoken to Saint Paul, and that henceforward he was to spend his life spreading God's kingdom upon earth.

In the following five or six years Hung Hsiu-Ch'uan and his friends built up a following in the southeast of China. They took a Chinese translation of the Bible as their textbook and the Ten Commandments as their rule of life. Their activities, especially the forcible destruction of images in local temples, brought them into some popular disfavor and led to a few clashes with the authorities, but at this stage they do not seem to have been planning anything other than a religious movement.

But the mid-19th century was not a period in which any substantial movement in China could remain isolated. Triad Society members were constantly at odds with the Manchu administration in the southeast; foreign soldiers had also recently been engaged there. Hung Hsiu-Ch'uan's "God Worshipers," as they were then called, were drawn into the local fighting between immigrant and indigenous Chinese. The government, thoroughly distrustful, resolved

太平天国癸好三年新刻

新遺詔聖書

Title page of part of the Taiping Bible, the "Holy Book of the Former Testament" (1853). Annotated by Hung Hsiu-Chuan, it contained all the books of the New Testament except *John*. As opponents of the Ch'ing dynasty, the Taipings drew support from many of the older rebel associations, but they alienated others (especially the educated classes) by their adoption of a foreign faith. One of the edicts issued by the Taiping generals at Nanking in 1858–9 urges young Triad members to sacrifice their scruples in the cause of freedom: "Why not reflect that the Hung smearing of blood on the mouth is really performed to show unity of heart and will to overthrow the Ch'ing? Men have never been known to join a society and become brethren and still render allegiance to the enemy. Now among the high-spirited people in the provinces, the number of distinguished renowned scholars is not small and that of heroes and warriors is also great. All that is wanted is that all fight for righteousness, vehemently wave their banners to revenge themselves on the enemy, and unite in the meritorious act of founding a dynasty. . . ."

to nip this new movement in the bud. Its attempt at suppression provoked a swift popular reaction, and by the end of 1850 Hung Hsiu-Chu'an found himself the leader of a full-scale armed revolt.

For the next 14 years the great Taiping Rebellion occupied most of the attention of the Manchu government and its armies. The Taipings, with the backing of an immense popular rising in the south and many of the numerous rebel associations, began with a series of startling military successes. By 1853 they were strong enough to capture Nanking, where Hung set up his capital and declared himself emperor, with the title "Heavenly Ruler." Other rebellious forces (notably the Triads) seized Shanghai, Amoy, and other important cities, and set siege to Kweilin and Canton. This massive rebellion was not crushed for another 10 years—and then only with foreign help, at the cost of an estimated 20,000 lives and the devastation of much of the richest land in China. At the height of his power, Hung Hsiu-Ch'uan ruled half China. He committed suicide in 1864, when his forces were crushed by those of General Gordon and the Chinese statesman Li Hung-Chang.

There followed 50 more years of economic, religious, social, and political decay. Those years saw not only the passive weakening of traditional Chinese institutions under one set of foreigners—the Manchus—but also their active erosion by the rapid encroachments of another, more alien set—the Westerners. Since the Taipings had failed (and failed partly through Western intervention), it was still necessary to drive out the Manchus, but it had become even more necessary to oust the other foreigners. This aim, as we have seen, was embodied

Above right, Chinese cartoon entitled "The lion [China] destroys the pigs and the goats [labeled Christians and Westerners]." Millions of similar cartoons were circulated in China during the early 1890s, when mounting xenophobia led to a series of riots in the Yangtze Valley, and Christian missions were attacked. The continued aggression of the Western powers, and the failure of the Taipings, had confirmed the Chinese in their traditional hostility toward Christianity—one of the foreign religions condemned as heterodox in the "sacred" Ming edicts of 1724. (Illustration from *Heresy Exposed in Respectful Obedience to the Sacred Edicts. A Complete Picture Gallery*, Hankow, 1891.)

General Gordon (1835-85) in command of the "Ever-Victorious Army," the multiracial force used by the Ch'ing to defeat the Taipings (newspaper illustration of 1884).

in another secret society that arose at the turn of the century—the Boxers. Far from being anti-Manchu, the Boxers were supporters of the Ch'ing dynasty, and were supported by them—at first clandestinely, later openly.

I Ho Chuan, the Chinese name for the Boxers, means literally "The Fists of Righteous Harmony." "The idea underlying the name" (the British Foreign Office was informed by the minister in Peking) "is that the members of the Society will unite to uphold the cause of righteousness, if necessary by force." Whether or not the Boxers were affiliated to other secret societies, in particular the White Lotus, has often been argued; the probability is that there was some connection, but that it consisted mainly in similarities of procedure.

The chief characteristic of the Boxer movement, apart from its extreme ferocity, was its reliance on supernatural powers. This took the form of faith in magic, with none of the spiritual overtones of Christian or Buddhist salvationism that distinguished the Taipings and the White Lotus groups. Such faith in magic, typical of the rank and file of almost all Chinese rebellious movements, appears to have been as strongly held by the Manchu court as by anyone else. The most important magical power was the gift of invulnerability. "This useful asset," writes Peter Fleming in his book *The Siege at Peking*, "was conferred on the Boxers by the spirits of the heroes, demigods and other legendary beings to whom they addressed their incantations, of which the following is a fair example:

> 'The Instructions from the God Mi T'o to his Disciples—proclaiming upon every mountain by the Ancient Teachers—reverently inviting the Gods from the central southern mountains, from the central eight caves—your Disciple is studying the Boxer art, to preserve China and destroy Foreigners. The Iron Lo Han, if cut with knife or chopped with axe, there will be no trace. Cannon cannot injure, water cannot drown. If I urgently invite the Gods they will quickly come, if I tardily invite them they will tardily come, from their seats in every mountain cave. Ancient Teachers, Venerable Mother, do swiftly as I command.'

"This abracadabra was uttered to the accompaniment of gestures and posturings. Facing towards the southeast (nobody knows why) the worshipper genuflected, stamped on a cross, knocked his head on the ground, bowed and made cabalistic signs with his hands."

On completing this ritual, the worshiper became possessed. After going through a series of violent spasms, twitching, foaming at the mouth and rolling his eyes, he would fall into a trance. After this, he was supposed to be invulnerable to both swords and bullets. Naturally these performances attracted many onlookers, who were deeply impressed by the demonstrations of invulnerability that followed. It was always possible to explain failures away by saying that the victims had failed to perform the rituals properly, or had broken one of the many taboos of the society.

The Boxers began their activities with attacks on small missionary outposts in Shantung, and soon discovered that far from being punished, they were to be encouraged. The 64-year-old empress dowager, who had assumed the regency and held on to it by actually deposing the young emperor, her nephew, had been the virtual ruler of China for nearly 40 years. She had always been superstitious; by 1900, she was (in the words of the British minister in Peking) "so influenced by the pretensions of the Boxers to supernatural powers as to believe that they could safely defy the rest of the world." For a while, the regular imperial forces worked with the Boxers, providing them with officers. Several hundred missionaries were massacred, a great deal of foreign property was destroyed, and finally the whole foreign legation area in Peking was put under siege. This policy gave the Manchus popularity with the masses in the north of the country—but only for a few months. Before the end of August, Peking was in foreign hands.

The Ch'ing dynasty lingered on, however, until 1911, when it was overthrown by Dr. Sun Yat-Sen's Republican Party, with the aid of the most prominent of Chinese secret societies: the Triad, or Heaven and Earth League.

As a political organization, the Triad Society, or group of societies, was similar to the White Lotus and its ramifications: to overthrow the Ch'ing dynasty was their common objective. The Triads eagerly exploited any and every opportunity to that end, as we have seen in the case of the Taiping Wars (p. 226). But it is the elaborate ritual and symbolism of the Triad Society, and its system of secret signs, rather than its political activities, that have always attracted the attention of Western scholars—notably the Freemasons G. Schlegel (*The Hung League*, 1866) and J. S. M. Ward and W. G. Stirling (*The Hung Society*, 1925). A brief account of Triad ritual claims a place in this chapter on at least two counts: firstly, because such rituals are still widely practiced among Chinese communities today; and secondly, because this ritual, rich in traditional elements, can be seen as a synthesis, if not a typical example, of the rituals of many Chinese secret societies.

The Triad ritual is based on the traditional story of the society's foundation in 1674. According to this story, the society was set up by five monks (now

The Revolution of 1911 fulfilled one of the Triad's traditional aims—*Overthrow Ch'ing*. Here President Sun Yat-Sen, himself a Triad official, visits the tombs of the Ming emperors to declare that the Ch'ing dynasty has finally been dethroned.

described as the "Five Ancestors" of the society) to avenge their betrayal by the Ch'ing emperor K'ang-Hsi. During the reign of K'ang-Hsi (1662-1722), rebels from the state of "Silu" threatened to invade the country. The emperor's appeal for help in suppressing the rebels came to the ears of a former Ming partisan called Cheng Kwan-Tat, who was then residing at "Shaolin" monastery, where he was taking instruction in the art of boxing. The result was that Cheng Kwan-Tat and 128 monks put themselves and their fighting skills at the service of the emperor. They routed the rebels in three months, declined the grateful emperor's offer of titles and official posts, and returned to their monastery. But two of the emperor's ministers, jealous of the honors shown to the monks, succeeded in persuading the emperor that the monks had returned to their monastery only in order to stir up a rebellion in the south. At this point, the emperor issued orders for the destruction of Shaolin monastery and the execution of Cheng Kwan-Tat.

With the aid of an unfrocked monk, the imperial troops surrounded the monastery and set fire to it. A hundred and ten monks were burned to death; 18, who prayed to Buddha for deliverance, were magically protected from the flames by a large yellow curtain that appeared in answer to their prayers; but only five of these (the Five Ancestors) survived. Their subsequent journey—and indeed most of this story—lies in the realms of allegory rather than those of fact. The Five Ancestors, fleeing from the burning monastery, found a three-legged incense pot on the shore of a river, inscribed with the words that were to become the Triad motto: *Overthrow Ch'ing; Restore Ming*. While they were offering prayers of gratitude, they were surprised by a band of imperial soldiers, and saved only by the sudden transformation of a sacred grass sandal into a boat, in which they crossed the river to safety. They lost the sandal and its partner in another brush with imperial troops, and eventually came to a two-planked bridge guarded by two more soldiers. Under cover of the bridge, they crossed the river by means of three large stones that were miraculously floating on the surface of the water.

A series of such ordeals, and a visit to the "White Stork Grotto" (described as a rebel stronghold near the borders of Honan and Shantung), eventually led the monks to a city in Fukien province, where they founded, and began to recruit for, the Triad Society. They held mass ceremonies at which new members swore an oath to overthrow the Ch'ing and restore the Ming; at the first of these ceremonies, a bright red glow appeared in the eastern sky. The color red ("Hung" in Chinese) has many favorable connotations in Chinese culture, including happiness, success, and riches. Traditionally a Chinese bride always wore red (and today, the value of the Communists' red flag to their cause in China is often remarked). Partly because of this, and partly because the word "Hung," written in a slightly different way, was the surname taken by the first Ming emperors, the Triads regarded this glow as a good omen, and decided to take the name of the "Hung Family."

Above, a 19th-century Chinese painting of the legendary monastery of Shaolin, home of the Five Ancestors of the Triad Society and traditionally the cradle of Chinese boxing. It was supposedly founded in sixth century by Bodhidharma, who gave the monks the 18 basic exercises of Shaolin boxing (an art still practiced today). Right, a scene from a filmed reconstruction of a Triad initiation rite in Hong Kong, 1957. The Incense Master dons a grass sandal representing the sandal that took the Five Ancestors across a river. It was said to be a relic of Bodhidharma (invoked in Triad ritual by his Chinese name, Tat Mo).

Tradition has it that soon after this the Triads attacked the Ch'ing and, after capturing the whole of Fukien province, were slaughtered in their thousands by the imperial troops. Western students of the Triad, having failed to agree on the year (or even the century) in which such a rising should be placed, have suggested that the incident may be an elaboration on the rest of the story, based on memories of the White Lotus rebellion of 1794 (p. 221). The rest of the Triad story tells how the Five Ancestors decided to scatter after the failure of this rising in order to organize simultaneous rebellions in different parts of the country, and how each founded a lodge in a different region or province. The exact locations of these five lodges are in doubt; indeed, most of the places mentioned in the story of the Five Ancestors cannot satisfactorily be identified.

The play on the word "Hung" is of particular interest because the Chinese language offers almost endless opportunities for puns and the manipulation of characters, and the secrecy of the Triads consists largely in knowing the right ones. In this context, it is interesting to recall that the leader of the Taiping movement (p. 224) also happened to have the name Hung. What is more, the top part of the Chinese character for the name Hung looks like the two characters for the number 21; 21 is the sum of the numbers 4, 8, and 9; and the code number 489 represents the Triad Society's highest rank. When it is realized that much of the symbolism in Chinese religions is of a similar punning nature, and that the art of numerology has also been deeply studied in China for over two thousand years, it can be seen that the esoteric implications of this kind of wordplay can become exceedingly complex.

The ceremonial robes of Triad officers are largely Buddhist in character, as are the furnishings and paraphernalia of their lodges. Most of these objects represent scenes in the story of the Five Ancestors, for every phase of this story and its ordeals is reenacted in the ritual by which candidates are admitted into the "Hung Family." At the climax of the initiation rite, candidates take an oath of blood brotherhood—a reminder of the oath taken by the three heroes in the peach garden nearly two thousand years ago.

Those Freemasons who have made a special study of the Triad have found striking similarities in the organization of the Triad and Masonic lodges, especially in their hierarchies of officers. They have also found that some of the numerous Triad signs, and their meanings, are remarkably similar to their own. But that is not the end of the Masonic claims. "Like Freemasonry in the West," writes J. S. M. Ward, "the Hung or Triad Society seems justly entitled to claim that it is a lineal descendant of the Ancient Mysteries. Its signs are of primeval antiquity, but it represents the Higher Degrees in Freemasonry rather than the Craft in that the main part of the ritual deals with what is supposed to befall a man after death. It has many striking analogies with ancient Egypt; for example, the Hung Boat is similar to the Solar Barque of Ra. . . . For all that, we are not entitled to assume that the

Chinese Society is an offshoot of Egypt. It seems much more probable that the Egyptian Mysteries have sprung from a common ancestor and have developed along slightly different lines."

Such conjectural attempts at historical explanation can only be confusing. Nevertheless, it is true that Triad practices show striking similarities to those of many other secret organizations. Oaths of initiation are commonly accompanied by the threat of death in the event of betrayal, as are the 36 initiatory oaths of the Triad. The oath of blood brotherhood is nearly everywhere accompanied by the shedding of blood and the sharing of it in a communal drink, as it is in the Triad ceremony. Common, too, is the baring of the candidate's knee—usually the left. But most widespread of all is the kind of symbolism found in the complex Triad ritual of initiation, with its mimed ordeals of death by fire and water, followed by the "rebirth" of the candidate, and his progress through three guarded gateways to the eastern "City of Willows"—the legendary heaven of the Hung heroes.

One of the most difficult questions concerning the Triad societies is the degree to which they were ever really organized as a single, centralized movement. Today, there is no single Triad movement, only a number of groups that are known collectively in English as Triads. Yet there is evidence that Sun Yat-Sen, founder of the Republic in 1911 and a Triad member of long standing, was able to make active use of the various Triad organizations overseas for the collection of funds and the dissemination of propaganda. Triad assistance in the Republican cause was rewarded by the virtual recognition of the society in China. In the following years it actually increased its membership still further, and became so powerful a pressure group that the majority of officials found themselves bound to join it in order to achieve their ends, while others (particularly employers of labor) found that membership increased their security and their profits.

From graft to outright crime is an easy step. In addition to their political activities, the Triads have acquired a reputation as criminal gangs. After the Republican Revolution they became more and more unequivocally criminal organizations; they also became increasingly fragmented, and added internecine fighting to their other activities. Obviously, only the overriding necessity for common action in the political field could bring about real coordination between them. Between 1946 and 1956 there were several attempts to unite the criminal Triad gangs in Hong Kong in the anti-Communist cause. They all failed.

It is largely because they were established by Chinese immigrants in such overseas centers that the Triads are the societies about which we have the most information. One of the fullest accounts of their history in the last five decades is W. P. Morgan's *Triad Societies in Hong Kong*, published in 1960.

Five stages in a Triad initiation ceremony (photographs from the filmed reconstruction of 1957). Above, the Incense Master kneels to invoke the spirits of the Hung heroes; he then offers them libations of tea and wine. A 489 official (usually one of the society leaders) stands beside the altar holding the yellow warrant flag that authorizes the Incense Master to begin the ceremony. His sword represents the sword of righteousness of the war-god Kwan-Ti; according to the ritual "it can be used to slay the officials of Ch'ing without incurring any loss to the Hung family." Left, before the lodge is opened, officials perform a series of boxing movements as a mark of respect for the society leader. Each makes the hand sign appropriate to his rank (the man in the foreground is making the "Head of Dragon and Tail of Phoenix" sign, which identifies a 489 official).

Right, a candidate for initiation is challenged at the entrance to the lodge by armed guards. After answering the ritual questions and paying the initiation fee, he crawls in under the crossed swords. In the course of the long rites (often abbreviated) he reenacts the ordeals of the Five Ancestors, takes the 36 Triad oaths, and learns the signs of identification. Below right, toward the close of the ceremony, the "Vanguard" beheads a cock to show him how traitors will die. Below, the Incense Master pricks his finger, again warning him that his blood will be shed if he betrays the society. The candidates then drink a mixture of wine, blood, cinnabar, sugar, and ashes. They receive paper coins bearing the motto *Overthrow Ch'ing; restore Ming*. They chant: "We swear loyalty like Liu, Kwan, and Chang. Loyalty and faithfulness will ensure us longevity."

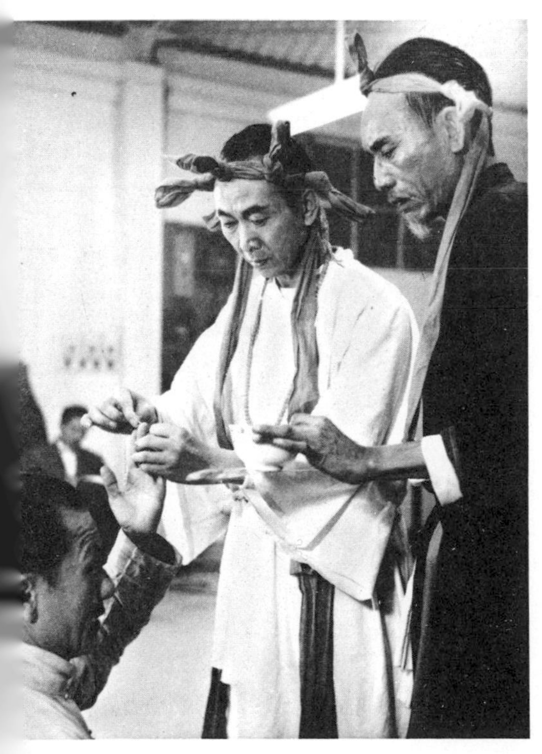

Morgan, a former inspector of police, describes the seven main Triad groups in the colony, each of which has its own special area of influence, its headquarters and sub-branches. Most of these groups operated at first under the guise of trade guilds, benevolent associations, or sports clubs. Thus, behind the façade of the officially registered Fuk Yee Industrial and Commercial General Association (which catered for the speakers of a particular dialect, Hoklo) lay the Fuk Yee Hing Triad Society; both societies shared the same officers, but the rituals, aims, and methods of the second were secret. The Fuk Yee Industrial and Commercial Association is known to have had at least 12 branch offices to administer its members. People joined the registered association because it was the chief agency dealing with the employment, welfare, and funeral problems of their dialect group. Their monthly subscription was $HK 1 (about 17 U.S. cents.) About 3000 of its 10,000 members were actually Triad members too. Through these fellow Triad members the officers of the two associations were able virtually to control the entire Hoklo-speaking community in Hong Kong.

With the increases in population, and in economic hardship, that affected practically all Chinese cities in this period, the officers' possibilities of making greater personal gains out of their positions increased too. New societies began to push their way in, and old ones started to encroach on one another's preserves. It was in these circumstances that the notorious protection rackets developed; people were forced to take the Triad oaths and pay their dues in order to save their jobs, their property (such as it was), and their lives. In Hong Kong, this great increase in criminal activity came during and immediately after the Japanese war. Before 1941, only eight or nine per cent of the Hong Kong population belonged to Triad societies; in 1958, it was nearer 15 per cent—though the island's total population had almost trebled during the interim period.

Three main streams of political thinking existed among Triad members in Hong Kong on the eve of the Japanese attack: some were pro-Chinese, some were pro-Japanese, and some were uncommitted. In the early days of the war, the first group helped a number of Chinese to escape into Free China; but with the success of the Japanese, the second group gained in importance, and the third was soon eager to join in. The Japanese made use of the secret societies in the task of keeping order and preventing sabotage and subversion. This, together with their open encouragement of prostitution, gambling, and drug peddling (from which the societies gained much of their income), put the Triads in an even stronger position. During the administrative uncertainties of the immediate postwar period, they were able to monopolize the organization of vice and the control of the labor force. There is every reason to believe that things were much the same in China itself. But peace with the Japanese did not bring an end to fighting in China. Civil war between the Communist and Nationalist (Kuomintang) armies continued until, in

1948-9, the Communists swept their opponents southward and (almost literally) into the sea. A vast influx of refugees entered Hong Kong, and with the refugees came more gangs. Among the southerners were more Triad members; among the Shanghaiers, and others who did not speak the southern dialects, members of the Green and Red Pang.

The *Green Pang* in particular soon became a serious menace. Members who were already in Hong Kong set themselves up as a reception committee for the northern strangers. They pretended to be in a special relationship with the Hong Kong administration, and let it be rumored that people who relied on their help would be offered housing and employment, licenses to trade, or even education for their children, while those who did not would be deported back to Shanghai. The previous experiences of these refugees (most of whom were unable to speak English, and unacquainted with any methods of government other than their own) were not such as to lead them to rely upon the disinterested integrity of any administrative official. It is not surprising that they were willing to pay out large sums in return for these false claims to give services and protection from deportation. At the same time the Green Pang began to organize prostitution and the narcotics racket on a scale larger than anything hitherto known in Hong Kong. It popularized the use of heroin, organized armed robberies, and started an epidemic of pickpocketing. In spite of much action by the Hong Kong police, members of the Green Pang are still active in the control of labor, the organization of prostitution, and the sale of drugs. They are also believed to have control of the unofficial guides and tailors' agents who specialize in meeting visitors to Hong Kong, especially United States servicemen.

The Green Pang concentrated rather more on the rich than on the poor; but the squatters in their wooden shanty-towns, who numbered something like 600,000 in the 1950s, had brought their own Triad with them. This, the so-called *14K Association*, had been founded to support the anti-Communist cause, and deliberately organized on Triad lines. After 1953 it degenerated into a particularly ruthless criminal gang, exploiting the very people it had originally been designed to help. By 1954, when its membership reached about 80,000, it had become a distinct threat not only to society at large, but also to the other, older-established Triad groups. As a result, they too felt themselves obliged to increase their membership. One outcome of this increase in Triad activity from about 1953 onward was the intensity of the rioting that broke out in Hong Kong in October 1956.

The riots, and the mass arrests that followed, shocked public opinion into trying to check Triad influence. For the first time there was a remarkable increase in the information forwarded to the authorities: the police, reorganized, were given new powers of detention. Nevertheless, the Triads remained strong, and are likely to remain so as long as the present economic conditions continue. It is hard for anyone who has not seen these societies at work to grasp how they affect ordinary people in their everyday lives. Take a small street hawker, for example; there are some 20,000 of them in Hong-Kong—some licensed, and many more unlicensed. To a street hawker, two things are of prime importance: security for his pitch, and security for his goods. In order to prevent the Triad "bully boys" from stealing his pitch or destroying his goods, a hawker must either join a Triad society and pay its dues himself, or pay a daily flat rate to its collectors. This often entails great sacrifice, but without it the street hawker would get no protection. It has been estimated that Triad societies in Hong Kong obtain a daily revenue of over $HK 10,000 ($U.S. 1750) from this source alone. This, combined with the estimated profits made from shoe-shine boys, prostitutes, dance-hall girls, restaurants, sale of black-market theatre and sports tickets, and membership fees, and the much larger sums made from the trade in drugs, protection of criminals, gambling, control of rickshaw coolies and laborers, and general extortion, would have given the Triads a revenue of about 40 million Hong Kong dollars ($U.S. 7,000,000) in 1958—and this from a total population of about three million people. For enforcement of their demands, the Triads rely upon violence and intimidation.

Though secret society control is usually illegal, it does not follow that it is always as antisocial as it has been in Hong Kong. There have been occasions, both in China and elsewhere, when the legal authorities have been as extortionate as any secret organization, and secret society control has at least been better than no control at all.

An example comes from the country around Dairen in the north of China in the early 20th century. Because the official administration was weak, a local secret society called the Red Beards was able to run what amounted to an alternative government; it exacted customs dues, issued licenses, and judged disputes. Such situations usually occurred in periods of governmental breakdown, corruption, and oppression, such as the last century of Ch'ing rule or the later years of the Kuomintang government.

At times, governments have deliberately decided to leave the local organization of Chinese communities to private enterprise. This was true when large-scale Chinese immigration into southeast Asia and the United States began in the mid-19th century. In Singapore, where official policy was to leave the Chinese to manage their own affairs, the secret societies became very powerful. Though most of them belonged to the Triad groupings of south China, the anti-Manchu aspect of the Triad lost its significance for them, at least until they were asked to provide monetary support for Sun Yat-Sen. At first, they operated openly and were secret only in the ritual sense. They were registered voluntary associations, to which newly arrived immigrants, whose passages they had usually arranged, turned for assistance of every kind. They acted as internal police for the Chinese community, settled disputes, and provided the administrative framework that the British did not provide. But in 1890, when

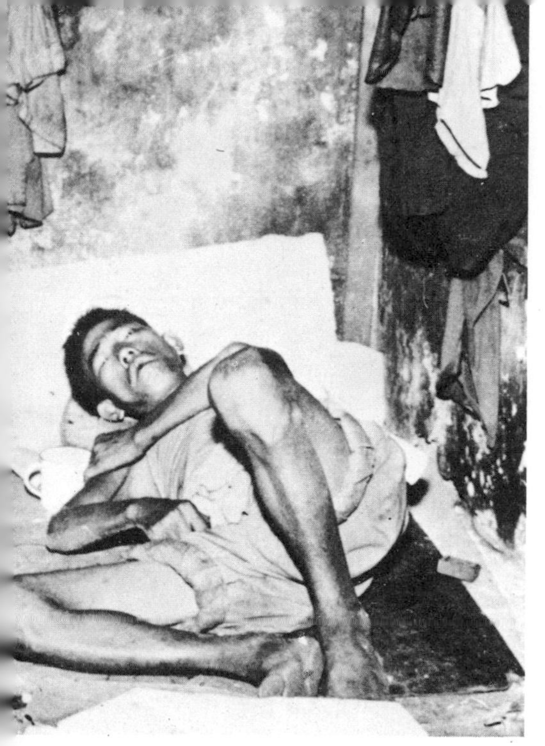

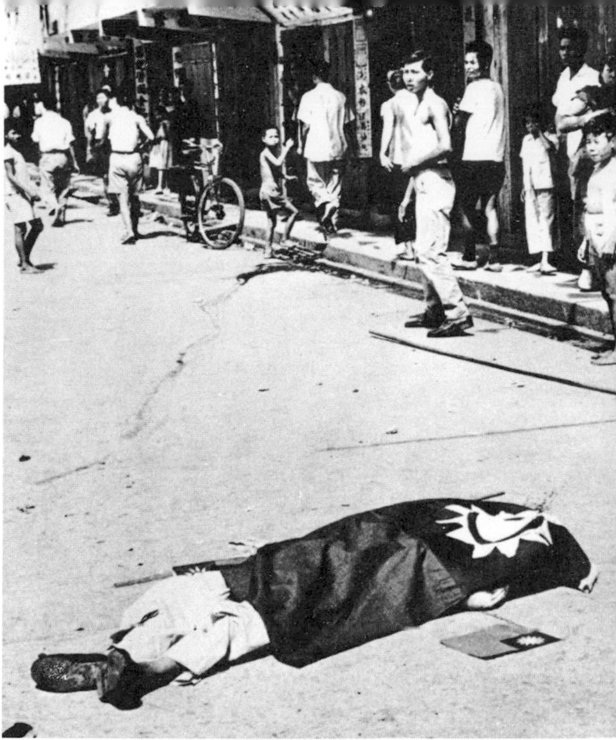

Above, a drug addict in Kowloon. Triad members now control many opium dens in Hong Kong. But some groups still have links with the Chinese Nationalists, and Triad members were involved in the Nationalist riots that broke out in Kowloon in October 1956. Above right, one of the 47 victims of the riots lying beneath the Nationalist flag. Right, a tattoo that identifies members of the Triad "108" group in Singapore (photograph from the secret society branch of the Singapore police).

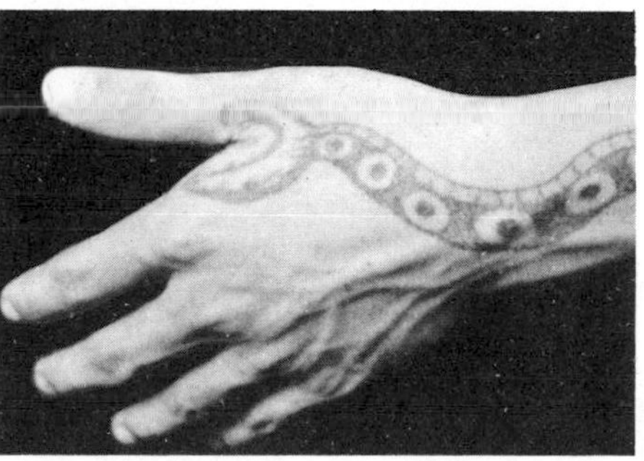

their independence seemed to be becoming too great, and their extortions too obvious, the British decided to outlaw them. The secret societies went underground, and followed much the same path as their brother societies in Hong Kong. Today there are six main secret society groups in Singapore, with a total membership of at least 9000. Police estimate that in 1957 there were some 400 clashes between rival secret society gangs, though the number dropped to 70 in 1965, after the introduction of more stringent laws.

Similar accounts could be given of most of the other centers of overseas Chinese settlement. Large numbers of Chinese workers, attracted by news of the gold discoveries, began to reach the west coast of the United States in the late 1840s. It was impossible for the authorities in Washington, or even in the new state of California itself, to control at all closely the internal affairs of the huge mining centers that sprang up almost overnight. These Chinese immigrants, herded together in a foreign country and completely at the mercy of those who had hired them and paid their passages, were a rich soil for activities of the Triad type. With astonishing speed, Triads sprang up in every place in the States in which the Chinese had settled. Among the first was the "Five Companies" (named after the five districts of China) which, by 1854, had a total membership of 35,000 in California—almost every male Chinese immigrant in the state. Many an apparently innocent benevolent association or social club was in fact the façade for the same mixture of criminal and organizational elements that was so common elsewhere. Only the name was different for, in the United States, Chinese secret societies came to be known as *Tongs*, from a Chinese word meaning "hall" or "meeting place" that is used quite frequently in the titles of all kinds of association.

In the 1850s rival Tongs fought miniature wars in the United States, their members wearing warpaint and wielding hatchets. These continued, in a less picturesque form, until recent years, though the federal and state authorities gradually gained a closer hold on administration. With this, the Tongs became more and more clearly criminal. As in Hong Kong and elsewhere,

San Francisco's Chinatown police squad in the 1900s. Despite its efforts, tongs led by highbinders or hired killers dominated Chinatown until its destruction in 1906.

splintering began to take place. At the same time, more and more immigrants began to realize that their future lay in the United States, rather than in a long-dreamed-of return to China, and (as in Singapore) the revolutionary aspects of the secret societies became less and less important. But here too, the traditional anti-Manchu ardor was revived at the turn of the century by the energy and devotion of Dr. Sun Yat-Sen, who spent 16 years of exile traveling in the cause of his revolution.

The heyday of the Chinese secret society as a political organization is over. It was linked with a particular stage in the development of Chinese social structure, and that stage has passed, though it lasted for some two thousand years. Since 1911, secret societies have played little part in Chinese politics, though Chiang Kai-Shek and Mao Tse-T'ung are known to have had dealings with them. The societies may give sporadic support to this or that political party, and there may even be occasions when such support is decisive, but in China today it is the political parties, not the secret societies, that are crucial. Modern politics are not simply about power, they are also about policy, and no White Lotus or Triad society ever produced a political program beyond that which was embodied in the slogan *Overthrow Ch'ing; Restore Ming.* By 1911 (even, as the Taipings saw, by 1850) the situation demanded more than a mere change of dynasty: it demanded revolution or, at the very least, drastic reform. A revolution (or even a reform) requires a competence in policy-making such as the secret societies never possessed; modern policy-making demands a rational approach that is ultimately incompatible with the kind of mystical ritualism that characterizes these Chinese societies and provides most of their secrets.

Changes in social structure are likely to affect the religious secret societies too. Modern technological and economic developments both demand and make possible far closer governmental control than in the old days, and there is less scope for private associations. In the Western world, though the state has increasingly entered fields that were previously not its concern, such as education, housing, and health, there are other fields that it has not touched. Religion remains outside its control, and ritual associations such as Freemasonry continue to flourish. A similar state of affairs is not likely to exist in People's China. Chinese societies are unlikely to survive as religious organizations, except among those overseas Chinese communities that are situated in countries with democratic traditions. It is possible that Chinese sects, secret only in the ritual sense, may long continue to flourish on the West Coast of the United States, for example.

As for the criminal societies, they too are likely to change, preserving their necessary secrecy but becoming more and more like criminal gangs in the rest of the world, with increasing organizational fragmentation. Though their ritualism may decline, much of it is likely to survive, for it has a proved contribution to make to group solidarity.

10 The Mafia

The word *mafia* probably comes from the same word in Arabic, which means "place of refuge." During the Arab rule of Sicily, which began in the 9th century, the land was split up into smallholdings; but when the Normans conquered the island in the 11th century, feudal overlords seized the land and ran it in estates as large and despotic as the Roman slave-farms denounced by Cicero. Many dispossessed smallholders ran to a *mafia* in the hills rather than become serfs on the estates that had swallowed up their fields.

When the Spaniards conquered the island in the 15th century, the Inquisition used heresy trials to torture and plunder both rich and poor. Then the outlaws in the hills represented the only resistance to despotic government. The bandits of the hill towns, invulnerable while they kept the respect of their local communities, became the champions of the poor and the oppressed. Thus the roots of the Mafia (known to Sicilians as the "Honored Society") lie in the millennia of misgovernment suffered at the hands of various invaders: Romans, Arabs, Normans, Spaniards, Neapolitan Bourbons, and, to a certain extent, Northern Italians. Though the modern Mafia dates only from the 19th century, its traditions stretch back to tribal days.

The strength of the Mafia lies in the fact that it is a family society. Bitterly hostile toward official government, the people of Sicily have clung for centuries to the family unit or tribe as the only source of protection and

Sicilian women weep for Mafia victims. Though the Mafia once had the character of a popular resistance movement, it has long terrorized the Sicilian peasant, enforcing its extortions by murder. Its members virtually control land, labor, and local government, and a conspiracy of silence blocks every attempt to bring them to trial.

morality. The discipline of the Mafia grew up because justice for the wrongs suffered by a member of a family could be expected only outside the official law. Where no one trusted the law of the invaders, the writ of family law ran.

This family discipline—similar in many ways to that of the Scottish clans—went under the name of *omertà* ("manliness"). It included the refusal to give any information to the authorities after an act of violence, because revenge was a family's duty, not the State's or God's; the exaction of an eye for an eye and a tooth for a tooth in a quarrel between families, until all the men of one family were dead; the stoic and bland acceptance of insults from the enemy or the oppressor, until the time was ripe for vengeance; the lifelong refusal to forgive or forget an injury; devotion to the welfare of the family, because the good fortune of one meant the good fortune of all, and a wealthy family could better withstand the attacks of the enemy; blind obedience to the head of the family, whose will was law; and a love of secrecy, because the official law was always hostile to any society within a society. Such a code produced in the families of the Mafia a great self-respect and sense of honor and duty; it also produced murders of a barbarity and meanness rarely equaled in modern times.

Police lead Rosa Messina to the corpse of her 13-year-old son, killed by mafiosi in 1963. Though she named the killers, she dared not testify against them in court.

The transformation of the Mafia families from outlaw bands into the real rulers of Sicily took place in the 19th century, when feudal power in the island disintegrated. The feudal landowners, who were becoming less and less interested in working their own land, began to employ agents called *gabellotti*, who agreed to work the land in return for the payment of a fixed yearly sum. The gabellotti, many of whom belonged to Mafia families, sublet the land to the peasants. When Garibaldi invaded the island with his Redshirts in 1860, this new Sicilian class of middlemen transferred its support from the Bourbon regime to him; and in the ensuing Republic, it controlled the politics of the island by force and by the intimidation of voters. The gabellotti had already hired other members of Mafia families to collect rents from the peasants and to protect the orange groves, sulfur mines, and property of the landowners; eventually, they bought the estates at low prices from the aristocrats, and consolidated their control over the town governments. Their rule was as oppressive, savage, and unjust as that of the former rulers. Their vengeance was as terrible and even more sure, because they were local people.

The reason why the Mafia and its family code still flourish in Sicily lies in the backwardness of the island. Deep suspicion of the law and the central government, an economy where a man may find work for only about a hundred days a year in times of sowing or harvest, the exclusion of women from social life, enormous overpopulation, and fanatic Catholicism, have allowed Mafia families to exploit their past traditions as champions of the people in order to become the present exploiters of the people, the funnels through which all jobs, all patronage, and all trade have to flow, in the name of a secret Sicilian government that rules far more effectively than the official government in Rome. The Mafia has preserved its secrecy by allowing no informer to live.

Though the Mafia is a protection racket that takes its percentage on practically every transaction made in the island, it remains a force of law and order—its own law and its own order. Sicilians have to pay a double tax, the first to the government to pay for the official police and the official judges, the second to the Mafia to pay for the real police and the real judges. For while petty crime would flourish in Sicily without the Mafia, the Mafia, which brooks no competition, has almost eliminated the petty criminal. Those who do not pay protection have the throats of their sheep cut, their olive trees chopped down, their automobiles bombed, and their homes burned; but those who pay—and that means nearly the whole population—have their stolen goods restored to them when even the police are ineffective.

The organization of the Mafia depends on a loose form of democracy within certain Sicilian families, but membership may also be conferred on outsiders of great daring and of Sicilian blood. One of the few known confessions of a Sicilian *mafioso*, that of the doctor Melchiore Allegra (made in 1937, but not published until 1962) told of an association split up into families, each one headed by an elected chief or *capofamiglia*. The family was made up of men from neighboring towns and villages who were connected either by blood ties or by their status in the community. The capofamiglia was the effective ruler of his area and was independent; but he was expected to cooperate with all the other local chieftains of the Mafia and to obey the elected head of them all, the *capo dei capi*. The association was not confined to Sicily; it had offshoots in Tunisia and Marseilles, as well as in North and South America.

Allegra also told of certain passwords and signs by which one mafioso might know another; these, however, were few, and were confined for the most part to the display and exchange of colored handkerchiefs. More interesting, perhaps, is Allegra's description of the ceremony by which he was initiated into the society. The tip of his middle finger was pierced by a needle and blood was squeezed from it onto the small paper image of a saint. The paper was burned and the ashes were put into the doctor's hand. He was then made to take this oath: "I swear to be loyal to my brothers, never to betray them, always to aid them, and if I fail may I burn and be turned to ashes like the ashes of the image."

Though the Mafia is a family society, internal feuds are common. Its efforts to keep the peace among its members are complicated by the code of the vendetta, which governs members and nonmembers alike. A Mafia member is bound to avenge not only the death of another Mafia member, but also the death of a blood relation. Frequently, mafiosi in various parts of

Left, the old hospital at Corleone, still in use in the 1960s, epitomizes the poverty and feudalism of Sicily—prolonged by the influence of the Mafia. The old Mafia, which prevented the cultivation of large areas of land, has also opposed some of the developments recently undertaken in Sicily by the Italian government. Right, the modern, government-financed hospital at Corleone, which stood unused for years because its construction was opposed by Dr. Michele Navarra, chairman of the hospital board and leader of the traditional Mafia.

Sicily have almost eliminated the organization by killing each other in blood feuds. Thus, 153 murders took place in the Mafia stronghold of Corleone between 1944 and 1948. Between 1918 and 1960, nearly one tenth of the population of the town of Godrano was killed in blood feuds, despite the capo dei capi's efforts to make peace. Such murders are often done in a spirit of resignation and despair; a peaceable farmer suddenly becomes head of his family and inherits the inescapable obligation to murder several of the opposing family to satisfy family honor and secure a corpse for a corpse.

Sicily, plundered through the centuries by invaders, eventually sent its own sons to plunder abroad. The mafiosi, who controlled most of the land in Sicily, left much of it to waste in order to drive up the prices of their products and to have a permanent pool of cheap labor under their control. In the late 19th and early 20th centuries, armies of jobless peasants discovered that the only way to feed themselves and their families was to emigrate, preferably to America, and to send money home until their families had enough to join them. During this period, more than a million Sicilians reached the United States; their exact number is hard to calculate because their country of origin was registered as Italy. These Sicilians found work as laborers, particularly in the docks.

For the immigrants, there were few ways of rising fast in the world, though these few were many more than in Sicily. But undoubtedly one of these ways was through crime, and soon Mafia chieftains were established in all the

little Italies of the big-city slums, where they enjoyed much the same respect as they had had in their own communities in Sicily. The American public first became aware of these new groups in 1890, when Italian gang warfare broke out in New Orleans. Two brothers from Palermo, called Matranga, had set up a protection racket over all cargo loaded or unloaded in the docks. Sicilian dockworkers, used to a similar extortion in Palermo and scarcely able to speak the American language, let alone understand American law, accepted the traditional system of paying tribute to mafiosi. But gang leaders from Naples had also moved into the New Orleans docks: the Provenzano brothers from the rival *Camorra*, a Neapolitan secret society that was wholly criminal. Soon, several murders a week were taking place by revolver, bomb, and dagger. The local chief of police, an Irishman called Hennessey, decided to investigate the murders instead of allowing Italian criminals to butcher one another and solve the law's problems outside the law. He learned so much about the organization of the Mafia and the Camorra (which was less rooted in the social fabric of its mother city) that he was shot down in October 1890, a few days before he was due to testify before a grand jury on the subject.

Left, New Orleanians fire on the mafiosi accused of police chief Hennessey's murder (*Harper's Weekly*, March 1891). Below, Uncle Sam asks Humbert of Italy to resume diplomatic relations (*Punch*, April 1891).

Indictments were eventually returned against 19 Sicilians; but at least half the jury was intimidated or bribed, and batteries of America's top lawyers were engaged for the defense. The result was that judgment was suspended on three of the defendants, while the rest were declared innocent. The familiar Sicilian pattern of trials of mafiosi seemed to have been established in America; but in Louisiana the custom of lynch law antedated the custom of Mafia law, and the Mafia had not allowed for the citizens taking the law into their own hands. A mob of several thousand gathered, dragged 11 of the mafiosi out of the city jail, strung them up in the street, and riddled them with bullets. The fact that the offenders were not prosecuted led to a break in diplomatic relations between the United States and Italy. The Italian foreign minister inferred that the Americans were barbarians, incapable of enforcing their own laws; the American secretary of state replied that the United States, though a relatively young country, did not have the criminal societies that seemed to flourish in Italy. Nevertheless, diplomatic relations and immigration were resumed, and the American Mafia developed into a brilliant and powerful organization, perfectly adapted to the techniques of American urban crime. Just as the Irish, in their secret political organizations at home, had developed the family political techniques that made them the bosses and policemen of the sprawling new American cities, so the Italians, and particularly the Mafia, were the natural inheritors and developers of organized crime in the United States (though, for individual acts of violence, the Western tradition was as bloody as anything from the Mediterranean, while the South had its own tradition of family vendettas). The immigrant Mafia had only to learn the techniques of bank and train robbery developed by the American outlaws and add them to its own expertise in the protection racket to create a far more profitable Mafia on American soil than was possible in the homeland.

The American Mafia, however, differed vastly from the Sicilian. The very virtues bred in the Mafia by the social situation in Sicily—the omertà caused by poverty, suspicion of the law, and hatred of the courts—were badly affected by the concept of the American melting pot. Slowly, the conspiracy of silence began to crack; informers on the Mafia have been found with far greater frequency among American citizens and the American mafiosi themselves than have ever been found in Sicily, even to this day. Moreover, the American Mafia could hardly claim that it was the defender of the people against government oppression. On the contrary, many mafiosi actually escaped from the electric chair because of legal snarls caused by the conflict between state and federal law.

The American Mafia soon bred imitators. In the 1900s, the United States became familiar with the phenomenon of the "Black Hand." Demands for protection money were sent out among the Italian community; on each demand was drawn a crude black hand. Children of the selected victims were threatened with kidnapping, murder, or mutilation if the ransom was not

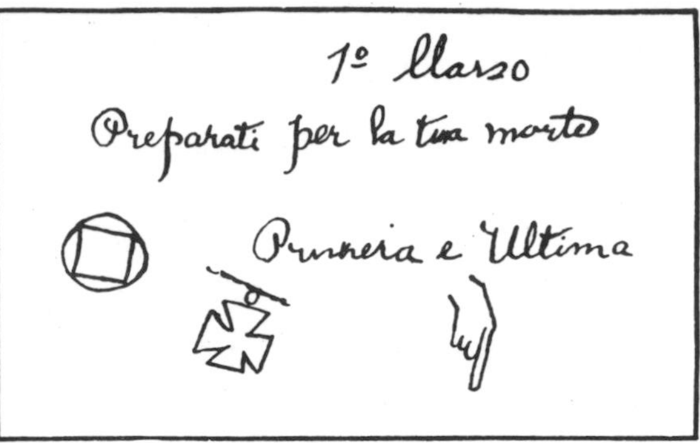
1º Marzo
Preparati per la tua morte
Primera e Ultima

Above, a death note signed with a "black hand"—a device widely used by American gangsters in the 1900s to enforce their threats of extortion. It reads "Prepare for your death." Right, a photograph of Joe Petrosino, the New York detective who investigated the demands and found that no organized "Black Hand" gang existed. His chief achievement was his exposure of Mafia activities; he was murdered by the Sicilian Mafia leader Don Vito in 1909.

paid. Americans already used a single name for all Italian immigrant gangs: the Italian Society. Now, they leaped to the conclusion that a single gang was behind the "Black Hand" demands. But the New York police department had an exceptionally persistent detective, Lieutenant Joe Petrosino. As he was of Italian origin, Petrosino could gain information from among the majority of Italian immigrants, who were honest working people. He discovered that there was no central Black Hand organization; any criminal who wished to terrify someone into paying protection used the warning tactics of the Mafia or the publicized symbol of the black hand.

Petrosino spent 20 years compiling huge dossiers on Italian criminal groups and secret societies, including the Mafia and the Camorra. The irony was that while disproving the myth of the international conspiracy of the Black Hand, he became the first victim of the international conspiracy of the Mafia. In 1909 he visited Italy to establish contact with the Italian police, so that the New York police could be warned when Italian criminals set sail for the United States. This pioneer in Interpol met his death at the hands of the pioneers in international crime syndicates. As soon as he landed in Palermo to check on the police records of the Mafia, he was killed by the capo dei capi of all Sicily, Don Vito Cascio Ferro himself. Don Vito, who was acquitted of 20 murders during his 25-year rule of the Mafia, used to boast of only one of them, the murder of Petrosino. He had taken time off from dinner with a member of parliament to kill Petrosino with a single pistol-shot as he came out of the Palermo docks. Don Vito's comment showed that he clearly recognized the importance of the detective's attempt to set up international police cooperation. "My action was a disinterested one," he used to explain, "and was taken in response to a challenge I could not afford to ignore." Don Vito was eventually jailed by Mussolini's chief of police on a false charge of smuggling, and died in prison.

Another outbreak of Sicilian and Neapolitan gang warfare in New York in the 1910s resulted in the emergence of Ignazio Saietta, known as Lupo the Wolf, as head of the city's Mafia. Saietta coined money by illegal lotteries, drug-peddling, and extortion from immigrants; his downfall took place when he literally began coining money, and the government gave him a 30-year sentence for forgery. After a struggle for the succession, he was succeeded by Giuseppe Masseria, known as Joe the Boss. Such internal wars were frequent, because the American Mafia lacked central control. As yet it had no equivalent to the Sicilian capo dei capi. Moreover, all the independent urban Mafias had to compete for the control of crime in their cities with various other gangs. "Diamond Jim" Colosimo, who ran a large vice empire based on prostitution and gambling in Chicago, had to leave large areas of the city in the hands of Irish and Jewish gangsters. In 1920 Colosimo was assassinated, probably by henchmen of Johnny Torrio, a rival mafioso from New York. Torrio, a man of vast ambition and ruthless efficiency, was himself superseded by the young man he took as his lieutenant—Alphonse Capone. Capone, though debarred by his Roman birth from becoming a true mafioso, became the head of Torrio's organization in 1925. It was he who gave the American Mafia the ideas that enabled it to expand.

The virtue of the Mafia in Sicily had been its extreme clannishness. But this quality proved a vice in the context of American crime. The Mafia's efforts were spent on fighting rival Neapolitan, Irish, or Jewish gangsters instead of on devising new ways to plunder the public. Once Capone had established himself as head of the Italian gangsters in Chicago, he began to demonstrate the virtues of cooperation. The hundreds of gangland killings in Chicago during prohibition, caused by the scramble for the huge profits from the sale of bootleg liquor by rival Italian, Irish, Jewish, and Polish gunmen, ended in a truce imposed by Capone. By this truce, the city was divided into territories, each under the control of a gang boss. But Capone's vision soon left Chicago to encompass the whole of the United States. In 1929 he organized a national convention of Mafia chiefs at Atlantic City, at which the whole United States was split into territories and assigned to gang leaders. Capone, who taught the close-knit Chicago Sicilians the wisdom of cooperating with gangsters of other ethnic groups, remained their effective boss, despite an attempt by a leading New York mafioso, Giuseppe Aiello, to murder him. Even Capone's downfall was an object lesson to the American Mafia; his love of the limelight and his contempt of the law led to his arrest and conviction on charges of filing false income-tax returns in 1931, and he was sent to jail, where he died in 1947.

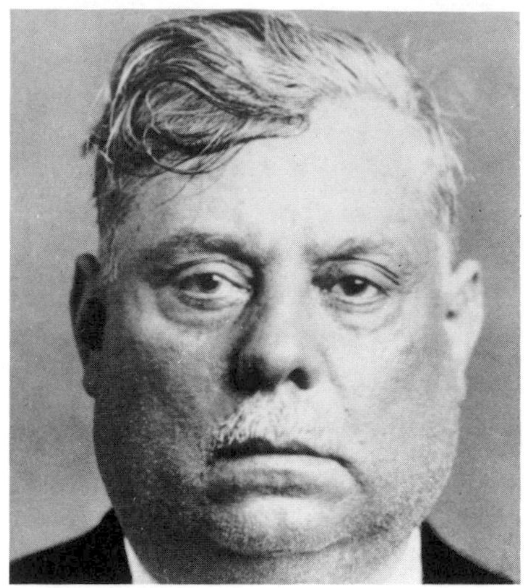

Notorious leaders of the U.S. Mafia, from the urban gangsters of the 1910s to the international entrepreneurs of the 1960s. Above left, Ignazio Saietta or "Lupo the Wolf," head of the New York Mafia in the 1920s, and one of the first "big bosses" of American crime. Above, his successor Giuseppe Masseria ("Joe the Boss"). Left, "Diamond Jim" Colosimo, head of the Chicago Mafia in the 1910s. Below left, Chicago Mafia leader Johnny Torrio, who seized Colosimo's empire in 1920. Below, Torrio's ambitious protégé Al Capone, who took control of crime in Chicago about 1925, and organized the rival leaders of city Mafias into a nationwide crime syndicate. Opposite page: Left, Giuseppe Aiello, the New York Mafia chief who tried to murder Capone in 1927. Right, Charles "Lucky" Luciano, leader of the new Mafia that emerged in the 1930s. It murdered many of the older chiefs, organized drug peddling and prostitution, and established itself as an international criminal network.

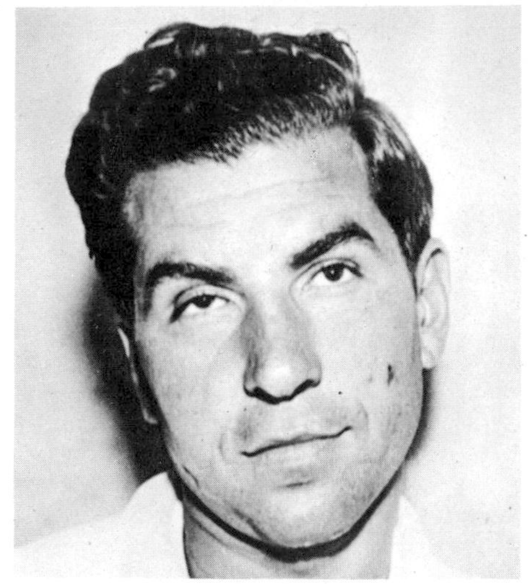

The new era of cooperation ushered in by Capone spawned the famous national network of killers called Murder Inc., which included non-Sicilians, and which killed for hire as the Assassins had done in their later degenerate days. For greed was exalted in the American mafioso over the discipline of omertà, and particularly over the concept of unquestioning obedience to the elder mafiosi. In their lust for a greater share of the spoils, the younger American mafiosi began ousting the older generation by murder. In 1931, led by Charles "Lucky" Luciano, they began a systematic elimination of the old mafiosi and their families, beginning with Joe the Boss in New York. With the help of non-mafiosi, they killed off some thirty or forty of their old chiefs. Their group, though known as the *Unione Siciliana*, was an entirely American criminal gang. One informer, Ernest Rupolo ("the Hawk"), has gone so far as to say that since 1931 the Unione has totally superseded the Mafia, and that any similarity between the two is purely imaginary.

With the destruction of the patriarchal and hereditary structure of the American Mafia, the social basis of omertà certainly disappeared. The life of rich Sicilian Americans in large cities had little in common with the life of small-town mafiosi in Sicily. The Americans were dealing with billions of dollars raised from an alien, industrial society; the Sicilians were dealing with much smaller sums raised from a backward and poverty-stricken rural society. The American Mafia became sophisticated; it learned how to move into legitimate industry and to work the levers of capitalism. While it kept those practices of the old Mafia that were useful for a criminal gang in the United States—vengeance on informers, the intimidation of juries, and corruption of the law—it abandoned the traditional Mafia philosophy. In Sicily, however, the Mafia has remained a way of life as well as a means of exploitation.

The Sicilian Mafia has survived many attacks, the most brutal of which was undoubtedly the campaign waged against it by Cesare Mori, Mussolini's chief of police, in the early 1920s. After flogging, maiming, flaying, and

Cesare Mori, Mussolini's chief of police in the 1920s, and organizer of the Fascist campaign against the Mafia, photographed in the Sicilian town of Piana dei Greci.

castrating hundreds of suspects, and deporting hundreds more, Mori declared in 1928 that the Mafia had been wiped out. His account of the campaign, though vainglorious and inaccurate, contains a few points of interest. "The most salient and perplexing factor in the psychology of the typical mafioso," Mori wrote, "is his conviction that he is doing no wrong. As long as he obeys the rules of omertà—whether he extorts, steals, or even murders—he is, to himself, as well as to his brethren, an honorable man. His conscience is at peace." The rules of war, by which a society allows members of its armed forces to murder and loot, are applied by members of the Mafia in times of peace, because they always feel themselves to be at war with the wider society. Nevertheless, Mori was not the man to moralize against the Mafia's correct view that the government at Rome was in a state of open and bloody warfare against its very existence.

Mori did not believe that the families of the Mafia elected their chiefs; he claimed that these chiefs chose themselves and imposed themselves. In a way he was right, for a family confirmed as its chief the one who showed most authority among them. Mori also recognized that the Mafia would absorb any talented Sicilian who had the qualifications it thought desirable; but once the Mafia thought one of its members might compromise the others, he was murdered or retired by force and threats. Mori emphasized that the Mafia was as much a philosophy as a society. It had little use for passwords and secret signs—the mafiosi knew one another by a way of speaking, a dignity and reserve of manner, a cold-eyed stare, an intuition. A recent witness, the

Protestant pastor Tullio Vinay, confirms this view, declaring that in Sicily, "the ideology of the people *is* the Mafia—to be strong, to be prepotent, to dominate. That is the first thing, and it is the effect of the history of Sicily, because the people of Sicily *need* to be somebody. And the Mafia is first the desire to dominate. To be the *lord of the situation.*"

In America, too, the Mafia had flourished because it met the immigrants' need for prestige. But the Sicilians' 19th-century tradition of extortion and robbery was an anachronism in a society where big business had outgrown its brutality and refined its techniques of success. As many Sicilians grew rich by legitimate means and joined the American middle classes, the old Mafia died; its successor became increasingly hard to differentiate from big business. The new American Mafia owns trucking businesses, hotels, casinos, jukebox firms, restaurants, whole resorts. It even organizes prostitution, a thing unthinkable to the old Sicilian mafiosi.

The successful American mafiosi, who had retained links with their homeland, eventually taught new techniques of extortion to the Sicilians. The beginnings of this influence lie in the Allied conquest of Sicily in 1943, when the Sicilian Mafia, so adept at picking winners, decided to take the advice of its American branch and allow the island to fall like a ripe plum into the hands of the invaders. For this purpose, the Allies enlisted the aid of "Lucky" Luciano, who was serving a 30-year jail sentence for the organization of prostitution, and who had already been used to stop Italian-American stevedores from sabotaging Allied ships in New York. The potent influence of the jailed head of the Mafia was evident. Hardly any cases of sabotage were reported from the New York docks, and resistance to Allied armies was negligible in Western and Central Sicily, where the Mafia was most powerful. Before the invasion, Calogero Vizzini, then capo dei capi of the Sicilian Mafia, was contacted in his home town of Villalba in Central Sicily by an airplane that dropped a packet wrapped in a yellow silk handkerchief marked with the letter "L"—presumably standing for Luciano. Vizzini, known as "Don Calò," allied himself with the invading American divisions, which contained nearly all the immigrant Sicilians in the American army. As a result of his orders to the local Mafia, nearly two thirds of the troops under Italian orders deserted; their commander was himself captured by the Mafia and handed over to the Americans.

The grateful Allies made Don Calò Mayor of Villalba and put into positions of power those mafiosi he recommended as anti-Fascists and true Italian patriots. Thus they delivered Sicily back into the hands of the Mafia, from which Mussolini had almost delivered it. It was ironical that the Allies should owe one of their cheapest and most decisive victories in World War II to the cooperation of American and Sicilian gangsters. The price of this victory, however, was paid in full. Luciano was paroled from prison and deported to Italy, where he became the acknowledged head of the international Mafia, while the old Mafia chieftains again assumed control of most of the small towns of Sicily and took their cut from nearly all Sicilian industry and agriculture.

From its experiences under Fascism and in America the Mafia had learned that the best climate for extortion was capitalism and the weakest system of law was under democracy. As one notable analyst of Italy, Luigi Barzini declares, "The Mafia sides with those in power. The Mafia was with the Bourbon kings before 1860 and immediately shifted its power, its loyalty, to Garibaldi when Garibaldi landed. The Mafia was on the side of the Americans when they landed in Sicily. The Mafia is siding with the Christian Democrats who are running the country now, at the present time."

The Christian Democrats soon found that the way to gain seats in Sicily and to keep back the Communist vote was to cooperate with the Mafia. This alliance led to the most tragic episode in Sicilian postwar history: the massacre of townspeople near Portella della Ginestra in 1947. The Christian Democrats had done badly in the Sicilian elections of that year; the townspeople near

Left and below, cheering Sicilians greet U.S. troops entering Monreale during the allied invasion of Sicily in 1943. In the words of the photographer, Robert Capa, "The road leading into the city was lined with tens of thousands of frantic Sicilians waving white sheets and home-made American flags. . . . Everyone had a cousin in 'Brook-a-leen.' " This warm reception was ensured by the efforts of Lucky Luciano, who threw the influence of the Sicilian Mafia on the side of the Allies as the price of his release from jail. After the war he settled in Naples and prospered, allegedly on the profits of international drug-peddling. He died in January 1962. Right, the funeral cortege of Luciano, who went to his grave like a national hero, in the hearse built for the funeral of Caruso.

Portella della Ginestra had voted for Popular Front candidates, and the powers-that-were in Sicily decided that the Reds needed a lesson. The agent of revenge chosen by the Mafia and the few aristocrats still powerful in Sicily was the successful bandit Salvatore Giuliano, a popular outlaw who had backed the Separatist movement in Sicily after the war and had even invited the United States to annex Sicily—a solution that would certainly have solved the Sicilians' problem of overcrowding and the Mafia's problem of getting its members from one country to the other. Giuliano (never actually a member of the Mafia) was promised a safe passage to Brazil with his men if he cooperated in the deterrence of the Reds. He duly opened fire with machine guns on the townsfolk celebrating May Day at Portella della Ginestra, killing 11 of them and wounding 55 others. The peasants in Sicily took this lesson to heart. In the next election, the vote for the Christian Democratic candidates climbed. Salvatore Giuliano, being of no further use to the Mafia, was then due to be eliminated.

But Giuliano was more difficult to eliminate than to employ. Warned of a Mafia plot, he tried to kidnap the capo dei capi, Don Calò, and also the Archbishop of Monreale. Far from submitting to the Mafia, he was actually trying to overthrow it. But the Mafia won over his lieutenant and cousin Pisciotta, who murdered Giuliano in July 1950. When tried for his part in the massacre at Portella della Ginestra, Pisciotta succinctly explained how the Sicilian Mafia, the police, and the bandits cooperated, rendering unto the government what was the government's—the votes—and rendering unto the rest what was theirs—a share of the loot. "We were a single body," Pisciotta testified, "bandits, police, and Mafia, like the Father, the Son, and the Holy Ghost." This trinity of power, linked and barely divisible, has ruled and still rules in Sicily, while the Sicilians who emigrate to the North to work become the staunchest supporters of the Communist Party.

The Mafia's ability to deliver the Sicilian vote has given it enormous influence in Rome. "This masonry of favors goes beyond Sicily," one commentator from Palermo says, "because those modern mafiosi who have transferred their activity to the mainland, to the areas round Naples and Rome, for instance, have been able to operate there with exactly the same favors and political protection that they've enjoyed here in Palermo." In Italy and in certain American states, the Mafia controls large sectors of power. Here, as in the small towns of Sicily, everyone knows perfectly well who the mafiosi are,

Opposite page, the celebrated Sicilian bandit Salvatore Giuliano (right) with his cousin Gaspare Pisciotta—the man who confessed to his murder in 1950. Right, women and children fleeing from the massacre at Portella della Ginestra on May Day 1947, carried out by Giuliano and his men at the command of the Mafia. Giuliano was killed in his bed on July 4, 1950, at the instigation of the Mafia and the police. Below, the courtyard death scene faked on the night of the murder to support the claim that police killed Giuliano in a gun battle. Below right, Giuliano's mother kisses the blood that surrounded her son's body (a traditional gesture of revenge).

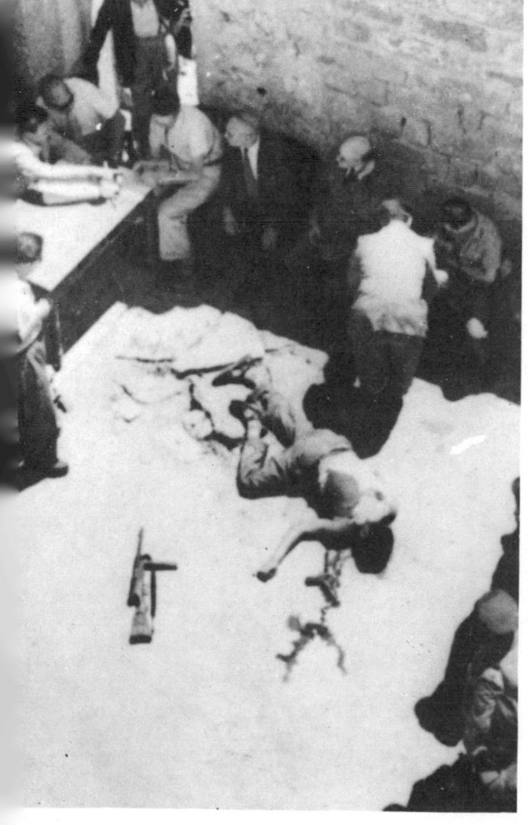

though their intrigues may remain secret. The fact that the Mafia chieftains are known, yet immune, is their most potent weapon; they seem able, in their chosen areas, to control industry, elections, and the processes of law. The very success of the new Mafia in industry and politics has done much to earn it the "respect" of the rich and powerful. The new Mafia has also earned the acquiescence of the wider society, which the old capi mafiosi sought so hard to gain in their small Sicilian towns.

One acute commentator on Italy talks of the Mafia as "a sort of habit, a moral habit. This is the danger, that now Mafia isn't any more what it used to be, a sort of organized delinquency. But now it has spread like an octopus, and the mentality of all business people and politicians especially—they do it openly, they blackmail, they keep you under their thumb. You see, they *use* their power." Perhaps, in many ways, outside Sicily the example of the Mafia has been even more dangerous than its practice. It has taught other American gangsters its protection rackets and its means of intimidation; it has taught Italian politicians how to get the votes they need. If the practice of

Representing Sicily's two governments, a carabiniere and a mafioso stand outside Brancaccio polling station to supervise elections to the Regional Assembly (1959).

the Mafia has been an education for American crime, its philosophy has been an education for Italian politics. Only the citizens and the process of democracy are the losers.

Nicola Gentile, formerly a leading American mafioso, told in 1963 of the increasing centralization of the Mafia; though local organizations were still autonomous, modern communications had given much more authority to the Sicilian capo dei capi and to the "king," his counterpart in the United States; the huge profits of international drug-smuggling demanded a far higher measure of cooperation and subordination. Contact with the American Mafia has enabled the Sicilian Mafia to exploit the industrialization that is slowly creeping into the island. Luciano and other expatriated American gangsters have advised on new techniques of extortion, and have masterminded them. The result is that new blocks of flats and new factories in Palermo are just as much under the control of the Mafia as the old orange groves and sulfur mines. A bandit in a pinstripe suit remains a bandit. When Brecht made Mack the Knife turn from burglary to business and asked his famous question, "What is robbing a bank compared with founding a bank?" he forecast the path the modern Mafia would take.

The slaughter of the old American Mafia by the new, and the breakdown of patriarchal control, have also been reenacted in Sicily in recent years. The new Mafia outlook percolated to the town of Corleone, where, in 1957, an American-style mafioso called Luciano Liggio declared war on the old-style Mafia, led by Dr. Michele Navarra. The issue was the construction of a dam nearby, which Navarra opposed for fear that irrigation would make the peasants prosperous and free them from the Mafia's domination. But Liggio wanted the quick profits from the construction of the dam, which he duly secured. In Navarra's world, all change was bad, even though it might be profitable; in Liggio's world, all profits were good, and change could always be exploited. Liggio would have none of the secrecy of the traditional Mafia, with its graduated system of warnings and covert killings; in a town where the murder rate was already swollen by old blood feuds, wars between shepherds and farmers, and attacks on the Communists, he and his men shot people down in broad daylight. Liggio shot Navarra, and was tried and convicted for the murder in his absence. Not until 1964 were he and 54 of his associates arrested. After an investigation that lasted more than a year, they were indicted on a lengthy list of charges.

A Sicilian mafioso with three sons tries to place one in the Church, one in the medical profession, and one in the law. The result is that churchmen in Sicily acquiesce to a great extent in the doings of the Mafia, while the capofamiglia of a district may even be the local priest. In 1962, four of the Franciscan monks of Mazzarino were tried for conspiracy, extortion, and manslaughter. While the interpenetration of the Church and the Mafia was obvious to all outside observers, fear of the Mafia's power kept the mouths of

Above, the body of Dr. Michele Navarra, head of Corleone's traditional Mafia, who was shot dead in his car by eight gunmen in August 1958. Above right, an early photograph of Luciano Liggio, the rival mafioso who engineered Navarra's death.

Right, Danilo Dolci's social study group meets at its headquarters in Partinico. Dolci (in glasses) was jailed in 1958 for attempting to find work for the unemployed, and tried in 1966 on 14 charges of libel arising from his anti-Mafia activities.

most of the vital witnesses sealed. A scapegoat was found in the gardener at the monastery, and the monks were acquitted for having acted under duress. But a year later, when a special commission was due to arrive from Rome to investigate the Mafia, an appeal by the prosecution was allowed. The monks were then re-tried, convicted, and sentenced to 13 years' imprisonment.

As once the Mafia became a force of law and order by eliminating rival bandits, so, when its members are well entrenched in a state, it merges itself with the state and sacrifices its less sophisticated followers. The high profits to be made by the legal exploitation of the city worker may even induce it to give up its grip on the Sicilian peasant, who is at last finding effective champions. The boldest of these is the Northern Italian reformer Danilo Dolci, who has married a Sicilian widow and settled among the peasants. Dolci has led the peasants in fights to take over unused land and build roads; he has become the gadfly and conscience of Italy over the problem of Sicily—and, despite many warnings from the Mafia, he has survived. Prodded on by public opinion, the government in Rome has begun land reform in Sicily, including the sale of unused land to the peasants. The new Palermo Mafia, more interested in its urban profits, has actually welcomed land reform as another means of raising revenue; it has taken its usual commission on all

sales of land, and has kept prices of farm products artificially low in the countryside and high on the Palermo markets. Better to exploit a small business than a peasant, better to exploit a big business than a small one, better to exploit the whole state than a big business.

The central government in Rome, urged on by inflamed opinion in the rest of Italy, sent its anti-Mafia Commission to Sicily in July 1963. Since then, the Sicilian police have been forced into action. There have been over 2000 arrests, and a truce on killing by the Mafia, which always lies low when the heat is on. However, the Mafia seems to be surviving the commission as it has survived many worse enemies. "It will take a generation to eradicate the Mafia," says Luigi Barzini, a member of the commission, "and even then, can we be sure that Sicilians, who have invented this terrific technique of living in a law-abiding state as if the law did not exist, can they forego it when it offers—even an honorable man—so many advantages?"

The only way to eradicate the Sicilian Mafia is to eradicate the poverty and rural morality that have spawned it. Prosperity will bring an end to the old Mafia, because the peasants will no longer need it to find jobs and the new city mafiosi will seek the respect of the rich and the urban rather than of their own kind. When the prosperity of Italy spreads south, the extortion of the

Mafia will merge into the extortion of big business, terror tactics will no longer be necessary to bring in the complacent Christian Democratic vote, and wealth will wither the brotherhood that poverty spawned, which had nothing but its fierce honor to cling to.

In the United States, this process has already begun. Leading gangsters are continually harried by the federal authorities. In 1957, about 60 Mafia chiefs were arrested when they met at Apalachin in Upper New York State; 20 of them were sentenced to prison terms of three to five years for conspiracy to thwart the law and for perjury. Though the Supreme Court, always jealous of the liberties of the individual, overturned the convictions, the new Mafia had actually been discovered in conference and sentenced. A special section of the F.B.I. and the Department of Justice, reinforced in 1961 when Robert Kennedy became Attorney General, has been set up to compile dossiers on all the major Sicilian and southern Italian criminals.

Moreover, in well-publicized hearings before a Senate committee, the federal authorities have produced an informer from the inner ranks of the Sicilian gangsters, Joe Valachi. It was Valachi who first referred to the newest of the Mafias as the *Cosa Nostra*, and who named Vito Genovese as its head. In 1962, after Genovese had given Valachi the ritual kiss of death in jail (the signal that Valachi's murder had been decided upon in council), Valachi desperately killed a fellow prisoner, whom he mistook for a Mafia agent. His only way out of the electric chair was to inform, and this he did with relish, enjoying the publicity of television and the dispassionate recounting of the many murders he had seen. Though Valachi's evidence has not yet

Left, the four Mafia monks of the Franciscan monastery of Mazzarino on trial at Messina in March 1962 on charges of conspiracy, extortion, and manslaughter. Though the monks' crimes were common knowledge, their power and prestige silenced the leading witnesses for the prosecution, including their victim's widow. They were convicted at a retrial in 1963.

Right, Joe Valachi, a former member of the U.S. Mafia or Cosa Nostra, testifies before a senate investigating committee in October 1963. Fear of the death penalty for killing a fellow prisoner in the Atlanta Federal Penitentiary prompted Valachi to break his oath of secrecy and to disclose details of Cosa Nostra crimes. He was convicted of murder in the second degree and sentenced to life imprisonment.

been corroborated, the new Mafia in the United States has remained quiescent in the east and has transferred many of its operations to such states as Nevada, where the law authorities are lax to the point of acceptance.

In the most famous exposé of the Mafia in the United States—the hearings before the Kefauver Committee in the Senate in 1951—the Senator found it "a fearful thing to contemplate how close America has come to the saturation point of criminal and political corruption. . . ." He forgot one thing. When saturation point is reached, the thing that saturates the body politic becomes the body politic. In the end, the American melting pot will work, and the United States will absorb the Sicilian Mafia, as once it absorbed the Irish Bowery Boys. As the Mafia families become part of big business, so the control of organized crime will slip to other underprivileged groups. Though the Mafia may teach the ruling Americans lessons about the ruthless use of power, these lessons cannot be wholly applied in a nation that has many of the genuine forms and traditions of democracy.

The aspirations of the new mafiosi—and perhaps the future of the Mafia—may be summed up in the words of "Lucky" Luciano (who, at the time of his death in 1962, was about to be arrested on charges of international drug-trafficking): "If I had my time over again," he said in 1960, "I'd do the same sort of thing, only I'd do it legal. Too late I learned that you need just as good a brain to make a crooked million as an honest million."

Crime does pay, as any study of the Mafia shows. But when crime pays really well, criminals become respectable; and the first to do so are those who became criminals only to win respect.

11 The Ku Klux Klan

"I, before the immaculate Judge of Heaven and Earth, and upon the Holy Evangelists of Almighty God, do, of my own free will and accord, subscribe to the following sacredly binding obligation:

"1. We are on the side of justice, humanity, and constitutional liberty, as bequeathed to us in its purity by our forefathers.

"2. We oppose and reject the principles of the radical party.

"3. We pledge mutual aid to each other in sickness, distress, and pecuniary embarrassment.

"4. Female friends, widows, and their households, shall ever be special objects of our regard and protection.

"Any member divulging, or causing to be divulged, any of the foregoing obligations, shall meet the fearful penalty and traitor's doom, which is Death! Death! Death!"

This was the oath of initiation that a former member of the Ku Klux Klan disclosed to an investigating committee of the United States Senate in 1871. The investigation revealed the extent and viciousness of the terror the defeated whites of the South were using against their conquerors from the North and their former Negro slaves, freed at the end of the Civil War. The Ku Klux Klan was a secret terrorist organization of white supremacists, who thought that violence was the only answer to the military and corrupt governments

Protesting the Civil Rights Act of 1964, Klan members parade in St. Augustine, Florida, with an inverted American flag. In defiance of federal law, the Southern remnants of the Klan still cling to their traditional objective—"the maintenance of the supremacy of the white race."

imposed on the defeated Southern States. In its beginning, the Klan could claim to be a resistance movement against intolerable oppression, even if it would end as the mere tool of hate, greed, and sadism.

General Nathan Bedford Forrest, who founded and ran the Klan, definitely thought of it as a temporary guerilla organization that would last only as long as Northern carpetbaggers and illiterate Negroes and Southern renegades, called scalawags, ruled the Southern States. Forrest was tall and black-bearded; he had been a death-and-glory commander in the Confederate cavalry. His maxim for winning cavalry actions had been: "Get there first with the most." At one time he had been a slave dealer, but he had bought himself into the plantation aristocracy. He had been accused during the Civil War of the atrocious massacre at Fort Pillow, where captured colored troops had been exterminated. He was not likely to accept the principle of Negroes representing white people in the legislatures of the South.

Forrest appeared in front of the Senate investigating committee and was questioned about the Klan. He never admitted to being its leader, though he had given interviews to the newspapers telling them of the Klan, and its rise in various Southern States had begun immediately after his travels through those States. He was, however, absolutely sure of the righteous purposes of the Klan and told the Senate committee of them: "There was a great deal of insecurity felt by the southern people. There were a great many northern men coming down there, forming Leagues all over the country. The negroes were holding night meetings; were going about; were becoming very insolent; and the southern people all over the State were very much alarmed. I think many of the organizations did not have any name; parties organized themselves so as to be ready in case they were attacked. Ladies were ravished by some of these negroes, who were tried and put in the penitentiary, but were turned out in a few days afterward. There was a great deal of insecurity in the country, and I think this organization was got up to protect the weak, with no political intention at all."

In his incoherent way, Forrest set out the haphazard social pressures that may lead to the foundation of secret societies—dislocation in a defeated group, the urge to resist tyranny, fear of humiliation at the hands of troops or servants become rulers, the excuse that a league of the enemy needs to be fought by a conspiracy of friends, and the dark sexual imaginings that seek revenge at the rumor of outrage. Forrest also showed that a particular secret society flourishes when little bands of rebels are widespread everywhere and are looking for a uniform and a leader who can cloak a political purpose under the hood of a benevolent society of brothers.

The oath a Klansman had to take on initiation hardly justified Forrest's mild description of the secret society. In fact, the Klan was a group of Democrats who hated Negroes, Northerners, and Republicans. After the Civil War, the defeated men of the South had found (in the words of their devastator,

Above, newly enfranchised Southern Negroes hold a political meeting before their first presidential election (*Harper's Weekly*, July 1868). Right, the first Negro representative, John W. Menard, arrives in Congress (*Frank Leslie's Illustrated Newspaper*, December 1868). Resentment of Negro power, and of the Republicans who favored it, was a major factor in the formation of the Klan. Below right, a heroic portrait of the Klan's founder, the ex-Confederate general Nathan Forrest. Below, a cartoon that betrays the Klan's role as a resistance movement against Northern rule. It shows "the fate in store for those great pests of Southern society —the carpet-bagger and the scalawag—if found in Dixie's land after the break of day on the 4th of March next." (*Independent Monitor*, Tuscaloosa, September 1, 1868.)

General Sherman): "Mourning in every household, desolation written in broad characters across the whole face of the country, cities in ashes and fields laid waste, their commerce gone, their system of labor annihilated and destroyed. Ruin, poverty, and distress everywhere." The Southerners had tried to seize back the government of their States and reduce the freed Negroes to serfdom through new laws that came to be known as "Black Codes"; but the radical Republican Congress had retaliated by imposing military rule on the South, after the murder of the moderate Lincoln and the ineffectiveness of his successor, Andrew Johnson. When, in 1868, the Northern Commander in Chief, General Grant, became president, there was no control over the radical Republicans in Congress. A reign of political corruption run by Northerners and freed slaves exploited the ruins of the South.

There was bound to be resistance on the part of the hundreds of Confederate veterans, who had little to do in the economic slump after the war in the South. In 1865, six young men in Pulaski, Tennessee, formed a hooded society of mock ghosts and ghouls; they called it Ku Klux Klan, derived from the Greek word *kuklos* meaning "circle," and the Scots word "clan." Wherever the original Klansmen rode by night in their shrouds on shrouded horses, they found that freed Negro slaves, uneducated and superstitious, were terrified by such sinister visitors, who often claimed to be the ghosts of the Confederate dead, pretended to drink a gallon of water at a gulp, and produced a skeleton hand out of their sleeves to grasp a Negro's palm. Forrest saw

Victims of the South's postwar poverty line up to collect rations from the Union army (*Harper's Weekly*, August 11, 1866).

immediately the possibility of using such practical jokes to terrorize the Southern countryside. He claimed 550,000 hooded riders in the South by 1868, under the name of Klansmen, Palefaces, the White Brotherhood, the White League, or Knights of the White Camellia.

Forrest, though aided by other ex-Confederate officers, did not have a proper military organization, and could not keep control of his men. He may have intended to be a Robin Hood, as the early Klan oath suggests, and he may have tried to protect the weak against the freebooters working in the name of government. But soon the local Klans degenerated into a horde of gangs, denounced by one of the Klan founders as often composed of "rash, imprudent, and bad men." These gangs rode at night for personal revenge, profit, or thrills. Any rogue could put on a hood, whether black or white man; the cloak over the face hid all responsibility. Secrecy, which had been the strength of the early Klan, became its weakness; the mystery of its organized terror, a license for the vengeance of anarchic criminals.

The number of murders and outrages committed by the Klan between 1868 and 1872 is impossible to establish. Every criminal or man who wanted to pursue a vendetta wore a hood. In almost all Southern counties there was sporadic warfare between the armed Negro militia and Southern veterans. Terror was used by both sides, though undeniably the Negroes suffered the worst. The Senate committee found that in nine counties of South Carolina, over a period of six months, the Klan had lynched and murdered 35 men,

New Orleans law officers arrest Negroes for vagrancy under the "Black Codes" (*Frank Leslie's Illustrated Newspaper*, May 1868).

whipped 262 men and women, and otherwise outraged, shot, mutilated, raped, or burned out 103 other people. During this time, Negroes had killed four men, beaten one man, and committed 16 other outrages; there was no known case of rape of a white woman. In the thousands of murders that took place in the South in the decade after the Civil War, white Southerners killed or attacked Negroes in nearly every case. The motive for this broadcast violence was simple; to keep the black man in his place and away from the polls. W. E. Du Bois, one of the great leaders and historians of the Negro people, summed up the "significantly varied" reasons for the Klan outrages: "the victims should suffer in revenge for killing, and for some cases of arson; they were Republicans; they were radical; they had attempted to hold elections; they were carrying arms; they were 'niggers'; they were 'damn niggers'; they boasted that they would own land . . . they were whipped for debt, for associating with white women, and for trying to vote."

The horror inspired by the Klan was due more to its haphazard assaults than to its State-wide organization. Though Forrest was never in control of his Klansmen, he organized the Klan on paper like a Southern army. The whole South was called the Invisible Empire; each State was a Realm, each congressional district a Dominion, each county a Province, and each

Disguised in the motley robes and masks of the early Klan, members of a North Carolina den prepare to hang a local Republican, John Campbell. He was rescued by federal agents. (Newspaper illustration of 1871.)

locality a Den. Forrest was the Grand Wizard, and his staff were the ten Genii; each Realm had a Grand Dragon and eight Hydras, each Dominion a Grand Titan and six Furies, each Province a Grand Giant and four Goblins, each Den a Grand Cyclops and two Night Hawks. This perfect hierarchy could have worked if the Klan had not been a hidden organization; but as it was, Forrest could not hold accountable any local Klan for senseless outrages committed by hooded riders in its area, because local Klansmen could always claim that the guilty hooded riders might have been Negroes in disguise. Forrest's failure to control his men was shown by the local Klans' refusal, in 1869, to obey his order to disband. Forrest himself had seen that they had got out of hand and were increasing the disorder of the South instead of putting an end to anarchy.

Once Forrest and the best of the Klan's military leaders had left the organization in disgust for its reckless acts of indiscriminate revenge, the sadism and childishness of local Klansmen had no restraints. The General Orders of the Klan in Tuscaloosa, Alabama, could be headed:

> Hollow Hell, Devil's Den, Horrible Shadows, Ghostly Sepulchres.
> Head Quarters of the Immortal Ate of the KKK
> Gloomy Month. Bloody Moon. Black Night. Last Hour.

But such an infant fantasy of Halloween gibberish could result in real murder and mutilation of Negroes and Republicans. While the Senate investigating committee sat, petitions from terrorized Negroes flooded into Congress. One from Kentucky Negroes asked for laws to suppress "the Ku Klux Klans riding nightly over the country going from County to County and in the County towns spreading terror wherever they go, by robbing whipping ravishing and killing our people without provocation, compelling Colored people to brake the ice and bathe in the Chilly waters of the Kentucky River."

President Grant was too much of a military man to support a guerilla insurrection. In 1870 and 1871 the "Ku-Klux Acts" were passed to put the federal government in charge of Southern elections; they also gave the president power to declare martial law in the Southern States and to suspend the writ of habeas corpus. Klansmen were frequently thrown into jail without trial for long periods, because they were usually acquitted by a jury—except when it happened to be a Negro jury. Excessive vengeance by lawlessness was now replaced by excessive vengeance by law.

Moderate Southern opinion supported the legal and illegal attack on the Klan. Many Southerners had had enough of anarchy; like one moderate Mississippi minister, they thought "that Ku Kluxing is unnecessary and foolish, whether engaged in by whites or blacks." In face of this public disapproval, and because white Democrats were gradually winning back control over State governments in the South, the Klan withered away. The white and red and black hoods were put away, the ghoulish jokes and outlandish costumes were once more confined to Halloween and to Mardi Gras in New Orleans.

How the first Klan entered into Southern folklore. Left, the frontispiece of Thomas Dixon's popular novel *The Clansman, A Historical Romance of the Ku Klux Klan* (1905). It glorified the Klan as a crusade against federal oppression and Negro power. Right, triumphant Klansmen scatter Negro federal troops in a scene from the film *The Birth of a Nation* (1915). Dixon's novel provided the inspiration and part of the plot.

By a tacit compromise in 1877, the Democrats were allowed to rule the South in the name of white supremacy in return for allowing the Republicans to rule the North in the name of big business. When the South was allowed by Congress to reduce the freed Negroes to voteless sharecroppers, there was no need for the Klan to ride. The carpetbaggers went back North to loot their fellows there; racism below the Potomac and corruption above lay down quietly side by side.

Southerners love the past, and they love gilding it. In their memory, a patch becomes a plantation and a cowed slave is transformed into a contented mammy. As Malory once turned the feudal robber barons of the Middle Ages into the Arthurian Knights of the Round Table, so white Southern memories transformed the brutal Klansmen into the white knights of chivalry and romance. There was much more Walter Scott in their fond folklore than actual fact. And when the cinema came to direct human imagination by visions on celluloid, a Southern genius called David Wark Griffith could conjure up millions of hooded riders merely by representing the first Ku Klux Klan as a group of chivalric heroes who hunted down a Negro murderer and rapist. If *Uncle Tom's Cabin* incited the Civil War in the North, *The Birth of a Nation* (1915) helped to revive the dead body of the Klan in South and West. Griffith, one Southerner noted, "made the Ku Klux as noble as Robert E. Lee."

In the year Griffith's film classic appeared, a racist sniffed the wind of reaction against alien influences and decided to become a second General Forrest for the sake of the Old South. William Joseph Simmons of Alabama, a one-time soldier and minister and drummer of ladies' garters, was a great

joiner. He had belonged to some fifteen fraternal organizations, including the Masons. "I believe in fraternal orders and fraternal relationships among men," he stated, "in a fraternity of nations." In the name of the fraternity of the white Protestant American people against the rising tide of color and Catholics and Jews and immigrants from southern Europe, Simmons strode to the top of Stone Mountain near Atlanta with 15 followers in 1915 and burned a fiery cross by night at the side of a rough stone altar, on which lay the American flag, an open Bible, a naked sword, and a canteen of "holy" river water. There, Simmons declared himself Grand Wizard of the revived Ku Klux Klan and administered the oath of allegiance to his kneeling disciples, who rose as Knights of the new Invisible Empire.

Yet Simmons was a failure as an organizer and as a salesman; the Hun in Europe seemed a more important enemy than the alien at home. Simmons nearly ruined himself in attracting a few thousand members to the cause of the revived Klan; but when he was on the point of bankruptcy, he met two of the most successful merchandisers of hate known in modern times. Edward Young Clarke and his mistress, Mrs. Elizabeth Tyler, ran a public relations and promotional business called the Southern Publicity Association. They raised funds for the Young Men's Christian Association and the Salvation Army; but they decided that the profits of bigotry might exceed the profits of brotherhood. Meeting Simmons in 1920, Clarke signed a contract by which the Grand Wizard remained the figurehead of the revived Klan, while the Clarke-Tyler combination took recruiting in hand and tapped the pockets of the Knights of the Invisible Empire.

With Klan hoods sold as ruthlessly as American flags during the Great War, membership of the Klan reached 100,000 by 1921 and about 4,000,000 by 1924. It captured the imaginations of the fearful small towns of the South and West, and even won adherents in the rural North. No other nativist movement had done so well since the Know Nothings and the American Protective Association of the 19th century. And the very success of the Klan's recruiting, which Clarke and Mrs. Tyler had seen merely as a method of bamboozling Babbitts into joining another nonsensical fraternity, changed the purpose of the Klan from a fund-raising racket to a political force inside many States and within the Democratic party. The second Ku Klux Klan had risen as the marketed shadow of the first; but when its members came to be numbered in millions, it was transformed into a nationwide threat to democracy, while the first Klan had only subverted popular government in the South.

The second Klan would have amounted to little, had not a politically conscious group of rebels led by a plump Texan dentist, Hiram Wesley Evans, seized control of the Klan from Simmons, Clarke, and Mrs. Tyler in 1922. Installed by Simmons as national secretary or Imperial Kligrapp of the order, Evans won enough support among Klan leaders to elevate Simmons to the powerless post of Emperor of the Klan, and to push out Clarke and Mrs. Tyler. These two had, anyway, been discovered half-dressed and drunk together and had been convicted of disorderly conduct. How could they claim to run an organization committed to fighting fornication and liquor?

Evans organized the Klan as a political power-group within the Southern Democratic party. Klan candidates reached the United States Senate and the governorship of several States. In Indiana, David C. Stephenson, who (like so many small-town dreamers) worshiped Napoleon and wanted to be president, was Grand Dragon of the State; he effectively took over the whole local government, appointing his henchmen to every office in the State. After the great Konklave at Kokomo on July 4, 1923, when Stephenson, clad in a purple robe, arrived in a gilded airplane to address the faithful, the Klan virtually ran Indiana, and some 500,000 people in the State wore Klan robes and supported the treasury and the policy of the hooded order. The Klan may have been secret, but it was never exclusive. It wanted all the members it could get, for both their money and their votes. "They just throwed the doors open," a disillusioned Texan Klansman declared, "and every man that had the money, they took him in to get his vote . . . and if he did not have any money, they took his note payable in the fall. . . ."

Simmons himself turned the gibberish of the old Klan into a new mumbo jumbo of idiocy. He was besotted with the magic of the letter K. The meeting of a Klan was called a Klonvokation; cases were tried at a Kloncilium. Under the Exalted Cyclops of each local Den, now called a Klavern, sat a Klaliff, a Klokard, a Kludd, a Kligrapp, a Klabee, a Kladd, Klageros, Klexters, and Klokann. The book of ritual of the new Klan was called the Kloran, a strange title for the bible of a Christian organization. The ritual itself was a hotchpotch of masonic rites and childish rhetoric put together by Simmons, whose one inspiration was to burn fiery crosses at each Konklave in order to spread terror and to prove faith in Christianity. Yet, in a curious way, the Klan's burning of the Cross was as blasphemous as the supposed spitting on the Cross by the Templars. The merciful side of Christ would be denied by any such action.

The Kloran preached a bastard Christian militant faith, that of white supremacists riding against the Jew, the Catholic, and the Negro, and imposing a Puritan law and order on backsliding Protestants. The catechism asked of a Klansman made it clear that the organization was for white Anglo-Saxon Protestant nationalists only.

"1. Is the motive prompting your ambition to be a klansman serious and unselfish?

"2. Are you a native born, white, Gentile American citizen?

"3. Are you absolutely opposed to and free of any allegiance of any nature to any cause, government, people, sect or ruler that is foreign to the United States of America?

"4. Do you believe in the tenets of the Christian religion?

"5. Do you esteem the United States of America and its institutions above any other government, civil, political, or ecclesiastical in the whole world?

"6. Will you, without mental reservation, take a solemn oath to defend, preserve, and enforce same?

"7. Do you believe in clanishness, and will you faithfully practice same towards klansmen?

"8. Do you believe in and will you faithfully strive for the eternal maintenance of white supremacy?

"9. Will you faithfully obey our constitution and laws, and conform willingly to all our usages, requirements, and regulations?

"10. Can you always be depended on?"

The oath of the second Klan showed significant differences from that of the first; it was nationalist rather than sectional, and overtly for white supremacy. Yet the terms of the oath were quite rational; this was not true of the secret code of the Klan, which was childish in the extreme. When two Klansmen met, they would give a Klasp of left hands after something like the following Klonversation:

"*Ayak?*" (Are you a Klansman?)

"*Akia.*" (A Klansman I am.)

"*Capowe.*" (Countersign and password or written evidence.)

"*Cygnar?*" (Can you give Number and Realm?)

"*No. 1, Atga.*" (Number One Klan of Atlanta, Georgia.)

"*Kigy.*" (Klansman, I greet you.)

"*Itsub.*" (In the sacred, unfailing bond.)

"*Sanbog.*" (Strangers are near, be on guard.)

Above, a complacent crowd below the corpse of a Negro lynch-mob victim in the Deep South. Racial hatred ran high when the second Klan rose to power in the 1920s; its crimes of violence were widely condoned.

Below, the organizers of the second Klan. (Left to right): Imperial Wizard Simmons, the ex-preacher who concocted Klan ritual; assistant publicity agent Elizabeth Tyler; publicity chief Edward Young Clarke.

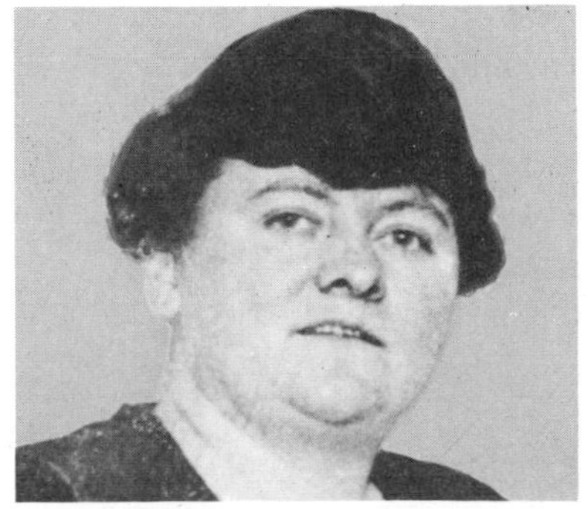

The Great War's ending led to a wave of reaction against alien Europe and to America's refusal to join the League of Nations. Under the banner of "one hundred per cent Americanism," the United States turned inward upon itself against foreigners and restricted immigration, while small-town America increasingly grew to loathe the cities with their ghettos of foreign-born Americans. The boom of the twenties was confined to the cities; the farmer and the townsman steadily lost influence and income. Small wonder that rural people saw in the hooded riders of *The Birth of a Nation* the rebirth of the old rural Protestant United States, which resisted the immoral and carpetbagging governments and manners of the big cities. Moreover, what could satisfy a small townsman more, frustrated as he was by his loss of national importance, than to put on rich robes and mumble long words and terrify those even worse off than himself? When men feel inadequate, they usually find inferiors to maltreat in order to regain their self-respect.

Wilbur Cash, most profound of all the analysts of the Southern mind, described the motives behind the revival of the Klan. "Here in ghostly rides through the moonlit, aromatic evening to whip a Negro or a prostitute or some poor white given to violating the Seventh Commandment or drinking up his scant earnings instead of clothing his children, or merely given to staying away from church; to tar and feather a labor organizer or a schoolmaster who had talked his new ideas too much—in slow, swaying noonday parades through the burning silence of towns where every Negro was gone from the streets, and the Jews and the Catholics and the aliens had their houses and shops shuttered—here was surcease for the personal frustrations and itches of the Klansman, of course. But also the old coveted, splendid sense of being a heroic blade, a crusader sweeping up mystical slopes for White Supremacy, religion, morality, and all that had made up the faith of the Fathers: of being the direct heir in continuous line of the Confederate soldiers at Gettysburg and of those old Klansmen who had once driven out the carpetbagger and tamed the scalawag; of participating in ritualistic assertion of the South's continuing identity, its will to remain unchanged and defy the ways of the Yankee and the world in favor of that one which had so long been its own.

"An authentic folk movement, beyond a doubt: such was the Klan."

The expertise of Clarke and Mrs. Tyler found a way to enrol rural nostalgia and discontent. Adding to the old organization of the first Klan, they put in the field hundreds of drummers called Kleagles. These traveled around the United States to sign up Klansmen; while $4.50 out of every $10 taken for an initiation fee went back to the Klan treasury at Atlanta and another $1.50 remained in the hands of the local Klan, the remaining $4 stuck to the Kleagle's palm. The Kleagles were encouraged first to sign up the leading figures in any small town, then to play on local prejudices in order to attract more and more people to the Klan; any bigot, sadist, or criminal was allowed to join as long as he had his $10.

VOL. 9, NO. 4 — WASHINGTON, D. C., SATURDAY, JULY 6, 1929 — PRICE FIVE CENTS

Roman Church and Press Start Campaign to Force America to

RECOGNIZE POPE AS KING

Vol. 9, No. 5 — WASHINGTON, D. C., SATURDAY, JULY 13, 1929 — PRICE FIVE CENTS

Imperial Wizard Opens Klan Drive to Repeal 15th Amendment and

PERPETUATE WHITE SUPREMACY

VOL. 5, NO. 15. — WASHINGTON, D. C. SATURDAY, SEPTEMBER 26, 1925. — PRICE FIVE CENTS.

NATIONAL DEFENSE IS IN HANDS OF ROMAN GENERALS

American Institutions Must Be Perpetuated

FOLLOWERS OF POPE IN KEY POSITIONS CONTROL AMERICA'S MILITARY FORCES

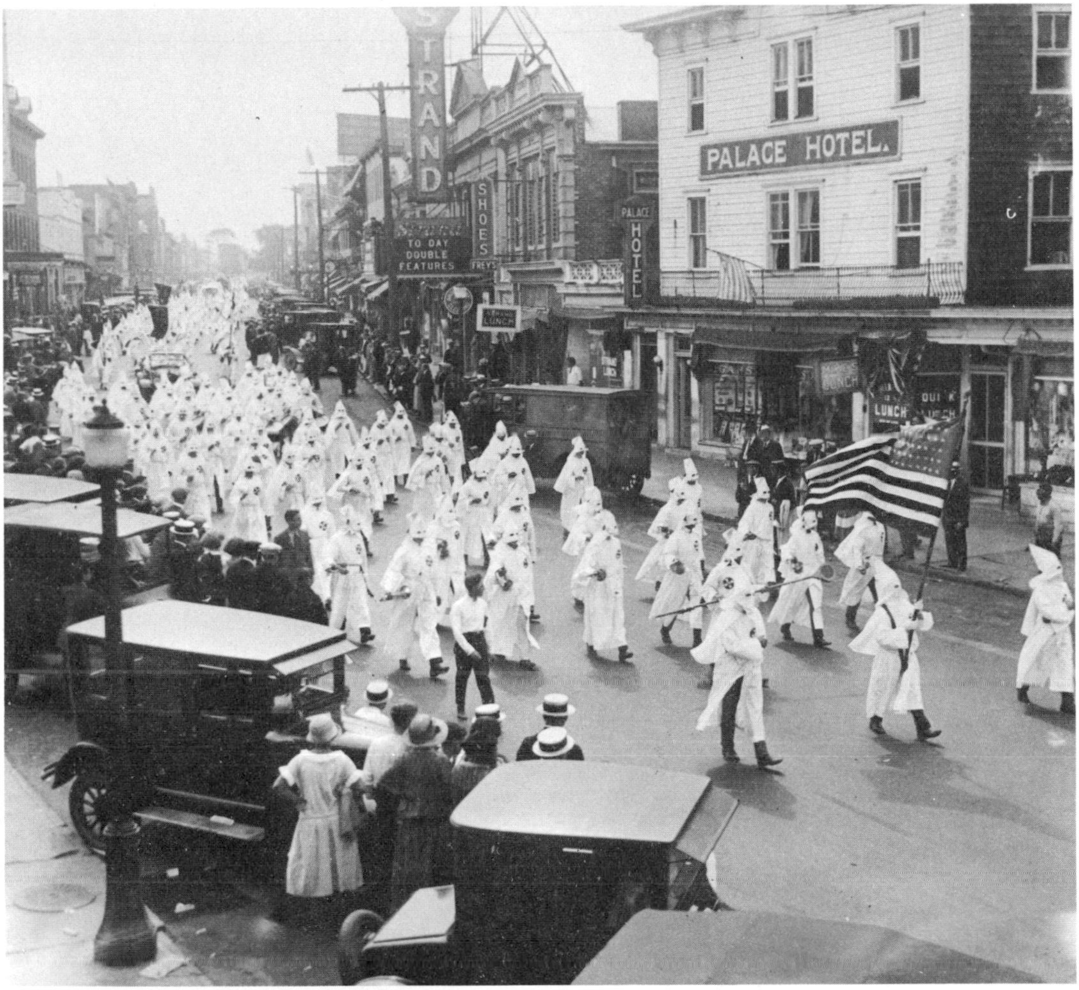

A wave of xenophobia swept the second Klan to power in the 1920s; intensive promotion helped. The Klan exploited small-town prejudice in a nationwide propaganda campaign, condemning Negroes, Jews, and Roman Catholics as "enemies of the state." Opposite page: upper left, anti-Catholic propaganda in a Klan newspaper of the period, *The Fellowship Forum.* Lower left, four hooded Klansmen pose in front of a biplane used for distributing propaganda leaflets. Center, above, and left, Klansmen parade openly with the fiery cross (a symbol of "the sacred traditions of the past"), and the national flag (a token of their vaunted "one hundred per cent Americanism").

The Klodes the Klan sang together were more like old school hymns than war cries. One Klansman testified to singing the following verse when he was initiated into the Klan beside the fiery cross:

We meet with cordial greetings
 In this our sacred cave,
To pledge anew our compact
 With hearts sincere and brave;
A band of faithful Klansmen,
 Knights of the KKK,
We will stand together
 For ever and for aye.

The Klan even organized the year into its own special Kalendar, based on the games of the old Klan. The year 1867, which marked the founding of many local Klans, replaced the birth of Christ as the starting point of the Kalendar; the seven days of the week were in order "dark, deadly, dismal, doleful, desolate, dreadful, and desperate"; the five weeks of the month were "woeful, weeping, wailing, wonderful, and weird"; the twelve months were "bloody, gloomy, hideous, fearful, furious, alarming, terrible, horrible, mournful, sorrowful, frightful, and appalling." This spookery in dating merely called up the ridicule of the Klan's enemies without concealing the dates of their meetings, for the order was too widespread to be truly secret.

The absurdity of the Klan's ritual made it attractive to those of limited mentality and education. There was also the added attraction, even to the moderately intelligent, of the Klansmen's petty secrecy. "Secrecy is an inherent and indispensable part of their equipment," wrote John Mecklin, the first analyst of the hooded order, "for without secrecy it would be vain to seek to escape the light of the drab and commonplace democratic day. The bar of secrecy makes possible a charmed land of mystery and imagination and intimate friendships. It is a make-believe land to be sure, often a cheap and tawdry substitute even for the uninteresting realities of small town existence. But the barrier of secrecy gives to this land of make-believe a fascinating charm.

It even lends to it in the minds of the initiated as well as of the 'aliens,' as the Klan calls outsiders, a sort of supernal reality. Whatever takes place within this veil of secrecy assumes a unique importance."

The initiation ceremony at the hands of shrouded Klansmen, with its use of the fiery cross, "holy" water, a Bible, and a naked sword, was awesome to the simple. And even the clever and the ambitious joined the Klan when it became a power in business and politics. There was no question that the Klan also appealed to many decent rural people, who vaguely wanted to "reform" the anarchy that seemed to be destroying the settled ways of village life in the days of bootlegging, prohibition, and city immorality, broadcast by the radio and cinema, and of the Model-T Ford, which one judge called "a house of prostitution on wheels." An old country tradition of vigilante attacks on local undesirables also gave the Klan a badge of respectability. Where the law in America was venal and inefficient, there was a long history of local townsmen cleaning up the district by lynch or mob action.

The Klan of the 1920s, indeed, was very different from the first Klan. While the original order had proceeded against Negroes and Republicans in the South, its imitator attacked Jews, Catholics, radicals, and immoralists as much as it attacked Negroes. The Negro had seemed the chief political and social threat after the Civil War; by the 1920s, he had been reduced to social insignificance outside the slums of the great cities. "Our antagonists are the lawbreaker, the prostitute, the Negro, the Jew, the Catholic, the foreigner, and the misguided Protestant," a Klan clergyman declared in full flower of faith, and then asked his congregation in Ohio to declare which side it supported.

Six handsigns from Klan ritual. Opposite page: to obtain admission to the den, the Klansman scratches a cross on the door. He holds the American flag to his heart and salutes it. After saluting the Confederate flag (on altar with sword and Bible), he extends his arms in the "sign of the cross."

This page: the Klansman makes the "sign of secrecy" by putting his finger to his lips, then gestures "off with his head" to remind him of the penalty for breaking the oath. Finally, he half raises his left hand to demonstrate the Klan "sign of greeting"—made by members when they enter the den.

Unless the Klan, despite its idiotic trappings, had appealed as a genuine reform movement and had tapped an urge toward a better Christian life, it would never have had the success it did in the Bible Belt of the United States. "The Ku Klux Klan is sweeping this great nation like a forest fire," a Klan newspaper declared. "Nothing of its kind ever has swept America like this wonderful movement for Christianity. . . . The fiery cross is moving on, spreading its beautiful light everywhere for the betterment of humanity and the triumph of those principles which have made this nation great. . . ."

The second Klan was both more bigoted and more of a revivalist movement than the first. The first Invisible Empire had a visible enemy, carpetbagger rule; the second Empire had an invisible foe, urban change. The new Klan preached at the simple choice of black and white in the rural Protestant mind. It was also spawned in the age of American fraternal organizations with new, efficient techniques for raising money through membership. Stephenson in Indiana became a millionaire through the Klan, while tens of millions of dollars poured through the treasury in Atlanta. The attraction of the Klan for the small-town businessman of the twenties is shown by the most effective of the new Klan's methods, that of economic boycott. Compared with the tens of thousands of outrages committed by the first Klan, the second seems a comparatively mild affair, even though hundreds of cases of murder, lynching, whipping, tarring and feathering, and running out of town were attributed to the Klan. Its new method of economic boycott, however, proved irresistible. The virtue of "clanishness" taught Klan members to deal only with fellow Klansmen. Signs reading TWK (Trade With Klan) appeared in the shop windows of Klansmen; undesirable shopkeepers were named at Klan meetings and boycotted until they went out of business. Many merchants joined the Ku Klux Klan for the same reason as they joined the Elks or the Oddfellows, for the benefit of their business—and to use the Klan to drive their competitors out of town.

The comparative sophistication of some of the techniques of the later Klan—boycotting, contributions to pro-Klan clergymen, and charity to Klan widows—did not prevent it from committing many horrible deeds. Mass conscription of anyone with $10 into Klan ranks gave sadists and criminals the opportunity to flog and torture any victim they chose. Hooded thugs could take the law into their own hands and call it moral justice. The resurgence of the Klan increased the number of lynchings of Negroes in the South; there were 135 cases of lynching in the Klan center of Georgia alone in the two years before 1922. The governor of Georgia declared: "In some counties the Negro is being driven out as though he were a wild beast. In others he is being sold as a slave. In others no Negroes remain. In only two of the 135 cases cited is the 'usual crime' [rape] involved." In fact, the attack on Negroes, as on Catholics or Jews, was now mainly for economic advantage, to get their business or land cheaply by forcing them out.

The sporadic anarchy of the Klan in the 1920s was less serious than its political organization as a potential group of American Fascists. Its successes in State politics reached their apogee in the Democratic presidential convention of 1924. The popular and anti-prohibitionist Catholic governor of New York, Alfred E. Smith, wanted the party's nomination for the White House; against him stood the Klan-backed William Gibbs McAdoo, a stern prohibitionist of good Protestant Anglo-Saxon stock. With the galleries howling for Smith and the Klansmen threatening Southern and Western delegates, the convention deadlocked for 102 ballots, before choosing a compromise candidate to lead the party to defeat. The great success of the Klan was to prevent Smith's supporters from passing a resolution condemning the Klan by name. The Klan already seemed powerful enough to have a veto over the candidates in one of the two major parties, as well as holding half-a-dozen State governments in its pocket. At least as powerful as Mussolini's Fascists before his takeover of the Italian government in 1922, the Klan could hope for great things in the future.

Yet American nativist movements, at the moment of their greatest strength, seem to wither suddenly. The Klan was no exception. Its very success led to arrogant and stupid behavior by its leaders and to a real assault on it by decent democrats and newspapers. Old-time politicians suddenly realized that a rival for power and patronage was demanding its slice of the pie, and that they would do better to eliminate the Klan than to share offices with it. The result was that when D. C. Stephenson mutilated and raped a girl on an express train, and was named by her before her death from taking poison, he was unexpectedly convicted of second-degree murder and sentenced to life imprisonment. This proof of bestial immorality on the part of the leading Klansman of the mid-West turned away the Knights in their millions. In

A picket line in Atlanta, Georgia, in 1964. Klansmen still engage in economic boycott, a ploy that proved its power in the 1920s.

David C. Stephenson, the former Grand Dragon of Indiana, photographed in 1950 when he was arrested for breaking parole. He was jailed for life in 1925 for the murder of a girl who had been raped and mutilated—a crime that caused nationwide revulsion and shattered the second Klan's image as a guardian of public morality.

Indiana itself, membership of the Klan dropped by three quarters in two years. "We have had some good men in the Klan," a minister from the mid-West told another Senate investigating committee in 1926. "They are not staying by it now."

The lechery and profiteering behind the hoods of the Klan were now exposed. Secrecy, which allows lack of responsibility, allows corruption; even the Grand Wizard, Dr. Evans, well knew the caliber of the people he attracted to his secret organization. When he was asked by an Exalted Cyclops in Indiana why he did not let the Klansmen parade with their hoods raised, he replied cynically, "The morale of the Klan would kill itself." The same Exalted Cyclops also admitted to the Senate committee the credulity that Evans exploited, by declaring that the Grand Wizard "could almost convince the average Klansman that we had in the State of Indiana that Jesus Christ was not a Jew."

Internal warfare for loot and political posts also shattered the Klan. Simmons, when pushed out of power, tried to found a rival Klan for women, called the Kamelia. The Klan killed off this project and also prevented Simmons from making a success of another group, the Knights of the Flaming Sword. In Texas, however, the Klan-backed candidate for the governorship in 1924 began denouncing the Klan bitterly when it threw its support to one of his rivals, and the vitriolic tongue of the colorful ex-governor of the State, "Farmer Jim" Ferguson, put his wife in the governor's seat against the new "Klandidate" of the hooded order, whom Ferguson called "the great grand gizzard mouthpiece of the Grand Dragon." The Klan was soon run out of Democratic party politics in Texas by a coalition of its enemies. Similar counterattacks took place in all the States where the Klan was powerful, and most Klansmen, seeing the way the political wind was blowing, put aside their robes and got out of the wind.

The end of the second period of the Klan was as sudden as its rise. Stephenson, brooding on the injustice of not being able to fix his release from jail, turned state evidence and exposed details of Klan corruption and graft in Indiana. His testimony jailed a congressman, the mayor of Indianapolis, the sheriff of Marion County, and other officials; the governor was saved only by the statute of limitations. By 1927, when Stephenson's testimony came out, the Klan had dwindled to a mere 350,000 members. The hysteria against aliens that had made it sprout was equaled only by the revulsion against corruption that made it wither.

When, in 1928, Alfred E. Smith ran as Democratic nominee for the presidency against Herbert Hoover, the Klan revived in the South to fight this threat "to put the pope in the White House." In Alabama, the Klan lynched a straw-filled effigy of Al Smith. Fiery crosses often greeted Smith's campaign train. "I would sooner go down to ignominious defeat than be elected to any office," Smith declared, "if to accomplish it I had to have the support of any group with such perverted ideas of Americanism." Smith would rather be anti-Klan than president; but, as a Catholic, he could be nothing else. The battle against Smith, who would anyway have been defeated by Hoover, bankrupted the Klan and removed the last purists from the organization. "We got so desperate for votes that we just took in anybody who had ten dollars," a Klan organizer confessed later. "Consequently, we wound up with all sorts of scum and riffraff. . . ." The businessmen left the Klan; those who remained were the out-and-out bigots, the red-necks, and the retarded. Irony of irony, the Klan's old Imperial Palace in Atlanta, Georgia, after changing hands many times, became the site for a Roman Catholic cathedral.

A rival Klan, called the Black Legion, boomed briefly in the mid-West during the 1930s; but the idealism of Franklin Roosevelt's New Deal led to the Legion's quick and ruthless suppression by the State governments. More political and Fascist organizations, such as Pelly's Silver Shirt Legion, took away funds and members from the Klan. And when the United States entered the war against Fascism in Europe, most of the members of right-wing organizations gave up their affiliations for fear of seeming unpatriotic. In 1944, when the United States Treasury assessed the Klan for over half a million dollars in back taxes, the organization went into liquidation. World War II officially put an end to the second Klan, which had risen again on the hatreds left after World War I.

Many Negroes served in the armed forces during World War II, or became used to high wages and good jobs in munitions factories. When the war ended, the South was faced with a Negro movement demanding civil rights and equal treatment. The Klan now rose for a third time in the South; its object was similar to that of the first Klan, to keep the Negro people in an inferior condition. Yet this time the Klan lacked the excuse that white Southerners did not control the government of the Southern States. They pretended that the federal government—and later the Supreme Court—was oppressing the governments of the States and forcing civil rights down the throats of the white majority in the South.

There were neither Northern troops nor Negro militiamen to resist the third group of Klansmen. In fact, in the more brutal and backward places of the Deep South the local sheriffs wore Klan hoods by night. As often as not, policemen in small Southern towns helped Klansmen terrorize local Negroes and keep out civil-rights workers. Before American presidents became aware of the power of the Negro vote in presidential elections and infiltrated the Klan with agents of the Federal Bureau of Investigation, those who labored to help the Negro in the Deep South had no hope of protection by law from assault and murder.

Though a majority of Americans opposed the thought of Negroes as neighbors or sons-in-law, and many feared the competition of Negroes economically and socially, the third eruption of the Ku Klux Klan was curiously unsuccessful. Briefly, it had an initial success in Georgia politics, after fiery crosses had burned on Stone Mountain again in 1945, and some 50,000 Klansmen had enrolled in the order once more. Yet horror at Nazi atrocities against the Jews made the Klan's anti-Semitism stink in the nostrils of the nation, especially as the Klan had been linked with the pro-Nazi *Bund* before World War II. Governments in various States refused to permit the chartering of the Klan. Even Georgia, after flagrant Klan intervention in an election for the governorship, forced the State Klan to surrender its charter. Thus the remnants of the national Klan, now banned in its headquarters, writhed on their own, like the

tentacles of an octopus chopped off from their parent body. Two Imperial Wizards, one Imperial Emperor, one Grand Dragon, and one National Adjutant competed for the leadership of the fragmented movement for white supremacy and spoils.

Sporadic Klan outbreaks still took place in the South, but lynchings by hooded men declined, as Southern legislatures passed laws forbidding the wearing of masks—except for Halloween or Mardi Gras, the riotous festivals that had first given the idea of the joke Klan to the six knights of Pulaski. Yet the Klan lingered on in the backwoods areas, where poor whites wanted to keep down "uppity" Negroes and felt safe only in hooded assault. One pregnant Negro girl who was whipped in North Carolina was told: "Niggers want to go to school with white folks, but the Klan's gonna see to it that they don't—nor ride school buses nor eat in the same cafés." The Southern poor white had only one feeling of superiority in the world: he was better than the Negro. If the Negro inched upward to his level of poverty, he himself would be reduced to the status of the most despised of all.

Yet the local Klans had a new enemy to fight, the Federal Bureau of Investigation. The Lindbergh kidnap case in 1932 had forced the FBI to take over investigations that had been the concern of the state police; its intervention was sanctioned by the federal Interstate Commerce Acts, which made the transportation of people across State borders for illegal purposes a federal crime. Political considerations also began to persuade presidents that they should proceed against the Klan to satisfy the powerful Negro vote in the Northern cities. FBI informers broke up the Klan in North Carolina and sent 23 Klansmen to jail. The Klan's weakness was that it was filled with poor people who could be bribed. When the FBI needed information, it could pay the necessary price or slip its own men into the hooded order.

Left, Governor Alfred E. Smith, Democratic nominee for the presidency in 1928, leaves Chicago by train with a band of supporters. As a Catholic and a liberal, he met with fierce opposition from the declining Klan.

Right, Arthur A. Bell, Grand Dragon of New York, poses with Arthur Klapprott of the German-American Bund during a combined rally of Bund and Klan members at Camp Nordland, New Jersey (August 18, 1940).

The Supreme Court decision to desegregate Southern schools made many Klansmen ride again—in cars now, loaded with shotguns and clubs. Yet the Klansmen moved in constant fear of treachery. Bombings of Negro schools and homes, murdered Negroes found in the mud of bayous, whippings of civil-rights workers, all these crimes happened in the Deep South in the late 1950s. There were riots like those in Little Rock, Arkansas, in 1957, when President Eisenhower called in federal troops to protect the few Negro children in white schools. Wherever there were riots, Klansmen were to be found among the rioters. It was six Klansmen who flogged and castrated the Negro called Judge Aaron in 1957; their action shocked the State authorities so much that four of them received jail sentences of 20 years for "the most cowardly, atrocious, and diabolical crime ever." Moderation had begun to creep into the South together with a higher standard of living based on industrialization; in the new South, the Klan seemed like a sheeted scarecrow gibbering in a corner at the feast.

Southern authorities, in fact, have not been sympathetic to the Klan in recent years. Every outrage makes it harder for the Southern States to attract the investment and personnel they need to bring factories to Dixie. With thousands of civil-rights workers visiting the Deep South, the Klan has been remarkably ineffective over the last decade. From 1955 to 1959, there were only 530 cases of intimidation or violence reported from the whole South—a pittance compared with the crimes of Reconstruction days. The Klan has been too scared of betrayal to attack the militant Negro workers who are trying to register the Negro vote in the Black Belt. It has also failed to attract many members because potential leaders of white resistance to Negro rights have joined the Citizens' Councils rather than the Klan. These councils have been called "the uptown Klan" or "the white-collar Klan." Businessmen and bankers, who were the backbone and milch cow of the second Klan, have preferred to join a "civic" organization rather than a splintered and hated group whose ritual is an insult to the intelligence. The Klan is too outdated for the complicated tactics within the law now needed to fight the Negro rights movement without scaring away Northern capital investment. In fact, many Klansmen have joined the Citizens' Councils to fight in the daylight against the Negroes' push for equality.

In 1960, when the Negro "sit-in" movement with its techniques of passive resistance reached the South, the split Klans held a convention and agreed on a loose federation. Klansmen under the Grand Dragon of Georgia were present at the riots that took place at the University of Georgia when Negro students were admitted for the first time. Robert Shelton, titular head of the United Klans, held recruiting drives; but these fizzled out, though Shelton's brand of hatred of Jews, Negroes, Communists, the Supreme Court, brain-washing through mental health, and fluoridization of water appealed to some of the lunatic fringe of the American right wing. In fact, when Barry Goldwater

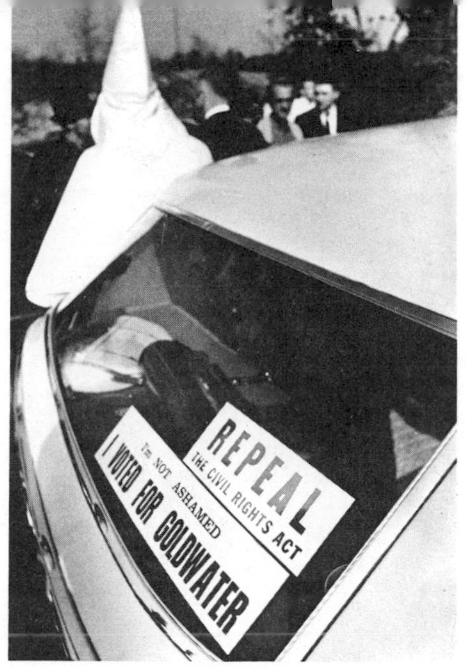

The 1960s saw the Klans in the forefront of the South's struggle against integration. Above, stickers on a Klansman's car in North Carolina protest the Civil Rights Act of 1964, which opened restaurants, hotels, cinemas, and barber shops, to Negroes. (A Mississippi Klan pamphlet averred "the black savages have threatened to turn the Gulf coast into the Congo coast.") Above right, police arrest a civil-rights demonstrator in Birmingham, Alabama. Right, they hose Negroes (1963).

Below, supporters of Martin Luther King's movement for Negro rights march from Selma to Montgomery in March 1965 to present a petition to Alabama's governor. Police brutality was one of their grievances.

Above, Neshoba county sheriff Lawrence Rainey and his deputy, Cecil Price, at their arraignment in Meridian, Mississippi, in connection with the murder of three civil-rights workers found in a dam (1964). The FBI held that the crime had been engineered by the Klan. Rainey, Price, and their 16 codefendants could not be charged with murder, which is not a federal crime. They were accused of conspiring to deprive the dead men of their civil rights, and the charges were dismissed. Left, Lemuel Penn, murdered in Georgia in 1964. The two Klansmen accused of the crime were acquitted by an all-white jury. Right, Mrs. Viola Liuzzo, the civil-rights supporter shot on the last day of the Selma-Montgomery march (1965). Far right, Collie Leroy Wilkins, the Klansman accused of her murder. Though acquitted on this charge, he was jailed for 10 years for conspiring to deprive her of civil rights.

became the candidate of the Republican party for the White House in 1964, the Klan thought that it had at last found a presidential candidate it could support. Goldwater's speech accepting the nomination declared that "extremism in the defense of liberty is no vice," and the Klan howled approval; but the defeated rival of Goldwater, Nelson Rockefeller, declared: "The extremism of the Communists, of the Ku Klux Klan and of the John Birch Society—like that of most tyrants—has always been claimed by such groups to be in defense of liberty."

In his stunning electoral defeat by Lyndon Johnson, Goldwater carried only six States—and five of these were in the Deep South. Southern poor white frustration helped him carry these States; but the Klan could now see clearly that even the South was divided. A moderate group of Southern States ringed the last hotbeds of the Klan; the movement was on its last legs as Negroes were slowly integrated into Southern schools. Even the Klan's official policy was affected by the success of the Negroes' tactics for getting their rights; imitating its enemies, the Klan began to use non-violent methods, such as picketing integrated stores and hotels. Shelton himself has taken to opposing Communism more than the Negro in an effort to win right-wing rather than anti-Negro support. "I don't hate the nigra," he says in a parody of Southern paternalism. "I feel sorry for him. He's been used as a tool by the forces that are trying to take over this country." He talks of finding a peaceful solution to the Negro problem and shipping all Negroes back to Africa in the mothball fleet left over from World War II.

The Klan's membership, now estimated at between 40,000 and 65,000, is concentrated almost exclusively in the rural districts of the Deep South. In the frequent bombings of churches and homes in the Natchez and McComb areas of Mississippi in 1964, local Klansmen were regularly implicated. One Klansman, wearing the black leather apron and black hood of the Klan executioner, was arrested with four rifles, an arsenal of clubs, a blackjack, a

hypodermic syringe—and a deputy sheriff's badge. After the killing of a Negro teacher, Lt. Col. Lemuel Penn, by a shotgun blast fired from a passing car as he drove through Georgia, one Klansman turned in two other Klansmen as the murderers, but both were acquitted by a local jury. In December 1964 three civil-rights workers, two white and one black, were killed near Philadelphia, Mississippi, and buried in a dam until discovered by the FBI. Twenty-one men, including two peace officers and a preacher, were accused by the FBI of the crime; many were Klansmen. Klansmen were also charged with the murder of Mrs. Liuzzo as she drove a civil-rights worker home after the peace march of Martin Luther King and his followers from Selma in March 1965. Since 1960, 27 civil-rights supporters had been murdered, yet no convictions had been secured in a Southern court. With the murder of Mrs. Liuzzo, President Johnson called for new legislation to wipe out the Klan, as Grant had done in 1872.

The present United Klans are a sorry vestige of the first and second Klans. They are fighting a losing battle against the advance of Southern urbanism and industrialization as well as against the progress of the Negro people. Their mumbo jumbo is out of touch with modern times, a hiccup rather than a roar of terror. Their appeal is only to the frustration of the poor white, who lacks the education necessary to keep up self-respect in the most automated society of our day. "The Jews have got the B'nai B'rith," a Klansman exploded as he filled up a reporter's car at a decayed petrol station. "The Catholics have got the Knights of Columbus. The niggers have got the N.A.A.C.P. Tell me what in hell the white man's got, besides the Klan? What has the white Protestant American Gentile got except the Klan? It's the poor bastard like me who pays the taxes. He keeps the wheels turning." Even the Deep South has become disenchanted with the hooded order. The South, preoccupied with the image it presents to the rest of the nation, and its need to attract capital for development, cannot afford the retrograde vendettas of the Klan.

The Klan is no longer a secret society; its membership and many of its plans are known to Washington. It is rather in the position of that "conspiracy against the American state," the American Communist party, which is said to be so penetrated by agents of the FBI that most of its party funds come from the government. Though the Klan is still capable of horrible crimes locally, its days even in the Deep South are numbered, merely because the poor whites are being pushed off their marginal farms into the city factories. The South is becoming less and less of a closed society; it is opening itself to innovation and change in order to become as rich as the North or the West. The Negroes have now spread themselves across the United States; only about half America's Negro population now lives in the South. Thus the Negro problem has become a national problem, not just a Southern one; the South need no longer feel isolated and misunderstood about its methods of dealing with its own particular society, split between black and white.

Right, Robert Shelton, Imperial Wizard of the United Klans of America, Knights of the Ku Klux Klan Inc., at a Klan rally in South Carolina (1964). Below, members of his audience, including a uniformed Klan "security guard." Shelton's organization, the largest surviving Klan, has "realms" in eight Southern states, and branches in New York, Wisconsin, and Pennsylvania.

It is ridiculous for the remnants of the Ku Klux Klan to claim that they still represent a majority in America. The majority in America is, indeed, white, Anglo-Saxon, and Protestant; but it does not feel in the least represented by the Klan, which stands for only a dwindling minority group. Imperial Wizard Shelton says that the Klan "is a religion, a faith, a belief. A man may subscribe to its principles and live under it, and in the heritage and background of the Klan—the *only* organization by and for Americans—sentimentally. In this way we are all members." But Shelton is not talking about the present day; he is referring to his nostalgia for a government by small farmers of British stock, something that has not existed in America for more than a hundred years.

The surviving Klan is the *reductio ad absurdum* of the secret society. It has turned impressive masonic ritual into a farcical flummery. The aggressive faith of the military orders of the Crusaders has been perverted into a petty, sadistic, and aimless vengeance, signifying nothing. The initiation ceremony and oath of secrecy that scared terrorist sects such as the Assassins into obedience unto death has become a smoking-room joke. In North Carolina, a prospective Klansman is shown a red-hot iron bar, is blindfolded, is told to bare his buttocks, and then yells when a piece of dry ice is put against his rump—to the delight of his fellow Klansmen.

The Klan is venal now, and no longer secret. Its members are known to Washington, and bought by it regularly. It no longer inspires fear outside the Southern backwoods; it provokes laughter and bad publicity. "We try," Shelton says, "to keep the Klan today on the same pedestal of history, of the Reconstruction past, when there were no laws to defend Southerners under the cruel heel of Federal oppression." But times are changing, and Shelton cannot clean up the rusty shield of the Klan. The secret society, which often overturned governments and terrified whole peoples, is reduced by the Klan to a rash of guttersnipe gangs, whose hoods strike no more terror in the average citizen than a dunce's cap.

Above left, scene at an inaugural meeting of a Klan branch in Birmingham, England (1965). Like other attempts to launch the Klan in Britain, it failed; the Klan's mythology, rooted in the traditions of the Deep South, has little propaganda value elsewhere. In America, President Johnson called for a congressional inquiry into the Klan after the murder of Mrs. Liuzzo in 1965. Left, the Un-American Activities Committee opens its investigation of the Klan in October of the same year. Shelton and six other Klansmen refused to hand over their records, and were sent for rial on charges of contempt of Congress.

Conclusion

We began this book by suggesting that there is a basic human need for secrecy. Without the ability to keep secrets, a man could not develop a distinct personality; and without the ability to respect the secrets of others, he would not make an acceptable member of any society. Nevertheless, secrecy arouses strong emotions. Most of us feel some resentment when a friend or colleague persists in withholding certain information from us, and we often react by disparaging the secret, as if to convince ourselves that it is not worth knowing. At this point, therefore, it may be useful to remember that there are two kinds of secrets: not only "artificial," or deliberately invented, secrets (such as code words and hand signs), but also "natural" secrets (such as the experience of initiation into a religious order or sect). If there is one thing we resent more than secrecy in those around us, it is intrusion on our own "natural" secrecy or privacy. But we all have to learn how to strike the balance between privacy and publicity that is appropriate to our own society.

What can it be that prompts people to join secret associations? Can we say that those who do so are people in whom the need for secrecy has been exaggerated? We know that some individuals are excessively secretive about personal matters. Others have the sense of being spied on, of having their thoughts laid bare; but this is a symptom of schizophrenia, and people who suffer this affliction are no longer integrated or social personalities. This cannot be generally true of people who join secret associations, for membership in any group, even a secret one, necessitates participation in the social life of that group. We might even ask whether a secret really remains a secret once it is shared among the members of a group. We might take the point further, and ask whether any *wholly* secret society could possibly exist. Any study of secret societies must show that their secrecy is only partial, and that they have something in common with open groups.

We may find the answer to our question not so much within the individuals or groups concerned, as in their relationship to the society at large. If we consider the examples described in this book, we shall see that most of them have emerged in periods of social disorganization and ideological conflict, when old ways of life were breaking down or new ways of life were emerging. The development of Mau Mau is a good case in point: Kikuyu tribal life was being subjected to intolerable strains and stresses in its attempt to adjust to the changes imposed by the white missionaries and farmer-settlers. The Knights Templar were founded in an effort to create order out of the chaos of the Crusades. The early history of Freemasonry is part of the story of the European Enlightenment—an attempt to establish a universal morality in an age of rationalism and religious doubt. The Ku Klux Klan emerged from the tensions of the South after the Civil War, the Mafia from the archaic social structure of an island forced into modern Europe by geography and politics. All the important nationalist secret societies, virtually by definition, grew up in periods of great unrest and social dislocation; the same is true of most revolutionary and subversive conspiracies. The racist and authoritarian cliques that take the form of secret societies also tend to draw their membership from people who are socially disturbed or uprooted.

We may say that those who join secret groups may be people who are clinging to old ways of life that have been disrupted; or they may, on the contrary, be people who are themselves in rebellion against the existing order, and find secrecy necessary as a cover for their activities. We can see examples of the former type in Mau Mau and the Mafia, and of the latter in the Illuminati, the Carbonari, the Clan-na-Gael, and the Bolsheviks. The emergence of secret societies, that is to say, is one indicator of social instability and conflict.

This does not necessarily mean that the whole of the wider society is unstable; particular strata of society, such as migrants and ethnic and religious minorities, may be peculiarly subject to disorganization. Many secret societies, or groups closely akin to them, seem to emerge in rural communities that are at the point of transition to modern industrial and commercial conditions, when established ways of life are being disrupted. Millenarian cults, for example, have often appeared in these circumstances, and the peasants recruited by contemporary communist organizations may be reacting more to this kind of pressure than to the ideological appeal of communism.

We can add that in urbanized or highly industrialized societies, secret associations of the fraternal, quasi-masonic type seem to be playing a stabilizing role, helping to fill the void that has been created by the sheer size, complexity, and fragmentation of urban living. Their hierarchies of titles and functions may compensate for the anonymity of the individual in such environments; their myth and ritual may provide relief from the constraints of rationalism; and their emphasis on charity, morality, or temperance may offer a necessary reassurance against unconscious desires for antisocial behavior.

The special environment of the secret society was well described by the great German sociologist Georg Simmel, whose article *The Sociology of Secrecy* was published at the beginning of this century. Simmel was one of the few social theorists who have tried to construct a theory of secret societies, and much of what he had to say remains helpful today. Secrecy offers, he suggested, "the possibility of a second world alongside of the obvious world." He also saw that there might be some constant ratio of secrecy in human life, that each of us might need to keep a due proportion of our lives concealed from others. He proposed that secrecy "procures an enormous extension of life, because with publicity many sorts of purposes could never arrive at realisation." But he pointed out that the purposes concealed would differ from one society to another, and would change over periods of time. In the tribal community, for example, very little of the individual's private life is concealed. Men, women, and children live in very close proximity, and the whole cycle of life from birth to death occurs in public intimacy. Yet there is, in such groups, a great deal of secrecy about matters that relate to the group as a whole. Its religious mysteries are jealously guarded by the medicine man, shaman, or priest, who is the intermediary between the tribe and the unseen powers. The magic of charisma is the prerogative of priests; and initiation is controlled by secret societies.

The opposite seems to be true in large modern societies, in which there is increasing emphasis on personal privacy, and a steady decline in group secrecy. Individuals learn to conceal their emotions, and their religious and political beliefs, from others. But they have come to expect that matters relating to the society as a whole should be disclosed. Presidents, politicians, and pop-singers must now lead public lives; the conduct of government, and the state of the nation's economy, are open to debate; and the evidence of scientists about the "mysteries" of nature gradually becomes part of the common stock of knowledge.

Simmel also observed that a secret gives the individual "a feeling of personal possession." Children, he noted, love a secret because it strengthens and aggrandizes them; they derive pleasure and a sense of power from resisting the ever-present temptation to reveal what they know. Secrecy, therefore, is "an individualising factor of the first rank." This is a different way of saying that it fosters one's sense of identity, and Simmel observed that the larger the social group, the more the individual feels the need to distinguish himself in some way from others. This is particularly true in contemporary industrial societies, which have placed a premium on individuality (it is part of the cultural background created by the rise of Protestantism and the rise of industrial capitalism) yet, at the same time, have imposed more conformity upon the mass of citizens.

The clues seem to be pointing to a relationship between secrecy and the sense of identity of an individual or a group. They seem to be indicating that where secrecy takes an organizational form there is some kind of disturbance, or threat of disturbance, in the identity-patterns of the groups or individuals concerned. Recent psychological writing, especially that of the American psychoanalyst Erik H. Erikson, has emphasized the relationship between the emotional crises of growing up and the discovery of a satisfactory identity that enables an individual to cope with the demands of adult life. Dr. Erikson describes the process by which the growing child seeks to identify himself with others—in the first place, with his parents, and with the values embodied in his family. Later, he extends that process to the wider society through school, work, and the accepted patterns of leisure, politics, and religion. If something necessary to that process is lacking—whether in his environment or in himself—he will go on attempting it throughout life. He will always be searching for recognition and support, for means to allay his loneliness and anxiety (and many of the crises of middle age in modern society stem from an effort finally to resolve identity-problems of this kind). This is why all human societies have some kind of technique for registering the transition from childhood to adult status. As Dr. Erikson observes in his book *Insight and Responsibility*, for "this very reason societies *confirm* an individual at this time in all kinds of ideological frameworks and assign roles and tasks to him in which he can *recognise* himself and *feel recognised*. Ritual confirmations, initiations, and indoctrinations only enhance an indispensable process by which healthy societies bestow traditional strength on the new generation and thereby bind to themselves the strength of youth."

The elements of this process are strongly marked in the initiation rites of tribal groups. But in modern industrial societies, where communities have been broken up, they are often missing; as a result, the accepted techniques of initiation lose much of their significance for the individual, and many people feel a sense of estrangement and a lack of real identity. It therefore seems likely that one of the major attractions of secret societies is their offer of an initiation that confers a specific role on the individual and relates him to a clearly defined group. In the environment of such a group, which has its own collective identity, the individual can indeed "recognise himself and feel recognised." It is as if the secret group is compensating for the inability of the wider society to bring up and educate its children with the sense of belonging that characterizes smaller, more stable, and less mobile communities.

The solidarity of the secret group is reinforced by the fact that its myth and ritual are private property, preserved and handed down within the group. The myth is the principle on which the special environment of the group is constructed, the ritual the technique by which the individual is integrated, or "reborn," into that environment. But the function of the ritual does not end here. It is usually rigid and unchanging, valid only if it is performed in the prescribed conditions, without a single error or variation. This means that the emotionally binding impact it makes on the individual member at his own initiation will be renewed when others are initiated. The repetition of the ritual continually locates him within the organization and in relation to his fellow members, reminding him both of his own obligations and of the common aim. While reawakening his sense of responsibility to the group, it also reminds him that he now operates within a structure on which he can depend.

The individual who formerly felt exposed and vulnerable is likely to find that membership in such a group gives him reassurance in the outer world. Though he may continue to live and work in that world, he no longer depends on it in the same way. He is able to withdraw from it, and to find the reciprocal confidence on which the existence of the secret society depends. This new sense of fellowship may create such powerful bonds that the member feels invulnerable to the outside world. We can observe this phenomenon in groups as diverse as the Jehovah's Witnesses, the Japanese *kamikaze* pilots of World War II, clandestine communist parties, or—to go back in time—the Assassins.

To observe that religious sects and racist or political secret societies have these features in common is not to draw an analogy between the two; we have emphasized the distinction between the natural secrecy of the first and the artificial secrecy of the second. Nevertheless, the impression of similarity is reinforced by the fact that many societies with essentially secular aims have adopted rituals based on the emotionally binding theme of rebirth, and hierarchies that have a religious flavor—as the Illuminati took titles like "Presbyter" and "Magus," dividing their ranks into "Greater and Lesser Mysteries." These superficial similarities are confusing, and it is hardly surprising that the wider society has often failed to see beyond them, and has tended to regard all secret groups with equal hostility and suspicion. Secret societies, and minority groups resembling them, have often been scapegoats for the failures and abuses of society as a whole. It is important, therefore, to realize that these groups may reflect as many different aspects of human thought and action as are found in society at large—and that each, in its own way, represents an attempt to solve the common human problem of identity.

Appendix 1

Masonic Ceremony of Raising to the Third Degree

The third, or Master's, degree of Freemasonry first appeared in Scotland in the 1720s, and was officially recognized in England in 1738. There is no absolute uniformity in the working of the degree (the texts used in Irish, Scottish, and American lodges vary considerably from those used in England), but all versions of the ritual are similar in content. and structure. This version is taken from Darkness Visible, A Revelation and Interpretation of Freemasonry *by Walton Hannah (1952).*

The Worshipful Master examines the Candidate.

W.M. Brethren, Bro. A.B. is this evening a Candidate to be raised to the Third Degree, but it is first requisite that he give proofs of proficiency in the Second. I shall therefore proceed to put the necessary questions. How were you prepared to be passed to the Second Degree?

Can. In a manner somewhat similar to the former, save that in this Degree I was not hoodwinked. My left arm, breast, and right knee were made bare, and my left heel was slipshod.

W.M. On what were you admitted?

Can. The Square.

W.M. What is a Square?

Can. An angle of 90 degrees, or the fourth part of a circle.

W.M. What are the peculiar objects of research in this Degree?

Can. The hidden mysteries of Nature and Science.

W.M. As it is the hope of reward that sweetens labour, where did our ancient Brethren go to receive their wages?

Can. Into the middle chamber of King Solomon's Temple.

W.M. How did they receive them?

Can. Without scruple or diffidence.

W.M. Why in this peculiar manner?

Can. Without scruple, well knowing they were justly entitled to them; and without diffidence, from the great reliance they placed on the integrity of their employers in those days.

W.M. What were the names of the two great pillars which were placed at the

Third-degree tracing board design (1825). "Let the emblems of mortality which lie before you lead you to contemplate on your inevitable destiny, and guide your reflections to that most interesting of all human studies, the knowledge of yourself."

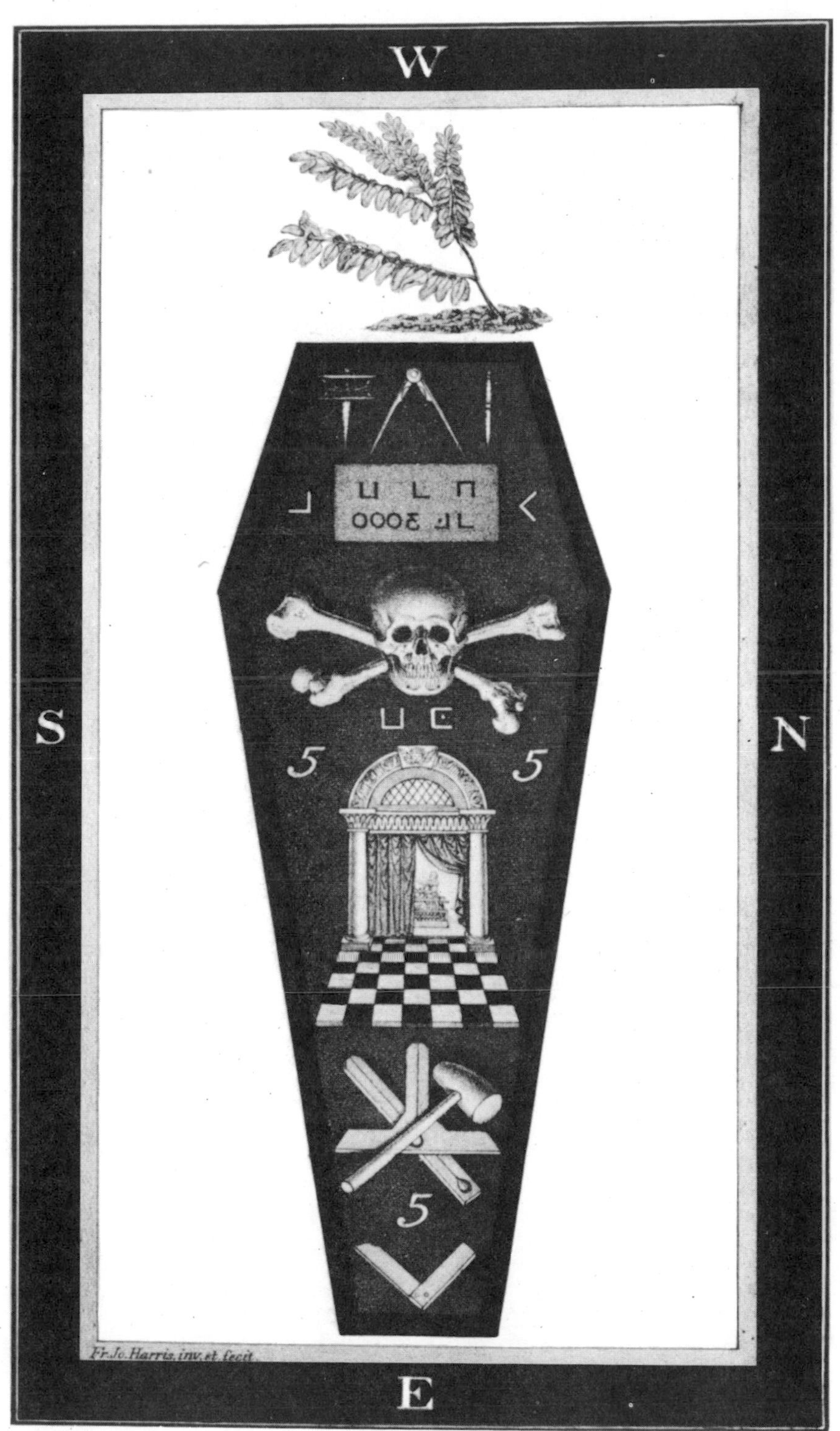
W
S
N
5
5
5
Fr. Jo. Harris. inv. et fecit.
E

porchway or entrance of King Solomon's Temple?

Can. That on the left was called Boaz, and that on the right, Jachin.

W.M. What are their separate and conjoint significations?

Can. The former denotes in strength, the latter, to establish; and when conjoined, stability, for God said, "In strength will I establish this Mine house to stand firm for ever."

W.M. These are the usual questions. I will put others if any Brother wishes me to do so.

Do you pledge your honour as a man and your fidelity as a Craftsman that you will steadily persevere through the ceremony of being raised to the sublime Degree of a Master Mason?

Can. I do.

W.M. Do you likewise pledge yourself, under the penalty of both your Obligations, that you will conceal what I shall now impart to you with the same strict caution as the other secrets in Masonry?

Can. I do.

W.M. Then I will entrust you with a test of merit, which is a pass grip and a pass word, leading to the degree to which you seek to be admitted. The pass grip is given by a distinct pressure of the thumb between the second and third joints of the hand. This pass grip demands a pass word, which is TUBAL CAIN. Tubal Cain was the first artificer in metals. The import of the word is worldly possessions. You must be particularly careful to remember this word, as without it you cannot gain admission into a Lodge in a superior Degree. Pass, Tubal Cain.

The Senior Deacon conducts the Candidate to the door, instructing him to salute the Worshipful Master with the signs of the first two Degrees. He retires to be prepared for the Third Degree: both arms, both breasts, and both knees are made bare, and both heels are slippered. He wears the Fellow-Crafts apron. In the meantime the Lodge is opened in the Third Degree. The Deacons lay a sheet along the mid line of the Lodge some five feet west of the Worshipful Master's pedestal: on this sheet is depicted the "open grave," surrounded by skulls and crossbones. In a few Lodges there is an actual grave-trap in the floor. The practice of using a real coffin is almost but not quite extinct. Sometimes real or plastic "emblems of mortality" are used. When all is ready the Tyler gives the Second-Degree knocks.

Inner Guard: (*With step and Penal sign of Third Degree*) Bro. Junior Warden, there is a report.

Junior Warden: (*With step and sign*) Worshipful Master, there is a report.

W.M. Brother Junior Warden, inquire who wants admission.

J.W. (*Cuts sign*) Bro. Inner Guard, see who wants admission.

I.G. (*Cuts sign, opens the door*) Whom have you there?

Tyler: Bro. A.B., who has been regularly initiated into Freemasonry, passed to the Degree of a Fellow-Craft, and has made such further progress as he hopes will entitle him to be raised to the sublime Degree of a Master

Mason, for which ceremony he is properly prepared.

I.G. How does he hope to obtain the privileges of the Third Degree?

Ty. By the help of God, the united aid of the Square and Compasses, and the benefit of a pass word.

I.G. Is he in possession of the pass word?

Ty. Will you prove him? (*The Inner Guard extends his right hand, and receives the pass grip and pass word from the Candidate*).

I.G. Halt, while I report to the Worshipful Master. (*Closes door, takes step and sign*) Worshipful Master, Bro. A.B. who has been regularly initiated into Freemasonry, passed to the Degree of a Fellow-Craft, and has made such further progress as he hopes will entitle him to be raised to the sublime Degree of a Master Mason, for which ceremony he is properly prepared.

W.M. How does he hope to obtain the privileges of the Third Degree?

I.G. By the help of God, the united aid of the Square and Compasses, and the benefit of a pass word.

W.M. We acknowledge the powerful aid by which he seeks admission; do you, Bro. Inner Guard, vouch that he is in possession of the pass word?

I.G. I do, Worshipful Master.

W.M. Then let him be admitted in due form. Brother Deacons.

At this point all lights are extinguished in the Lodge except the candle by the Worshipful Master's pedestal. The Junior Deacon places the kneeling stool in position, and both Deacons proceed to the door. The Inner Guard opens it, presents the extended points of a pair of compasses to the Candidate's breasts, and holds the compasses above his head to show that he has done so. The Senior Deacon leads the Candidate to the kneeling stool.

Senior Deacon: Advance as a Fellow-Craft, first as an Entered Apprentice.

Candidate takes step and gives First-Degree sign then another step and the sign of the Second Degree.

W.M. Let the Candidate kneel while the blessing of Heaven is invoked on what we are about to do.

Worshipful Master gives one knock, repeated by the Wardens. All stand with sign of Reverence, and the Deacons cross their wands over the Candidate's head.

W.M. (or Chaplain) Almighty and Eternal God, Architect and Ruler of the Universe at whose creative fiat all things first were made, we, the frail creatures of Thy providence, humbly implore Thee to pour down on this convocation assembled in Thy Holy Name the continual dew of Thy blessing. Especially, we beseech Thee, to impart Thy grace to this Thy servant, who offers himself a Candidate to partake with us the mysterious secrets of a Master Mason. Endue him with such fortitude that in the hour of trial he fail not, but that, passing safely under Thy protection through the valley of the shadow of death, he may finally rise from the tomb of transgression, to shine as the stars for ever and ever.

Immediate Past Master: So mote it be. (*The Deacons lower their wands, and the Brethren dismiss sign.*)

W.M. Let the Candidate rise.

He does so. The kneeling stool is removed and placed before the Worshipful Master's pedestal. The Senior Deacon takes the Candidate by the right hand, and begins the perambulations of the Lodge, carefully squaring it at the corners. A halt is made before the pedestal in the East, and the Senior Deacon instructs the Candidate to salute the Worshipful Master as a Mason. They then proceed to the Junior Warden's pedestal in the South.

S.D. Advance to the Junior Warden as such, showing the sign and communicating the token and word. (*Candidate takes step and gives sign of First Degree.*)

J.W. Have you anything to communicate?

Can. I have. (*Gives First-Degree grip.*)

J.W. What is this?

Can. The grip or token of an Entered Apprentice Freemason.

J.W. What does it demand?

Can. A word.

J.W. Give me that word, freely and at length.

Can. BOAZ.

J.W. Pass, Boaz.

The Senior Deacon continues round the Lodge with the Candidate, and halts in front of the Senior Warden, whom the Candidate is instructed to salute as a Mason with step and sign of the First Degree. The perambulation is continued, squaring the Lodge, and the Candidate is directed to salute the Worshipful Master as a Fellow-Craft, which he does with step and sign of the Second Degree. Continuing round the Lodge, he next salutes the Junior Warden as a Fellow-Craft, and on to the Senior Warden again.

S.D. Advance to the Senior Warden as such, showing the sign, and communicating the token and word of that Degree. (*Candidate takes step and gives sign.*)

Senior Warden: Have you anything to communicate?

Can. I have. (*Gives grip.*)

S.W. What is this?

Can. The grip or token of a Fellow-Craft Freemason.

S.W. What does it demand?

Can. A word.

S.W. Give me that word freely and at length.

Can. JACHIN.

S.W. Pass, Jachin.

W.M. (*Gives single knock, repeated by the Wardens*) The Brethren will take notice that Bro. A.B., who has been regularly initiated into Freemasonry, and passed to the Degree of a Fellow-Craft, is about to pass in view before them, to show that he is the Candidate properly prepared to be raised to the Sublime Degree of a Master Mason.

The Senior Deacon conducts the Candidate round the Lodge the third time, followed by the Junior Deacon. They halt before the Worshipful Master's pedestal, where the Senior Deacon instructs the Candidate to salute as a Fellow-Craft, then on to the Junior Warden, who is similarly saluted. They then proceed to the right of the Senior Warden.

S.D. Advance to the Senior Warden as such, showing the sign and communicating the pass grip and pass word you received from the Worshipful Master previously to leaving the Lodge. (*Candidate takes step and gives Fellow-Craft sign.*)

S.W. Have you anything to communicate?

Can. I have. (*Gives pass grip to the Third Degree.*)

S.W. What is this?

Can. The pass grip leading from the Second to the Third Degree.

S.W. What does this pass grip demand?

Can. A pass word.

S.W. Give me that pass word.

Can. TUBAL CAIN.

S.W. What was Tubal Cain?

Can. The first artificer in metals.

S.W. The import of the word?

Can. Worldly possessions.

S.W. Pass, Tubal Cain. (*Senior Warden takes step and Penal sign of the Third Degree.*) Worshipful Master I present Bro. A.B., a Candidate properly prepared to be raised to the Third Degree.

W.M. Bro. Senior Warden, you will direct the Deacons to instruct the Candidate to advance to the East by the proper steps.

S.W. Bro. Deacons, it is the Worshipful Master's command that you instruct the Candidate to advance to the East by the proper steps.

S.D. The method of advancing from West to East in this Degree is by seven steps, the first three as if stepping over a grave. For your information I will go through them, and you will afterwards copy me.

The steps are taken diagonally back and forth; starting at the West or head of the grave as depicted on the sheet, the first step is taken in a North Easterly direction, the second South Easterly, and the third brings the Candidate to the foot of the grave, facing due East. After each separate step the heels are brought together with the feet squared. Four ordinary walking steps, described in some workings as "bold marching steps," taken due East, bring the Candidate into position before the Worshipful Master's pedestal.

W.M. It is but fair to inform you that a most serious trial of your fortitude and fidelity and a more solemn Obligation await you. Are you prepared to meet them as you ought?

Can. I am.

W.M. Then you will kneel on both knees, place both hands on the Volume of the Sacred Law. (*Candidate does so. The Worshipful Master gives one knock, followed by the Wardens, the Brethren stand to order with the Penal sign of the Third Degree, and the Deacons cross their wands over the Candidate's head.*)

Repeat your name at length, and say after me:-

OBLIGATION

Can. I, A.B., in the presence of the Most High, and of this worthy and worshipful Lodge of Master Masons, duly constituted, regularly assembled, and properly dedicated, of my own free will and accord, do hereby (*Worshipful Master touches Candidate's hands with his left hand*) and hereon (*Worshipful Master touches the Bible with his left hand*) most solemnly promise and swear that I will always hele, conceal, and never reveal any or either of the secrets or mysteries of or belonging to the Degree of a Master Mason to anyone in the world, unless it be to him or them to whom the same may justly and lawfully belong, and not even to him or them until after due trial, strict examination, or full conviction that he or they are worthy of that confidence, or in the body of a Master Masons' Lodge duly opened on the Centre. I further solemnly pledge myself to adhere to the principles of the Square and Compasses, answer and obey all lawful signs and summonses sent to me from a Master Masons' Lodge, if within the length of my cable-tow, and plead no excuse except sickness or the pressing emergencies of my own public or private avocations.

I further solemnly engage myself to maintain and uphold the Five Points of Fellowship in act as well as in word; that my hand, given to a Master Mason, shall be a sure pledge of brotherhood; that my feet shall travel through dangers and difficulties to unite with his in forming a column of mutual defence and support; that the posture of my daily supplications shall remind me of his wants and dispose my heart to succour his weakness and relieve his necessities, so far as may fairly be done without detriment to myself or connections; that my breast shall be the sacred repository of his secrets when entrusted to my care—murder, treason, felony, and all other offences contrary to the laws of God and the ordinances of the realm being at all times most especially excepted. And finally, that I will maintain a Master Mason's honour and carefully preserve it as my own; I will not injure him myself, or knowingly suffer it to be done by others if in my power to prevent it; but on the contrary, will boldly repel the slanderer of his good name, and most strictly respect the chastity of those nearest and dearest to him, in the persons of his wife, his sister, and his child.

All these points I solemnly swear to observe, without evasion, equivocation, or mental reservation of any kind, under no less a penalty, on the violation of any of them, than that of being severed in two, my bowels burned to ashes, and those ashes scattered over the face of the earth, and wafted by the four cardinal winds of heaven, that no trace or remembrance of so vile a wretch may longer be found among men, particularly Master Masons.

So help me the Most High, and keep me steadfast in this my solemn Obligation of a Master Mason.

W.M. As a pledge of your fidelity and to render this binding as a Solemn Obligation for so long as you shall live, you will seal it with your lips thrice on the Volume of the Sacred Law. (*Candidate does so.*) Let me once more call your attention to the position of the Square and Compasses. When you were made an Entered Apprentice, both points were hid; in the Second Degree one was disclosed, in this the whole is exhibited, implying that you are now at liberty to work with both those points in order to render the circle of your Masonic duties complete. Rise, newly obligated Master Mason. (*Deacons and Candidate step back to the foot of the grave.*)

Having entered upon the Solemn Obligation of a Master Mason, you are now entitled to demand that last and greatest trial, by which alone you can be admitted to a participation of the secrets of this Degree. But it is first my duty to call your attention to a retrospect of those Degrees in Freemasonry through which you have already passed, that you may the better be enabled to distinguish and appreciate the connection of our whole system, and the relative dependency of its several parts.

Your admission among Masons in a state of helpless indigence was an emblematical representation of the entrance of all men on this, their mortal existence. It inculcated the useful lessons of natural equality and mutual dependence. It instructed you in the active principles of universal beneficence and charity, to seek the solace of your own distress by extending relief and consolation to your fellow-creatures in the hour of their affliction. Above all, it taught you to bend with humility and resignation to the will of the Great Architect of the Universe; to dedicate your heart, thus purified from every baneful and malignant passion, fitted only for the reception of truth and wisdom, to His glory and the welfare of your fellow-mortals.

Proceeding onwards, still guiding your progress by the principles of moral truth, you were led in the Second Degree to contemplate the intellectual faculty, and to trace it from its development, through the paths of heavenly science, even to the Throne of God himself. The secrets of Nature and the principles of intellectual truth were then unveiled to your view. To your mind, thus modelled by virtue and science, Nature, however, presents one great and useful lesson more. She prepares you, by contemplation, for the closing hour of existence; and when by means of that contemplation she has conducted you through the intricate windings of this mortal life, she finally instructs you how to die.

Such, my Brother, are the peculiar objects of the Third Degree in Freemasonry; they invite you to reflect on this awful subject and teach you to feel, that, to the just and virtuous man, death has no terrors equal to the stain of falsehood and dishonour. Of this great truth the annals of Masonry afford a glorious example in the unshaken fidelity and noble death of our Master, Hiram Abiff, who was slain just before the completion of King Solomon's Temple, at the construction of which he was, as no doubt you are well aware, the principal architect. The manner of his death was as follows. Brother Wardens.

The Wardens come up and stand on either side of the Candidate, who is instructed to cross his feet right over left.

W.M. Fifteen Fellow Crafts of that superior class appointed to preside over the rest, finding that the work was nearly completed and that they were not in possession of the secrets of the Third Degree, conspired to obtain them by any means, even to have recourse to violence. At the moment, however, of carrying their conspiracy into execution, twelve of the fifteen recanted, but three, of a more determined and atrocious character than the rest, persisted in their impious design, in the prosecution of which they planted themselves respectively at the East, North and South entrances of the Temple, whither our Master had retired to pay his adoration to the Most High, as was his wonted custom at the hour of high twelve. Having finished his devotions, he attempted to return by the South entrance, where he was opposed by the first of those ruffians, who, for want of other weapon, had armed himself with a heavy Plumb Rule, and in a threatening manner demanded the secrets of a Master Mason, warning him that death would be the consequence of a refusal. Our Master, true to his Obligation, answered that those secrets were known to but three in the world, and that without the consent and cooperation of the other two he neither could nor would divulge them, but intimated that he had no doubt patience and industry would, in due time, entitle the worthy Mason to a participation of them, but that, for his own part, he would rather suffer death than betray the sacred trust reposed in him.

This answer not proving satisfactory, the ruffian aimed a violent blow at the head of our Master, but, being startled at the firmness of his demeanour, it missed his forehead and only glanced on his right temple (*here the Junior Warden touches the Candidate's right temple with the Plumb Rule*) but with such force as to cause him to reel and sink on his left knee (*the Candidate goes down on his left knee*). Recovering from the shock (*Candidate rises*) he made for the North entrance, where he was accosted by the second of those ruffians, to whom he gave a similar answer with undiminished firmness, when the ruffian, who was armed with a Level, struck him a violent blow on the left temple (*the Senior Warden touches the Candidate's left temple with the Level*) which brought him to the ground on his right knee (*here the Candidate goes down on his right knee, and recovers*).

Finding his retreat cut off at both these points, he staggered faint and bleeding to the East entrance, where the third ruffian was posted, who received a similar answer to his insolent demand (for even at this trying moment our Master remained firm and unshaken), when the villain, who was armed with a heavy Maul, struck him a violent blow on the forehead (*Here, according to Emulation Workings, the Worshipful Master makes a gesture only from his seat of slaying the Candidate with the Maul; in some workings he leaves his place and touches the Candidate's forehead*) which laid him lifeless at his feet. (*The Wardens lower the Candidate backwards into the grave.*)

The Brethren will take notice that in the recent ceremony, as well as in his present situation, our Brother has been made to represent one of the brightest characters recorded in the annals of Masonry, namely, Hiram Abiff, who lost his life in consequence of his unshaken fidelity to the sacred trust reposed in him, and I hope this will make a lasting impression on his and your minds, should you ever be placed in a similar state of trial.

Brother Junior Warden, you will endeavour to raise the representative of our Master by the Entered Apprentice's grip.

The Junior Warden raises the Candidate's right arm with his left, gives the First-Degree grip with his right hand and lets it slip, then lowers the Candidate's arm again.

J.W. (*With step and sign*) Worshipful Master, it proves a slip. (*Cuts sign.*)

W.M. Brother Senior Warden, you will try the Fellow-Crafts'. (*The Senior Warden attempts the Second-Degree grip and lets it slip, in the same way as the Junior Warden did*)

S.W. (*With step and sign*) Worshipful Master, it proves a slip likewise. (*Cuts sign.*)

W.M. Brother Wardens, having both failed in your attempts, there remains a third method, by taking a more firm hold of the sinews of the hand and raising him on the Five Points of Fellowship, which, with your assistance, I will make trial of.

The Worshipful Master leaves his chair and advances to the Candidate's feet, which he uncrosses. He then takes the Candidate's right hand in the Third-Degree grip, places his right foot to the Candidate's right foot, and then, as the Wardens lift the Candidate, places right knee to right knee, right breast to right breast, and left hand over the Candidate's back.

W.M. (*Still holding the Five Points of Fellowship*) It is thus all Master Masons are raised from a figurative death to a reunion with the former companions of their toils. Brother Wardens, resume your seats.

Let me now beg you to observe that the light of a Master Mason is darkness visible, serving only to express that gloom which rests on the prospect of futurity. It is that mysterious veil which the eye of human reason cannot penetrate unless assisted by that light which is from above. Yet, even by this glimmering ray, you may perceive that you stand on the very brink of the grave into which you have just figuratively descended, and which, when this transitory life shall have passed away, will again receive you into its cold bosom. Let the emblems of mortality which lie before you lead you to contemplate on your inevitable destiny, and guide your reflections to that most interesting of all human studies, the knowledge of yourself. Be careful to perform your allotted task while it is yet day; continue to listen to the voice of Nature, which bears witness, that even in this perishable frame resides a vital and immortal principle, which inspires a holy confidence that the Lord of Life will enable us to trample the King of Terror beneath our feet, and lift our eyes to that bright Morning Star, whose rising brings peace and salvation to the faithful and obedient of the human race.

The Worshipful Master changes places with the Candidate; the former is in the North facing South, the latter in the South facing North.

W.M. I cannot better reward the attention you have paid to this exhortation and charge than by entrusting you with the secrets of the Degree. You will therefore advance to me as a Fellow-Craft, first as an Entered Apprentice. (*Candidate takes step and gives First-Degree sign, then another step and the sign of the Second Degree.*) You will now take another short pace towards me with your left foot, bringing the right heel into its hollow as before. That is the third regular step in Freemasonry, and it is in this position that the secrets of the degree are communicated. They consist of signs, a token and word.

Of the signs, the first and second are Casual, the third Penal. The first Casual sign is called the sign of Horror, and is given from the Fellow-Crafts. Stand to order as a Fellow-Craft, by dropping the left hand into this position (*down, with palm outwards as if shielding the eyes from some object on the ground*), elevating the right (*with the back of the hand to the face, shielding the eyes*) with the head turned over the right shoulder, as if struck with horror at some dreadful and afflicting sight.

The second Casual sign is called the Sign of Sympathy, and is given by bending the head forward, and smiting the forehead gently with the right hand.

Place your hand in this position (*that is, with the forearm parallel with the ground and in line with the navel, palm downwards*) with the thumb extended in the form of a square. (*The tip of the thumb touching the body.*) The Penal sign is given by drawing the hand smartly across the body, dropping it to the side, and recovering with the thumb to the navel. This is in allusion to the penalty of your obligation, implying that as a man of honour and a Master Mason you would rather be severed in two than improperly disclose the secrets entrusted to you. (*In each case the Worshipful Master demonstrates the signs, and the Candidate copies him.*)

The grip or token is the first of the Five Points of Fellowship. They are hand to hand, foot to foot, knee to knee, breast to breast, and hand over back. (*Worshipful Master demonstrates with Candidate, and disengages*) and may be thus briefly explained. (*He again demonstrates each point with the Candidate as he explains it.*)

Hand to hand, I greet you as a brother; foot to foot I will support you in all your laudable undertakings; knee to knee, the posture of my daily supplications shall remind me of your wants; breast to breast, your lawful secrets when entrusted to me as such I will keep as my own; and hand over back, I will support your character in your absence as in your presence. It is in this position, and this only, and then only in a whisper, except in open Lodge, that the word is given; it is MACHABEN or MACHBINNA.

You are now at liberty to retire in order to restore yourself to your personal comforts, and on your return to the Lodge the sign, tokens, and word will be further explained.

The Senior Deacon conducts the Candidate to the door, instructing him to salute the Worshipful Master in the three Degrees, but only with the Penal sign in the Third Degree. The Candidate dresses himself, and in the Lodge meanwhile the lights are fully restored. When the Candidate is ready, the Tyler gives the Third-Degree knocks.

I.G. (*With step and sign*) Bro. Junior Warden, there is a report. (*Junior Warden gives one knock, and the Inner Guard opens the door.*)

Ty. The Candidate on his return. (*I.G. closes door.*)

I.G. (*With step and sign*) Worshipful Master, the Candidate on his return.

W.M. Admit him. (*Inner Guard opens door, the Senior Deacon takes the Candidate and leads him to the North of the Senior Warden.*)

S.D. Salute the Worshipful Master in the three degrees. (*Which the Candidate does, with full signs.*)

S.W. (*With step and sign*) Worshipful Master, I present to you Bro. A.B., on his being raised to the Third Degree, for some further mark of your favour.

W.M. Brother Senior Warden, I delegate you to invest him with the distinguishing badge of a Master Mason. (*The Senior Warden cuts the sign, and invests the Candidate with the apron, the right hand corner of which he holds with his left hand during his next speech.*)

S.W. Bro. A.B., by the Worshipful Master's command I invest you with the distinguishing badge of a Master Mason to mark the further progress you have made in the science.

W.M. I must state that the badge with which you have now been invested not only points out your rank as a Master Mason, but is meant to remind you of those great duties you have just solemnly engaged yourself to observe, and whilst it marks your own superiority, it calls on you to afford assistance and instruction to the Brethren in the inferior degrees.

We left off at that part of our traditional history which mentions the death of our Master Hiram Abiff. A loss so important as that of the principal architect could not fail of being generally and severely felt. The want of those plans and designs which had hitherto been regularly supplied to the different classes of workmen was the first indication that some heavy calamity had befallen our Master. The Menatschin or prefects, or more familiarly speaking, the overseers, deputed some of the most eminent of their number to acquaint King Solomon with the utter confusion into which the absence of Hiram had plunged them, and to express their apprehension that to some fatal catastrophe must be attributed his sudden and mysterious disappearance. King Solomon immediately ordered a general muster of the workmen throughout the different departments, when three of the same class of overseers were not to be found. On the same day the twelve Craftsmen who had originally joined in the conspiracy came before the King and made a voluntary confession of all they knew, down to the time of withdrawing themselves from the number of conspirators. This naturally increased the fears of King Solomon for the safety of his chief artist. He therefore selected fifteen trusty Fellow-Crafts, and ordered them to make diligent search after the person of our Master, to ascertain if he were yet alive, or had suffered death in the attempt to extort from him the secrets of his exalted Degree.

Accordingly, a stated day having been appointed for their return to Jerusalem, they formed themselves into three Fellow-Craft Lodges, and departed from the three entrances of the Temple. Many days were spent in fruitless search; indeed, one class returned without having made any discovery of importance. A second, however, were more fortunate, for on the evening of a certain day, after having suffered the greatest privations and personal fatigues, one of the Brethren, who had rested himself in a reclining posture, to assist his rising caught hold of a shrub that grew near, which to his surprise came easily out of the ground. On a closer examination he found that the earth had been recently disturbed. He therefore hailed his companions and with their united endeavours re-opened the ground, and there found the body of our Master very indecently interred. They covered it again with all respect and reverence, and to distinguish the spot, stuck a spring of acacia at the head of the grave.

They then hastened to Jerusalem to impart the afflicting intelligence to King Solomon. He, when the first emotions of his grief had subsided, ordered them to return and raise our Master to such a sepulture, as became his rank and exalted talents, at the same time informing them that by his untimely death the secrets of a Master Mason were lost. He therefore charged them to be particularly careful in observing whatever casual sign, token, or word might occur whilst paying this last sad tribute of respect to departed merit.

They performed their task with the utmost fidelity, and on re-opening the ground one of the Brethren looking round observed some of his companions in this position (*Worshipful Master demonstrates sign of Horror*) struck with horror at the dreadful and afflicting sight, while others viewing the ghastly wound still visible on his forehead, smote their own in sympathy with his sufferings. (*Worshipful Master demonstrates sign of Sympathy.*) Two of the Brethren then descended the grave and endeavoured to raise him by the Entered Apprentice's grip, which proved a slip. They then tried the Fellow-Crafts' which proved a slip likewise. Having both failed in their attempts, a zealous and expert brother took a more firm hold on the sinews of the hand, and with their assistance raised him on the Five Points of Fellowship; while others, more animated, exclaimed MACHABEN or MACHBINNA, both words having a nearly similar import, one signifying the death of the builder, the other the builder is smitten. King Solomon therefore ordered that those casual signs, and that token and word, should designate all Master Masons throughout the universe, until time or circumstances should restore the genuine.

It only remains to account for the third class, who had pursued their researches in the direction of Joppa, and were meditating their return to Jerusalem, when, accidentally passing the mouth of a cavern, they heard sounds of deep lamentation and regret. On entering the cave to ascertain the cause, they found three men answering the description of those missing, who, on being charged with the murder, and finding all chance of escape cut off, made a full confession of their guilt. They were then bound and led to Jerusalem, when King Solomon sentenced them to that death the heinousness of their crime so amply merited.

The remainder of the traditional history is given from the tracing board:

Our Master was ordered to be re-interred as near to the Sanctum Sanctorum as the Israelitish law would permit; there in a grave, from the centre three feet East and three feet West, three feet between North and South, and five feet or more perpendicular. He was not buried in the Sanctum Sanctorum, because nothing common or unclean was allowed to enter there; not even the High Priest, but once a year; nor then until after many washings and purifications against the great day of expiation for sins; for by Israelitish law, all flesh was deemed unclean. The same fifteen trusty Fellow-Crafts were ordered to attend the funeral, clothed in white aprons and gloves as emblems of their innocence.

You have already been informed that the working tools with which our Master was slain were the Plumb Rule, Level, and heavy Maul. The ornaments of a Master Masons' Lodge are the Porch, Dormer, and Square Pavement. The Porch was the entrance to the Sanctum Sanctorum, the Dormer the window that gave light to the same, and the Square Pavement for the High Priest to walk on. The High Priest's office was to burn incense to the honour and glory of the Most High, and to pray fervently that the Almighty, of His unbounded wisdom and goodness, would be pleased to bestow peace and tranquillity on the Israelitish nation during the ensuing year. The coffin, skull and cross-bones, being emblems of mortality, allude to the untimely death of our Master Hiram Abiff. He was slain three thousand years after the creation of the world.

This ends the tracing-board explanation.

In the course of the ceremony you have been informed of three signs in this Degree. The whole of them are five, corresponding in number with the Five Points of Fellowship. They are the sign of Horror, the sign of Sympathy, the Penal sign, the sign of Grief and Distress, and the sign of Joy and Exultation, likewise called the Grand or Royal sign. For the sake of regularity I will go through them again, and you will copy me.

This is the sign of Horror; this, of Sympathy; this, the Penal sign. The sign of Grief and Distress is given by passing the right hand across the face, and dropping it over the left eyebrow in the form of a square. This took its rise at the time our Master was making his way from the North to the East entrance of the Temple, when his agony was so great that the perspiration stood in large drops in his forehead, and he made use of this sign (*demonstrates it again, and Candidate copies it*) as a temporary relief to his sufferings. This is the sign of Joy and Exultation. (*The hands are raised above the head, with the palms facing each other.*) It took its rise at the time the Temple was completed, and King Solomon with the princes of his household went to view it, when they were so struck with its magnificence that with one simultaneous motion they exclaimed, O wonderful Masons.

On the continent of Europe the sign of Grief and Distress is given in a different manner, by clasping the hands and elevating them with their backs to the forehead, exclaiming, "Come to my assistance, ye children of the widow" on the supposition that all Master Masons are Brothers to Hiram Abiff, who was a widow's son. In Scotland, Ireland and the States of America the sign of Grief and Distress is given in a still different manner by throwing up the hands with the palms extended towards the heavens, and dropping them, with three distinct movements, to the sides, exclaiming, "O Lord my God, O Lord my God, O Lord my God, is there no help for the widow's son?"

The Candidate copies these signs as they are demonstrated.

I now present to you the working tools of a Master Mason. They are

the Skirret, Pencil, and Compasses. The Skirret is an implement which acts on a centre pin, whence a line is drawn to mark out ground for the foundation of the intended structure. With the Pencil the skilful artist delineates the building in a draft or plan for the instruction and guidance of the workman. The Compasses enable him, with accuracy and precision, to ascertain and determine the limits and proportions of its several parts. But as we are not all operative, but rather free and accepted, or speculative, we apply these tools to our morals.
In this sense, the Skirret points out that straight and undeviating line of conduct laid down for our pursuit in the Volume of the Sacred Law. The Pencil teaches us that our words and actions are observed and recorded by the Almighty Architect, to whom we must give an account to our conduct through life. The Compasses remind us of His unerring and impartial justice, who, having defined for our instruction the limits of good and evil, will reward or punish, as we have obeyed or disregarded His Divine commands. Thus the working tools of a Master Mason teach us to bear in mind, and act according to, the laws of our Divine Creator, that when we shall be summoned from this sublunary abode, we may ascend to the Grand Lodge above, where the world's Great Architect lives and reigns for ever.

Appendix 2

The Reception of an Apprentice Carbonaro

In the early 19th century there were only two classes of members among the Neapolitan Carbonari, Apprentices and Masters. The form of their rituals varied considerably from lodge to lodge. This text, the earliest known record of the Apprentice's initiation ceremony, was first published in Memoirs of the Secret Societies of the South of Italy, *attributed to Baron Bertholdi, in 1821.*

The Preparatore (*preparer*) *leads the* Pagan (*uninitiated*) *who is to become a member, blindfold, from the closet of reflexion to the door of the* Baracca (*hut*). *He knocks irregularly; the* Copritore (*coverer*) *says to the second assistant,* "A Pagan knocks at the door." *The second assistant repeats this to the first, who repeats it to the Grand Master; at every communication the Grand Master strikes a blow with an axe.*

G.M. See who is the rash being, who dares to trouble our sacred labours.

This question having passed through the assistants and Copritore to the Preparatore, he answers through an opening in the door.

Prep. It is a man whom I have found wandering in the forest.

G.M. Ask his name, country and profession.

The secretary writes the answer.

G.M. Ask him his habitation—his religion.

The secretary notes them.

G.M. What is it he seeks among us?

Prep. Light; and to become a member of our society.

G.M. Let him enter.

The Pagan is led into the middle of the assembly; and his answers are compared with what the secretary had noted.

G.M. Mortal, the first qualities which we require, are frankness, and contempt of danger. Do you feel that you are capable of practising them?

After the answer, the Grand Master questions the candidate on morality and benevolence; and he is asked, if he has any effects, and wishes to dispose of them, being at the moment in danger of death; after being satisfied of his conduct, the Grand Master continues,

Well, we will expose you to trials that have some meaning—let him make the first journey.

A Carbonari lodge meeting (1821). "The first qualities which we require are frankness and contempt of danger . . . weak as we are, and struggling in this vale of tears, we can only attain virtue by good works, and under the guidance of reason."

He is led out of the Baracca—he is made to journey through the forest—he hears the rustling of leaves—he is then led back to the door, as at his first entrance.

G.M. What have you remarked during this first journey?

The Pagan relates accordingly.

G.M. The first journey is the symbol of human virtue: the rustling of leaves, and the obstacles you have met in the road, indicate to you, that weak as we are, and struggling in this vale of tears, we can only attain virtue by good works, and under the guidance of reason, etc. Let him make the second journey.

The Pagan is led away, and is made to pass through fire; he is made acquainted with the chastisement of perjury; and, if there is an opportunity, he is shown a head severed from the body, etc. He is again conducted into the Baracca.

G.M. The fire through which you have passed is the symbol of that flame of charity, which should be always kindled in our hearts, to efface the stains of the seven capital sins, etc.

Make him approach the sacred throne, etc.

You must take an irrevocable oath; it offends neither religion nor the state, nor the rights of individuals; but forget not, that its violation is punished with death.

The Pagan declares that he will submit to it; the Master of the Ceremonies leads him to the throne, and makes him kneel on the white cloth.

G.M. Order!

THE OATH

I, N.N., promise and swear, upon the general statutes of the order, and upon this steel, the avenging instrument of the perjured, scrupulously to keep the secret of Carbonarism; and neither to write, engrave, or paint any thing concerning it, without having obtained a written permission. I swear to help my Good Cousins in case of need, as much as in me lies, and not to attempt any thing against the honour of their families. I consent, and wish, if I perjure myself, that my body may be cut in pieces, then burnt, and my ashes scattered to the wind, in order that my name may be held up to the execration of the Good Cousins throughout the earth. So help me God.

G.M. Lead him into the middle of the ranks. (*This is done.*) What do you wish? (*The Master of the Ceremonies suggests to the Pagan, to say* Light.)

It will be granted to you by the blows of my axe.

The Grand Master strikes with the axe—this action is repeated by all the Apprentices—the bandage is removed from the eyes of the Pagan—the Grand Master and the Good Cousins hold their axes raised.

G.M. These axes will surely put you to death, if you become perjured. On the other hand, they will all strike in your defence, when you need them, and if you remain faithful. (*To the Master of the Ceremonies,*) Bring him near the throne, and make him kneel.

Repeat your oath to me, and swear to observe exactly the private institutions of this respectable Vendita.

Candidate: I ratify it and swear.

G.M. *Holding the specimen of wood in his left hand, and suspending the axe over the head of the candidate with his right, says:* To the great and divine Grand Master of the universe, and to St. Theobald, our protector—In the name and under the auspices of the Supreme Vendita of Naples, and in virtue of the power which has been conferred upon me in this respectable Vendita, I make, name and create you an Apprentice Carbonaro.

The Grand Master strikes the specimen which is held over the Apprentice's head, thrice; he then causes him to rise, and instructs him in the sacred words and touch.

G.M. Master of the Ceremonies, let him be acknowledged by the Apprentices.

The Assistants anticipate the execution of this order, by saying to the Grand Master: All is according to rule, just and perfect.

G.M. Assistants, tell the respective orders to acknowledge, henceforth, the Good Cousin N.N. as an active member of this Vendita, etc.

The Symbolical Picture is explained to the new Apprentice.

G.M. At what hour do the Carbonari terminate their sacred labours?

First Assistant: As soon as the Sun no longer enlightens our forest.

G.M. What hour is it?

Second Assistant: The Sun no longer enlightens our forest.

G.M. Good Cousins, as the Sun no longer enlightens our forest, it is my intention to terminate our sacred labours. First, let us make a triple salutation (*Vantaggio*), to our Grand Master, divine and human, (*Jesus Christ*).—To St. Theobald, our protector, who has assisted us and preserved us from the eyes of the pagans—Order! To me,— etc. (*The signs and salutations* (Vantaggi) *are performed.*)

G.M. I declare the labours ended; retire to your Baracche—retire in peace.

Appendix 3

Ku Klux Klan Initiation Ceremony

A complete record of Ku Klux Klan ceremonial is contained in the Kloran, *the manual issued by Colonel Simmons when he revived the moribund Klan in 1915. The source of the text reproduced here is a 21-page manuscript copy of the Kloran in the possession of the Department of Special Collections, University of Kansas Library.*

When the ceremony of naturalization shall have been reached in the regular order of business the Klarogo will signal by Allw *to the Klexter, who will repeat the signal to the Night-Hawk in the outer den with candidates. Prior to the signal the Night-Hawk will have presented a blank petition of citizenship to each candidate, requesting him to read and sign name. (Said petition to be witnessed by the Night-Hawk.) He will collect from each candidate the klectokon, if same has not been previously paid. On hearing the signal of the Klexter he will excuse himself from the candidates and will approach the outer door of the inner den and give thereon seven raps (having in his possession the petition of the candidates and the klectokons by him collected).*

Klexter: Who dares to approach so near the entrance of this klavern?

N.H. The Night-Hawk of the klan.

Klexter: Advance with the countersign.

The N.H. will then give the countersign in a low whisper through the wicket.

Klexter: (*Will open the outer door and say*) Pass.

*The N.H. passes the outer door into the inner den of the klavern and at once enrobes completely and then approaches and signals on the inner door***X. The Klarogo will open the wicket. When the wicket is opened the N.H. will* Gallw.

Klarogo: Who seeks entrance to the klavern?

N.H. The Night Hawk of the klan with important information and documents from the alien world for His Excellency.

The Klarogo secures the wicket, salutes and reports to the Exalted Cyclops.

Klarogo: Your Excellency: The N.H. of the klan is respectfully waiting to enter the klavern with important information and documents from the alien world.

E.C. You will permit him to enter.

Klarogo: (*Through the wicket* Gallw. *which is answered by the N.H. with* Allw,

The initiation of Klan candidates in Georgia (1946). " 'Neath the uplifted fiery cross . . . I dedicate you in body, in mind, in spirit, and in life, to the holy service of our country, our klan, our homes, each other, and humanity."

and gives the password through the wicket. Then the Klarogo opens the door and says) : You have his Excellency's permission to enter.

The N.H. enters, steps across the threshold of the klavern, stands erect and Gtosog; *all will answer by the same from their seats. The N.H. will then proceed to the altar. Arriving at the altar, he* Gtnh, *then* Gtsof-c, *then removes his helmet and* Gtsok-c, *and stands erect and steady.*

E.C. Faithful N.H., you may now speak and impart to us the important information in your possession.

N.H. (*bows and speaks*) Your Excellency; Sir, pursuant to my duty in seeking laudable adventure in the alien world, I found these men. (*here he gives their names.*) They having read the Imperial Proclamation of our Emperor, and prompted by unselfish motives, desire a nobler life. In consequence they have made the honorable decision to forsake the world of selfishness and fraternal alienation and emigrate to the delectable bounds of the Invisible Empire and become loyal citizens of the same.

E.C. Faithful N.H., this is indeed important information and most pleasant to hear. Important, in that it evidences human progress; most pleasant, in that it reveals through you a klansman's sincere appreciation of his sacred mission among men and his fidelity to duty in the betterment of mankind. Their respective petitions will be received and justly considered.

N.H. (*bows and says*): Sir, I have in my possession the required petitions for citizenship of the men named, together with their klecktokon.

E.C. Then you will approach and deliver same to the Kligrapp who will publish them to all klansmen in klonklave assembled.

The N.H., will deliver the petitions and klectokons to the Kligrapp and resume his position at the altar. The Kligrapp will then arise and publish the names of the petitioners and hand the petitions to the E.C. and resume his seat. The E.C. will say:

E.C. Klansmen, you have heard the publication of the petitions for citizenship in the Invisible Empire of. . . . Does any klansman, on his oath of allegiance, know of any just reason why these aliens, or any of them, should be denied citizenship in the Invisible Empire?

If there be no objections, the E.C. will address the N.H.

E.C. Faithful N.H., you will inform these alien petitioners from me: That it is the constant disposition of a klansman to assist those who aspire to things noble in thought and conduct, and to extend a helping hand to the worthy. That their desires are sincerely respected, their manly petitions are being seriously considered in the light of justice and honor. With true faith a man may expect just answer to his prayers and his virtuous hopes will ultimately ripen into a sublime fruition.

The N.H. bows and says: I have your orders, Sir: *and retires to the outer door of the inner den of the klavern and through the wicket of the outer door and informs the candidates as follows:*

N.H. Worthy Aliens: His Excellency, the Exalted Cyclops, being the direct representative of His Majesty, our Emperor, and chief guardian of the portal of the Invisible Empire, has officially instructed me to inform you that it is the constant disposition of a Klansman to assist those who aspire to things noble in thought and conduct and to extend a helping hand to the worthy. Therefore your desires are sincerely respected and your manly petitions are being seriously considered in the light of justice and honor. With true faith you may expect a just answer to your prayers, and your virtuous hopes will ultimately ripen into a sublime fruition. This is the decision of His Excellency, the E.C., with all his klan concurring.

The N.H. returns to his station in the klavern without form.

E.C. Faithful Klokard: You will examine under witness the alien petitioners, as to their qualifications.

The Klokard, with his assistants, the Klaliff and the Kludd, retires to the outer den and will propound to the candidates in waiting the following required "Qualifying Interrogatories", and then immediately administer Sections I and II of the Oath of Allegiance, requiring each candidate to place his left hand over his heart and raise his right hand to heaven. The Klokard will first ask each candidate his name and then speak to the candidates in the outer den as follows:

Sirs: The Kns. of the KKK, as a great and essentially a patriotic, fraternal, benevolent Order, does not discriminate against a man on account of his religious or political creed, when same does not conflict with or antagonize the sacred rights and privileges guaranteed by our civil govt., and Christian ideals and institutions.

Therefore, to avoid any misunderstanding and as evidence that we do not seek to impose unjustly the requirements of this Order upon anyone who cannot, on account of his religious or political scruples, voluntarily meet our requirements and faithfully practice our principles, and as proof that we respect all honest men in their sacred convictions, whether same are agreeable with our requirements or not, we require as an absolute necessity on the part of each of you an affirmative answer to each of the following questions:

Each of the following questions must be answered by (each of) you with an emphatic "Yes."

1st. Is the motive prompting your ambition to be a klansman serious and unselfish?

2nd. Are you a native born white, Gentile, American citizen?

3rd. Are you absolutely opposed to and free of any allegiance of any nature to any cause, government, people, sect or ruler that is foreign to the U.S.A.?

4th. Do you believe in the tenets of the Christian religion?
5th. Do you esteem the U.S.A. and its institutions above any other government, civil, political, or ecclesiastical in the whole world?
6th. Will you, without mental reservation, take a solemn oath to defend, preserve, and enforce same?
7th. Do you believe in clanishness and will you faithfully practice same towards klansmen?
8th. Do you believe in and will you faithfully strive for the eternal maintenance of white supremacy?
9th. Will you faithfully obey our constitution and laws, and conform willingly to all our usages, requirements and regulations?
10th. Can you always be depended on?

He then administers sections 1 and 2 of the oath.

This done, he, with his assistants, will return to the s.a., he will salute and report as follows:

Your Excellency: (number) men in waiting have each duly qualified to enter our klavern to journey thru the mystic cave in quest of citizenship in the Inv. Emp.

E.C. Faithful Klikard, you and your assistants will resume your stations. The Kladd of the Klan! *The Kladd will arise and advance to a position immediately in front of the E.C. and about 5 ft. from his station, and salute and say:*

Kladd: The Kladd, Your Excellency.

E.C. You will retire under special orders to the outer premises of the klavern, assume charge of the worthy aliens in waiting, and afford them a safe journey from the world of selfishness and fraternal alienation to the s.a. of the empire of chivalry, industry, honor and love.

Kladd: *Salutes the E.C. and says:* I have your orders, Sir! *He retires to the room where the candidates are. Lines them up in single file, the left hand of the rear man on the left shoulder of the man in front. He then takes his place in front of them and says:* Follow me and be (a man) men! *He proceeds to the outer door of the inner den and gives thereon*.*

Klexter: (*Opens the wicket and says*) Who and what is your business?

Kladd: I am the Kladd of Klan No.... Realm of......, acting under special order of His Excellency, our E.C.; I am in charge of a party!

Klexter: What be the nature of your party?

Kladd: Worthy aliens from the world of selfishness and fraternal alienation prompted by unselfish motive, desire the honor of citizenship in the Inv. Emp. and the fellowship of klansmen.

Klexter: Has your party been selected with care?

Kladd: These men (or this man) are (or is) known and vouched for by klansmen in klonklave assembled.

Klexter: Have they (or has he) the marks?

Kladd: The dist. marks of a klansman are not found in the fibre of his garments or his social or financial standing, but are spiritual; namely, a chivalric head, a compassionate heart, a prudent tongue and a courageous will. All devoted to our country, our klan, our homes and each other; these are the dist. marks of a klansman, oh, Faithful Klexter! And these men claim the marks.

Klexter: What if one of your party should prove himself a traitor?

Kladd: He would be immediately banished in disgrace from the Inv. Emp. without fear or favor, conscience would tenaciously torment him, remorse would repeatedly revile him, and direful things would befall him.

Klexter: Do they know all this?

Kladd: All this he now knows. He has heard, and they must heed.

Klexter: Faithful Kladd, you speak the truth.

Kladd: Faithful Klexter, a klansman speaketh the truth in and from his heart. A lying scoundrel may wrap his disgraceful from within the sacred folds of a klansman's robe and deceive the very elect, but only a klansman possesses a klansman's heart and a klansman's soul.

Klexter: Advance with the countersign.

The Kladd advances and whispers the countersign through the wicket to the Klexter.

Klexter: (*Opens the door and says*): With heart and soul, I, the Klexter of the Klan, welcome you and open the way for you to attain the most noble achievement in your earthly career. Be faithful and true unto death and all will be well and your reward will be sure. Noble Kladd, pass with your party!

The Kladd, with his party will pass the outer door and stop. He will then give Allw. *The Klarogo, upon hearing the* Llw, *will announce:*

Klarogo: Your Excellency and klansmen assembled. I hear from the watch the signal of the Kladd of the klan with a party.

E.C. My Terrors and klansmen, one and all; make ready.

Each k. present will put on his helmet, both aprons dropped down, robes completely buttoned and girdles tied and capes adjusted; all light must be turned down so as to make the klavern almost dark. All must remain as still and as quiet as possible; there must be no moving, talking or noise only as the ceremony requires. Striking matches and smoking during the ceremony is absolutely prohibited. If an officer has to read he must use an electric flash light, and throw the light only on the page he is reading. When all are ready the Klarogo will answer the signal of the Kladd with Allw *and begin to* Otds.

Kladd: (*On* Stdos, *the Kladd will say to his party*): Sirs The Portal of the Inv. Em. is being opened for you. Your righteous prayer has been answered and you have found favor in the sight of the E.C. and his k. assembled. Follow me and be prudent!

As the Kladd approaches with his party the treshold of the inner door, the Klarogo will stop them by facing them with Tsotf-c. *He will then recover* Tsotf-c, *face inward and stand erect and steady.* (*The Klokard, or person selected, just previous to this has stationed himself near the door where he can be heard by the candidates but not seen by them.*)

Klokard: God give us men! The I. E. demands strong
Minds, great hearts, true faith and ready hands.
Men whom the lust of office does not kill;
Men whom the spoils of office cannot buy;
Men who possess opinions and a will;
Men who have Honor; men who will not lie;
Men who can stand before a demagogue
And Damn his treacherous flatteries without winking!
Tall men, sun-crowned, who live above the fog
in public duty and in private thinking;
For while the rabble, with their thumb-worn creeds,
Their large professions and their little deeds,
Mingle in selfish strife, Lo! freedom weeps,
Wrong rules the land, and waiting justice sleeps.
God give us men!
Men who serve not for selfish booty,
But real men, courageous, who flinch not at duty;
Men of dependable character; men of sterling worth;
Then wrongs will be redressed, and right will rule the earth;
God give us men!

After a pause, the Klarogo faces the candidates and says:

Klarogo: Your Excellency, and fellow klansmen: Just such men are standing without the portal of the I.E., desiring the lofty honor of citizenship therein, and ready and willing to unflinchingly face every duty on him imposed.

E.C. Faithful Klarogo and klansmen: Let them enter the klavern in quest of citizenship, but keep you a klansman's eye of scrutiny upon them, and if they, or one of them, should flinch at duty or show himself a cowardly weakling or a treacherous scalawag, at this time or in the future, it will be your sworn duty to eject him or them from the portal of the I.E. without fear or favor and do so without delay; be thou not recreant to duty's demand!

While the above prayer is being said the N.H. takes the f.c. from the a, lights it and takes a position immediately in front of and about 4 ft. from the Klaliff's station, facing the Klarago, holding the f.c. above his head.

Klarogo: (*Steps aside and says to the Kladd*): Pass.

When the Klad crosses the threshold of the klavern he will stop and give Tsog. *All k., except the station officers, will arise, face the Kladd and give* Tsog, *then face the a. and remain standing with* Tsoc-l. *The Kladd will then proceed with his party toward the N.H. As the Kladd approaches the N.H. with his party and gets in about six ft. of him the H.H. will about face and march in front of the Kladd about 6 ft. from him on the journey, until he is halted by the signal* Allw *from the E.C. When he hears the signal he will stop his party, answer the signal with* Allw, *then face his party toward the sacred a. When this is done the N.H. with the f.c. takes a position in front of and about six ft. from the party, facing this position until he hears the 2nd signal of* Allw *from the E.C., when he will resume his position at the head of the party in front of the Kladd and move on. When the Kladd hears the second signal he will face his party as they were, answer the signal with* Allw, *and follow the N.H.*

When the first signal of Allw *of the E.C. is given, all klansmen, except the station officers, Klarogo and Klexter, will form from their seats, march around the hall in single file, the Klokard leading to his right, pass in front along the line of the party, between the party and the N.H., each klansman will look the party squarely in the eyes, but continue moving; after passing the party the Klokard will form the klansmen in a double line with open ranks about 6 ft. apart and facing each other, holding* Tsoc-l, *and standing steady, on the opposite side of the klavern; the E.C. then gives the second signal of* Allw, *The N.H. will lead the Kladd and his party on their journey by way of the E.C. station and through the formation of klansmen. All this must be done quietly, with dignity and with a steady pace. After the Kladd and his party shall have passed the formation of klansmen, all klansmen will, without signal return to their seats, but remain standing until the Kladd presents his party to the E.C., when they quietly sit down.*

As the Kladd approaches the station of the Klaliff after he has passed the formation of klansmen, the Klaliff will arise and Gtsog *and halt him with* Allw. *On hearing the* Llw, *the Kladd stops and answers with same. The N.H. also stops.*

Klaliff: Who are you that walk in the klavern at this hour?

Kladd: The Kladd of the klan with a party whom the eye of the unknown has seen and doth constantly observe.

Klaliff: What be the nature of your party?

Kladd: Faithful Klaliff: These are men (or man) as the Inv. Emp. and a time like this demands; men of strong minds, great hearts, true faith and ready hands. Worthy aliens known and vouched for by klansmen in klonklave assembled, and by order of His Excellency, I, the Kladd of the klan, am their guide to the s.a.

Klaliff: Pass on.

The journey from the entrance of the klavern to the E.C. station must be made in a circle around the klavern.

The N.H. will move on, followed by the Kladd with his party, and will then continue his journey until he arrives at the station of the E.C., when he shall stop and line his co. up in a straight line immediately in front of the station. The N.H. stops but does not change position. The Kladd steps to the rear of his party and will address the E.C. as follows:

Kladd: Your Excellency, Sir, pursuant to your orders, I present to you these alien aspirants, men of dependable character and courage, who aspire to the noble life and the high honor of citizens in the Inv. Emp.

The E.C. will arise and address the candidates as follows:

Sirs: Is the motive prompting your presence here serious and unselfish?

It is indeed refreshing to meet face to face with men like you who, actuated by manly motives, aspire to all things noble for yourselves and humanity.

The luster of the holy light of chivalry has lost its former glory and is sadly dimmed by the choking dust of selfish, sordid gain. Pass on!

The E.C. will resume his seat and the Kladd will face his party toward the N.H. and advance behind the N.H. until he hears the signal of Allw *from the Klokard. On hearing the signal from the Klo. the N.H. stops and stands steady; the Kladd will also stop his party immediately in front of the Klokard's station and face them to the Klokard's station and answer the signal by the same. On receiving the answer the Klo. will arise and address the party as follows:*

Real fraternity, by shameful neglect, has been starved until so weak that her voice is lost in the courts of her own castle, and she passes unnoticed by her sworn subjects as she moves along the market place. Man's valuation of man is by the standard of wealth and not worth; selfishness is the festive queen among human kind, and multitudes forget honor, justice, love, and God and ever religious conviction to do homage to her, and yet with the cruel heart of Jezebel she slaughters the souls of thousands of her devotees daily. Pass on!

The Klo. will resume his seat and the Kladd will face his party as before and advance behind the N.H. until he hears the signal of Allw *from the Klaliff. On hearing the signal of the Klal. the N.H. stops and stands steady; the Kladd will also stop his party immediately in front of the Klaliff's station, facing them to the Klal., and answering the signal by the same. On receiving the answer the Klal. will arise and address the party as follows:*

The unsatiated thirst for gain is dethroning reason and judgment in the citadel of the human soul, and men maddened thereby, forget their patriotic, domestic and social obligations and duties, and fiendishly fight for a place in the favor of the goddess of glittering gold; they starve their own souls, and make sport of spiritual devotion. Pass on.

The Klal. will resume his seat and the Kladd will face his party as before and advance behind the N.H. until he hears the signal of Allw *from the Kludd. On hearing the signal the N.H. stops and stands steady; the Kladd will also stop his party immediately in front of the Kludd's station, facing them to the Kludd, and then answers the signal by the same. On receiving the answer the Kludd will arise and address the party as follows:*

Men speak of love and live in hate!
Men talk of faith and trust to fate!

Oh, might men do the things they teach
Oh, might men live the life they preach
Then the throne of avarice would fall and the clangor
Of grim selfishness o'er the earth would cease;
Love would tread out the baleful fire of anger,
And in its ashes plant the lily of peace.
Pass on.

This is followed by a repetition of the party's marching, and then the E.C. speaks:

E.C. Sirs: We congratulate you on your manly decision to forsake the world of selfishness and fraternal alienation and emigrate to the delectable bounds of the Inv. Emp. and become loyal citizens of the same. The prime purpose of this great Order is to develop character, to practice clanishness, to protect the home and chastity of womanhood, and to exemplify a pure patriotism toward our glorious country.

You, as citizens of the I.E., must be actively patriotic toward our country and constantly clanish toward klansmen socially, physically, morally, and vocationally; will you assume this obligation of citizenship?—

You must unflinchingly conform to our requirements, regulations and usages in every detail, and prove yourselves worthy to have and to hold the honors we bestow; do you freely and faithfully assume to do this?—

Sirs: If you have any doubt as to your ability to qualify, either in body or character, as citizens of the I.E., you now have an opportunity to retire from this place with the good will of the klan to attend you; for I warn you now, if you falter or fail at this time or in the future as a k., in klonklave or in life, you will be banished from citizenship in the I.E. without fear or favor.

This is a serious undertaking; we are not here to make sport of you, nor indulge in the silly frivolity of circus clowns. Be you well assured that "he that putteth his hand to the plow and looketh back is not fit for the kingdom of Heaven" or worthy of the high honor of citizenship in the I.E., or the fervent fellowship of klansmen. Don't deceive yourselves; you cannot deceive us, and we will not be mocked. Do you wish to retire?—

Faithful Kladd, you will direct the way for these worthy aliens to the sacred alter of the empire of chivalry, honor, industry and love, in order that they may make further progress toward attaining citizenship in the I.E. of the KKK.

The Kladd will conduct his party to the s.a. by way of the Klo's station. When he has arrived within about 6 ft. of the Klo's station he will turn square to his left and continue in a straight direction until he reaches a point about 6 ft. of the s.a. alt. toward the station of the E.C.; he will then turn square to his right and continue until he has passed the s.a. about 4 ft.; he will then turn square to his left and continue about 6 ft. then he will turn square to his left and bring his party into the formation of a 3/4 hollow square and will face them towards the s.a.

The N.H. takes his place with the fiery cross held aloft just from the corner of the s.a. to the right of the E.C. he stands within the wuadrate. The f.c. is held aloft during the administration of the oath and dedication ceremony.

When the Kladd has perfected the 3/4 quarter hollow square formation, he will advance to a point about midway between the alter and the station of the E.C., salute and in a strong, clear voice say:

Kladd: Your Excellency, the Aliens in our midst from the world of selfishness and fraternal alienation, forsake the past and are now ready and willing to bind themselves by an unyielding tie to the I.E., KKK.

The Kladd will about face and advance to his position opposite of the center and to the rear of the line of candidates toward the station of the Klaliff and await orders. The Klo., with his assistants, the Klaliff and the Kludd, now administer the oath, sections 3 and 4.

Klokard: Your Excellency: the worthy aspirants at the s.a. of the klan have each voluntarily assumed, without mental reservation the sol. and thrice binding oath of allegiance to the I.E., KKK, and are awaiting to be dedicated to the holy service of our country, the klan, each other, our homes, and humanity.

E.C. Faithful Klo. You and your assistants, have performed your duty well; now you may rest; but stand by in readiness to perform other duties, if such arise.

The E.C. then proceeds to the s.a. to perform the following ceremony of dedication.

DEDICATION

E.C. Sirs: Have you assumed without mental reservation your oath of allegiance to the I.E.?—

Mortal man cannot assume a more binding oath; character and courage alone will enable you to keep it. Always remember that to keep this oath means to you honor, happiness, and life; but to violate it means disgrace, dishonor, and death. May honor, happiness, and life be yours.

Then he holds up the vessel from the s.a., containing the dedication fluid, and addresses the candidates as follows:

With this transparent, life-giving, powerful God-given fluid, more precious and far more significant than all the sacred oils of the ancients, I set you apart from the men of your daily association to the great and honorable task you have voluntarily allotted yourselves as citizens of the I.E., KKK.

As a klansman, may your character be as trans. your life purpose as powerful, your motive in all things as magnanimous and as pure, and your clanishness as real and as faithful as the manifold drops herein, and you a vital being as useful to humanity as is pure water to mankind.

You will kneel upon your right knee.

At this point a stanza is softly sung, to the tune "Just as I am Without One Plea."

E.C. Sirs: 'neath the uplifted f.c. which by its holy light looks down upon you to bless with its sacred traditions of the past, I dedicate you in body, in mind, in spirit, and in life, to the holy service of our country, our klan, our homes, each other, and humanity.

He advances to the candidates and pours a few drops of the dedication fluid on each candidate's back and says: "In Body", pours a few drops on his head and says: "In Mind," places a few drops on his own hand and tosses it upward and says: "In Spirit", then moves his hand in a horizontal circular motion around the candidate's head and says: "And in Life". After this he says:

Thus dedicated by us, now consecrate yourselves to the sacred cause you have entered.

To All he will say: My terrors and Klansmen: Let us pray.

Immediately after the prayer the E.C. addresses the candidates as follows:

Sirs: You are no longer strangers or aliens among us, but are citizens with us; and with confidence in your character that you have not sworn falsely or deceitfully in the assumption of your oath, I, on behalf of our Emperor and all klansmen, welcome you to citizenship in the empire of chivalry, honor, industry, and love.

After saying this the E.C. will raise the front apron of his helmet (and all klansmen will do the same) and as a token of welcome he will greet each of the candidates with Tcok, *and then returns to his position at the altar and says:*

By authority vested in me by our Emperor, I now declare and proclaim you a citizen of the I.E., KKK, and invest you with the title of Klansman, the most honorable title among men.

Index

Page numbers in *italics* refer to captions

Acknowledgments

Key to picture positions: (T) top (C) centre (B) bottom; and combinations, e.g. (TL) top left. British Museum photographs reproduced by courtesy of the trustees.

21 courtesy The Museum of the American Indian, Heye Foundation, New York
24 Biblioteca Apostolica Vaticana
27 (L) artwork David Litchfield (R) Royal Geographical Society, London
28 (L) Prof. d'Azevedo, Mexico City (R) Royal Geographical Society, London
29–30 photos Prof. V. R. Dorjahn, Oregon
33 (T) photo Chester Sprague, Massachusetts (BL) artwork David Litchfield (BR) courtesy Field Museum of Natural History, Chicago
34 courtesy Field Museum of Natural History, Chicago
35 (L) artwork David Litchfield (R) Smithsonian Institution, Washington
36 (T & B) courtesy The American Museum of Natural History, New York
39 photo George Rodger, courtesy Magnum Photos
41 photo courtesy Rev. H. D. Hooper, Church Missionary Society, London
42–3 artwork Gordon Cramp
44 Paul Popper Ltd., London
45 (L) Central Press Photos Ltd., London (R) British & Foreign Bible Society, London
47–8 Radio Times Hulton Picture Library, London
52–3 Central Press Photos Ltd., London
54 United Press International (U.K.) Ltd., London
57 photo Keystone, London
59 photo George Rodger, courtesy Magnum Photos and Camera Press Ltd., London
61 Camera Press Ltd., London
62 United Press International (U.K.) Ltd., London
63 (T) Central Press Photos Ltd., London (B) United Press International (U.K.) Ltd., London
65 courtesy Victoria and Albert Museum, London: photo Mike Busselle, London
68–9 photos Brit. Mus. (TL) photo John Freeman, London
72 Brit. Mus.: photo John Freeman, London
73 photo Mike Busselle: courtesy Brigadier J. C. Sleeman
74–5 artwork Jill Mackley
76 courtesy Victoria and Albert Museum, London: photo John Freeman, London
79 Brit. Mus.: photo John Freeman, London
80 reproduced by courtesy of the Secretary of State for Commonwealth Relations
81 reproduced by gracious permission of Her Majesty the Queen
83 Mansell Collection, London
85 National Archaeological Museum, Athens: photo Emile Serafis, Athens
87 (L) Mansell Collection, London (R) photo Edwin Smith, London
88 (T) Bibliothèque Nationale, Paris
88–9 (B) Museo Profano Lateranense, Rome: Mansell Collection, London: photo Alinari
90 Mansell Collection, London: photo Alinari
93 (T) Mansell Collection, London: photo Anderson (B) Museum für Völkerkunde, Berlin
96 (T) Bibliothèque Nationale, Paris (B) Brit. Mus.: photo William Rhodes, London
97 Mansell Collection, London: photo Anderson
99 Römisch-Germanisches Museum, Köln
101 (T) Zemaljski Musej, Sarajevo (B) photo André Held, Switzerland
102 André Held, Switzerland
103 photo Scala, Florence
105 André Held, Switzerland
107 photo José de Prado Herranz, Madrid
110 (T & B) photos Mike Busselle: courtesy Peter Willey
111 (T & TC) photos Peter Willey (B) redrawn by Jill Mackley from *The Castles of the Assassins* by Peter Willey, George G. Harrap & Co. Ltd., London, 1963
113 (T) Bibliothèque Nationale, Paris (B) Edinburgh University Library
116 Bibliothèque Nationale, Paris
118 Bibliothèque Nationale, Paris: photo Studios Josse-Lalance & Cie, Paris
120 (TL) Musée de Chantilly: photo Giraudon, Paris
120–1 (TC) Bibliothèque Nationale, Paris
121 (TR) Bibliothèque Nationale, Paris
124 (T) photo Patrick Guilbert, Paris

(B) Musée du Louvre, Paris: photo Giraudon, Paris
125 Biblioteca Apostolica Vaticana
126 photo Claude Michaelides, Paris
128–31 photos Brit. Mus.
133 (T) Lutherhalle, Wittenberg (B) Rijksmuseum, Amsterdam
135 Brit. Mus.
136 Brit. Mus.: photo John Freeman, London
138 (L) photo John Freeman: courtesy Warburg Institute Library, London (R) Marburg Library, Germany: photo John Freeman, London
141 (L) Brit. Mus.: photo John Freeman, London (R) Bodleian Library, Oxford (MS. Ashmole 1459, fol. 284)
143 Bibliothèque Nationale, Paris
145 (T & B) Brit. Mus.: photo John Freeman, London
148–9 courtesy Frater Volo Intellegere
150–1 Supreme Grand Lodge of AMORC, Rosicrucian Park, San Jose, California
153 Brit. Mus.
156 photos Mike Busselle, London
157 (T) photos Mike Busselle, London (B) Brit. Mus.
160 Brit. Mus.
163 Brit. Mus.: photo John Freeman, London
164–5 courtesy Parker Gallery, London: photos Mike Busselle, London
168–9 Mansell Collection, London
171 Brit. Mus.: photo John Freeman, London
174 courtesy Victoria and Albert Museum, London
175 (L) Bibliothèque Nationale, Paris (R) Brit. Mus.: photo John Freeman, London
176 Life © (1956) Time Inc.
177 photo Grey Villet, Life © (1956) Time Inc.
179 Galleria del deposito, Gnova-Boccadesse: photo Fotosport, Rapallo
181 by permission of the Comptroller of H.M. Stationery Office
182 courtesy Parker Gallery, London: photo John Freeman, London
184 (TR & L) National Library of Ireland (B) artwork Gordon Cramp
185 photos John Freeman, London
186 Radio Times Hulton Picture Library, London
187 Mansell Collection, London
189 (T) Historical Pictures Service, Chicago (B) Mansell Collection, London
191 Imperial War Museum, London
192 photo The Press Association Ltd., London
193 photo J. Cashman, Dublin
194 (L) Brit. Mus.: photo John Freeman, London (R) photo Giraudon, Paris
195 photo Giraudon, Paris
196 photo John Freeman, London: courtesy London Library
197 Museo Centrale del Risorgimento, Vittoriano, Rome
198 (T) State Historical Museum, Moscow: Novosti Press Agency, London (B) Musée du Louvre, Paris: photo Giraudon, Paris
199 photo courtesy Hamburger Kunsthalle
200 (R) Radio Times Hulton Picture Library, London (L) courtesy Ben Shahn, New Jersey
202–4 Institute of Contemporary History, The Wiener Library, London
205 United Press International (U.K.) Ltd., London
209 Life © (1965) Time Inc.
211 Musée Guimet, Paris: photo Giraudon
212 (L) redrawn by Gordon Cramp from *The Siege at Peking* by Peter Fleming, Rupert Hart-Davis Ltd., London, 1959 (R) photo Roger Viollet, Paris
213 photo H. Bristow, courtesy Mrs. K. F. Newton, England
215 artwork David Litchfield
217 (TL) Nationalmuseum, Stockholm (TR) Brit. Mus.: photos John Freeman, London (BR) School of Oriental & African Studies Library, London: photo John Freeman, London
218 redrawn by Gordon Cramp from Albert Herrmann's *Historical and Commercial Atlas of China* (Yenching Monograph Series Vol. I), Harvard University Press, U.S.A., 1935
221 (L) in the collection of the National Palace Museum, Taipei, Taiwan, Republic of China (R) from *East Asia, the Great Tradition*, by Edwin O. Reischauer and John Fairbank, Houghton Mifflin Company, Boston, 1960
223–5 Brit. Mus.: photos John Freeman, London
226 Radio Times Hulton Picture Library, London
227 photo John Freeman, London
229 Radio Times Hulton Picture Library, London

231 (T) Ecole Française d'Extrême-Orient, Saigon : photo Leon Comber, Hong Kong (B) reproduced by permission of the Hong Kong Government

234–5 reproduced by permission of the Hong Kong Government

239 (TL) United Press International (U.K.) Ltd., London (TR) photo Keystone, London (B) courtesy Commissioner of Police, Government of the State of Singapore

240 courtesy Society of California Pioneers

243–4 photos Nicola Scafidi, Palermo

246–7 photos James McNeish, author of *Fire under the Ashes* : Press Feature Service, London

248 (L) Culver Pictures Inc., New York (R) courtesy Punch Publications Ltd.

250 (TL) Brown Brothers, New York (TR) Keystone, U.S.A.

252 (TL, CL & BL) United Press International (U.K.) Ltd., London (TR) New York Daily News Photo (BR) Keystone, London

253 (TR) Associated Press Ltd., London (TL) United Press International (U.K.) Ltd., London

254 photo Rizzoli : Hecht Photo Features, Como

256 Robert Capa : Magnum Photos

257 Life © (1962) Time Inc.

258 photo Ivo Mildolese : Sandro Vespasiani, Rome

259 (TR) photo Nicola Scafidi, Palermo (BL) photo Pippo Stella, Sicily (BR) photo Sandro Vespasiani, Rome

260 Sergio Larrain : Magnum Photos

262 photos Nicola Scafidi, Palermo

263 Sergio Larrain : Magnum Photos

264 European Picture Service, New York

265 United Press International (U.K.) Ltd., London

267 Camera Press, London : photo Lynn Pelham, Florida

269–72 Culver Pictures Inc., New York

274 Brit. Mus. : photo John Freeman, London

275 Culver Pictures Inc., New York

276 (T) from *The Movement* by Lorraine Hansberry, Simon and Schuster Inc., New York (BL) United Press International (U.K.) Ltd., London (CB) Brown Brothers, New York (BR) New York World-Telegram

280 (TL) from Eugen Lennhoff, *Politische Geheimebünde*, Amalthea Verlag, Wien, 1932 (TR) Radio Times Hulton Picture Library, London (B) Culver Pictures Inc., New York

281 (T) Brown Brothers, New York

282–3 Life © (1946) Time Inc.

285 photo Danny Lyon, Chicago

286 Brown Brothers, New York

288–9 Culver Pictures Inc., New York

291 (TL) Rapho Guillumette Pictures, New York : photo David Cupp (TR & CR) Black Star, New York : photo Charles Moore (B) Black Star, New York : photo Matt Herron

292 (T) Black Star, New York : photo Bill Read (BL) Camera Press, London : photo Vernon Merritt III

293 United Press International (U.K.) Ltd., London

295 Lynn Pelham : Rapho Guillumette Pictures, © Curtis Publishing Co., New York

296 (T) Beaverbrook Newspapers Ltd., London (B) United Press International (U.K.) Ltd., London

307 Brit. Mus. : photo John Freeman, London

325 courtesy London Library : photo John Freeman, London

331 Life © (1958) Time Inc.

Text credits

Acknowledgment is made for permission to reprint excerpts from the following works :

Social Organization by Robert Lowie (U.K. : Routledge & Kegan Paul Ltd. U.S.A. : Holt, Rinehart and Winston Inc., 1948)

Mau Mau and the Kikuyu by L. S. B. Leakey (Methuen & Co. Ltd., 1952)

"Mau Mau" Detainee by J. M. Kariuki (Oxford University Press, 1963)

Darkness Visible by Walton Hannah (Britons Publishing Company, 1952)

Hofmeyr by Alan Paton (Oxford University Press, Cape Town, 1964)

The Hung Society by J. S. M. Ward & W. G. Stirling (The Baskerville Press, 1925)

The Siege at Peking by Peter Fleming (Rupert Hart-Davis Ltd., 1959)

Mind of the South by Wilbur Cash (Alfred A. Knopf Inc., 1960)

Insight and Responsibility by Erik H. Erikson (U.K. : Faber & Faber Ltd. U.S.A : W. W. Norton & Co. Inc., 1964)

If the publishers have unwittingly infringed copyright in any picture or photograph reproduced in this book, they offer their apologies and—upon being satisfied as to the owner's title—will pay an appropriate fee.